PERSONS OF COLOR AND
RELIGIOUS AT THE SAME TIME

Persons of Color and Religious at the Same Time

THE OBLATE SISTERS OF PROVIDENCE, 1828–1860

DIANE BATTS MORROW

The University of North Carolina Press

Chapel Hill and London

Designed by April Leidig-Higgins
Set in Monotype Centaur by Copperline Book Services, Inc.

The paper in this book meets the guidelines for permanence
and durability of the Committee on Production Guidelines
for Book Longevity of the Council on Library Resources.

Library of Congress Cataloging-in-Publication Data
Morrow, Diane Batts, 1947–
Persons of color and religious at the same time: the Oblate
Sisters of Providence, 1828–1860 / Diane Batts Morrow.
p. cm. Includes bibliographical references and index.
ISBN 0-8078-2726-6 (cloth: alk. paper)
ISBN 0-8078-5401-8 (pbk.: alk. paper)
1. Oblate Sisters of Providence—History—19th century.
2. African American Catholics—History—19th century.
I. Title.
BX4412 .M67 2002   271'.97—dc21   2001059759

cloth 06 05 04 03 02   5 4 3 2 1
paper 06 05 04 03 02   5 4 3 2 1

Portions of this book appeared earlier, in somewhat different
form, in Diane Batts Morrow, "Francophone Residents of
Antebellum Baltimore and the Origins of the Oblate Sisters
of Providence," in *Slavery in the Caribbean Francophone World: Distant Voices, Forgotten Acts, Forged Identities*, ed. Doris Kadish
(Athens: University of Georgia Press, 2000), 122–39 (© University of Georgia Press; reprinted by permission); " 'Our
Convent': The Oblate Sisters of Providence and the Antebellum Black Community," in *Dealing with the Powers That Be: Negotiating the Boundaries of Southern Womanhood*, ed. Janet Coryell et
al. (Columbia: University of Missouri Press, 2000), 27–47
(reprinted by permission); and "Outsiders Within: The
Oblate Sisters of Providence in 1830s Church and Society,"
U.S. Catholic Historian 15, no. 2 (Spring 1997): 35–54 (© 1997
by Our Sunday Visitor, Inc.; reprinted by permission).

Frontispiece: An unidentified Oblate Sister of Providence,
professed before 1906 (Courtesy of Archives of the Oblate
Sisters of Providence, Baltimore, Md.)

To my mother, Ruth Violet Batts,
my father, James Alexander Batts (1913–92),
and my husband, John Howard Morrow Jr.

CONTENTS

ILLUSTRATIONS

ACKNOWLEDGMENTS

Many individuals have contributed significantly to the completion of this book. I thank the Oblate Sisters of Providence, whose existence inspired this study, for the gracious hospitality they extended to me during the summers of 1994, 1997, 2000, and 2001 when I conducted research in their archives. I thank Dr. Christopher J. Kauffman, whom I met fortuitously at the Sulpician Archives in Baltimore the summer of 1994. He has graciously suggested fruitful avenues of inquiry, provided important sources, and offered valuable insights about my work. I am also deeply indebted to Elaine Maisner, editor at the University of North Carolina Press, for her faith in my work and encouragement throughout the acquisition process.

Archivists Sisters M. Reparata Clarke, O.S.P., and M. Reginald Gerdes, O.S.P., of the Oblate Sisters of Providence Archives, the Reverend John W. Bowen, S.S., of the Sulpician Archives in Baltimore, the Reverend Peter E. Hogan, S.S.J., and his wonderful staff at the Josephite Fathers Archives in Baltimore, and the Reverend Paul K. Thomas of the Archives of the Archdiocese of Baltimore all provided documents readily, answered my incessant questions patiently and informatively—both during my visits to their respective archives and afterward in correspondence—and in general assisted my research efforts with their interest, encouragement, and expertise. African American Collection specialist Eva Slezak at the Enoch Pratt Free Library and reference librarian F. P. O'Neill at the Maryland Historical Society in Baltimore also gave generously of their time to facilitate my work.

Archivists Sisters Genevieve Mary Simons, I.H.M., of the Villa Maria House of Studies, Mada-Anne Gell, V.H.M., of the Visitation Sisters, Constance Fitzgerald, O.C.D., of the Baltimore Carmelite Monastery, Betty Ann McNeil,

D.C., of the Daughters of Charity, Emmitsburg, Dr. W. Kevin Cawley of the University of Notre Dame Archives, and the Reverend Carl Hoegerl, C.SS.R., of the Redemptorist Provincial Archives, Baltimore Province, all responded promptly, graciously, and productively to my research inquiries by mail.

Several colleagues at the University of Georgia assisted my postdissertation professional development significantly. They include Professors Joseph R. Berrigan (emeritus), John C. Inscoe, Doris Kadish, Sandy D. Martin, Barbara McCaskill, and R. Baxter Miller. I thank the reference librarians and the inter-library loan staff of the University of Georgia Library, without whose courteous and able assistance my research would have proven impossible.

Individuals beyond the University of Georgia have improved my work with their thoughtful commentaries at professional meetings, editorial suggestions, perceptive insights offered in conversations, valuable contribution of sources, or warm encouragement. They include Christine Anderson, Richard J. Blackett, John E. Bodnar, Patricia Byrne, Emily Clark, Carol Coburn, Janet Coryell, Cyprian Davis, Florence Deacon, Susanna Delfino, Mary Anne Foley, Michele Gillespie, Michael Gomez, Mary Hayes, Michael W. Harris, Darlene Clark Hine, Suellen Hoy, Paula Kane, Karen M. Kennelly, Delores Liptak, Joseph G. Mannard, Elizabeth McGahan, Jo Ann Kay McNamara, Randall Miller, Barbara Misner, Cecilia Moore, Paul Noonan, Stephen Ochs, Regina Siegfried, Martha Smith, Elizabeth Smyth, Rosalyn Terborg-Penn, Sandra Gioia Treadway, Judith Weisenfeld, and Marcia Wright.

I thank all the members of the Batts and Morrow families for their loving support, encouragement, and tolerance throughout this process. My husband's late aunt, Mrs. Nellie K. Parker, extended her hospitality and love to me during my first research summer in Baltimore in 1994. My sister, Denise I. Batts, has provided invaluable technical assistance to her frequently desperate, computer-phobic sister throughout the years. My parents, Ruth V. Batts and the late Dr. James A. Batts, have always provided me with unconditional love, support, and a firm belief in the value of education, for which I will always remain grateful. My mother remains my first and most enduring model of black female agency. My children, Kieran and Evan, aided my research efforts as much with their love, patience, and understanding as they did with French or Latin translations and computer assistance. Finally, my husband, John, anchored my existence during this experience. His love, support, and perceptive intelligence unfailingly guided me through the dark and difficult times. I have appreciated his constructive comments on my work as much as his emotional support of my person. Without him, I would have neither undertaken nor completed this journey.

PERSONS OF COLOR AND
RELIGIOUS AT THE SAME TIME

INTRODUCTION

"Women without Virtue" was the title of the radio broadcast announced unexpectedly one Sunday morning. I listened intently as the *Sound and Spirit* program celebrated in word and song the various means African American women
had used historically to transcend white America's damningly exclusionary categorization of them as "women without virtue."[1] The program's theme resonated strongly in my own research on the Oblate Sisters of Providence, the
first permanent community of Roman Catholic women religious of African descent in the United States.[2] Organized in Baltimore, Maryland, in 1828, this pioneering Roman Catholic sisterhood defined itself as "a Religious society of
Coloured Women, established in Baltimore with the approbation of the Most
Reverend Archbishop, [who] renounce the world to consecrate themselves to
God, and to the Christian education of young girls of color."[3] The broadcast's
focus on black women redefining righteous behavior or generating alternative
standards of morality reinforced my appreciation of the exceptionalism of the
antebellum Oblate endeavor. In forming themselves into a religious sisterhood,
these women of color identified themselves—and demanded recognition from
white American society—as women of virtue who embodied standards of
morality previously ascribed to white middle-class women exclusively.

Elizabeth Clarisse Lange and James Hector Nicholas Joubert de la Muraille,
the two individuals recognized as cofounders of the Oblate Sisters of Providence, shared as well a French cultural heritage, Caribbean refugee status, a fervent devotion to the Roman Catholic faith, and an abiding commitment to the
education of black children. Nevertheless, within the contexts of the antebellum South and the Roman Catholic Church, defining differences of race and
gender separated the lives of these two people more than their mutual experi-

ences united them. Theirs proved to be a collaboration of extraordinary individuals. In aspiring to establish a black sisterhood, Elizabeth Lange defied both the denigration of black women's virtue and the subordinate status ascribed her as a free woman of color in a slave society. As a Roman Catholic priest and white male in the antebellum South, James Joubert transcended prevailing institutional and social attitudes toward both black people and women in organizing the Oblate Sisters of Providence.

More comprehensive in scope than a standard institutional history of the Oblate community, this study analyzes critical aspects of the reciprocal relationships of the Oblate Sisters, the Roman Catholic Church, and antebellum southern society. It highlights the complexities and nuances of the early development of the Oblate community and the critical role the sisters played in their own history.

Although spirituality constitutes a fundamental component of Oblate identity, this book in no way purports to be a treatise on Oblate spirituality. The decidedly sociocultural perspective of this work implies no intentional denial or diminution of the fervent piety that has suffused the Oblate foundation since its inception. The study does address significant aspects of Oblate spirituality, where and as appropriate to its thesis. However, this book emphasizes the societal and cultural experiences the Oblate Sisters shared with their black and female contemporaries in a racist and sexist society and the Oblate educational mission. Indeed, broadening the definition of spirituality beyond an exclusive focus on prayer life and ritual allows the inclusion of active ministry as a critical spiritual dimension. One source has observed, "In the parish ministry in their chapel and in their teaching ministry in their schools these black women religious directly and indirectly achieved religious meanings."[4] From this perspective, Oblate ministry forms a fundamental component of Oblate spirituality.

This study posits the centrality of race in the antebellum Oblate experience. The Oblate Sisters' color informed how they perceived themselves, as well as how others perceived them. The black racial identity of the Oblate Sisters remains the defining characteristic distinguishing them from the other communities of women religious functioning within the archdiocese of Baltimore during the nineteenth century. Black feminist thought differentiates black women's empowerment and prevailing models of power as domination. It offers "an alternative vision of power based on a humanist vision of self-actualization, self-definition, and self-determination."[5] Sociologist Patricia Hill Collins maintains that "empowerment involves rejecting the dimensions of knowledge, whether personal, cultural, or institutional, that perpetuate objectification and dehumanization."[6] This book argues that the Oblate Sisters, by associating in community as women religious and by executing their teaching ministry, defined themselves positively as a black sisterhood, in spite of their experience of socially ascribed derogation based on their identities as black women in antebellum American society. It further contends that the actions and initiatives of the Oblate Sisters fully conformed to what historian Rosalyn Terborg-Penn has identified as "perhaps the two most dominant values in the African feminist theory . . . developing survival strategies and encouraging self-reliance through female networks."[7]

TWO STREAMS OF immigration that converged in Baltimore in the 1790s enabled the formation of the Oblate Sisters almost forty years later. As the see, or official seat, of the first diocese of the Roman Catholic Church formed in the United States in 1789, Baltimore provided a logical haven for Catholics fleeing revolutions in France and the Caribbean. The extreme anticlericalism espoused by the proponents of the French Revolution prompted a group of French diocesan priests, the Society of St. Sulpice, to establish a mission on more hospitable shores. Between 1791 and 1793 nine Sulpician priests and seven seminarians arrived in Baltimore. The priests fulfilled their society's mission by establishing St. Mary's Seminary to educate priests and St. Mary's College as a preparatory institution for the seminary. They also augmented Bishop John Carroll's inadequate complement of thirty-five priests to minister to the 30,000 Catholics nationwide who initially composed the diocese of Baltimore.[8]

The second stream of immigration began in 1793 and spanned almost twenty years, as several contingents of San Domingan exiles arrived in Baltimore to escape the retributions of the former slave revolutionaries in St. Domingue. Located on the western third of the Caribbean island of Hispaniola, the colony of St. Domingue had developed into France's most profitable overseas possession in the eighteenth century. The labor of African slaves on San Domingan plantations enriched French planter and empire alike. In 1791 San Domingan slaves seized the opportunity and the inspiration provided by the revolution in France to strike for freedom. Toussaint L'Ouverture conquered the entire island of Hispaniola but maintained colonial ties with France. Jean Jacques Dessalines assumed leadership of the black forces after Toussaint's capture in 1803. Having defeated the invading French military expedition, Dessalines declared the independence of the island as Haiti in 1804.

French Caribbean exiles sought refuge in New Orleans, Charleston, Philadelphia, and other port cities in the United States. However, well-established commercial relations between Maryland planters and merchants and Caribbean planters made Baltimore a particularly logical haven for the émigrés. Hundreds of black and mulatto refugees, many of whom belonged to or identified with the Caribbean planter class in terms of sympathies, self-interest, education, and wealth, composed a significant portion of these successive waves of French Caribbean immigration.[9] In Baltimore, shared traditions attracted Sulpicians and San Domingans to each other, bound together by their French language and cultural heritage, their profession of the Roman Catholic faith, and their common experience of flight from radical revolutions at home that undermined their privileged positions.[10]

Starting in 1796 the Sulpician priests conducted Sunday catechetical classes, or religious instruction, in French for the community of black San Domingan émigrés who congregated in St. Mary's Lower Chapel at the Sulpician seminary on Paca Street. In 1827 James Joubert inherited responsibility for these catechetical classes and conceived the idea of a school to facilitate religious instruction. Fellow Sulpicians Ambrose Maréchal, archbishop of Baltimore, and Jean Tessier, superior of St. Mary's Seminary and vicar-general of the archdiocese of Baltimore, approved Joubert's school project in principle but opposed its immediate implementation, ostensibly because of lack of funds.[11]

Joubert persisted. When the Englishman James Whitfield became the fourth archbishop of Baltimore following Maréchal's death in January 1828, Joubert submitted his school proposal to him. Whitfield approved the plan. To staff his school Joubert approached Caribbean émigrés Elizabeth Lange and Marie Balas, two educated women of color and experienced teachers who already conducted their own school for children of their race. Lange and Balas informed Joubert of their enduring religious vocations, and the Sulpician decided, after consulting with Archbishop Whitfield, that a black sisterhood would suit his purposes as well.[12]

During the 1830s the Oblate Sisters of Providence forged the patterns of their communal life, executed their teaching ministry, defined their relationship as black women religious to the black lay community, and sought acceptance as a legitimate constituency within both the antebellum Roman Catholic Church and southern society. The Oblate Sisters functioned in a climate of heightened racial tensions in both society and church. Nevertheless, even in their first decade, the Oblate Sisters demonstrated "the utility of Black women's relationships with one another in providing a community for Black women's activism and self-determination."[13]

During the 1840s the Oblate Sisters confronted a series of crises: the death of cofounder James Joubert, the first departures and dismissal of professed members, and apparent desertion by church authorities. From November 1843 until

October 1847 the Oblate Sisters persevered in their observance of religious life and in the conduct of their school without benefit of official clerical sponsorship. Oblate steadfastness finally attracted the support of the German Redemptorist priests, who, beginning with Thaddeus Anwander, assumed the spiritual direction of the Oblate Sisters in 1847.

During the 1850s, conditions for free black people in general deteriorated as both abolitionists and apologists for slavery advanced to the polar extremes of their adversarial positions. Yet, Oblate status within the Baltimore religious community improved significantly with the succession of Francis Patrick Kenrick to the archiepiscopacy of Baltimore in 1851. The Oblate Sisters expanded their teaching mission, refined their relationship to the black lay community, and reformulated their school curriculum and prospectus to reflect their status as a tested and mature religious community. Student enrollment in the Oblate schools grew steadily in the antebellum period. In 1839 the Oblate Sisters taught 56 pupils; in 1850, 120 students; by 1855, between 250 and 300 students.[14]

OBLATE PROVENANCE in Baltimore proved to be a defining feature of the sisters' nineteenth-century experience. "Baltimore has, not improperly, been styled the Rome of the United States,"[15] boasted an 1830 Catholic publication of the city's status as literally the capital of the Catholic United States. The Oblate Sisters joined three other communities of women religious previously established in the archdiocese: the Carmelite Nuns (1790), the Visitation Sisters of Georgetown (1800), and the Sisters of Charity of St. Joseph, Emmitsburg (1809). By 1837 all four communities maintained establishments in the city of Baltimore. The School Sisters of Notre Dame (1847), the Sisters of Mercy (1855), and the Sisters of the Holy Cross (1859) complete the roster of sisterhoods functioning in antebellum Baltimore. As did the other women religious located in Baltimore, the Oblate Sisters enjoyed exceptional exposure to and recognition from national and international church dignitaries and officials who visited the premier see of the Catholic Church in the United States.[16]

As the "free black capital of America" after 1820, Baltimore offered the Oblate Sisters a potentially critical base of black community support. In 1790 Baltimore claimed approximately 300 free black residents; in 1820, over 10,000. Between 1800 and 1850 the free black population of Baltimore increased by more than 22,000 people, representing a growth rate in excess of 800 percent during the first half of the nineteenth century. Several developments between 1780 and 1820 had contributed to the burgeoning free black population in the Upper South in general and in Maryland in particular. Black military service in the

American War of Independence, revolutionary ideology proclaiming liberty, and religious enthusiasm espousing equality and fraternity had motivated significant numbers of eighteenth-century slaveholders to manumit their slaves. The supplanting of tobacco by wheat cultivation and the consequent reduced need for large slaveholdings further decreased the number of slaves in the region. Finally, the swelling tide of San Domingan refugees between 1790 and 1810 significantly augmented the ranks of free black people in Baltimore.[17]

Few reliable sources documented black Catholic demographics in antebellum Baltimore. In 1785, eight years before the first wave of San Domingan emigration, Bishop John Carroll estimated that 3,000 black Catholics—slave and free—lived in the state of Maryland. By 1865 black Catholics in Maryland numbered 16,000, and nationally, 100,000. No reliable statistics documented the actual number of black San Domingan émigrés entering Baltimore between 1793 and 1810, but sources estimate between 500 and 1,000 black Francophone refugees. The significance of the influx of black San Domingan refugees lay in their ethnic consciousness and consequent formation of a discrete black Catholic congregation at St. Mary's Lower Chapel, served by the French Sulpician priests. Before the Francophone black emigration, Baltimore black Catholics "were absorbed in the parish churches and were taken for granted."[18]

But this self-conscious black San Domingan refugee community remains largely lost in the historical record. In sharp contrast to its reception of the white San Domingan refugees, white American society received the darker-skinned Francophone immigrants from the Caribbean in the late eighteenth and early nineteenth centuries inhospitably. In significant ways the hostile reception white American society accorded Haitian refugees in the 1990s replicated their reception in the 1790s. For black San Domingan refugees, "as second-class citizens in the slaveholding sections of the United States, their contributions to antebellum society were dutifully ignored or purposefully misattributed by unsympathetic whites in the nineteenth century."[19]

By the 1820s Anglophone black Catholics had joined the second-generation, American-born children of émigré parents attending the Sulpician classes in religious instruction, now conducted in English. In 1832 Archbishop James Whitfield claimed 300 to 400 regular black Catholic communicants in Baltimore alone. Thus, a significant number of black Catholics of both Anglophone and Francophone cultural origin and the largest free black population base in the antebellum United States provided the Oblate Sisters of Providence with a decided demographic advantage in antebellum Baltimore.[20]

As befitted its reputation as the nineteenth-century free black capital, Baltimore sustained a vital, varied, and self-empowered antebellum black community. Black Baltimoreans created and supported a nexus of religious, social, and educational institutions undergirding their community life.[21] Previous accounts of the Oblate experience have essentially ignored the complex, nuanced interactions between this pioneering sisterhood and the community the sisters dedicated themselves to serve. This study explores the mutually supportive relationship the Oblate Sisters and the black laity forged during the antebellum period.

Antebellum Baltimore further influenced the existence of the Oblate Sisters as free women of color in a slaveholding city that occasionally noted their "of color" designation more rigorously than it honored their free status. Baltimore was "in but not of slave society" and as such embodied the "middle ground" between the commercial North and plantation South that Maryland occupied.[22] A vital urban center, Baltimore emerged as the industrial and commercial capital of Maryland, thoroughly integrated into the commercial economy of the North and only vestigially dependent on the South's slave economy. However, the powerful commercial interests of Baltimore and northern Maryland failed to supplant the political dominance of eastern shore and southern Maryland planters in the state. The state legislature severely underrepresented the city of Baltimore.[23]

The tenuous position of Maryland's free black population—economically essential and socially anomalous—reflected the inherent volatility of Maryland's dualistic slave and free political economy. Free black labor proved economically desirable to both slaveholders and nonslaveholders in Maryland. Declining slaveholdings forced planters to depend on the seasonal hiring of free black workers. Furthermore, planters preferred free black to white workers, as the latter—enfranchised and hostile to slavery—posed a potentially formidable challenge to the continued existence of the peculiar institution. Nonslaveholders, resentful of planter political dominance and confronted with a declining slave labor pool for hiring, readily employed free black workers for their casual, seasonal labor needs. Thus, although white Americans frequently despised and feared them, free black people nevertheless served a crucial economic function in antebellum Maryland society.[24]

The pervasive debasement of all black people ensuing from the racial basis of slavery in the United States convinced most white Americans of universal black inferiority. The city of Baltimore differed in degree, but not in kind, in this pattern of white thought about black people. White Baltimoreans' ambivalence toward free black people interpolated their perceptions of and responses to the Oblate Sisters of Providence. Baltimore figured prominently in antebellum Oblate life, less as a topographical construct distinguished by its peculiar spatial arrangement of streets and buildings and more essentially as a social construct, the locus of a unique confluence of attitudes, beliefs, people, and experiences. Whether as Roman Catholic see, free black capital, or anomalous slaveholding metropolis, Baltimore provided the locality and context that structured both the opportunities and the restrictions the Oblate Sisters of Providence encountered in their early years.

ISSUES OF RACE, gender, and ethnicity informed the Oblate Sisters' position within the nineteenth-century Roman Catholic Church in the United States, as it confronted significant challenges in its own evolution as an institution in American society. A relatively recent and understaffed mission of the ancient and universal church, the Catholic Church in the United States struggled to reconcile its duties of subordination and submission to Rome with its need to establish a national identity responsive to the issues and conditions inherent in the American environment. From 1789 through the 1830s the church in the South remained the foundation of American Roman Catholicism. In 1789 over half of the 35,000 Roman Catholics in the United States lived in the South, the largest number by far in Maryland. Waves of European Catholic immigrants— 250,000 in the 1830s; 700,000 in the 1840s; 1,000,000 in the 1850s—shifted the concentration of the American Catholic population from Maryland to the cities of the Northeast beginning in the 1840s.[25]

But the Catholic Church in the United States retained the imprint of its southern origins through the nineteenth century. In fully embracing the tenets of southern nationalism, the Catholic Church in the South accommodated racism and the institution of slavery. Questions of race occasionally strained relations between the American hierarchy and authorities in Rome. Throughout the antebellum era several bishops and clergy defended the peculiar institution of slavery, although the papacy had condemned the slave trade in 1839. Such contemporary racial attitudes influenced the specific relationships and interactions between the Oblate Sisters and members of the American clergy.[26]

As women religious, the Oblate Sisters shared with other sisterhoods an ascribed social status within the patriarchal and hierarchical Roman Catholic Church. Indeed, the institutionalized subordination of women provided one instance in which the orientation of the Catholic Church accorded well with that of nineteenth-century American society. Nineteenth-century sisters often accommodated male dominance in the church, home, and workplace and inculcated conventional pedagogical ideals of republican motherhood and domesticity in their female convent school pupils. Yet, convent life itself offered nineteenth-century young women unique countercultural opportunities to inhabit an environment of relative female autonomy. Furthermore, women religious often opposed male clerical superiors in order to protect the integrity of their distinctive missions as they understood them. During this era most service communities of women religious struggled to reconcile the realities of their active ministries requiring interaction with the secular world and the ideal of cloistered contemplation promoted by church authorities in Rome. As did their peer active sisterhoods throughout the world, the Oblate Sisters experienced the dynamic tension between the realities imposed by their social environment and the spiritual ideals upheld by the Roman Catholic Church's preference for the contemplative tradition.[27]

Issues of race, gender, ethnicity, and religion informed the position of the Oblate Sisters of Providence within antebellum southern society. Their Roman Catholic identity potentially estranged these black sisters from the sympathies of a substantially Protestant nation, which viewed the Catholic Church alternately as the perpetrator of a popish plot to conquer the United States and as the evil genius holding in thrall the teeming masses of immigrants invading America. Nativism, in both its anti-Catholic and anti-immigrant aspects, flourished in antebellum Baltimore.

As a sisterhood whose charter members had emigrated from Saint Domingue, the Oblate Sisters themselves claimed immigrant roots. The standard chronicle of the Oblate experience, disregarding the sisters' African ancestry, characterizes them as "French in language, in sympathy, and in habit of life."[28] However, this study contends that elements of traditional African cultures plausibly influenced the foundation of the Oblate community in important, if previously unrecognized, ways.

As black women religious, members of the Oblate community observed the vow of chastity in a society that denigrated the virtue of all black women—slave or free—and consequently considered the concept of chaste black women an oxymoron. Indeed, the commitment to celibacy embraced by all sisterhoods would have found favor with few nineteenth-century Americans who subscribed to the cult of domesticity and its promulgation of the goals of matrimony and maternity. While issues of gender woven into the nineteenth-century social context affected the Oblate Sisters and their peer white sisterhoods comparably, the pervasive strands of racism woven warp and woof into the American social fabric ensnared the Oblate community alone. The ways in which issues of race, gender, ethnicity, and religion informed the antebellum experience of the Oblate Sisters of Providence constitute a recurring theme of this work.

THE ANNALS, or the original diary of the Oblate Sisters of Providence, form the principal primary source for this study. Generally formal and impersonal in its language, this official community record reflects the priorities of the Roman Catholic institutionalized religious life for women it so faithfully chronicles by supplanting individual and personal perspectives with communal and spiritual ones. Nevertheless, the Oblate annals contain revealing glimpses of the tensions, opposition, challenges, and triumphs this community of black women religious experienced. The Oblate Rule and Constitutions, account books and ledgers, parish sacramental records, episcopal correspondence, census materials, city directories, and newspaper accounts provide additional information.

The historical record includes virtually no information about the lives of individual Oblate Sisters beyond the material found in the annals. The early Oblate Sisters do not number among the historic founders and members of congregations of women religious who have bequeathed posterity written personal accounts, correspondence, scholarly treatises, or mystical writings. Whereas the Protestant tradition, particularly Calvinism, encouraged journal or diary keeping as a gauge of individual progress toward spiritual perfection, the Catholic tradition deemed neither literacy nor individual written records essential to salvation.[29]

Although literate, the women who joined the Oblate community lacked both the religious imperative and probably the leisure for diary keeping. Sisterhoods often practiced anonymity and self-effacement in pursuit of the religious ideal of loss of self in community. Like some other communities of women religious, the Oblate Sisters tolerated only minimal, censored, external correspondence, even with immediate family members, to subordinate familial to communal allegiance.[30] Even as this regulation facilitated communal bonding, it deprived the historical record of a potentially rich source of information about the Oblate antebellum experience. As an indigenous religious community independent of European attachment, the Oblate Sisters never amassed the body of correspondence and reports characteristic of the many American sisterhoods affiliated with European motherhouses. Furthermore, the Oblate Sisters did not establish missions or foundations beyond their Baltimore motherhouse during the antebellum era; consequently, they did not generate the written documentation produced by sisterhoods with multiple locations within the United States.

A detailed analysis of the critical first decade in the Oblate community's existence forms the major focus of the first half of this book. The first six chapters identify the roots of the Oblate community. In 1914 Oblate Sister Mary Petra Boston entitled her book on the Oblate Sisters *Blossoms Gathered from the Lower Branches*.[31] Pursuing the floral metaphor suggested by that title, this study conceptualizes its treatment of the Oblate experience in the 1830s as a blossom examined from the inside out. This approach appropriately highlights the study's fundamental thesis that the Oblate Sisters exercised self-definition and self-empowerment as it attempts to reconstruct the Oblate antebellum experience from the perspective of the sisters themselves.

The first chapter examines the salient personal characteristics and pre-Oblate experiences of the four charter Oblate members: Elizabeth Clarisse Lange, Marie Magdelaine Balas, Rosine Boegue, and Marie Therese Duchemin. Chapter 2 examines the essential role of Oblate cofounder and Sulpician priest James Joubert in the formulation of the Oblate Rule and his tireless efforts to legitimize this community of black women religious within the Roman Catholic Church. Chapter 3 examines the development of Oblate communal life, the sisters' sense of communal identity and their collective consciousness as a society of black women religious, and the articulation of a statement of philosophy for the Oblate school.

Chapters 4, 5, and 6 represent three concentric rings of petals to continue the floral motif. They shift the focus of the study from the internal Oblate community to those external elements forming the historical context within which the Oblate Sisters functioned. Chapter 4 examines the Oblate Sisters' relationship with the black community; Chapter 5, Oblate interaction with the institutional church; Chapter 6, Oblate interaction with white society. Chapters 7, 8, 9, 10, and 11 examine the impact of these root forces from the 1830s on Oblate experiences in the 1840s and 1850s.

Recent scholarship investigating the experiences of black women has essentially redressed the state of historiography indicted in the title of the 1982 study *All the Women Are White, All the Blacks are Men, But Some of Us Are Brave.*[32] However, as free black people, as women, as Roman Catholics, and as a religious institute, the Oblate Sisters of Providence have eluded serious scholarly attention, perhaps because they confound conventional historiographical categorization. Scholars researching nineteenth-century black religious history have focused almost exclusively on Protestant denominations; those in black women's history, on issues of slavery, family, sexual relations, and work; those in Roman Catholic history, on European immigrants, nativism, and institutional histories of white religious communities. As this study clearly indicates, however, the antebellum experience of the Oblate Sisters embodied the issues of race, gender, religion, education, and immigration animating nineteenth-century American society.

Conceived as a response to scholar Cyprian Davis's assertion that no adequate history of any of the black Catholic sisterhoods exists, this study aspires to be a contribution toward rectifying such an egregious omission.[33] Among recent studies of nineteenth-century Baltimore, Christopher Phillip's *Freedom's Port* focuses on the development of black community institutions but slights the role of black women in general and fails to acknowledge the existence of the Oblate Sisters of Providence in particular.[34] No monographic treatment of the Oblate Sisters of Providence has appeared since Grace Sherwood's out-of-print and nonscholarly work, *The Oblates' Hundred and One Years*, published in 1931. Sympathetic but dated, Sherwood's treatment minimizes the agency of the Oblate Sisters in their own history and that of black people in general. The Oblate story merits both a more nuanced treatment and wider inclusion in the annals of American history than it currently enjoys.

CHAPTER ONE

Persons of Color and Religious at the Same Time

THE CHARTER MEMBERS OF
THE OBLATE SISTERS

❖ ❖ ❖ ❖ ❖ ❖ ❖ ❖ ❖ ❖ ❖ ❖ ❖ ❖ ❖ ❖ ❖ ❖ ❖ ❖

Roman Catholic reference sources define the term "charism" as a spiritual gift, talent, or grace that God gives individuals to use for the spiritual welfare and benefit of the Christian community. These sources consider charisms manifestations of the Holy Spirit animating the church; as such, charisms constitute social graces in that they lead their recipients to the total service of Christ in the church. Church sources maintain that in every age the Holy Spirit has endowed saints, founders of religious orders and movements, and individuals from both the clergy and the laity with charisms to speak to their own age.[1]

Historically, founders of religious societies imprinted their respective communities with their personal charisms. The secular definition of the term "charism"—a special quality of leadership that captures the popular imagination and inspires unswerving loyalty—reflects this essential relationship between religious founders and their communities. This integral component of religious formation also occurred in the Oblate experience. Much of the life of Elizabeth Clarisse Lange, Oblate cofounder with James Joubert, remains undocumented prior to 1828. However, two salient characteristics of her pre-

Oblate life prove verifiable: her fervent devotion to the Roman Catholic faith, noted by both her confessor and her cofounder, and her vocation to teach.[2] The Oblate Sisters incorporated these personal qualities of Elizabeth Lange in their community identity.

The historical and sociocultural contexts in which sisterhoods formed also influenced their respective identities. As did all societies of women religious in the nineteenth-century United States, the Oblates contended with both the entrenched, male-centered orientation of the Roman Catholic Church and the encroachments of patriarchal tendencies in American society. In studying nineteenth-century women in general as well as the histories of communities of women religious operating within the concentric circles of male-dominated church and society, determining female agency frequently proves challenging. Standard histories customarily credit men with the foundation of women's teaching communities. Indeed, for the first decade of Oblate existence, their Sulpician cofounder James Joubert personally maintained the Oblate annals, imposing a male perspective on the only extant account of the community's history. Furthermore, two of the earliest histories of the community, written by Oblate Sisters, followed the annals closely and portrayed Joubert as the sole founder and Elizabeth Lange merely as a charter member and first superior of the community.[3]

But the Oblate Sisters formed one of four sisterhoods founded in the United States between 1809 and 1829 that evolved from previously existing associations of lay women teachers organized in response to perceived community needs. Reinterpreting James Joubert's role as more that of a facilitator and less that of a micromanager of daily Oblate affairs restores focus on the original personal charisms of Elizabeth Lange and Marie Balas.[4]

The fact that Lange and Balas had independently established a school in Baltimore demonstrated their determination to address a perceived need for education in their new country without seeking white, male, or institutional approval to proceed. Circumstantial evidence suggests the Fells Point area in east Baltimore as the probable location of their home-based school. Lange and Balas had discussed with Reverend John Francis Moranvillé, pastor of St. Patrick Church in Fells Point, prospects for establishing a school for colored people at the Point, "the home of many French sea-captains engaged in trade with the West Indies, and they, with their families and slaves, made up the early congregation."[5]

Oblate member and Superior Sister Mary Theresa Catherine Willigman, generally recognized as the first Oblate historian, recalled in her late-nineteenth-century accounts that black Caribbean émigré parents "lost no time in placing their children in Miss Lange's school," which was "filled with the children of the most intelligent families of Baltimore." Significantly, Willigman continued,

"However, let me add here that no distinction whatever was made among the pupils, and a very large number of the poorer class who had no means of paying for their tuition was admitted."[6] Lange's school evidently served a broad spectrum of the black Francophone community, from poor families to those enjoying sufficiently comfortable circumstances to finance their children's education at the school.[7]

Joubert's own account of his first meeting with Elizabeth Lange and Marie Balas in 1828 clearly indicated his full appreciation of their teaching competence and their independent means. He further acknowledged that Lange and Balas revealed to him spontaneously and unsolicited their pre-existing religious vocations:

> In consequence I imparted my plans on this subject to two excellent colored girls, well thought of and very capable of keeping this school. Both of them told me that for more than ten years they wished to consecrate themselves to God for this good work, waiting patiently that in His own infinite goodness He would show them a way of giving themselves to Him. . . . They promised to do everything that I should think of to further this work, and they put themselves and all that they had entirely at my disposal, which necessitated their discontinuing a small free school which they had been having for a number of years at their home.[8]

After Lange and Balas declared their religious vocations, Joubert asserted, "Up to this time I had been thinking of just founding a school." Citing considerations of stability and efficiency, he concluded, "I thought of founding a kind of religious society. . . . Hence it was then that I conceived the idea of founding the Sisters of Providence. I declare before God that I had no other desire than to advance His glory."[9] Beneath the veneer of his exclusive assumption of the credit for the Oblate foundation, Joubert's account suggests that he himself remained fully cognizant of the collaborative, mutually advantageous nature of the Oblate venture. Joubert acquired the services of experienced teachers while Lange and Balas gained official church sanction of their teaching endeavors and the realization of their religious vocations.

That these two black Catholic women persisted in their religious vocations for a decade prior to fulfillment reveals much about the personal charisms of two of the charter members of the Oblate Sisters of Providence. In common with the lives of founders of other religious communities, the lives of Lange and Balas embodied the charismatic model of the "grace of constant, lifelong fidelity to the living of the Christian life in one's state in the Church, despite trials and difficulties of every type."[10] Unaided by external acknowledgment or official encouragement, Lange and Balas relied exclusively on their internalized commitments to their religious vocations based on their faith that God would provide.

Joubert himself may have sensed this wellspring of black Catholic female activism at the inception of the Oblate community. The Oblate Sisters of Providence adopted as a patron St. Frances of Rome, who in the fifteenth century had founded an oblate community of women religious engaged in charitable works in the world. The term "oblate" means "one offered" or "made over to God." Throughout church history, oblate has referred variously to children dedicated to monasteries by their parents, to laymen and -women who did not take the vows binding religious but affiliated and worked with monks or nuns, and to several different societies and congregations of priests and nuns.[11]

St. Frances of Rome organized a group of Roman noblewomen already engaged in charitable hospital work into a religious community that received papal approval of their constitutions in 1433. She ranked among the first female founders of a church-sanctioned service sisterhood who both institutionalized a preexisting mission in the identity of her community and earned recognition as the exclusive founder of her community, without male collaboration.[12] While apparently conforming to contemporary social conventions and expectations about white male dominance, Joubert nevertheless acknowledged black female initiative within southern U.S. society and the patriarchal Roman Catholic Church. Elizabeth Lange and Marie Balas had already committed themselves to religious vocations and engaged in the Oblate community's defining mission: the education of children of color. The choice of St. Frances of Rome as an Oblate patron consequently reflected the seminal roles of these two women in the formation of the Oblate Sisters of Providence.

On 13 June 1828 San Domingan émigré Rosine Boegue joined Elizabeth Lange and Marie Balas to begin their novitiate, or period of spiritual preparation and training prior to professing the vows of a full member of a religious community. During this trial year the sisters collaborated with Joubert in the formulation of the Oblate Rule and Constitutions, the customized set of regulations guiding all facets of behavior for members of religious communities. That same day the School for Colored Girls opened with eleven boarding and nine day students. A rented residence at 5 St. Mary's Court, in close proximity to St. Mary's Seminary and Lower Chapel, served as both Oblate convent and school that first year.

A year later, on 2 July 1829, in their second rented residence at 610 George Street, James Joubert received the professions of the four charter members of the Oblate Sisters of Providence. The fourth candidate, Almaide Duchemin, although born in Baltimore, claimed San Domingan ancestry through her mother, Betsy Maxis Duchemin. Elizabeth Lange became Sister Mary Elizabeth; Marie Balas, Sister Mary Frances; Rosine Boegue, Sister Mary Rose; and Almaide Duchemin, Sister Mary Therese.[13]

No extant record reveals the self-perceptions or understandings of Elizabeth Lange, Marie Balas, Rosine Boegue, and Almaide Duchemin about their own roles in the founding of the Oblate Sisters of Providence. But the racial prejudice prevalent in American church and society precluded "their taking the direct and public initiative to start an order of black religious women."[14] The Roman Catholic Church required all communities of women religious to function under the spiritual directorship of a priest. For the black Oblate Sisters, considerations of race compounded their gender status, doubly requiring the intervention and sponsorship of the white Sulpician priest James Joubert to validate their existence as constituencies in both the Roman Catholic Church and antebellum American society.

In fulfilling their missions, founders of nineteenth-century American sisterhoods established schools, hospitals, or orphanages. These institutions had such obvious social utility that the general public patronized and recognized them as both serving a public need and consonant with social values. However, unlike founders of white communities serving white society, Elizabeth Lange and James Joubert proposed to provide for the despised black population both a corps of teachers from its own ranks and an education, neither of which the general public considered serving a public need or consonant with prevailing social values. Indeed, some segments of American society objected to education for free black people as much as for slaves.[15] The Oblate Sisters' very existence as free women of color organized into a religious community to educate black children challenged prevailing social and episcopal attitudes about race and gender. If not revolutionary, Lange's and Joubert's foundation of the Oblate Sisters constituted a heroic feat.

THE DEARTH OF extant evidence frustrates efforts to reconstruct the pre-Oblate lives of the charter members of the Oblate community in detail. Nevertheless, sufficient evidence survives to document a broad outline of some of their personal histories. Born of racially mixed parentage probably in the 1780s in either Saint Domingue or Cuba,[16] Elizabeth Clarisse Lange apparently enjoyed a relatively privileged life, including a formal education. The Sisters of Notre Dame du Cap-Français had established an academy for girls in Le Cap, St. Domingue, in 1733. The sisters had intended to educate young girls of both races originally, but the white colonists objected so strenuously to the prospect of racial integration that the sisters acquiesced to their demands that even catechetical instruction occur only on a segregated basis. However, in 1774 the English fleet lay siege to the city and Mother de Columbas, superior of the Sisters of Notre Dame du Cap-Français in that mission, vowed to institute special classes for mulatto and black girls if Le Cap escaped destruction. According to the Notre Dame du Cap-Français annals, a fierce storm arose and destroyed the English fleet in the harbor. Mother de Columbas fulfilled her vow, and from 1774 the sisters' school accepted mulatto and black pupils as well.[17] Elizabeth Lange and other early Oblate members of Caribbean origin may have enrolled in this convent school. Such an educational experience would have exposed these young girls of color to the religious life as an appropriate and viable vocation.

Lange emigrated with her mother to the United States, where she may have resided briefly in Charleston, South Carolina, and Norfolk, Virginia. Only the friendly intervention of certain ship captains who were indebted to Lange's mother enabled the two émigrés to circumvent Charleston's restrictions on the admission of colored people. Elizabeth Lange resided in Baltimore from at least 1813.[18] Financial support from her father's estate allowed Lange to maintain her independence in the slave city of Baltimore. The Oblate Sisters of Providence did not own slaves. But Elizabeth Lange, and later the Oblate community through her inheritance, clearly benefited from the institution of slavery, which generated planter wealth. Oblate accounts note that "Sister Mary [Lange] especially was very often the recipient of large sums of money, sent from her home in Santiago" and that Lange had inherited "$2000 left her by Monsieur Lange her father" and had "received in settlement $1411.59 which was due her" in 1832 and 1833, respectively.[19] Like James Joubert, Elizabeth Lange probably maintained more direct connections with slave society than acknowledged in previous accounts. Unlike Joubert, Lange became an anomaly in her adopted home of Baltimore. Elizabeth Lange was a genuine victim of the slave insurrection so constantly feared yet seldom realized in U.S. slave society. But as a free woman of color, she elicited little sympathy from southern slaveholders or other white people who noted her "of color" designation more assiduously than either her planter connections or her free status.

The appearance of the names of Elizabeth Clarisse Lange and Marie Magdelaine Balas on the registers of three religious confraternities or devotional societies proves instructive. Within the universal Roman Church, religious confraternities were literally catholic in their membership, encompassing laity, clergy, and religious, male and female, rich and poor, young and old alike. Each confraternity selected one act, such as reciting a specific prayer, wearing a

Sister Mary Elizabeth Lange, O.S.P., Oblate cofounder and first superior, photographed in her later years (Courtesy of Archives of the Oblate Sisters of Providence, Baltimore, Md.)

certain medal, or regular assistance at Mass as its distinguishing feature or bond of association. Such groups might also hold regular, exclusive meetings or weekly rites, thus fostering a sense of bonding and cohesion.[20]

Entries in the registers of three religious confraternities cite the names Elizabeth Clarisse Lange and Marie Magdelaine Balas adjacent to each other. This consistent pairing of their names in the registers documented their close pre-Oblate collaboration. Early in his association with these two women Joubert had described them as "two persons so close one was not able to do without the other,"[21] a characterization as revealing as it may have been patronizing. Lange and Balas lived and worked together, hoped to realize religious vocations, and even joined confraternities together. But Elizabeth Lange and Marie Balas exhibited distinctly different personalities.

Their multiple memberships in these devotional societies from as early as 1813 indicate the depth of Lange's and Balas's religious piety and dedication to devotional life fifteen years prior to commencing their Oblate novitiate. The names of Rosine Boegue and Marie Therese Duchemin, the two other charter Oblate members, appeared on the registers of two of three of these religious confraternities as well. Their commitment corroborated the endorsement of the Sulpician priest Jean Tessier, Joubert's mentor and predecessor in ministering to the black congregation of St. Mary's Lower Chapel from 1796 to 1827. Tessier deemed all four charter Oblate members "his spiritual daughters," qualified to form the religious society of Oblates.[22]

The available evidence does not indicate in any detail the specific nature of the Baltimore confraternities to which Lange, Balas, Boegue, and Duchemin belonged. Written in French, the registers identified nonwhite members as "Negresse libre" or "Mulatresse libre" for free black or mulatto women; "Negre libre" or "Mulatre libre" for free black or mulatto men; "Negre de," "Negresse de," or "Mulatre de," or "Mulatresse de" for slaves. In part recorded by Jean Tessier, the confraternity registers listed the members' names indiscriminately. Such egalitarian listing—the rich among the poor, the French among the Anglo-American, the slave among the free, the black and mulatto among the white, clerics among laity, and children among adults—implied a degree of universal fellowship that in reality may have consisted of little more than the proximity of the names on the pages. Given the racial and social proscriptions of antebellum Baltimore, these confraternal members probably inhabited discrete, parallel social universes.

Circumstantial evidence suggests as much. Tessier's egalitarian system of recording the confraternity registers stood in sharp contrast to his recording of St. Mary's Lower Chapel Easter Duty Lists, which noted those Catholics who fulfilled their annual spiritual obligations of going to confession and receiving Holy Communion during the Easter season. In the Easter Duty Lists Tessier segregated white from black and male from female, and after 1825 further distinguished between French and American white "women" and between mulatto and black "girls." Significantly, Tessier's lists, extant between 1809 and 1833, suggest that—if these penitents and communicants prove representative of the larger group—black members consistently formed a significant component and occasionally the majority of the colored worshipers. Furthermore, slaves as well as free black people belonged to this congregation.[23] The black Catholics who congregated at St. Mary's Lower Chapel constituted no color or class elite.

Contrary to claims that the Catholic Church did not countenance racial segregation in the nineteenth century, "in accordance with a social convention, the colored worshipers in most Catholic Churches occupied a place by themselves and were not allowed to mix indiscriminately with the whites at divine services."[24] The Lower Chapel of St. Mary's Seminary served as a parish church for white and black laity alike, but not as a unified community. The two races either attended devotions at different times or maintained segregated seating at the same services.[25] The degree of social interaction or associational bonding the confreres of these devotional societies actually experienced remains unclear. The fact that the Catholic Church considered black and white, slave and free equally eligible for membership in these societies remains significant, a testimony to the church's spiritual—if not social—egalitarianism.

For Elizabeth Lange, Marie Balas, Rosine Boegue, and Therese Duchemin, membership in these religious confraternities proved especially vital. The lives of these women embodied the requisite middle-class values and virtues, but their race excluded them from joining existing Roman Catholic sisterhoods. Their Francophone Roman Catholicism precluded their membership in the women's societies associated with Baltimore's Anglophone black Protestant denominations. The Roman Catholic Church discouraged—when it did not explicitly forbid—Catholic participation in non-Catholic church activities and organizations.[26] Their residence in the slaveholding South obviated their membership in the nascent voluntary associations and moral reform societies of the urban, northern industrializing middle class.

From the 1790s through the antebellum period, voluntary female associations proliferated in the North. White women organized church-related and maternal groups, focusing on social and domestic reform. In contrast, northern free black women organized mutual benefit societies to extend financial assistance to members and their families. Free women of color in some cities of the Upper South also participated in such economic self-help initiatives. By 1838 black women in Baltimore had formed nine different mutual benefit groups associated with various Protestant church denominations.[27]

Roman Catholic free black women in Baltimore and Washington, D.C., also organized mutual aid societies. "The good coloured women [who] appear not to be outdone by the ladies of Baltimore" formed the church-sanctioned Tobias Society around 1827 to assist the sick and bury the dead of their own race "in the most solemn and religious manner." Tobias Society members distinguished themselves by their clothing of "deep black with white cuffs, and a white badge on the breast." They received communion once a month to commemorate the deceased.[28] Significantly, in its report of the activities of the Tobias Society, the *Metropolitan*, a Roman Catholic Baltimore publication, juxtaposed "good coloured women" to the "ladies of Baltimore." The report thus reflected conventional gender distinctions derived from racial identities: the females of color were "women," regardless of their class status; "ladies" required no color clarification since the term in conventional usage referred only to white females.

In 1828 free black women in Washington, D.C., organized the citywide Coloured Female Roman Catholic Beneficial Society. Although "having for a long time labored under very great disadvantages, arising from a state of ignorance existing among us," these women formed a mutual benefit society "for the further suppression of vice and immorality, the diffusion of knowledge, and that we may be enabled to stretch forth the hand of benevolence." Criteria for membership included status as a free colored woman or her descendant and residency within the incorporated city of Washington. No women "addicted to inebriety, or who have a plurality of husbands" qualified for membership. A member could receive benefits after regular payment of the $0.125 monthly dues for eighteen months and after the determination of the society's board of directors that her affliction "render[ed] her incapable of following her occupation, or of gaining a livelihood for the space of one week." Sickness benefits consisted of $1 a week for six weeks or longer, funds permitting; burial benefits "shall not exceed eight dollars, while the funds remain in their present state." Cause for membership termination included delinquency in payment of dues beyond three months, fraudulent receipt of benefits while gainfully employed, and "convict[ion] in a court of justice of any scandalous offence, or for being guilty of any disreputable conduct."[29]

Their printed constitution revealed that these women recognized the low esteem in which white society generally held black women and that they resolved both to ameliorate their condition and to hold their membership accountable to certain standards of decency and propriety. Members were working women of modest means, as their minimal dues and expressed concern about the state of the organization's funds suggested. Although organized under the auspices of the Roman Catholic Church, the society's constitution mandated no religious obligation or observance beyond burial: economic survival, not religious devotional practice, concerned the membership primarily. The organization, purpose, and membership of the Coloured Female Roman Catholic Beneficial Society of Washington City may reflect quite accurately those of many antebellum black women's beneficial societies.

Roman Catholic black women in the South confronted a void of socially, racially, and religiously sanctioned associations available to them. The religious confraternities and the spiritual egalitarianism their open membership implied, consequently, became even more compelling to especially pious and devout women of color. But devotional societies ultimately proved insufficient for Elizabeth Lange, Marie Balas, Rosine Boegue, and Therese Duchemin in 1820s Baltimore. These women and others sought a total immersion in the spiritual dimension of their lives, that neither devotional societies, nor inherently part-time voluntary associations, nor mutual benefit societies could provide.

OBLATE HISTORIAN Willigman provides the most comprehensive and reliable information on the nineteenth-century Oblate experience in general and individual Oblate members Lange and Duchemin in particular. She also translated the annals from their original French into English. Willigman's knowledge of Lange derived from personal experience, as she had lived in the Oblate community from the age of five years. Lange served as surrogate mother, teacher, and novice mistress to Sarah Willigman, the future Oblate Sister Mary Theresa Catherine.[30]

Four significant traits of Sister Mary Lange emerge from Willigman's portrayal of the Oblate cofounder. Willigman recalled that "Sister Mary never spared herself." "If there was any work to be done," she continued, "she would be first to give example." "Work held no terrors for her; very seldom did she rest." Even in advanced age, Lange "still continued taking part in the work of the Community, especially sewing, and when her strength permitted, manual labor." Lange was among the first of the sisters to volunteer to nurse the cholera victims at the Almshouse in 1832.[31] Lange's leadership by example, her demonstrated principle of requiring no more from another sister than she demanded of herself, probably made another Lange trait more palatable to the other sisters.

Willigman remembered that "Sister Mary was very good but a very strict observer of the Rule and made no allowance for small omissions." Lange's mother, who had retired to the Oblate community as a boarder the year before she died, "was afraid of her daughter and called her Mistress." A student "was mortally afraid of Sister Mary." The following excerpt from Willigman's account further suggests draconian tendencies in Lange's leadership compared to that of her successor, Sister Frances Balas, Lange's constant companion of pre-Oblate days: "When [Lange's] first term of office expired, she was succeeded by Sister Frances, the favorite of all the Community. Even the children would crowd around Sister Frances and look up lovingly for a smile or caress. Those who remember her have only the most pleasant of recollections."[32]

Willigman recalled that Sister Mary was a strict novice mistress, although one who "did her duty well to those she was placed over." Furthermore Willigman maintained, "I know that very often Father Joubert would take the young Sisters' part, though Sister Mary was a good, kind Mother and when anyone was sick or in pain, she would do the last thing to give them ease and comfort."[33] That Joubert's occasional intervention or exceptional circumstances of pain or illness alone elicited a maternal response from her reinforce the impression of Lange's severity.

Willigman was not the only one of Sister Mary's contemporaries to comment on her leadership style. In 1833 Joubert and the Oblate community revised and amended the original Oblate Rule. These revisions entailed minor adjustments suggested by four years of growth and lived experience as a community. They codified practices that had developed experientially and adapted the community's structure to resemble that of peer congregations of sisters. In ten articles, this revision essentially bureaucratized community governance and the functions of daily living and discipline. In delineating the specific duties and responsibilities associated with the office of superior, the revision included the following admonition: "Let the superior seek less to have herself feared by those who are in her charge than to be useful to them. Let her learn that she ought to be the mother and not the mistress of her subjects and if there be a need sometime to use severity, let it be the severity of the mother and not that of the tyrant."[34]

None of the descriptions of the remaining nine offices included such specific references to appropriate attitude and demeanor. Joubert undertook the revisions "at the repeated request of many of the Sisters, wishing to put an end to the different abuses which had been introduced not long ago among them" and "after having sought the advice of all of the Sisters."[35] The revisions occurred the year following the completion of Sister Mary's first term as superior. Even as the 1833 revisions aligned the Oblate Constitutions more closely to those of their contemporary sisterhoods, such circumstantial evidence suggests that these amendments also referred specifically to the experience of Lange's tenure in office.

In 1839, during Sister Mary's third term as superior, Joubert again addressed the community on the subject of severity: "He said that generally the Superiors and those who have to direct others, should not exact from them more virtue than they practice themselves, that they should above all preach by example, and in a word she should be severe with herself and full of indulgence for others."[36] Sister Mary probably was a relentlessly demanding individual who tolerated no deviation from the rule. But she also exercised executive skills of strength, forcefulness, and decisiveness that nineteenth-century American society and the Catholic Church deemed "severe" when associated with a woman. Evidently, the discipline, organization, attentiveness to detail and administrative skills so highly praised when associated with men transmogrified into symptoms of severity when possessed by Sister Mary Lange, a woman.

The fact that the only appropriate model of female leadership either Joubert or Willigman cited was that of mother proves as insightful as it is restrictive. U.S. social culture valued a multitude of roles for men—patriarch, patriot, soldier, scholar, farmer, merchant, laborer, breadwinner—but exalted primarily and ultimately for women the single icon of maternity. Perhaps the historical record distorted Sister Mary Lange's strength into severity on the Procrustean bed of a woefully inadequate social paradigm that failed to acknowledge or sanction in women personality traits or behavior beyond the solitary rubric of motherhood.

Notwithstanding concerns they may have entertained about the severity of her style, Lange's sister Oblates functionally endorsed her leadership. Between 1828 and 1841, by means of secret ballot, the community elected Lange superior for three terms, a total of ten years. Evidently the Oblate Sisters appreciated Lange's strength and recognized that her "severe" approach stabilized their fledgling community.

Strict observance of the Oblate Rule constitutes the third Lange trait emphasized in Willigman's account. Even while absent from the convent from 1842 until 1850 working at the Sulpician seminary, "Sister Mary . . . was faithful to the duties of a Religious." Upon Lange's return to the convent in 1850, Thaddeus Anwander, the Redemptorist priest who served as the second spiritual director of the Oblate Sisters from 1847 to 1855, corroborated Willigman's assessment: "About Sisters Mary and Rose I must remark that never in any community have Sisters shown a better spirit than these two under the circumstances; for after having been more or less independent at the Seminary for several years, when they returned to the community their zeal for the observance of the rules was most conspicuous."[37]

Even in her advanced years Lange "was exact to the regular daily exercises." She enjoyed reminiscing about her life in the West Indies, "but no matter how interesting the fact was she was telling, if the bell for silence rang, there was an end for that time." Yet, Lange's devotion to regulatory observance represented no simplistic obsession with ritual. She fully comprehended the spiritual component embodied in the rule. Lange once admonished a sister not to focus on the ritual of rosary recitation in the chapel to the neglect of her spiritual communion with the presence of God in the Blessed Sacrament.[38]

Every religious community requires a strict observance of its rules from every member. Yet, because the social order of the Caribbean with which Lange was familiar no longer obtained in Baltimore, she may have sought in her strict personal observance of the Oblate Rule not only the customary assurance of pursuing the path toward spiritual perfection but also some sense of social stability. In her native country—whether Saint Domingue or Cuba—Lange had probably enjoyed a doubly privileged status as functions of her freedom and her color. The privileged position of free mulattoes in a three-tiered caste system pervaded slave society in the Caribbean and Latin America whether under French, Spanish, or British rule.[39]

In Saint Domingue the French Black Code of 1685 had guaranteed the validity of interracial marriages, had established legal parity among free mulatto people, free black people, and white citizens, and had secured rights of unlimited property acquisition for mulattoes. In the next one hundred years, fearful and jealous white colonists had responded to the rising numbers and prosperity of the free mulattoes with social proscriptions and harassment. The revised French Black Code of 1724 prohibited intermarriage between peoples of French and African descent. Nevertheless, by the mid-eighteenth century the free mulattoes constituted an assertive, wealthy, and entrenched middle tier in the color-based, three-tiered caste system characteristic of Caribbean plantation societies.[40]

Upon arriving in the American South, Caribbean refugee Lange undoubtedly experienced a cultural assault on two significant determinants of her social identity. Unlike the free black populations in the Caribbean, or even in New Orleans, Charleston, or Savannah, Baltimore's black residents maintained no color hierarchy in which light-skinned mulattoes dominated darker-skinned people.[41] Baltimore's less color-striated black community diminished Lange's formerly privileged social status based on color.

White mainland society delivered a double blow to Lange's previous social status by disallowing both her color and freedom as sources of privilege. She soon discovered that United States society discriminated against nonwhite people categorically—slave or free, mulatto or black. The diminished capacities of both freedom and color to guarantee her personal social status in Baltimore probably increased the appeal of institutionalized religious life for Lange.

Finally, Willigman particularly noted Lange's resistance or aversion to the English language: "Sister Mary was a very accomplished scholar in French and Spanish; she never tried to acquire English; she however spoke and understood the language well enough to direct the Community, though in business matters Sister James Noel of Wilmington, Delaware was her auxiliary. After Sister James' death Sisters Theresa Duchemin and Louisa Noel did the work." On another occasion, Willigman recalled that Lange proclaimed herself "French to her soul."[42]

Lange personally preferred French to the English language, perhaps in response to her novel and unwelcome experience of the pervasive and indiscriminate racism present in mainland American society. To Lange, the English language symbolized most palpably the society that rejected her humanity. If Anglo-American culture promulgated such attitudes, Lange countered it with her "French soul": the pursuit of spiritual perfection and egalitarianism and immersion in her Francophone cultural identity.

Several of the traits attributed to Sister Mary Lange in Willigman's commemorative account of the Oblate cofounder resonate in the only extant correspondence Lange authored. Originally written in French in 1835, this letter responded to Louis Deluol, the Sulpician superior of St. Mary's Seminary, who had proposed that the Sulpicians pay the Oblate community $120 annually as compensation for the services of two sisters to manage the household and infirmary duties at the seminary.[43] Lange responded to this request with a letter that reflected her astute grasp of both the promise and the perils of the Oblate community's anomalous position within antebellum southern church and society: "We do not conceal the difficulty of our situation [a]s persons of color and religious at the same time, and we wish to conciliate these two qualities in such a manner as not to appear too arrogant on the one hand and on the other, not to miss the respect which is due to the state we have embraced and the holy habit which we have the honor to wear. Our intention in consenting to your request is not to neglect the religious profession which we have embraced."[44]

Lange insisted on the guaranteed integrity of the Oblate religious state as a precondition to Oblate employment at the seminary, asserting that "we cannot give our consent but under certain conditions, our sole wish is to do the Will of God." She requested separate accommodations and eating facilities for the sisters and the exclusion of visitors from the seminary kitchen. Her stipulation "not to have any other relation with the other servants and outside people than our obligations require" certainly referred primarily to the partial cloister required for congregations of sisters.[45] But this condition may also have represented her personal response to her experience of social dislocation in a Maryland that disallowed her former advantaged social position as a free woman of color. In requesting seclusion from the other seminary servants—black and white, slave and free—Lange reclaimed for the Oblate Sisters a distinctive social position—now based on their status as women religious—in reference to other people within the seminary household.

In the final portion of her letter, Lange exhibited her innate executive and managerial skills, attention to detail, and sense of organization—all valuable qualities of leadership. She reserved for the Oblate community the authority to choose the sisters for the seminary and to determine their length of service, to augment their number and to approve the selection of other kitchen personnel to insure domestic tranquility. She offered to expand Oblate responsibilities in exchange for additional staff and requested a written copy of the terms of the agreement for the Oblate convent records.

Lange responded to Deluol's seemingly routine request for traditional woman's-sphere services with a nontraditional manifesto declaring the Oblate Sisters' religious, racial, and social positions in the cosmos as they perceived them. Lange's self-possession, positive conviction of the Oblate religious vocation, and authority emanate from this letter. If, as Oblate chronicler Grace Sherwood contends, Deluol "was a little taken aback by so many restrictions,"[46] he may have found Lange's tone "severe"; he certainly could not have considered it maternal. The collective signature suggested the letter's collaborative nature, the hallmark of Oblate governance. But Lange's individual signature as superior literally verified the imprint of her personal charism, not only on this letter but also on the evolving Oblate communal identity. This single document amply indicated the intelligence, determination, conviction, spiritual commitment, strength— and vulnerability of Sister Mary Lange.

Mother superior of the Oblates from 1828 to 1832 and then from 1835 to 1841, Lange then served as part of the Oblate staff at St. Mary's Seminary until 1850. When she returned to the convent from the seminary, Lange became novice mistress from 1850 until 1855, assistant superior from 1857, and from 1858, director of an Oblate school at Fells Point in east Baltimore. Her personal qualities, example, and leadership incorporated in the Oblate communal identity fortified the sisterhood in its encounters with trials, challenges, and rejection throughout its first half century.

MARIE MAGDELAINE BALAS, Elizabeth Lange's pre-Oblate companion and fellow teacher, assumed the name Sister Mary Frances as an Oblate Sister of Providence. Her membership in devotional societies and commitment to a religious vocation equalled those of Elizabeth Lange, although Willigman's account indicates that her personality and demeanor stood in sharp relief to those of Lange. Sister Frances served one term as Oblate superior from 1832 to 1835. The annals recorded that "Sister Frances at the feet of Our Lord made the promise to govern the house according to the spirit of the rules (of which she knew as well as the other Sisters) and to conform to all of the constitutions given by the Archbishop."[47]

Like Lange, Balas bequeathed the historical record one extant document, a thank you note that in purpose and tone contrasted as sharply to Lange's business letter as did the personalities of their respective authors. In 1833, during Balas's tenure as superior, the Baltimore Oblate Sisters received from the Oblates of St. Frances of Rome relics, or fragments of the physical remains of St. Frances, whom both communities claimed in common as their "good mother and patroness." Humility, a hallmark virtue of St. Frances of Rome, emanated from Balas's letter. Reiterating themes of Baltimore Oblate unworthiness, Balas assumed the tone of the supplicant, reassuring the Roman Oblates that their Baltimore counterparts are "without doubt, far from daring to compare ourselves to you very reverend ladies, and we acknowledge our unworthiness of so great an honor." Maternal images resonated through the letter as Balas twice begged the protection of the Roman community, twice referred to our good or common mother, and called her sisters St. Frances's "poor daughters of Baltimore." Only the rather cryptic statement about Jesus not being a respecter of persons—an image frequently invoked in contemporary abolitionist discourse expounding the religious origin of the argument for racial equality—could have implied an assertion of self-worth by the Baltimore community. The complimentary closing, "with sentiments of respect and submission," could not have been more modest.[48]

The deferential tone of Balas's letter proves unremarkable in the context of the conventionally self-effacing style of nineteenth-century women's correspondence. However, in juxtaposition to the authoritative tone of Lange's letter, it demonstrates the contrasting personal styles of the first two Oblate superiors. When her term as superior expired in June 1835, Balas served as assistant superior. From 29 September 1835 until her death in 1845, Sister Frances Balas served at St. Mary's Seminary as one of the Oblate Sisters supervising the seminary household and infirmary; consequently, she remained physically separated from the Oblate community.

Rosine Boegue, who took the name Sister Mary Rose as an Oblate Sister, left little evidence concerning her pre-Oblate life beyond her personal copy of a book of scriptural commentaries written in French, signed and dated 29 August 1823. Devotional society registers placed her in Baltimore at least by 15 August 1823. On 16 December 1838 "the reading of the rules was made in French because by chance Sister Rose presented them." This remark suggests that Sister Mary Rose Boegue may have been monolingual or—like Sister Mary Lange— may have preferred to express herself in her native French rather than in English. Sister Rose accompanied Sister Frances to serve at St. Mary's Seminary until the termination of Oblate employment there in 1850. Spiritual director Anwander remarked on the faithfulness of both Sisters Mary and Rose to the Oblate Rule during and after their extended absences from the community. Of the four charter Oblate members, only Sister Rose did not serve as superior of the community. Sister Rose Boegue died 26 December 1871. According to

Willigman's account, she "had been Sister Mary's lifelong friend, at least during her religious life. It was noted after Sister Rose's death, Sister Mary began to fail."[49]

Considerable evidence documents the pre-Oblate life of the fourth and youngest charter Oblate member, Sister Marie Therese, or Almaide Duchemin, in part because of her later departure from the Oblate Sisters to found a white sisterhood, the Sisters, Servants of the Immaculate Heart of Mary (I.H.M.).[50] Oblate and I.H.M. sources differ dramatically in their respective foci on Duchemin. Antebellum Oblate records rarely mention a person's color. In fact, they contain only one explicit reference to an Oblate member's skin tone, which I discuss in Chapter 8. Color proved an arbitrary designation that white people ascribed. The French priest Jean Tessier, certain I.H.M. sources, and white male census takers characterized some Oblate members by color. The Oblate sources do not allude to Duchemin's physical appearance or family history but rather emphasize her personal piety, intellect, educational advantages, and great utility to the Oblate institution.[51]

By contrast, the older I.H.M. sources appear preoccupied with the physical traits of Duchemin's mother, Betsy or Anne Marie Maxis, "a mulatto of very light complexion" in whose "veins . . . flowed the finest blood of France, except that her paternal grandfather had been a negro, Maxis by name."[52] These sources also dwell on the social pedigree of Duchemin's reputed father and her physical appearance, reiterating that she "displayed none of the physical evidences of her mixed blood. She was fair, had blond hair and blue eyes."[53]

On 1 June 1829 Joubert recorded in the Oblate annals that Lange, Balas, and Boegue presented to him "as a novice a young lady of 19 years whom they had raised, and who had been living with them for some years." "It had been six months since they had notified me that Almaide Duchemin wished to join the three other Sisters," Joubert continued. "Since this young person was very pious and also was very capable of rendering great services to the institution, I thought, after the consent of Monsieur Tessier, that I should consent to the wish of these good persons and permit this young girl who had been following all the exercises of the community for a year, to do as the three first, and make her vows on July 2nd."[54]

Although raised by Elizabeth Lange and Marie Balas, Duchemin was no orphan. Her mother, Anne Marie Maxis, had lost her parents in the San Domingan Revolution in 1793 and emigrated to the environs of Baltimore in the care of a prominent family, the Duchemins, who managed to escape Saint Domingue with their fortune intact. Sources differ about whether the Duchemins were white or mulatto and whether they maintained a familial or employer relationship with Anne Marie Maxis. Sources agree that Anne Marie Maxis adopted the Duchemin name as her own and used the familiar Betsy rather than Anne Marie as her given name. Beginning in 1812, the Baltimore confraternity registers listed a "Marie Anne Betsy," designated a mulatto, undoubtedly referring to Betsy Duchemin. Furthermore, Tessier's Easter Duty List included a "Betsy, M[ulatto]" from 1812 through 1831. Betsy Duchemin received a good education that included training as a nurse, a profession she continued to practice even after entering the Oblate community in 1831. While employed as a nurse in the household of the socially prominent Howard family, Betsy met British major Arthur Howard, the man who, while visiting his American relatives in Baltimore, fathered her daughter, born in 1809.[55]

Late in her life Sister Therese Duchemin revealed her personal recollections of her early years to Sister Mary James, I.H.M., in conversations that occurred between 1885 and 1892, the year of Duchemin's death. She maintained that at her baptism she received only the name Mary as her Christian name. Even recent I.H.M. sources maintain that exhaustive searches in Baltimore archdiocesan records for Sister Therese's baptismal registration under the surnames "Duchemin" or "Maxis" remain unproductive.[56] These researchers have failed to account for the antebellum practice of omitting surnames when recording transactions involving black people—slave or free. This demeaning practice of recording only given names for people of color emphasized the chattel status of slaves and the subaltern status of free black people, whose racial identity supplanted their identities as individuals with both given and surnames. Listings of free black Baltimoreans in the 1790 federal census document this practice: while some white census takers did include both given and surnames for black residents, others regularly recorded black heads of households as "yellow George" or "Harry, negro" or even merely as "Free Negroes," with no names indicated at all.[57]

Baltimore baptismal records for 1809–11 contain duplicate entries in January and June 1810 for the baptism of "Mary, of colour . . . baptized by Rev. Dr. O'Brien . . . born 9ber last . . . natural daughter of Betsy, a coloured woman—Sponsor Clotilda, a coloured woman." They also list a "Mary (mulatto)" baptized on 3 April 1809, "about 2 months old, natural daughter of Betsy, free negro [crossed out] mulatto.—Sponsors Jean Baptiste and Antoinette." No other citations juxtaposed a free colored Mary as child and Betsy as mother. All citations dated the year of Therese Duchemin's birth as 1809, not 1810 as commonly accepted. The duplicated citation indicating Mary's birth in the fall of 1809 conforms to Joubert's reference to a nineteen-year-old Almaide Duchemin in June 1829.[58]

Concerning Duchemin's relationship with her father, Sister Mary James recorded that "later on when she saw her father (for the only time in her life) she was taken to the door of a drawing room in the Howard home outside of Baltimore, and told that the visiting English Major was her father. It seems she did not speak to him, but she went back again and again to look at him. She never mentioned whether he saw her or not, or even whether he knew of her existence. . . . But all her life she instinctively disliked the English and loved the French passionately."[59] This same source stated that Sister Therese "always insisted that in spirit she was like her mother whom she idolized." Willigman corroborated this fact by noting that when Sister Anthony Duchemin died in 1832 nursing a victim of the cholera epidemic, "Sister Therese felt her mother's death very keenly as it was the last tie on earth."[60]

Sister Mary James further noted of Duchemin that "Almaide received an even better education than her mother, and she was placed in the care of some French ladies who trained her so carefully that later on those who met her believed her to have come from France. Later some of these ladies formed a Community known as the Oblates of Saint Charles, which Mother Theresa says she joined as one of the first members."[61] Sister Therese firmly endorsed the quality education she received from Elizabeth Lange and Marie Balas over sixty years after the fact and forty years after her estrangement from the Oblate community. Furthermore, the mistaken impression that she had attended school in France echoed the frequently cited assertion that the original Oblate members "were from San Domingo, though they had some of them, certainly, been educated in France."[62] Wealthy black and mulatto residents of Saint Domingue frequently sent their daughters to school in France. Had either Lange or Duchemin studied abroad, however, they would undoubtedly have acknowledged it, given their Francophile tendencies. Significantly, Duchemin identified the Oblate Sisters exclusively as French, avoiding any reference to their racial identity in her recollections.

Some sources state that Duchemin briefly attended the Sisters of Charity school in Emmitsburg, Maryland. Willigman's account supports this assertion indirectly, stating that "Sister Therese was a very useful member as she had a good English education, she was a kind of amanuensis, also secretary, and she was appointed Teacher of the school in the English Branches."[63] Given Elizabeth Lange's aversion to speaking English, it seems improbable that Almaide Duchemin would have mastered the English language under Miss Lange's tutelage.

The exact year Elizabeth Lange and Marie Balas assumed custody of Almaide Duchemin remains uncertain. Devotional society registers place Almaide in the city of Baltimore in 1822 when she was twelve years old, so she may have lived with them at that time. One older I.H.M. source asserted, "At times, Mother

Theresa was her mother's child, humble, industrious, self-effacing, devoted, and deeply religious. Again, she became the leader, unbending, enterprising, dominant, a living exponent of her father's British insularity, for he was a Major in the service of His Majesty, George III."[64]

Duchemin's own recollection of her estrangement from her father and of her superior education under Lange and Balas challenge the preceding assertion, suffused with racial and gender stereotypes. Indeed, Sister Mary Lange demonstrated ample strength and leadership in her own life to have provided a sufficient role model of a "leading, unbending, enterprising, dominant" demeanor for Duchemin to emulate without recourse to a phantom, ephemeral father figure. The constant example of both her teachers' lives undoubtedly inspired Duchemin to profess herself as a religious. But Sister Mary Lange evinced intelligence, determination, initiative, leadership—and deeply felt personal reasons for preferring Francophone to Anglophone culture. In Lange, Duchemin probably recognized a kindred spirit.

Adherence to the Roman Catholic faith and a French cultural identity informed the responses of all four charter Oblate members to life in Anglophone, slaveholding Baltimore. Nevertheless, their African ancestry and Caribbean origins positioned these women genealogically in a diaspora within a diaspora: from Africa to the Caribbean to the United States, what historian Colin Palmer has identified respectively as the fourth and fifth major African diasporic streams.[65] In her 1931 account of the Oblate experience, Grace Sherwood characterized the sisters as "French in language, in sympathy, and in habit of life."[66] She may have employed this Eurocentric and proprietary perspective to legitimize this black sisterhood to a presumably white readership. Yet, elements of traditional African cultures plausibly influenced the foundation of the Oblate community as well.

From the 1500s African peoples transported in the Atlantic slave trade to the New World repeatedly demonstrated the complexity, resilience, viability, and dynamism of their traditional cultures in interaction with European peoples. Numerous examples of syncretism occurred between components of traditional African religious beliefs, practices, and icons and corresponding aspects of Roman Catholicism. The practice of *vaudou* (voodoo) that evolved in the French Caribbean colony of Saint Domingue constitutes perhaps the single most celebrated example of the syncretic fusion of elements of traditional African religions and Roman Catholicism. Dahomean peoples formed a significant component of the slave population in Saint Domingue and exerted major influence on the development of *vaudou*.[67]

The demographic and cultural prominence of Dahomean peoples in Saint

Domingan life proves particularly significant because women—in Dahomean society in particular and throughout West African societies in general—exerted significant agency in their cultures. Historians Sylvia Frey and Betty Wood explain that, in contrast to Western Christianity, "the participation of women in religious activities was built into the West African cosmological system" and that West African traditional religions "recognized the female as participating in the divine and thus allowed for the parallel and complementary development of male and female ritual leaders."[68] Historian Michael Gomez discusses the Sande, female secret societies widely institutionalized among the peoples of Sierre Leone that exercised important religious functions. He describes initiation into the Sande as "a celebration of death to life through spiritual rebirth" involving the assumption of new names that symbolize the members' new lives within the society. Gomez further observes that as members of Sande societies, "Senufo women in general, 'to a far greater degree than men, assume roles as ritual mediators between humankind and the supernatural world of spirits and deities.'"[69]

In the Dahomean religious belief system, the preeminence of Mawu, the Moon Goddess, among the pantheons of gods ascribed both power and divinity to women. In addition to fulfilling customary social functions of reproduction and nurture, Dahomean women also performed vital economic, political, and military functions throughout their society. They controlled local trade markets, served as recorders responsible for memorizing and retaining vital governmental procedures in a preliterate society, supervised male government officials at court, and served as special units in the royal army.[70] Women in European society enjoyed few analogous experiences.

Dahomean women enslaved in the New World transplanted directly to Saint Domingan *vaudou* the prominence of women, who were crucial in their service as divine interpreters, mediators, and subjects of possession, among devotees to the Dahomean gods. This traditional West African antecedent of woman exerting significant influence in the religious life of their society corresponded with the vital role European sisterhoods fulfilled in Roman Catholic countries. As Africans and Europeans interacted, black people creatively recast "European forms [to] serve African functions."[71] Certainly the concept of a group of women engaged in cooperative living and forging a communal identity as "Brides of Christ" resonated in the cultural traditions of West African women from societies that practiced polygyny. Similarly, Roman Catholic ceremonies of religious profession in which women renounced their former lives and received new names symbolizing their rebirth as new members of spiritual communities corresponded to the initiation rites inducting West African women into the Sande secret societies.

Over time in Saint Domingue, Dahomean and other West African cultural traditions and continuities incorporating female authority and agency merged with French cultural elements, including Roman Catholicism. During the fifth stage of the African diaspora from the Caribbean to Baltimore, women emigrants established the Oblate Sisters of Providence. Oblate community-building efforts replicated the experiences of diasporic Africans throughout the New World and reflected traditional African as well as European cultural elements. A synergistic fusion of both African and French traditions contributed the crucial components of faith and female empowerment facilitating their accomplishment.

PREVIOUS CHRONICLERS of the Oblate experience have emphasized the noteworthy educational and spiritual components of the Oblate community's accomplishments in the nineteenth century.[72] They have not considered the critical impact of the individual charisms and personalities of the founding Oblate Sisters that empowered and impelled the fledging community toward such achievements. These black women aspired to and realized religious vocations in a slaveholding society that denigrated the virtue of all black women—slave or free.

Antebellum American society ostracized black women beyond the pale of the social construction of gender. From the early days of slavery, white public thought rendered black women the antithesis of women of virtue, the social construct that defined white gender differences, justified the cult of domesticity, and sanctioned socially ascribed separate spheres for men and women. The image of black women as the sexually promiscuous Jezebel became fixated in the white public consciousness. Negative stereotypes of black women remained so pervasive in American culture that long after the abolition of slavery in 1865 a white observer accurately reflected public sentiment when she asserted in 1904, "I cannot imagine such a creation as a virtuous black woman."[73] Only the equally dysfunctional slave stereotype of black women as mammy, the asexual caretaker devoted to the nurture of her white family to the detriment of her own, challenged the Jezebel image of black women in white public opinion.[74]

Refusing to accept such societal derogation, the Oblate Sisters demonstrated self-empowerment instead, by defining themselves primarily in terms of their disciplined exercise of piety and virtue. As teachers, the Oblate Sisters effectively countered the mammy stereotype's neglect of her own offspring with their collective ministrations to the intellectual, spiritual, and social nurture of black children. In dedicating themselves to the religious state, these first Oblate Sisters offered their lives to God, "no respecter of persons." As women religious, the Oblate Sisters at least partially transcended their social marginalization in claiming "the respect which is due to the state we have embraced and the holy habit which we have the honor to wear," the same respect, virtue, and honor normally reserved for white middle-class women alone. A religious community formally established within the Roman Catholic Church, the Oblate Sisters of Providence indemnified the virtue of black women and by extension—according to the tenets of the social utility of women's sphere—the entire black race. By their very existence and commitment to the education of black children, the Oblate community epitomized the relationship black feminist thinker and educator Anna Julia Cooper would articulate so eloquently in 1892: "Only the BLACK WOMAN can say 'when and where I enter in the quiet, undisputed dignity of my womanhood . . . there and then the whole *Negro race enters with me.'"[75]

Deprived of the opportunity to replicate in her adopted state of Maryland her accustomed, socially privileged status as a free woman of color, Elizabeth Lange asserted herself through total immersion in the spiritual and cultural dimensions of her identity. She rejected the English language, symbol of the culture that denied her humanity, and fervently embraced institutionalized religious life, which promised spiritual perfection and spiritual, if not social, egalitarianism within that most stable and enduring of social institutions, the Roman Catholic Church.

Sister Mary Lange presaged by several generations the response of another brilliant and sensitive African American who decried racism's denial of his humanity in the United States, W. E. B. Du Bois. Lange was female; Du Bois, male. She was Roman Catholic; he, Protestant. She endured exquisitely in silence; he wrote exquisitely to expose and to confront the problem. Lange responded by taking the veil; Du Bois strove mightily to transcend the veil.[76]

Yet Sister Mary Lange and W. E. B. Du Bois responded analogously to the denigration of black people's humanity perpetrated by a racist society. They both chose to develop and perfect a component of their humanity that white racism disallowed black people. Lange's commitment to virtue and the disciplined pursuit of spiritual perfection within the institutional Roman Catholic Church defied the moral dimension of racist stereotypes of black people as inveterate wantons. Du Bois's cultivation of his superior intellect within institutional academe defied the intellectual dimension of racist stereotypes of black people as insentient brutes.

If Lange presaged Du Bois, he expressed eloquently in his classic work, *The Souls of Black Folk*, the intellectual analogue to Lange's spiritual quest for equality and acknowledgment of her humanity:

> Herein the longing of black men must have respect. . . . And to themselves in these the days that try their souls, the chance to soar in the dim blue air above the smoke is to their finer spirits boon and guerdon for what they lose on earth by being black. I sit with Shakespeare and he winces not. Across the color line I move arm in arm with Balzac and Dumas, where smiling men and welcoming women glide in gilded halls. From out the caves of evening that swing between the strong-limbed earth and the tracery of the stars, I summon Aristotle and Aurelius and what soul I will, and they come all graciously with no scorn nor condescension. So, wed with Truth, I dwell above the veil.[77]

Lange and Du Bois sought refuge from the temporal and spatial constraints a racist society imposed on their self-realization by pursuing timeless and universal ideals of virtue, knowledge, and service to humankind. Significantly, the enrollment of Du Bois's granddaughter in the Oblate St. Frances Academy in Baltimore in the 1940s would give solid form to the associational bonds uniting Lange and Du Bois posited here.[78] From different eras, experiences, and institutions, and employing different methods, Sister Mary Lange and W. E. B. Du Bois each strove literally to liberate the souls of black folk from the bondage of racism.

CHAPTER TWO

James Hector Joubert's a Kind of Religious Society

❖ ❖ ❖ ❖ ❖ ❖ ❖ ❖ ❖ ❖ ❖ ❖ ❖ ❖ ❖ ❖ ❖ ❖ ❖ ❖

The spiritual commitment and determination of Elizabeth Lange, Marie Balas, Rosine Boegue, and Therese Duchemin alone could not have accomplished the foundation of the Oblate Sisters of Providence in 1828. Societal and episcopal attitudes and traditions regarding race and gender necessitated white male advocacy to validate this black sisterhood in antebellum America. The Oblate community, the Roman Catholic Church, and Baltimore society produced extraordinary individuals who transcended contemporary prejudices and proscriptions to advance the Oblate cause. James Joubert proved to be one of the most exceptional of these individuals.

Born in France of a noble family in 1777, James Hector Nicholas Joubert de la Muraille attempted careers as a soldier and as a tax official in France. From 1800 to 1803, Joubert served as a tax official in St. Domingue. He fled from there to Cuba in 1803 as a refugee from the slave revolution. In 1804 he emigrated to Baltimore, where he taught French for a year at Madame Lacombe's, a fashionable girls' school on South Calvert Street. Joubert entered St. Mary's Seminary to study for the priesthood in 1805 and joined the Society of St. Sulpice shortly after his ordination in Baltimore in 1810. He served as disciplinarian and treasurer of St. Mary's College and instructed its students in both French and geography. Joubert eventually realized his life's vocation ministering to the needs of the black French Caribbean refugee community in Baltimore.[1]

Joubert's three-year sojourn in St. Domingue exposed him to a slave society that allowed a modicum of social and civil parity between white citizens and free people of color. In St. Domingue he experienced the social analogue of the Roman Catholic Church's spiritual approach to the institution of slavery: although a social evil, slavery in principle did not constitute a sin; enslaved status—however socially degrading—did not deprive an individual of her or his humanity or spiritual equality before God.[2] Informed by both his San Domingan social experience and the church's nuanced distinctions between social and spiritual equality, Joubert advocated forcefully for the cause of the free Oblate Sisters in antebellum Baltimore, where a racially based slave culture denigrated all black people, slave and free.

Joubert brought to his new vocation finely honed administrative skills of discipline, attention to detail, and organization developed in his previous careers as soldier, tax official, and teacher. One source has characterized him as "not the person to shirk difficulties when he had made up his mind that something ought to be done, his training and experience having made him a man of determination, whom obstacles rather attracted than discouraged." The source continued, "His character and career pointed him out to his superiors as a man of business, likely to enforce order."[3]

Joubert's noteworthy skills recommended him to secular and sacred agencies beyond the Sulpician community. He represented the French government in extended negotiations with the Haitian regime for payment of indemnities owed San Domingan refugees. Between 1832 and 1842 the Holy See twice considered installing Joubert as bishop and vicar apostolic to Haiti.[4] His poor health and Haiti's opposition to the appointment of a vicar apostolic defeated the efforts to elevate Joubert. Nevertheless, in his mission to legitimize the first community of black women religious in the eyes of both church and society, Joubert would utilize fully his diplomatic skills.

Joubert's attitude toward the Oblate Sisters as women in the nineteenth-century patriarchal American South proved exceptional in some respects. The Oblate Sisters of Providence constituted a truly collaborative enterprise from their inception. In their democratic style of governance the Oblates "reflected Sulpician collegiality."[5] The Oblate annals contain numerous examples of the "communal nature of the decision making and the revisions of regulations."[6] In almost any development in the Oblate experience necessitating a choice or decision, Joubert invariably commented that as the director he acted either at the request of or in consultation with the sisters. He sought substantive and sub-

The Reverend James Hector Joubert, S.S., Oblate cofounder and first director (Courtesy of Archives of the Oblate Sisters of Providence, Baltimore, Md.)

stantial participation from the sisters in these deliberations rather than perfunctory responses: "Before taking the votes of the Sisters, the Director made an observation and a reproach to the Sisters for not giving their way of thinking candidly in the assemblies, and that in general they all said 'Yes' or 'No.'"[7]

Although Joubert encouraged the sisters to participate in their own governance, he did not espouse gender equality. Oblate annals, the Rule, and other extant records fully attest that his relationship with the sisters remained well within the socially and episcopally sanctioned patriarchal paradigm. Chronologically only seven years Elizabeth Lange's senior, the fifty-year-old Joubert referred to her and her colleagues as "these good girls" or "these poor girls."[8]

For the Oblate Sisters and all their peer communities of women religious, the familial foundation resonating in the titles "Mother," "Father," and "Sister" with which community members addressed each other suggested the presumed nature of the relationship between women religious and their male spiritual directors. Perceived spiritual or temporal failings on the part of the sisters elicited scoldings, reproaches, and reprimands from "Father" Joubert. As was true in their peer communities, neither Joubert nor the Oblate Sisters intentionally challenged the gender restrictions imposed by church and society alike. Yet, the sisters enjoyed an extraordinarily harmonious relationship with their first spiritual director during his fifteen-year tenure in the position. Indeed, compared to those sisterhoods experiencing turbulent relationships with their directors, the Oblate Sisters appear advantaged in their relationship with Joubert.[9]

A fierce factional struggle within the Baltimore Sulpician mission from 1827 through 1829, concurrent with the founding of the Oblate community, involved philosophical differences, opposing styles of leadership, and deep personality conflicts. These Sulpician factions affected the experiences of the Oblate Sisters for the first two decades of their existence. The faction of Jean-Marie Tessier, superior of St. Mary's Seminary, consisted of Jean-Baptiste Damphoux, the mercurial president of Saint Mary's College; the American Michael Wheeler, St. Mary's College faculty member and spiritual director of the Visitation Sisters of Georgetown; and Joubert. These priests represented a traditionalist view characterized as "introverted, rigorous, and narrow minded" in its monolithic focus on the Sulpician mission in the United States to train seminarians.[10] Nevertheless, Tessier, Joubert, Wheeler, and Damphoux constituted the most devoted advocates for the Oblate Sisters within the Sulpician community.

The faction of Louis Regis Deluol consisted of the American Samuel Eccleston, future archbishop of Baltimore, and John Joseph Chanche, future president of St. Mary's College, adjunct to the seminary. Although born in Maryland, Chanche claimed French ancestry through his parents, who, as had Joubert, fled St. Domingue during the revolution. This alliance represented an "Americanist" position characterized as cosmopolitan, expansively open to American culture, and intimate with the Baltimore social elite—both Catholic and Protestant. Although the "Americanist" Sulpicians endorsed undertaking external ministries beyond the Sulpician mission of the seminary, Deluol's faction consistently refrained from overt demonstrations of support for the Oblate community.[11] In its openness to American culture, Deluol's faction may have absorbed the pervasive influence of racism as well. Ethnicity evidently played no pivotal role in these coalitions, as each one claimed both French and American members.

The frequency and intensity of the conflicts between these two factions accelerated from June 1827 in escalating cycles of resignations, dismissals, and appointments to various college and seminary positions. In July 1828 Joubert wrote the Sulpician superior in France opposing Deluol's plan to "appoint young Americans to positions of power and thereby become 'absolute master of the

Community and its institutions.'"[12] Deluol and Eccleston instigated an official visitation from Sulpician headquarters in France on 29 August 1829 that led to Tessier's replacement by Deluol as superior of St. Mary's Seminary in September 1829. The French superior also appointed Eccleston and Chanche president and vice president, respectively, of St. Mary's College. In response, Damphoux left the society permanently and both Wheeler and Joubert wrote the Sulpician superior general protesting the new administration. This sequence of events constituted "the Sulpician 'Revolution,'" a "watershed in the history of the American Sulpicians."[13]

Joubert's fears of a "young American" usurpation of Sulpician directorship proved prescient, for Eccleston, Deluol, and Chanche "constituted the triumvirate that would rule the archdiocese until Chanche's elevation to the see of Natchez in 1840."[14] Certainly in his lifetime the fifty-year-old Joubert—former soldier, bureaucrat, teacher, and survivor of both the French and San Domingan revolutions—had witnessed the human cost of promulgating social and political ideologies. Perhaps he surmised the grave ramifications of the Deluol coalition's eager embrace of a racist American culture for his ministry to black people in general and the fledgling Oblate community in particular. Indeed, Joubert's awareness of indifference and antipathy toward the Oblate Sisters within the Sulpician community, in addition to concern about his health, may have dissuaded him from accepting the bishopric of Haiti proposed in 1833.[15]

Tessier, Damphoux, Wheeler, and Joubert nurtured and validated the nascent Oblate community in several different ways over the years. Jean Tessier owned or had owned slaves. Yet he, like his colleague James Joubert—and innumerable antebellum clerics and ministers of both Catholic and Protestant persuasions—sought to address at some level the spiritual needs of black people.[16] Tessier had supervised the Sunday religious instruction classes for black émigré children—slave and free—at St. Mary's Lower Chapel from 1796 until 1827, when he surrendered this ministry to Joubert. He mentored Joubert in formulating the Oblate Rule, supported the sisters financially, subsidized student tuitions at the Oblate school, donated generously to the Oblate chapel reliquaries, and frequently presided at Masses and religious devotions for the Oblate Sisters before his death in 1840. Michael Wheeler procured papal favors and indulgences for the Oblate community. Wheeler's move to Washington, D.C., and his untimely death in 1832 at the young age of thirty-six precluded his figuring more prominently in Oblate history. Damphoux subsidized the community generously, presided at school functions, and officiated at Masses and religious services for the Oblate Sisters in Joubert's infirmity.[17]

Conversely, Deluol, Eccleston, and Chanche remained ambivalent, indifferent, or hostile toward the Oblate community. Subsequent chapters in this book examine in detail the relationships of Deluol and Eccleston with the Oblate Sisters; however, John Chanche was the first to demonstrate antipathy toward the Oblate community. In June 1829 Deluol noted in his diary, "M. Chanche turned down M. Joubert's request that he translate the prospectus of the Mulatto Ladies, called the Oblates or Sisters of Providence. M. Joubert was amazed and mortified at that refusal."[18]

Racial considerations or personal animosity toward Joubert motivated John Chanche's rebuff. No opposition to female education provoked Chanche's refusal of Joubert's request on behalf of the Oblate Sisters. In 1828 Chanche had proposed a more rigorous academic course of study including "the higher branches of Rhetoric, Philosophy, Chemistry, Botany, Algebra, Astronomy, etc."[19] for the young ladies attending St. Joseph's Academy under the direction of the Sisters of Charity of St. Joseph, Emmitsburg. In the 1830s the Carmelite Nuns recognized John Chanche alone by name from among the Sulpician priests who "encouraged and aided the Sisters very much with their school, instructing the teachers to enable them better to perform their duties."[20] Their race distinguished the Oblate Sisters and their pupils from the white Sisters of Charity and the Carmelite Nuns and their charges. Chanche's refusal to assist the Oblate Sisters demonstrated that opposition to a society of black women religious existed even within the Sulpician community.

THE ROMAN CATHOLIC CHURCH in the United States provided religious training for slaves and free black people at least from the early eighteenth century. Slaveholding priests and sisters instructed their own property in the basic tenets of the Roman Catholic faith and prepared them to receive the sacraments. Their ministry frequently extended to neighboring slaves of cooperative owners. Sources occasionally have designated as schools programs of mere religious instruction, conflating rote memorization in Sunday catechetical settings and a regular program of common school education emphasizing literacy and basic mathematical skills. The important distinction between evangelization and education merits inclusion in any discussion of antebellum Roman Catholic educational efforts directed at the black population throughout the antebellum South.

Ursuline Nuns from France arrived in New Orleans in 1727 to establish a boarding and day school for girls. In addition, they conducted daily a separate, ninety-minute "class to instruct the girls and women, Negro and Indian."[21] By the 1820s the Ursulines had reduced their religious instruction to "Negresses of the district" to Sunday and feast-day catechetical lessons.[22] The nuns also organized a lay confraternity of women, the Children of Mary, charged with the religious instruction of their children and their slaves. As historian Emily Clark has observed, considerations of both race and caste informed Ursuline school admission policies by the 1790s. The sisters continued to admit the few biracial applicants born of legitimate marriages to full participation in the school but admitted mulatto girls, presumed illegitimate, only on a segregated basis.[23] The determination of biracial admissions on an individual-case basis reflected racial tolerance, if not racial inclusiveness, on the part of the Ursuline Nuns.

A deliberate, more comprehensive program of formal education for black pupils under Catholic auspices in New Orleans began in the nineteenth century. French émigrés Sister Marthe Fortière, a member of the Dames Hospitalier, and Adele Aliquot opened a school for girls of color on St. Claude Street in 1823. Fortière returned to France in 1831, and the Ursuline Nuns assumed direction of the school between 1831 and 1838, when they relinquished it to the Sisters of Mt. Carmel. The New Orleans black community initiated and financed the St. Louis School for the Colored in 1837. After overcoming legal obstacles, the school opened in 1847, staffed with lay teachers and under the direction of the Catholic Society for the Instruction of Indigent Orphans.[24]

Efforts to educate black people in the archdiocese of Baltimore, encompassing Maryland and the District of Columbia, antedated the Oblate school. In 1800 the black population of Washington, D.C., consisted of 780 free black people and 3,220 slaves in a total population of 14,000 people. By 1850, 10,000 free black people and 3,000 slaves contributed to the total population of 51,000 people in the nation's capital. Between 1807 and 1830 residents of the District of Columbia supported no fewer than eighteen schools—both secular and denominational—of varying sizes for black pupils. Black people established and maintained eleven of these schools, including the Resolute Beneficial Society, which advertised openly its acceptance of both slave and free patrons, instituted in 1818. At least two schools operated under Catholic auspices, including a Sunday school established at Holy Trinity Church for both slave and free black pupils, which may have taught reading and writing as well as religion from 1818 to 1838.[25]

Several schools for black students existed in the city of Baltimore as well before the Oblate school opened in 1828. As was true in the nation's capital, the black community itself established over half of these schools. Unlike the situation in Washington, religious denominations initiated all of the permanent schools for black children before 1830. The most noteworthy Baltimore schools included the Sharp Street Methodist Episcopal Church's Free African School

(1802), which apparently enrolled both slave and free black pupils, Daniel Coker's Bethel Charity School (c. 1812), St. James Protestant Episcopal Day School (1824), which may also have served both a slave and a free black clientele, and William Lively's Union Seminary (1825).[26]

In promoting his idea of a school "mainly for colored girls,"[27] Joubert reasoned that knowledge of reading and writing would facilitate the children's learning their lessons in religion. The black congregation at St. Mary's Lower Chapel consisted of both free and slave members and significantly more female than male penitents and communicants. Joubert's proposal of a girls' school suggested that free black girls composed a substantial segment of the catechetical, or religious instruction, classes. It further suggested that a significant number of girls came from families sufficiently affluent to absorb both the financial expenditure and the loss of the child's labor entailed in school attendance. Females predominated in all antebellum free black urban populations.[28] Joubert's proposal of a school for free black girls consequently reflected a national as well as a local urban demographic condition. Gender considerations other than demographic distribution also informed Joubert's proposal of a girls' school under Oblate direction. The Catholic Church preferred models of single-sex education in which sisterhoods conducted schools for girls and clergy or lay teachers directed schools for boys.

The state of Maryland had instituted no legal restrictions on black education, slave or free. Nevertheless, an inhospitable climate of opinion prevailed toward educating even free black people, undoubtedly because of the close association in the white public mind among slaves, free black people, education, and insurrection.[29] Consequently, the proposal that even some black children receive formal education to enhance religious instruction represented a bold position in slaveholding Baltimore.

The Oblate School for Colored Girls was the first formal day—not Sunday—school for black pupils established under Roman Catholic auspices in the archdiocese of Baltimore. A frequently cited source erroneously claimed that the Sulpicians had established schools for the black San Domingan refugees prior to the organization of the Oblate community, an example of conflating religious training and formal education.[30] Unlike any of its predecessors, the Oblate school enrolled girls exclusively. But the most significant aspect of the collaboration of Lange and Joubert was the combination of establishing a school for black girls and creating a black religious community to staff it. This signal act committed in a slaveholding city simultaneously recognized the potential and the reality of black female agency and institutionalized it within the structure of the Roman Catholic Church. The tentativeness implied in Joubert's own words recalling his intention to found "a kind of religious society" indicated his awareness that in proposing this black sisterhood he ventured into uncharted territory. When the Oblate community began, Joubert was not certain church authorities would sanction these black women religious.[31]

AS A TEACHING community, the Oblate Sisters endured with other sisterhoods throughout the world who engaged in ministries of service the subordinate status ascribed them in the ecclesial hierarchy. Many sisterhoods incorporated teaching, nursing, or caring for orphans into their missions as their primary means of financial support. Such professions differentiated these active sisterhoods in both the United States and Europe from regular orders of nuns whose substantial endowments allowed them the choice of cloistered contemplation as their exclusive occupation. Church authorities in Rome promoted cloistered contemplation as the preferred model for female religious communities universally. In contending with opposing goals of spiritual isolation and worldly involvement, the Oblate community and its peer service sisterhoods throughout the world experienced the dynamic tension between the realities imposed by their active ministries and the rigid standards for legitimacy imposed by the church hierarchy.[32]

From the thirteenth century the Roman Catholic Church had issued a series of papal bulls, edicts, and conciliar decrees with a decidedly male-centered, if not misogynistic, orientation to regulate the status of women religious within the church.[33] Through the nineteenth century, the church restricted its definition of women religious to those orders of nuns who kept strict cloister—the physical separation of the nuns from the rest of the world—and professed solemn vows. It thus excluded congregations of sisters with simple vows who had organized to perform charitable works in the world. This official purpose as a community to which such sisterhoods adhered necessarily precluded the observance of strict cloister.

While remaining intransigent in its insistence on cloister and solemn vows as criteria for true women religious until 1900, the church recognized the tremendous social benefits it accrued from the works of these apostolic communities of sisters. Over the centuries the church attempted to reconcile its rigid stance on cloister and solemn vows with the legitimate requests of these service communities for formal recognition of their ministry and lifestyle. Between 1700 and 1900 the papacy modified its position from tacit toleration of active, or noncloistered, congregations with simple vows approved by their local bishops, to the confirmation and approbation of the constitutions of these secular institutions. But "it was the *constitutions* of congregations with simple vows, not the institutes themselves, which Rome approved prior to 1900; the congregations themselves were merely tolerated as societies of pious women."[34]

Several other permanent communities of women religious preceded the Oblate Sisters of Providence in the United States. The Ursulines (1727), the Carmelites (1790), the Sisters of the Visitation (1795), and the Religious of the Sacred Heart of Jesus (1818) all replicated in the United States the missions and Rules of their respective European motherhouses. Essentially contemplative orders that observed cloister and professed solemn vows, these four groups fit well within the church's narrowly constructed definition of women religious before 1900. Except for the Carmelite Nuns, these first congregations all included teaching in their founding apostolate or mission. They accommodated the dualities implicit in the simultaneous observance of cloister and performance of teaching duties with a hierarchical mixed religious lifestyle combining prayerful contemplation by their strictly cloistered members and secular instruction by their semicloistered and noncloistered members.[35]

The dispensations requested by their respective American bishops and most routinely granted by papal authorities involved a relaxation of the requirements of strict cloister to allow the nuns to teach or nurse or care for orphans as a source of income, if their respective ways of life did not already mandate such activities. Furthermore, all of the communities of women religious in the United States subsidized their education of orphans and indigent children with the tuition charged their more affluent patrons. These modifications represented the most substantive adaptations of these transplanted European communities to their new environment.[36]

Mother Elizabeth Seton organized the Sisters of Charity of St. Joseph, Emmitsburg in 1809, distinguished as both the first foundation of American women religious and the first exclusively active, noncontemplative congregation in the nation. From their inception these American Sisters of Charity considered their institute "the same in substance as that of the Sisters of Charity of France," although independent of any "connection whatever with the Company or Government of the said Sisters in France or any European country." In 1810 they adopted as their own the Rule and Constitutions of the French Daughters of Charity of Saint Vincent de Paul, incorporating an elastic clause allowing "such modifications in the Rules as the difference of country, habits, customs, and manners may require."[37] In 1850 Mother Seton's community formally united with the French Daughters of Charity. Like the Sisters of Charity, Emmitsburg, the Sisters of Charity of Nazareth, Kentucky (1812) followed the French Rule of the Daughters of Charity. The most substantive variation between the European and American Sisters of Charity again involved the latters' need to establish schools charging tuition as their primary means of self-support. In compliance with the original mission of the French community, the American Sisters of Charity also established orphan asylums and hospitals.[38]

Three communities—the Sisters of Loretto in Kentucky (1812), the Dominican Sisters of St. Catharine in Kentucky (1822), and the Oblate Sisters of Providence (1829)—followed constitutions specifically written for them by their founders in the United States. Charles Nerinckx, the Belgian priest who founded the Sisters of Loretto, envisioned a community of teaching sisters. But his sternly ascetic rule, that the papacy approved in 1816, was ill-suited to conditions in Kentucky. Its austerity proved so extreme that it resulted in a high mortality among the sisters. The Dominican priest Thomas Wilson, founder of the Dominican Sisters of St. Catharine in Kentucky, devised a rule for the community that said "more about the ascetical life than apostolic work even though educational needs seem to have been a primary purpose in their coming together."[39] Both Nerinckx and Wilson had apparently failed to reconcile the reality of a teaching mission with the persistent ideal of contemplative cloister.[40]

By contrast, Oblate regulatory efforts achieved a judicious balance between contemplative and service orientations. The Oblate Rule constituted "a succinct, carefully written document" that "clearly stated the purpose of this religious community and gave directives for carrying it out." It included "specific directives for the educational work of the sisters and their relationship with parents and the general public." The "very realistic constitutions" of the Oblate community helped the sisters surmount the difficulties engendered by their black racial identity in a racist, slaveholding society.[41]

Joubert crafted the Oblate Rule in consultation with his mentor, the Sulpician Superior Jean-Marie Tessier, and the Oblate Sisters themselves. Scholars disagree about the originality of the Oblate Constitutions formulated in 1829.[42] Had Joubert substantially duplicated a conventional religious rule, he himself would have publicized that fact to expedite ecclesial recognition of the Oblate community. The Sisters of Charity of Saint Joseph, as an American community dedicated to an active or service ministry and organized in the archdiocese of Baltimore under Sulpician auspices only twenty years earlier, provided the closest analogue to the Oblate Sisters of Providence. Both Joubert and Tessier knew of the Rule and Constitutions of the Sisters of Charity because of the long and intimate association of the Sulpician priests with that sisterhood. However, the original Oblate Rule and Constitutions distinguished themselves from those of the Sisters of Charity in numerous ways, including the omission of the Sulpician superior from Oblate governance, no formal Oblate association with an existing community, a specified Oblate dowry amount, and the annual Oblate spiritual commitment in the form of promises, not vows.

Aware of the antipathy Deluol, Eccleston, and Chanche felt toward the Oblate Sisters and wary of this triumvirate's potential to gain administrative control of the Baltimore Sulpician mission, Joubert did not replicate in the Oblate Rule the imposition of the Sulpician superior as "the head of the whole company" of the Sisters of Charity.[43] The racial identity of the Oblate membership may have convinced Joubert of the appropriateness—if not the necessity—of formulating a rule to accommodate the peculiar Oblate situation within the antebellum church and southern society.

The first paragraph of the original Oblate Rule stated the nature and purpose of the institute: "The Oblate Sisters of Providence are a Religious Society of Coloured Women, established in Baltimore with the approbation of the Most Reverend Archbishop. The Oblates renounce the world to consecrate themselves to God and to the Christian education of young girls of color."[44] The explicit racial self-identification incorporated into their rule differentiated the Oblate Sisters from all other sisterhoods at the time. Simultaneously, the Oblate mandate both to renounce the world and to teach united this black religious community with all sisterhoods engaged in service ministries and challenged to reconcile seclusion from and interaction with the secular world.

The original Oblate Rule established the sisterhood as an indigenous religious community with only a tenuous association with a European institute, the Oblates of St. Frances of Rome. The Oblate Rule included no explicit statement corresponding to the regulatory declarations of the American Sisters of Charity characterizing their respective communities as "the same in substance as that of the Sisters of Charity of France." The inclusion of the "ninth of March, the feast of St. Frances, foundress of the Oblates at Rome, under whose protection the school is established"[45] among the patronal feast days of recreation observed by the Oblate Sisters constitutes the only mention of either St. Frances or the Roman Oblate community in the original Baltimore Oblate Rule and Constitutions. While the American Sisters of Charity closely modeled their Rule and Constitutions on those of the French Daughters of Charity of St. Vincent de Paul, the Oblate Sisters had neither knowledge nor a copy of the governing regulations of the Oblates of St. Frances of Rome as late as 21 October 1834.[46]

The Oblate Rule, unlike the rules of their white contemporaries, stated a specific dollar amount for the dowry, requiring prospective candidates to advance four hundred dollars. Archbishop James Whitfield, not Joubert or Lange, had fixed the dowry amount. The archdiocese contributed nothing to the maintenance of communities of women religious. Because financial constraints engendered by the racial identity of the Oblate membership and their proposed clientele had threatened the Oblate project from its conception, Whitfield undoubtedly intended to bolster the community's financial self-sufficiency. Depending on the circumstances and qualifications of the candidate, the community could waive this requirement.[47]

Finally, the Oblate Rule of 1829 stipulated that the sisters "make no vows, but merely a promise of obedience. . . . Hence their annual engagement, instead of profession, is called oblation."[48] The Sisters of Charity made annual simple vows of poverty, chastity, and obedience. Available sources do not reveal whether Archbishop Whitfield rejected an initial proposal from Joubert of vow status for the Oblate community or whether Joubert requested only the lesser promise status for the Oblate Sisters in an effort to deflect anticipated social and ecclesial objections to the establishment of a black sisterhood. Regardless of what Joubert may have proposed, Whitfield retained the ultimate power to dispose: on 5 June 1829 Whitfield approved the Oblate community at the promise status of religious commitment. This distinction in the degree of commitment to religious life that archdiocesan authorities sanctioned for these respective sisterhoods constituted the most substantive difference between the black Oblate Sisters and the white Sisters of Charity.

Clerical confusion concerning the precise nature of the religious status of the Oblate Sisters soon occurred. Bishop John England of Charleston edited the *United States Catholic Miscellany*, the first Catholic newspaper in the United States. Its 12 February 1830 issue included the following notice about the Oblate community: "*The Oblates* This is a religious society of coloured females who bind themselves by annual vows." . . . "Note.—We doubt if the Oblates are permitted to make vows.—Edit. Miscel."[49] The unidentified Baltimore cleric responsible for submitting the Oblate notice to the newspaper claimed the Oblate community made vows. Bishop England, who had carefully scrutinized the Oblate Rule and Constitutions the previous year, exercised his editorial prerogative and corrected the error. Clerical assumption of initial Oblate vow status proved a recurring phenomenon.

FROM THE BEGINNING, Joubert's goal had been full ecclesiastical recognition of the Oblate Sisters of Providence. On 28 October 1828 Louis Deluol noted in his diary that Joubert "told Sister Felicite [a Sister of Charity] of his plans concerning his mulatto Sisters. He would first get the sanction of the Archbishop and then, in Rome, papal approval."[50] When Joubert presented the Oblate Rule to Archbishop Whitfield for his formal approbation on 5 June 1829, Whitfield was already thoroughly familiar with the project. Joubert had sought and received Whitfield's approval at each stage of his plan to establish a school for colored girls and to found a community of black women religious. In Joubert's words, "I followed constantly the advice of the Archbishop in all I did."[51] Joubert's disclaimer and the established pattern of consultation with Whitfield from 1828 suggest that Whitfield condoned and may even have suggested Joubert's initiative to seek papal approval for the Oblate community.

Archbishop Whitfield certainly knew that validation of active, not contemplative, religious communities required only the approval of a diocesan bishop in the nineteenth century.[52] He once described himself as "averse to unnecessary agitation and excitement" and the pursuit of "noisy, stirring courses."[53] He may well have concluded that the racial identity of the Oblate Sisters in antebellum Baltimore would generate sufficient agitation and excitement to necessitate some form of papal endorsement to reinforce his unprecedented approbation of a black sisterhood.

To effect papal approval of the Oblate community, Joubert solicited the help of Michael Wheeler, fellow Sulpician priest and traditionalist faction ally. As early as 10 November 1829, Wheeler had written to the Congregation of the Propaganda Fide in Rome about the formation of the Oblate community in Baltimore to minister to the Christian and elementary education of black girls. He further informed Rome of Archbishop Whitfield's sanction of the society, of the generally enthusiastic endorsement of the Oblate enterprise from the American bishops recently convened in Baltimore for the First Provincial Council, and of the support the Oblate Sisters attracted, even from wealthy Protestants. Wheeler mistakenly claimed that the Oblate Sisters professed simple vows in this letter.[54] An unidentified Propaganda Fide official replied to Wheeler on 9 January 1830, noting "with considerable pleasure what you wrote me about the new establishment there of a group of black religious with the purpose of seeing to the Christian education of black girls."[55]

The Roman Catholic Church had established the Congregation of the Propaganda Fide in the seventeenth century to centralize control of foreign missions in the papacy. This papal bureaucracy exercised exclusive power to invest authority in and allocate funds to missionaries in the field. The United States retained its status as a foreign mission until 1908. During the antebellum period the papacy regarded black people more sympathetically than did the American Catholic hierarchy. Black priests from Africa and the Caribbean ministered to congregations in their respective homelands. As early as 1807 Pope Pius VII, motivated in part by his disapproval of the African slave trade, had canonized Benedict the Moor, a saint of both African and slave ancestry.[56]

Pope Gregory XVI, a personal acquaintance of Wheeler, succeeded to the papacy in 1831. Although theologically conservative and politically reactionary, Gregory XVI had served, while cardinal, as prefect of the Propaganda Fide. In this capacity the future pope had developed significant interest in and sympathy for the problems missionaries encountered in foreign lands, particularly those associated with the African slave trade.[57] In 1839 Pope Gregory XVI unequivocally condemned the African slave trade in an official letter. He enjoined true Christians not "to exercise that inhuman trade by which Negroes, as if they were not men, but mere animals, howsoever reduced into slavery, are, without any distinction, contrary to the laws of justice and humanity, bought, sold, and doomed sometimes to the most severe and exhausting labors."[58]

ON 6 AUGUST 1831 Michael Wheeler wrote to Anthony Kohlmann, Joubert's Jesuit friend at the Roman College "to obtain from the Holy See, in the name of the Oblate Sisters of Providence and their Director, certain particular graces and a confirmation of their society." In the original Latin text of his petition, Wheeler emphasized the racial identity of the Oblate Sisters in explicit references to them as "a certain society of religious ladies of color, organized for the instruction of girls of their own race" and as "women born of mixed marriages, commonly mulattoes" and referred to their pupils as "girls of a black color."[59]

For the second time, Wheeler erred in observing that "the Sisters of said congregation are accustomed to make simple vows, in the same manner as the Sisters of Charity, instituted by St. Vincent de Paul." His claim of Oblate similarity to the Sisters of Charity in this regard served to associate the Oblate community with a traditional and highly esteemed service sisterhood. Wheeler's assertion that the black women "have adopted as their patroness and foundress St. Frances of Rome and are generally called Oblates" further linked this new American community with another well-established, active European sisterhood. The specific favors sought included "all the graces granted to the Oblates of St. Frances of Rome" and plenary indulgences for those entering the community, when "they make their profession or pronounce their vows" and on Oblate feast days—all standard requests of religious communities.[60]

The Oblate archives preserve the original rescript from Rome granting the community the graces and privileges Wheeler had requested on their behalf. On 2 October 1831, "His Holiness granted the following graces to the Sisters of the said congregation: . . . all and every grace and privilege already granted to the Oblates of St. Frances of Rome" and all the other requested plenary indulgences.[61] Evidently Joubert left no record of his own response or that of the Oblate Sisters to the joyful news of the papal blessings bestowed on their community. Nevertheless, he carefully documented the response of Archbishop Whitfield: "The Archbishop, to whom I had made known the favors received from Rome, gave permission today to keep the Blessed Sacrament in the chapel of the Oblate Sisters. 'These same being recognized by the Holy See, I cannot now refuse this favor; they are all religious and I shall have nothing more to say. I permitted their establishment, but today they are confirmed by the Pope; the thing is indeed more serious. May these good girls whom I esteem very much, continue to render themselves more and more worthy of the graces of God.'"[62]

Clearly, Whitfield viewed the papal favors granted the Oblates as an official vindication of his approbation of the community. The first Oblate prospectus published in the official Catholic directory in 1834 reinforced this perspective: "The Sisters of Providence are a religious society of coloured women, established in Baltimore on the 5th of June, 1829, with the approbation of the Most Reverend Archbishop Whitfield; under the direction of the Reverend Hector Joubert, St. Mary's College, Baltimore; and have been acknowledged as such by the Holy See."[63] Whitfield's eager response to and publicizing of papal recognition of the Oblate community contributed to the process of conflating papal acknowledgment of the Oblate Sisters with formal papal approval of the Oblate Institute and Rule, a confusion that persisted through the nineteenth century.

Wheeler's formulation of the petition emphasized Oblate racial identity and linked the black women with two prominent active sisterhoods. It implied a critical question: would the papacy condone the concept of black women religious? The most crucial component of the papal response proved less the substance of the favors and indulgences sought and granted the Oblate community than the papal affirmation implied in the words, "His Holiness granted the following graces to the Sisters of the said congregation." A papal blessing connotes papal approval. In 1831 Roman Catholic clergy from the antebellum South sought and inferred papal approval of the racial identity of the Oblate Sisters, what a twentieth-century Oblate source would term "a friendly wave of recognition" from the Holy See.[64]

Formal papal approval of religious institutes and rules involved an elaborate process including the submission of community constitutions.[65] Both Wheeler and Whitfield knew of this constitutional requirement for formal papal approbation. Wheeler had executed the procedure for the Visitation Nuns in 1829. Whitfield had sought cloistral dispensations in the Carmelite Rule to allow them to teach in 1831. No evidence suggests that Whitfield communicated with Rome about the Oblate Rule. No Oblate Rule accompanied Wheeler's petition, nor did Whitfield refer to the Oblate Rule in his response. Throughout the antebellum period, the black Oblate Sisters remained the only community of women religious within the archdiocese of Baltimore not designated a pontifical institute, that is, one whose constitutions the papacy had formally approved.[66]

That Wheeler structured the Oblate petition as he did and that the papacy responded with a rescript prove instructive. Motivated by insecurities because of perceived problems in their canonical status, religious communities—or, as in the case of the Oblate Sisters, their clerical superiors—occasionally sought and received papal blessings and acknowledgment of the sort Wheeler requested as validation. The racial identity and consequent pioneering nature of the Oblate community evidently caused sufficient insecurity in Archbishop Whitfield to warrant such a petition. In the hierarchy of papal decrees and grants, rescripts represented one of the simplest papal documents, used to reply to matters considered of lesser importance by either granting requests or empowering local bishops to do so.[67]

Not until 1903 did the Oblate community receive clarification of their papal recognition from Joseph Wissel, a Redemptorist priest friend, contributor, and adviser to the Oblate Sisters in the postbellum era. Wissel carefully examined Oblate annals, Wheeler's petition, and the papal rescript of 1831. His analysis included notice of Wheeler's mistaken claim of initial Oblate vow status and of the pivotal agency of Archbishop Whitfield in inferring papal approval of the Oblate institute. Wissel submitted his findings to the Oblate superior:

> What purports to be the approbation of Gregory XVI of your Institute, amounts to nothing more than the granting of certain indulgences to the members of the Community. . . . The approbation of the Institute is neither included in the petition nor in the grant. Such indulgences may be granted to any altar society of secular ladies or some other aggregation. Nevertheless, even Archbishop Whitfield seems to have regarded the document as a sort of indirect approbation. . . .
>
> This grant of indulgences cannot be called an approbation of the Institute and of the Rules. . . . There is no need of being in a hurry to obtain the approbation of the Holy See. You are a Religious Institute, approved by the Archbishop of Baltimore, and you can go on doing all the good you can and become great Saints.[68]

Joubert never considered the Oblate Sisters other than religious from their inception. He had even insisted in 1829 that the Oblate residence first undergo renovations "absolutely indispensable for making this house a convent for religious."[69] Nevertheless, Oblate annals on 2 July 1832 noted of the first annual renewal ceremony after papal recognition: "Until now the Oblates had made but one oblation of themselves and simple promises, but because of the graces accorded them by the Holy See and the recognition of their society as a religious society, as appeared on the document of the Sacred Congregation of the Propaganda of the Faith, dated 2 October 1831, in future they shall renew every year, on the same date, the simple vows of poverty, chastity, and obedience."[70]

The Oblate Sisters formed a diocesan community subject to regulation by their archbishop. Archbishop Whitfield had effected this change in the Oblate spiritual engagement from the simple promise to the simple vow formula. Papal acceptance had convinced Whitfield that the Oblate Sisters were indeed religious and "the thing is more serious." Papal recognition served as a catalyst emboldening Whitfield to exercise what had always been his prerogative: to permit the black Oblate Sisters to profess simple vows—as did the white Sisters of Charity—in the antebellum South.

HAVING SECURED BOTH diocesan approval and papal acknowledgment of the Oblate community by 1832, the indefatigable Joubert persisted in his mission to legitimize the first permanent community of black women religious in the eyes of the church. Expressing both his understandable pride and confidence in the viability of the Oblate community, Joubert revealed to Anthony Kohlmann his hope to establish an Oblate mission in Haiti one day. In the same letter, written on 10 March 1833, Joubert requested for the Baltimore Oblate community a copy of the Rule of the Oblates of St. Frances of Rome and both a relic and a portrait of that saint, their mutual patron.[71] Joubert hoped to promote the affiliation between the Baltimore and Rome Oblate communities and to acquaint himself and the Baltimore sisters with the precise nature of the graces and privileges the papal indulgence had granted them.

A second request sought in this letter affected not only the Oblate Sisters but Baltimore's black Catholics as well. Joubert had observed the widespread devotion of black Catholics to St. Benedict of San Philadelpho, known as the Moor. Born in Sicily in 1526, Benedict and his parents belonged to the significant population of African slaves who labored on Sicilian plantations. Benedict's remarkable piety from his youth earned him his freedom. He joined a band of hermits, eventually affiliated with a branch of the Franciscan order, and served his religious community as both superior and novice master. His piety and wisdom attracted the attention of both clerical and public officials who sought his counsel. He died in 1589, already widely acclaimed for his holiness. Popular devotion to Benedict the Moor developed first in Italy and Spain and then spread to the New World, where the black, mostly slave, population claimed him as their special patron. From 1833 the Oblate Sisters claimed St. Benedict as the fourth special patron of their house, after the Blessed Virgin Mary, St. Joseph, and St. Frances of Rome. Joubert requested a plenary indulgence for the Oblate Sisters and all Catholics celebrating St. Benedict's Feast Day in the Oblate chapel. Rome granted Joubert's request in May 1833.[72]

In presenting his case for the indulgence celebrating St. Benedict the Moor, Joubert revealed aspects of his own thinking about race and religion. Socially conservative if spiritually egalitarian, Joubert accommodated slavery, as did virtually the entire American church establishment. Indeed, recently rediscovered evidence indicates that Joubert himself may have owned a slave in 1808. Joubert commended St. Benedict as a role model to black people for transcending temporal inequities, pursuing a life of Christian perfection, and earning his spiritual reward in heaven. On occasion Joubert criticized his black congregation. In 1832 he complained that "our good colored people . . . often go beyond their means for pure vanity and ostentation." In 1839 he noted reprovingly "the indifference of the parents because they were not present" at the distribution of prizes marking the end of the school year.[73]

Yet, Joubert was personally very sympathetic to black people both as individuals and as a despised minority. Throughout his ministry Joubert demonstrated a marked respect for the humanity of black people and treated them as active agents in their own salvation rather than as passive recipients of an externally imposed regimen. His response to the black Catholics' expressed devotion to St. Benedict the Moor demonstrated his ability to consider black people collaborators in formulating a more personalized religious environment. His sensitivity to the crucial importance for black Catholics to identify with a fellow black person revered and canonized by the institutional church revealed Joubert's spiritual egalitarianism. The existence of a black canonized saint indicated the Catholic Church's commitment to the concept of the spiritual, if not the social, equality of black and white members. Joubert recognized and addressed black Catholic emotional and psychological as well as spiritual and temporal needs.

Joubert's pastoral concern for his black congregation prompted him to establish the Holy Family Society in St. Mary's Lower Chapel on 25 December 1827. This religious devotional society, formed with the approval of Archbishop

Ambrose Maréchal, enrolled black members exclusively. In 1833 Joubert sought and received special indulgences and papal favors for the Holy Family Society as well as for the Oblate Sisters of Providence.[74]

As a Roman Catholic priest and white male in the antebellum South, James Joubert transcended prevailing institutional and social attitudes toward black people and women. The Sulpicians subscribed to a modified form of Gallicanism, a French clerical movement that promoted the development of particular, autonomous, national churches over a culturally homogeneous, universal structure centralized under papal authority.[75] With the establishment of the Oblate Sisters of Providence Joubert transposed Gallican encouragement of national peculiarities into the incorporation of racial peculiarities in the evolving American Catholic identity. He cofounded the Oblate community and collaboratively designed a rule with them that reflected their anomalous position within church and society. He argued effectively for the right of black women—a doubly despised minority—to have access to formal education.

Joubert validated this first community of African American Catholic sisters in the eyes of the institutional church. Without benefit of guiding precedent he deftly negotiated uncharted paths to legitimize the Oblate community as a congregation of sisters. Joubert secured diocesan approbation of the Oblate Rule from a skittish Archbishop James Whitfield. He then orchestrated papal recognition of the black Oblate Sisters as a community of women religious.

He was as sympathetic to the Oblate Sisters as women as he was to black people as human beings. The sisters reciprocated by appreciating the true mettle of the man. The love, loyalty, respect, and gratitude they consistently accorded Joubert in his lifetime and thereafter eloquently testified to an enduring Oblate belief: in James Hector Nicholas Joubert de la Muraille, a providential God had sent them an advocate and indeed a champion. Joubert promoted the Oblate cause and advanced their mission in the frequently hostile environment of the antebellum South and the American Roman Catholic Church.

CHAPTER THREE

The Respect Which Is Due to the State We Have Embraced

THE DEVELOPMENT OF OBLATE COMMUNITY LIFE AND GROUP IDENTITY

✦ ✦

Historically, black people have marshaled their spiritual resources to assert their personal worth. Whether slave or free, black people in the Protestant tradition utilized religion both as individuals and collectively in congregations to counter the onslaughts of a racist society disallowing black humanity. The formation of the Oblate community provided another incarnation of black religious piety. The Oblate Sisters of Providence distinguished themselves by their collective profession and practice of spirituality as the first black women in the United States to pursue religious communal life in the Roman Catholic tradition.

As black women religious, the Oblate Sisters claimed for themselves the traditional entitlements of respectability and societal exemption inherent in the religious state. In community, black women felt empowered to transcend mere social opposition to their divinely mandated mission: their own personal spiritual perfection and the education of black children. To women circumscribed and demeaned by white society because of their racial identity the appeal of membership in such an organization proved significant. The Oblate Sisters forged their unique communal charism, or spiritual identity, during the first decade of their existence. In the process they incorporated new members, defined cardinal Oblate virtues and spiritual attributes, achieved economic self-sufficiency, determined their communal ethnic identity, experienced generation-gap tensions, contended with both physical and spiritual needs, conducted a school, and defined their relationship as black women religious to the black lay community.

Nineteenth-century Roman Catholic sisterhoods followed a general pattern of developing a functional community life that they continuously refined over time and with experience. The socialization process and strict daily regimen designed to facilitate each religious community member's quest for spiritual perfection and union with God resulted in often rigorous initiation experiences. Spending from six months to a year as a postulant and then from one to two years as a novice, a candidate tested her vocation while learning the fundamentals of religious life. Strict novice mistresses inculcated the obligations imposed by the religious vows of poverty, chastity, and obedience.

To maintain discipline religious communities enforced unquestioning obedience to superiors, a demanding schedule of religious exercises, periods of silence, and the chapter of faults, or weekly assemblies, where each member publicly acknowledged any infractions against the community rules she might have committed. To sustain community life among individuals not related by blood, religious communities often restricted both close personal relationships within the membership and most social contact between the sisters, their family members and friends, and the general laity. Their fervent piety and focus on spirituality sustained the large numbers of women who persevered in their commitment to the rigors of religious communal life.[1]

The Oblate Sisters of Providence conformed to this general pattern of religious life with some exceptions. From 1828 through 1833 small community size, pre-existing familiarity among the membership, and the mature age of the candidates allowed less formality in community structure. Elizabeth Lange, Marie Balas, and Almaide Duchemin had already lived together for some years prior to the beginning of the Oblate novitiate on 13 June 1828. These three women readily absorbed the one additional charter Oblate member, Rosine Boegue. The sisters adopted a simple dress "of black woolen stuff for winter and summer" and a white cap for housewear, that they exchanged for a black bonnet for streetwear. Only the black band of the cap and the cross suspended from a neck chain adorning the dress of professed sisters distinguished their habit from that worn by the novices.[2]

In October 1829 Archbishop James Whitfield accompanied three prelates attending the First Provincial Council in Baltimore to visit the Oblate convent and school on George Street. At the conclusion of the visit Benedict Flaget of Kentucky blessed the four charter Oblate Sisters and predicted that the community would number twelve members in two years. In 1830 four women entered the Oblate community as candidates; in 1831, four more. Entering candidates in 1830 included Anne Marie Barclay and Cassandra Butler, the first Oblate candidates not of Francophone ethnic origin, Rose Rock, and Clara Bourgoin. Oblate aspirants in 1831 included Anne Marie Becraft, who had established a school for black girls in Washington, D.C., before joining the Oblate community; Betsy Duchemin, skilled nurse and mother of charter Oblate Sister Marie Therese Duchemin; and Claire Bourgoin, Clara's aunt. By October 1831 the Oblate community had trebled in size to twelve members and candidates, accomplishing Flaget's prediction of 1829. In 1832 candidates Cecile Bourgoin, niece of Claire and either sister or cousin to Clara, and Eugenie LeBarth entered the Oblate community.[3]

Through 1832 Oblate members and applicants ranged in age from sixteen to forty-eight years old. Although the original Oblate Rule of 1829 referred to postulants, community size and maturity did not warrant use of this category for five years. On Christmas Day 1833, the Oblate Sisters received their first class of postulants to accommodate four Oblate pupils under sixteen years of age who wished to become sisters. The annals chronicler reported:

> After the last Mass, Susan Becraft, Helen Thomas, Hospiliene Deshais, and Mary Louise James were admitted as postulants and took the chain of the Holy Slavery of Mary. These four young persons who were pupils of the Sisters, attained their desire of attaching themselves to the institute, but their age did not permit them to be admitted as novices. In order to correspond with their good will we agreed that they should be separated from the rest of the young girls of the school, and that they should be given a special dress to wear so that they could be distinguished at the same time from the novices. We adopted a brown color for Sunday and feasts and blue for the other days. They shall be henceforth under the special care and direction of the Mistress of Novices.
>
> N.B. It was Msgr. L'Abbe Odin of the diocese of St. Louis who gave the first idea of establishing this society of postulants.[4]

Of the first four Oblate postulants, Susan Becraft (a sister of Anne Marie) died prematurely and Hospiliene Deshais did not persevere in her religious vocation. Oblate Superior Lange stood as godmother to Marie Helen Thomas, a convert to Roman Catholicism in 1830. Circumstantial evidence identifies Marie Helen as Anne, daughter of Helen Thomas, who in June 1829 paid tuition for

Anne for two quarters as a day student at the Oblate school. Apparently rather than incur debt, Thomas withdrew Anne from the school in 1830. After converting to Roman Catholicism in July 1830 and receiving her First Communion in June 1831, Anne reentered the school as a boarding student, free of charge in 1832.[5] Anne's baptismal name, Marie Helen, honored both her godmother, Sister Mary, and her birth mother, Helen. Thomas belonged to the Confirmation class of 1833. An exceptional student, she received prizes for excellence in both 1832 and 1833. Thomas, with fellow postulants James and Amanda, began her Oblate novitiate in 1835, having come of age that year. According to U.S. census data, Thomas would have been eleven years old at her baptism in 1830, fourteen years old as a postulant in 1833, and sixteen years old as a novice in 1835. As Sister Gertrude Thomas, she would serve as superior of the Oblate community for three terms, from 1851 to 1860.[6]

Josephine Amanda, a pupil in the Oblate school from 1828, had also converted to Catholicism. James Joubert had stood as her godfather at baptism and had presented her with a small holy water font that had belonged to his mother. Josephine Amanda joined the Oblate postulant class in 1834, began her Oblate novitiate as the second Sister Stanislaus in 1835, and professed her vows in 1836. Despite such an auspicious beginning, Sister Stanislaus would leave the Oblate community in 1845.[7]

In 1834 Jane Laurette and her mother, Laurette Jane Noel of Wilmington, Delaware, joined the Oblate community as novices. In 1835 the second Noel daughter, Marie Louise, joined the three rising postulants, Thomas, James, and Amanda, and one other candidate to form the largest group to enter the Oblate community in a single year. Marie Germaine, a "child of the house" whom the Oblate community educated and raised free of charge from 1828, applied as the community's only candidate in 1836. In 1838 applicants Marie West and Charlotte Schaaf joined the community. Laura Johnson and Angelica Gideon, both Oblate school pupils, completed the Oblate community's first-decade roster of members in 1839.

The Oblate Sisters accepted thirty applicants between 1829 and 1839. Twenty-five women actually entered the novitiate during this period. Because the sisters received no more than one to five new members in any given year of their first decade and suffered six deaths during this period, the complement of active Oblate Sisters in any year between 1828 and 1839 did not exceed sixteen members. Yet, from a global perspective the Oblate community, numbering twelve members in 1831, compared favorably with sisterhoods pursuing educational and medical ministries throughout the world. Characteristically, in most rural areas and missions, and occasionally in Europe, very small religious communities—frequently numbering fewer than six women—proved the norm.[8]

WITHIN THEIR FIRST DECADE the Oblate Sisters of Providence defined those distinctive personal qualities they sought in their members. Being women of color and certifiably pious proved necessary but not sufficient attributes for Oblate membership. Aspirants had to be women "capable of rendering great service to the institution," "well fitted for teaching," "of talents and ability suitable for any employment," and "useful for sewing." The Oblate Sisters accepted well-educated or skilled, disciplined members willing and able to contribute substantively to the community's advancement.[9]

The resources and assets the Oblate Sisters expected from prospective members did not necessarily include money. Anne Marie Barclay's application for admission in 1830 provided the first occasion for the sisters to implement the dowry waiver. In their assembly of 17 February 1830 to consider Barclay's application, the sisters listed the essential traits of a qualified Oblate candidate: "It was decided that the lack of a dowry should not present any difficulty provided the person be well known, of good reputation, being pious, experienced and virtuous, and that she be able to render service to the institution. Anne Marie Barclay fulfilled all these conditions, and we consented unanimously to admit her." Of the twenty-five candidates who entered the Oblate novitiate between 1828 and 1839, five brought no dowry.[10]

In 1834 and 1835 three other candidates, members of the Andrew Noel family of Wilmington, Delaware, compensated the Oblate community for the straitened finances of these five. The Noels had risen veritably from rags to riches, in the cherished American tradition. Parents Andrew and Laurette Noel arrived in Wilmington, Delaware, in 1804 as slaves in the Garesche household, all San Domingan refugees. After their owner had manumitted them, he endowed them with a significant amount of money. Extant evidence does not reveal the reason for the beneficence of their former owner toward the Noels.

The Noels purchased extensive plots of prime Wilmington real estate. They operated an inn at one end of their property and lived comfortably among "the French nobility and Wilmington wealthy." The enterprising Andrew Noel also opened a barber shop. He secured his position as a respected member of the Wilmington Francophone community by renting one of only fourteen pews— the socially prominent DuPont family rented another—in St. Mary's of Coffee Run, the first Catholic church in Delaware. Noel's untimely death sometime after 1820 left Laurette Jane Noel a prosperous, if bereaved, widow. The death of her only son soon compounded Laurette Noel's grief.[11]

For at least five years, from the time of her husband's death until she joined the Oblate community in 1835, Laurette Noel successfully managed the considerable business interests she had inherited from her husband. The Noel inn proved a favorite retreat for several distinguished clerics who vacationed or convalesced there. Francis Patrick Kenrick, bishop of Philadelphia and future archbishop of Baltimore; his brother Peter Richard Kenrick, future archbishop of St. Louis; George Carrell, future bishop of Covington, Kentucky; and Michael O'Connor, bishop of Pittsburgh and future Jesuit priest in Baltimore, all enjoyed the hospitality of the solicitous Laurette Noel. The Noel women established a nexus of clerical friendships and contacts that at critical times throughout the nineteenth century would benefit the Oblate community.[12]

In membership, contacts, and financial resources the three Noel women trebly endowed the Oblate Sisters. The mother, Laurette Jane Noel, brought significant business skills to the community. The daughters, Jane Laurette and Marie Louise, enriched the Oblate order with the benefits of their solid education. Barred by racial restrictions from attending Catholic school in Wilmington, the two sisters had enrolled in a Wilmington Quaker school, where they received instruction in art and fancy needlework as well as the standard curriculum. Finally, the Noel family endowed the Oblate community with notable wealth.[13]

The annals entry of 1 June 1833 said of the nineteen-year-old Jane Laurette that "if she is received she will bring with her more than the required dowry, her father having left her a small fortune at his death."[14] Two years later, in 1835, mother Laurette and daughter Marie Louise applied for Oblate membership. The Oblate annalist reported: "As soon as Mde. Noel was informed of the good intentions of the Sisters in her regard, she turned over to the Sister Superior the deeds of a property which she had conjointly with her two daughters in the City of Wilmington in the State of Delaware. This property is worth $1,500 or $2,000. Moreover they have in the bank $300 and she remitted to the Director $360 which is to be her dowry; and each of her two daughters has more than $700. In addition they brought with them considerable personal property."[15]

As Oblate Sisters, the Noel women assumed leadership roles. The mother, Sister Chantal Noel, served in 1836 for three months as superior during Sister Mary Lange's illness. When Lange resumed her duties as superior, Sister Chantal replaced the ailing assistant superior, Sister Frances Balas. In 1838 the Oblate community elected Sister Chantal to a full three-year term as assistant superior. She died in that office on the eve of the next election, which "would have made

*Sister Marie Louise Noel, O.S.P.,
Oblate superior, 1844–51 and
1861–85 (Courtesy of Archives
of the Oblate Sisters of Providence,
Baltimore, Md.)*

her Mother Superior."[16] Noel daughters, Sisters Mary James and Marie Louise,
acted as Lange's business auxiliaries. Sister Marie Louise Noel would serve the
Oblate community as superior from 1844 to 1851, as assistant superior from 1851
to 1857, and again as superior from 1861 until her death in 1885.[17]

The Oblate Sisters did not accept as a member every woman they admitted
as a candidate. Stated reasons for rejecting applicants often provide insights into
the evolving Oblate charism and sense of community identity. The ability to
pay the dowry in full did not compensate for perceived deficiencies of character. Jeanne Capot applied for Oblate membership in October 1831, fulfilling
Bishop Flaget's prediction of twelve Oblate members and candidates by that
time. Nevertheless, the Oblate Sisters did not hesitate to return Capot's dowry
and reject her candidacy one year later because "the hesitation which this young
person made, and the flightiness of her conduct filled us with doubts." The sisters determined that "the respect she owed their state and the good reputation
of their establishment" precluded Capot's admission into Oblate membership.[18]
The evolving Oblate communal identity demanded of prospective members
conviction and focused concentration on the Oblate mission. After her dis-

missal, Capot maintained cordial relations with the Oblate Sisters. She partic-ipated in the fund-raising fair that the black lay community organized for the new Oblate chapel in 1837.[19]

In 1833 the Oblate Sisters experienced an incident recurrent throughout church history in which parents attempted to impose religious life on uncom-mitted daughters. Mr. John Lee of Frederick County, Maryland, arranged to board his married daughter, Mary Tritt, with the Oblate Sisters and paid the $72 year's board in advance, a sum Oblate records listed as a dowry installment. Evidently, he hoped that after either the annulment of her marriage or the death of her husband, Mary would embrace the religious life. A mere five days after her arrival, Mary, "who it seemed came only to please her father . . . could not become accustomed to the manner of life of the Sisters and communicated to the Director her desire of returning to Georgetown. She left this morning."[20] The Oblate Sisters made no effort to convince, cajole, or coerce one who could not become accustomed to the manner of life of the sisters. They supplied Mary Tritt with $5 for the return trip to Washington, D.C. Her family donated the remaining $67 to the Oblate school.[21]

The Oblate community extended the probationary period required of some candidates. Marie Germaine lived in the Oblate community as a "child of the house" from 1828 to 1833. Then seventeen years old, she asked to enter the con-vent. The Oblate Sisters "did not judge it wise to accede to her request, but to wait and prove the fidelity of her vocation."[22] Age played no role in their deci-sion; at seventeen, Marie Germaine certainly qualified in years to begin her novitiate. Evidently, the sisters' close association with this candidate over a five-year period had raised concerns about her personality, her abilities, or her reli-gious commitment. They required Marie Germaine to lead a blameless life for two years in the outside world as a test. During this trial period, Marie Ger-maine acquired sufficient funds to allow her to lend the Oblate community $103 on 5 May 1834. In 1835 the Oblate Sisters unanimously accepted the nineteen-year-old Marie Germaine as a candidate. In February 1836 she entered the con-vent as just a postulant. Marie Germaine at last began her novitiate as Sister Clotilde in July 1836. In 1839 the sisters admitted their pupil, Angelica Gideon, into the community on her second attempt to join. Although this candidate re-ceived the unanimous consent of the community this time, the sisters accepted her only "on condition that she should be tried until the Feast of St. Benedict when she should receive the habit," several months later.[23]

Nineteenth-century white attitudes denigrated the virtue of all black women and consequently impugned the concept of a community of black women re-ligious. White supporters and detractors of the Oblate cause alike wondered,

"Where could be found the pious young women needed for it, who would consent to persevere in virginity and who would be satisfied with the meagre support to be derived from teaching the poorest of the poor?"[24]

In the 1830s the Oblate Sisters themselves demonstrated no such concern or preoccupation about the pool of prospective Oblate candidates. From their inception, the sisters established rigorous and highly selective standards for Oblate membership. They sought quality rather than quantity in their ranks and resisted opportunities to augment membership with candidates less than totally dedicated to the Oblate cause.

Religious vocations prove elitist by definition. Like the Marine Corps in search of a few good women and men, religious communities challenge adherents to live lives of hardship and service, bolstered by their faith and commitment. Attracting a mass membership was not a priority of the Oblate sisterhood. Indeed, amassing sufficient resources to support the significant number of devout women aspiring to Oblate membership remained a major Oblate concern throughout the antebellum period.

DURING THEIR FIRST DECADE, the Oblate Sisters determined crucial aspects of their evolving community charism. Humility formed an essential component of the Oblate spiritual identity. Joubert frequently charged the Oblate Sisters "to act with all humility and confidence in God" or to comport themselves with "the humility which should characterize religious."[25] On 9 March 1834—the feast day of the sisters' major patron, St. Frances of Rome—Louis Deluol, superior of the Sulpician seminary and vicar-general of the archdiocese of Baltimore, celebrated Mass in the Oblate chapel. In his sermon, Deluol "urged the Sisters to imitate in their holy Mother her humility and renunciation of self, virtues which shone in her in a very special manner." On the same feast day five years later, Joubert's Sulpician colleague Edward Damphoux preached a sermon that "pleased the Director very much, since he tended to inspire us with the virtues which he ceases not to inculcate in us and which he desires to see us practice, chiefly humility."[26]

In a worldly context, humility denotes a demeanor of deference from an inferior toward a superior, a socially hierarchical relationship between people. However, in a religious sense, humility signifies primarily a voluntary submission of self to God, a spiritual relationship between the individual and the divine. In practice, the moral virtue of humility "avoids inflation of one's worth or talents on the one hand, and avoids excessive devaluation of oneself on the other. Humility requires a dispassionate and honest appreciation of the self in relationship to others and to God."[27] Certainly Oblate Superior Lange articulated the very essence of the challenging practice of humility—framed in reference to Oblate consciousness of their racial identity—in her concern "not to appear too arrogant on the one hand and on the other, not to miss the respect which is due to the state we have embraced and the holy habit which we have the honor to wear."[28]

In its focus centered on the divine, humility involves a renunciation of the world, a rejection of secular concerns and status. Nineteenth-century communal religious life for women required members to reject their former worldly identities, symbolized in their acceptance of new names conferred by their new family, the religious community. While distinctions between the secular and spiritual connotations of humility applied generally to all religious congregations, they acquired particular racial significance for the black Oblate Sisters in the antebellum South. Embracing the religious state and rejecting secular concerns and status could prove both liberating and empowering to black women debased by the worldly social order. In renouncing the world to consecrate themselves to God, the Oblate Sisters of Providence achieved symbolic release from socially ascribed derogation based on their identities as black women. As the Oblate Sisters of Providence, women of color in the antebellum South utilized their piety and spiritual fervor to defy their socially ascribed inferior status and to act assertively in service to others.

Two aspects of Oblate spirituality established during the sisters' first decade resonate with racial meaning. From 1833 the Oblate Sisters claimed St. Benedict the Moor as the fourth special patron of their house, after the Blessed Virgin Mary, St. Joseph, and St. Frances of Rome.[29] This designation represents the only explicit element of African identity in their spirituality, as historian Cyprian Davis has noted.[30] The animosity surrounding their formation plausibly explains why the Oblate Sisters postponed claiming this black saint formally as a community patron until after papal recognition had secured their status as women religious in antebellum Baltimore.

On 2 July 1830 Oblate spiritual director James Joubert, the four charter Oblate members, and the three Oblate novices enrolled in the Association of Holy Slavery of the Mother of God, receiving the symbolic chain of membership. Future Oblate members were to enroll in the association the day they received their habits. Oblate affiliation with this devotional society initially appears problematic for black sisters in the context of the antebellum South. However, their allegiance to this devotional society conformed completely to the centrality of devotion to the Blessed Virgin in the Oblate charism. Davis treats this association as a development from seventeenth-century French devotional practices and states that the metaphor "holy slavery" enjoyed widespread usage in church devotional circles. Theologian Thaddeus Posey asserts that "to freely give oneself to a slavery that would secure a constant union with Christ was in complete harmony with the Oblate Rule" and that "these freed women took the classic model of the abused of the black community and turned it into a mode of service and a model of grace."[31]

This study concurs with Posey's first assessment; however, it contends that Oblate membership in the Association of Holy Slavery of the Mother of God represented no embrace of slavery as "the classic model of the abused of the black community" but rather a conversion—if not subversion—of the specific secular connotations of the institution of slavery in the antebellum South. The spiritual slavery with which the Oblate Sisters associated differed critically from its social analogue of involuntary subjugation to an owner, both in its voluntary nature and sole purpose of personal spiritual benefit. Oblate membership in this devotional society reflected the degree to which these black sisters successfully dissociated themselves spiritually—if not physically—from their immediate social context to divest the term slavery of its dehumanizing connotations.

The Oblate community further sought to divest the institution of slavery of its dehumanizing faculty in their membership policy. Oblate Sisters Chantal (Laurette Noel), Helen Joseph (Mary West), Clotilde (Marie Germaine), and Angelica (Angelica Gideon) all began life as slaves. Of the forty women who entered the Oblate novitiate in the antebellum period, eight had risen from slave origins.[32] The Oblate Sisters of Providence did not consider a candidate's previous condition of servitude a liability for Oblate membership. The Oblate Rule did not explicitly address the issue of slavery. The general requirement that candidates "be free from debts and detained in the world by no hindrance whatsoever"[33] commonly appeared in the regulations of religious congregations. Only in the context of the racial identity of the Oblate Sisters did this requirement mean that candidates had to be free black women.

It hardly proves surprising that the Oblate Sisters neither expressed abolitionist sentiments nor engaged in antislavery activities, whatever their private feelings about slavery might have been. Oblate silence about slavery occurred within the context of an American Roman Catholic Church whose clergy and hierarchy not only frequently and vociferously defended the institution of slavery but also participated in and profited from it. As a religious society within the Roman Catholic Church, the Oblate Sisters—and all sisterhoods—adhered to official church policy of nonintervention in social and political matters. The Oblate Rule required that "[the sisters] will not take the liberty of condemning others, though these may be really wrong. They will endeavor as much as possible to live at peace with everyone; they must strive to conciliate the goodwill of all."[34] Clearly this policy referred to the obligation of the Oblate membership to maintain the goodwill of the parents of their pupils; nevertheless, it applied with equal validity to Oblate abstention from public debate about social and political issues confronting antebellum society.

Convent life ostensibly offered young women exceptional countercultural opportunities in antebellum American society. It provided freedom from marital and maternal obligations and sororal community living outside the constraints of the conventional nuclear household, the functioning unit of the ideal of domesticity. Roman Catholic sisters participated in antebellum public life to an unprecedented extent, working outside the home on a permanent basis and pioneering in such professions as teaching and nursing. Sisters serving as convent superiors, school directors, or hospital administrators wielded exceptional authority in patriarchal American society. In the foundation, internal administration, and direction of their respective congregations, sisters exercised significant initiative and independence. Furthermore, sisters could and did resist the demands of male clerical authority when they obstructed the sisters' execution of the will of God or intruded on the realization of their communal missions as they understood them. However, as historian Joseph Mannard has perceptively observed, even as Roman Catholic sisters broadened the meaning of the female sphere by expanding traditional gender-role definitions, they did not explicitly challenge the male exclusiveness of the Catholic clergy, their own subordination within the church, or that of women to men in general. Sisters generally accepted gender distinctions and the tenets of the cult of domesticity and, by their practice of "maternity of the spirit," promoted the ideals of republican motherhood in their schools.[35]

In September 1833 the Oblate Sisters and their spiritual director James Joubert collaborated on revisions to the original Oblate Rule. These additions further disclosed the Oblate community's evolving charism. The revised Rule specified the duties of the novice mistress—an office only then incorporated into the administrative structure of the Oblate community. It charged the novice mistress with "the good formation of the novices [on whom] depend the well being and the conservation of the congregation of tomorrow." She was to impress on her charges that their commitment to the religious life entailed "a perfect abnegation of their own will, engraving well in their spirit and their heart that the Society of the Oblates of Providence is founded spiritually on the Mount of Calvary for the service of Jesus Christ Crucified, in the imitation of whom all Sisters must crucify their senses, their inclinations, their imagination, their passions, their aversions, and honors for the love of the Heavenly Father." The revision further enumerated cardinal Oblate virtues and attributes, enjoining the novice mistress to "exercise then the novices in humility, obedience, gentleness and modesty, increasing their courage in order that, like strong young women, they might do good works with a solid and powerful perfection."[36]

The Oblate community's explication of the office of novice mistress inadvertently raised issues of gender roles in both church and society. It juxtaposed seemingly conflicting goals in urging the training of humble, obedient, gentle, modest women who nevertheless evinced courage, strength, solidity, and power —in sum, agency. This statement embodied a dichotomy not peculiar to the Oblate community but rather endemic in nineteenth-century society and church, institutions that sought simultaneously to subordinate women and to exploit their strength and capabilities. As did other congregations of sisters, the Oblate Sisters dichotomized their efforts to resolve this apparent duality. They channeled their cultivation of humility, obedience, modesty, and gentleness into their quest for spiritual perfection. Simultaneously they demonstrated courage, strength, power, and solidity in the establishment of their institution, in their conduct and administration of their internal communal life, and in their execution of their teaching ministry.

During their first decade, the Oblate Sisters demonstrated courage and a sense of empowerment as a community on several occasions. In 1832 a cholera epidemic ravaged several eastern cities, including Baltimore. The Trustees of the Bureau of the Poor requested eight Sisters of Charity to nurse indigent cholera victims at the city almshouse in Calverton, a few miles from the populated areas of Baltimore. Supplied with only four Sisters of Charity, the trustees then approached Joubert on 26 August 1832 to request four Oblate Sisters to nurse the sick. Evidently, the Trustees of the Bureau of the Poor had not known of the Oblate Sisters of Providence until the Sisters of Charity informed them of the existence of that "society of religious colored women." Joubert informed "these gentlemen that the Sisters of Charity were by the spirit of their institute obliged to look after the sick; but that the Sisters of Providence were not, as they are obliged to the education of young girls of their color." Cautioning the officials that "my authority over them [the sisters] did not allow that I should force them to obey in a thing other than the spirit of their institute," Joubert nevertheless hoped to "find four among them who were willing, and who felt courage enough to expose themselves to possible contagion; these were to give me their names." In response, the entire Oblate membership of eleven sisters volunteered "and filled with joy and happiness, they all cried that they were ready to undertake it, that they should find much happiness in being able to serve our Lord in the person of the sick; all I had to do was to make a choice."[37] Joubert chose

Sisters Mary Lange, Anthony Duchemin, Magdalene Barclay, and Scholastica Bourgoin to nurse at the almshouse for a month. Oblate nursing at the almshouse earned a formal letter of thanks from Archibald Stirling, secretary of the Trustees of the Bureau of the Poor.

In July 1833 a clergyman from the diocese of Mobile, Alabama, where "the population was for the greater part colored," proposed the establishment of an Oblate mission in that city. The Oblate Sisters' response, although couched in deferential terms acknowledging the authority of clerical superiors to initiate and sanction such activity, revealed their burgeoning missionary zeal and sense of empowerment. The sisters "all unanimously declared that they had given themselves to God in the religious state to work more efficaciously for their sanctification and to contribute all the means in their power for the glory of God and the religious education of the girls of their race." Therefore the Oblates "at all times" stood "ready to go anywhere" that their clerical superiors "should judge the Holy Will of God called them." On 16 June 1834 Mathias Loras, vicar-general of the diocese of Mobile, again inquired about the feasibility of an Oblate mission in Mobile and "appeared very happy with the good will which the Sisters manifested at this time."[38] Although the Oblate Sisters had responded positively and eagerly to both inquiries, Bishop Michael Portier of Mobile never acted on his clerics' initiatives. When Portier finally decided to establish a school for free black girls in the 1840s, he invited the white Sisters of Charity of St. Joseph, Emmitsburg, not the Oblate Sisters of Providence, to staff it.[39]

Whether or not others chose to profit from it, the Oblate Sisters had demonstrated their apostolic enthusiasm. Their willingness to subject themselves to fatal diseases and to go wherever sent to advance the education of girls of color embodied that agency stipulated in their 1833 constitutional revision requiring "courage in order that, like strong young women, they might do good works with a solid and powerful perfection."

BECAUSE THE ARCHDIOCESE committed no financial resources to the maintenance of any of its sisterhoods, business and financial concerns formed an integral part of Oblate community life. Dowries provided a significant source of income for Baltimore's antebellum sisterhoods. The three white sisterhoods that preceded the Oblate community in the archdiocese had not stipulated specific required amounts for dowries. However, the dowry of £2,000 that candidate Jane Hamersley brought to the Carmelite Nuns in 1794 and that of $3,000 in cash plus real estate holdings candidate Elizabeth Neale surrendered to the Visitation Sisters of Georgetown around 1818 both reflected and typified the familial ties to Maryland's planter aristocracy and the wealth a significant portion of the membership of these two communities of women religious enjoyed.[40] In comparison to the dowries some of the white sisterhoods received, the inherited wealth Lange and the Noels brought to the young Oblate community proved modest.

As did their antebellum peer sisterhoods, the Oblate Sisters relied on dowries and tuition as their primary sources of income. The economic status of the Oblate membership varied. The stipulated $400 dowry could prove prohibitive for black candidates who lacked family affluence and who worked in a society that curtailed their economic options. As previously noted, five sisters invoked the dowry waiver clause incorporated in the original Oblate Rule during the sisterhood's first decade. Most candidates, however, presented at least a token dowry, if not the full stipulated sum. The annals' cumulative account from 17 May 1828 through 1 January 1836 cited $4,429.30 income from dowries, representing some nineteen entering candidates, averaging a $233 dowry per capita.[41]

Some Oblate candidates presenting the full dowry sum had earned the money themselves from working. Betsy Duchemin apparently financed her daughter Therese's education and Oblate dowry from her earnings as a nurse. She declared her own intention to join the Oblate community in September 1829 but delayed her entrance since her "affairs would still keep her in the world for about two years."[42] Evidently, Duchemin had to continue her work as a nurse to amass her dowry, $200 of which she advanced on 9 September 1829.[43] Even after entering the Oblate community as Sister Anthony in 1831, Betsy Duchemin continued to practice nursing professionally.

Historian Barbara Misner characterizes one-third of the Oblate membership before 1850 as middle class in socioeconomic background.[44] Black and white populations employed different criteria in determining middle-class status. Generally, black people considered not only family wealth but also free lineage, reputation, material possessions, and color in ascribing middle-class status. As noted earlier, Baltimore's black community proved exceptional in not privileging color as a criterion of social status. Black barbers, caterers, and tradespeople serving a white clientele exclusively and black people in personal service to prominent families from white society formed important elements of the black middle class. Although Baltimore's free black population also supported a small professional elite of physicians, ministers, lawyers, and teachers who served the black community, no evidence documents that Oblate members derived from this portion of the black middle class. Oblate family backgrounds more often included barbers and tradespeople, many of whom achieved a comfortable standard of living in antebellum Baltimore. A sufficient segment of the Baltimore black community proved prosperous enough to support a private school for girls and the black religious community founded to staff it.

The teaching sisterhoods conducting schools in antebellum American society derived much of their income from tuition. The young ladies' academies established in the archdiocese of Baltimore numbered among their pupils and alumna the daughters of both Roman Catholic and Protestant planter elite, affluent businessmen, and influential politicians as well as middle-class families. In 1809 the Sisters of Charity of St. Joseph, Emmitsburg, had intended to educate poor girls exclusively but experienced such financial straits within their first year of operation that they reluctantly consented to establish an elite academy. From its inception in 1810 the academy generated sufficient income not only to sustain itself but also to subsidize the sisters' instructional efforts for poor girls as well.[45]

The Oblate Sisters also realized a significant portion of their income from tuition charges. In 1829 Joubert twice noted, with evident satisfaction, that student enrollment proved sufficient to meet all Oblate expenses. In contrast to the affluence associated with the white Baltimore-area academies, however, the racially based comparative economic disadvantage of the Oblate target population restricted both the amount and the regular receipt of tuition income the Oblate Sisters could expect.[46]

On 28 May 1833 at an executive meeting attended by Director Joubert, Mother Superior Frances Balas, Assistant Superior Magdalene Barclay, and Sister Mary Lange, "it was decided that no extraordinary expenses should be incurred without the consent of the Superior, the Assistant, and Sister Mary."[47] This group appointed a treasurer, an office later formally incorporated into the Rule in the amendments of 1833. The sister treasurer assumed responsibility for all receipts and disbursements and for submitting monthly financial statements to the director. The fact that this executive committee included Lange, who then held no formal office in the community, undoubtedly reflected both her preeminent status as founder within the community as well as her proven proficiency in managing her personal estate.

The Oblate Sisters accommodated a limited number of paying female boarders, more as a service to such patrons than as a source of significant income. Younger women seriously contemplating a religious vocation and elderly pensioners lacking family providers for their care typified the Oblate boarder. Between 1829 and 1839 the Sisters received five boarders who paid $6 per month for room and board. From 1829 Betsy Duchemin and Eugenie LeBarth boarded two and four years, respectively, while working in the outside world, before joining the Oblate community as members. Both the Oblate Sisters and Mary Tritt's father had viewed her boarding with the community in 1833 as a preliminary step to her eventual religious profession. The sisters stipulated as a condition of Tritt's admission that she pay the annual board fee "until a change in her state would enable her to embrace definitely the religious life."[48]

The elderly Elizabeth DuMoulin boarded with the Oblate Sisters from 1831 until her death in 1837. She bequeathed all her possessions to the second Sister Stanislaus (Josephine Amanda), "her godchild whom she loved more . . . than if she were her own daughter."[49] In 1833 Helen Bourgoin, "sister of Sister Scholastica who is the aunt of Sisters Elizabeth and Bridget," arranged to board with the Oblate Sisters, "when the infirmities of age should make it impossible for her to gain a living by working." Helen Bourgoin had worked as a domestic servant for many years and agreed to surrender to the Oblate community all her present and future savings in return for perpetual care. Bourgoin's agreement with the Oblate community stipulated that "in case of the death of Helen Bourgoin before her entry in the house, the money she had thus given should be left as a gift to the community from her, so that her heirs could never claim anything."[50] By 17 June 1833 Bourgoin had paid the Oblate community $350. The 27 January 1839 annals entry indicated that Bourgoin also lent the Oblate Sisters money in addition to paying her accustomed fees for room and board.[51]

In July 1833 Sister Mary Elizabeth Lange donated $1,411.59 to the Oblate community. In return she requested that the sisters agree to shelter her mother, Nannette Lange, on the same conditions as Helen Bourgoin. Nanette Lange arrived from Matanzas, Cuba, and lived in the Oblate community for a little more than a year before her death in 1837. Elizabeth DuMoulin, Helen Bourgoin, and Nanette Lange undoubtedly remained indebted to the Oblate community for offering a viable alternative to the municipal almshouse's attic "chronic hospital for aged colored women."[52]

Sewing provided a significant source of income for the Oblate Sisters from 1834. The first Oblate prospectus published in the *Laity's Directory* concluded with the notice: "N.B. At the suggestion of several Right Reverend Bishops and Clergymen who attended the Provincial Council, the Sisters of Providence have taken measures for furnishing the different Dioceses of the United States with Clerical Vestments of all sorts, at the lowest prices, and on the shortest possible notice."[53] Evidently, the Oblate Sisters' skilled needlework displayed at their convent so impressed visiting clergy that it precipitated a business opportunity for the community. The Sulpician priest Pierre Babad had initiated negotiations with the Didier Petit Company in Lyons, France, to supply ornaments and cloth on credit until the Oblate Sisters had made, sold, and received payment for the vestments. When the cloth did not arrive and the clergy began ordering vestments, "the Director, after taking counsel with the Sisters, decided to write again to ask them to send the cloth."[54]

This entrepreneurial venture proved a lucrative enterprise for the Oblate Sisters from 1834 to 1844. Sister M. Theresa Catherine Willigman recalled that "for a number of years the Sisters had as many orders as they could fill. Sets of vestments of the best material were always on hand, and the writer saw, when a child, a complete set worth hundreds of dollars. As there was no other establishment at this time, of this kind, this was a good revenue for the Sisters." The itemized list of vestments the Oblate Sisters offered filled two pages in the national Catholic directory from 1836 through 1839 and corroborated Willigman's recollection of "vestments of the best material."[55] Items ranged from a complete set of vestments in red damask silk richly embroidered with fine gold, adorned with lace and fine gold fringe, and completely lined in silk for $750 to pastoral stoles edged with mock gold or silk and silk-lined for $5.[56]

The Oblate financial statement of 1 January 1836 listed annual income from sewing as $440, second only to income from boarding students at $540. Sewing formed such a significant aspect of Oblate community life that sometime later in the nineteenth century the Oblate Rule temporarily incorporated it as part of the community's mission: "*Note (a). Sewing* in all its branches has been an auxiliary activity from the beginning, ecclesiastically approved, and occupies those incapacitated to teach and to prevent idleness and to contribute to the support of the community."[57]

The comprehensive financial statement issued on 1 January 1836 represented all the income and disbursements of the Oblate institute from 17 May 1828 to date. The figures portrayed a picture of sound financial management and fiscal responsibility. Long term, the sisters maintained a deficit of only $5.775 despite a series of real estate transactions, renovations, and building on their Richmond Street property to accommodate the steadily growing Oblate community and school. Short term, the sisters balanced annual expenditures of $1,000 against an annual income of $1,305.

Significantly, gifts or donations from external sources amounted to only $360 for the eight-year period.[58] Only rarely did individuals like Elizabeth Lange and Laurette, Jane, and Marie Louise Noel endow the Oblate community with personal wealth. Neither large infusions of wealth from generous patrons nor personal fortunes of heiress members loomed large on the Oblate fiscal horizon during the 1830s. They maintained solvency through hard work, discipline, sound management, and self-reliance. The Oblate Sisters sustained their economic self-sufficiency a lesson, a stitch, and a prayer at a time.

ISSUES OF ETHNIC IDENTITY informed not only the individual charisms of charter Oblate members Lange and Duchemin; they also influenced the evolving collective charism of the Oblate community. Because the charter Oblate members "were French in language, in sympathy, and habit of life,"[59] the French language figured prominently in Oblate communal affairs. English-speaking sisters and students acquired at least a rudimentary knowledge of French to communicate effectively with Sister Mary Lange, Sister Rose Boegue, and Elizabeth DuMoulin, the elderly widow who boarded at the Oblate convent and spoke only French. As part of the daily regimen of sister and student alike, Lange read a chapter of the New Testament in French before the noon meal. From the foundation of the school the sisters taught the French language as an integral part of their school's basic curriculum.[60]

But the Oblate community and school did not function in a Francophone cultural vacuum in 1830s Baltimore. By the 1820s the Sulpician priests conducted religious education in English to accommodate the black Anglophone Catholics who also attended these classes. James Joubert had provided both English- and French-language versions of the Oblate Rule and Constitutions. Oblate Sister and historian Willigman maintained that Oblate Superior Lange spoke and understood English well enough to direct the community.[61]

Evidently all twelve Oblate sisters in 1832 understood and conversed in the English language. In describing the death of the first Sister Stanislaus (Cassandra Butler) on 29 September 1932, the Oblate annalist noted, "Just before she died the Sisters all gathered around her bed; she recognized among them Madame DuMoulin and she remembered that this lady did not speak English. So she addressed a few words to her in French."[62] In spite of its Francophone origins, the Oblate community functioned bilingually virtually from its inception.

Several annals entries noted the singing of hymns in French during Masses or other liturgical services. As their first decade progressed, the Oblate Sisters documented an increasingly pronounced preference for sermons in French. An annals entry of 1833 reported the delivery of a sermon in French without comment; but an entry of 1837 reported a sermon "in French to the great satisfaction of the Sisters." In 1838 some Oblate Sisters assisted Mass at St. Mary's Seminary to hear a sermon in French since "it was preached here [St. Frances Chapel] in English."[63]

In September 1839 the Oblate annalist reported that "something that was very remarkable was that contrary to custom there was a sermon in French, and though it had not been announced the chapel was filled, above all with those who understood French and who were very much impressed and benefited by the advantage offered to them."[64] In October and again in November the same

French missionary, Rev. Delaune, "preached a fine sermon on the gospel of the day to the great satisfaction of the French people."[65] Although in the 1830s French sermons in the Oblate chapel proved exceptional, the Oblate Sisters nevertheless attempted to accord the French language a significant presence in the evolving cultural life of their community.[66]

From the 1840s German Catholic immigrants in Baltimore interposed native-language parishes and social, educational, and cultural institutions between themselves and the frequently hostile American environment. The Oblate Sisters of Providence, like the German immigrants in Baltimore, preferred to practice their Catholicism in their native language whenever possible and sought refuge in their Francophone cultural tradition from the religious hostility of a fundamentally anti-Catholic society. Unlike the Catholic German immigrants, the Oblate Sisters also sought refuge in their Francophone cultural tradition from the racial hostility of a fundamentally racist society. The French language and Roman Catholicism reinforced each other as cultural as well as religious traditions and served to distinguish the Oblate Sisters from white, Anglophone, Protestant, and racist American society. Such cultural distinctions formed a buffer, analogous to what historian John Blassingame described for slaves when he argued that the more the slaves' cultural forms differed from those of their owners, the more the slaves gained in personal autonomy and positive self-concepts.[67]

However, neither the Oblate annals nor their Rule indicated that the sisters ever considered an exclusively Francophone ethnic identity an intrinsic component of the Oblate charism. While the Oblate Rule explicitly identified community members racially as women of color, it contained no corresponding statement concerning ethnic origin. In February 1830 the Oblate community concluded "that the institution needed some American Sisters" and unanimously accepted Anne Marie Barclay, the first non-Francophone applicant. After entering the Oblate community as Sister Magdalene, Barclay served as assistant superior from 1832 to 1835 and then as mistress of novices from 1835 until her death in 1838. Sister Magdalene's early assumption of responsible office within the Oblate community demonstrated that Anglophone ancestry was not a disadvantage for "American" Oblate Sisters. By 1839 English-speaking women constituted nine of the thirty applicants accepted for Oblate membership and three of the five novices received without dowry.[68]

CONTEMPLATIVE AND MIXED religious orders incorporated three distinct ranks of sisters in a socially stratified internal hierarchy reflecting the European social order functioning at the time of their establishment. The choir nuns drew membership from the privileged, literate class and formed the elite who devoted themselves exclusively to prayer and meditation. The lay sisters derived from the servant class and performed all the domestic labor. The externs, frequently literate if less privileged, lived outside the cloister and conducted the community's business affairs. During the antebellum period, five of the seven sisterhoods serving in the archdiocese of Baltimore—the Carmelite and Visitation Nuns, the School Sisters of Notre Dame, and the Sisters of Mercy and of the Holy Cross—observed rank distinctions practiced in their respective European motherhouses. Only the Sisters of Charity of St. Joseph and the Oblate Sisters of Providence institutionalized no such class stratifications.[69]

By not only accommodating but also participating in and profiting from the institution of slavery in antebellum America, white women religious further distinguished themselves from the Oblate Sisters of Providence. Members of at least nine communities of sisters established in the United States by 1825 owned slaves. Unlike all the white sisterhoods serving the archdiocese of Baltimore before them—the Carmelite Nuns, the Georgetown Sisters of the Visitation, and the Sisters of Charity—the Oblate Sisters owned no slaves to labor for their benefit. The Oblate Sisters performed all the cooking, cleaning, and laundry tasks of the household themselves, in addition to their teaching duties, on a rotating basis as far as the skills of the individual sisters permitted. Willigman remembered, "In the first early years of the community it was no uncommon thing to see the Sisters piling wood in the yard, taking care of the stable, milking the cow, and other labors."[70]

During their first decade the Oblate community did not experience the class tensions that occurred in some of the other American congregations of sisters. The tensions in Oblate community life revealed in the annals occurred more along generational lines. The first example of institutional adaptation to accommodate age differences was the introduction of the rank of postulant in December 1833. In September 1836 the Oblate community implemented a policy to utilize the skills of the young sisters and to incorporate them into the work of the community. The Oblate Sisters assigned "the young Sisters, novices" certain classes to teach "so that they might be employed usefully in the work of the house, and might relieve some of the older Sisters who are overburdened because of their ill health."[71]

In January 1838 a significant procedural modification occurred in Oblate community life. Joubert decided to hold weekly communal assemblies on Sunday to discuss with the sisters specific articles of their Rule, to dispense spiritual advice, and to conduct the routine administrative tasks of community life.

The annals themselves reflected this change. Future entries focused primarily on matters discussed in the weekly assemblies. Although the implied new Rule or amendments prove elusive, the central role allotted to discussion of the Rule in these assemblies suggested recent, significant constitutional amendments or revisions. Comments such as "part of the generous advice contained in the rule was read and the Director added his advice which was better understood than that written in the book" and "we read today some of the articles added to the rule" indicated significant constitutional change.[72] At this time the Baltimore Oblate community may have incorporated part of the Rule of the Oblates of St. Frances of Rome. Joubert had first requested a copy of the Roman Oblate Rule through Anthony Kohlmann, his Jesuit friend in Rome, in 1833 and then again through Rev. Adolph Williamson in late 1834.

The condition of the younger Oblate Sisters continued to generate discussion. In February 1838 the assembly of sisters demonstrated a solicitous concern for the well-being of the community's youthful members. They modified the rigorous devotional regimen "found to be very fatiguing above all for the young Sisters who needed more recreation because of their age."[73]

The 1829 Oblate Rule, like those of all sisterhoods, mandated a highly regimented order of the day. Rising at 4:30 A.M., the sisters spent time in meditation, prayer, and attending daily Mass before the boarding students rose at 6:00. After completing household chores, sisters and students ate breakfast at 7:30, sisters sitting with students "to maintain order and preside over the children." Morning classes began with prayers at 9:00 and concluded three and one-half hours later in the same fashion. At 12:45 P.M. the sisters and students recited the rosary, listened to a chapter of the New Testament—read in French by Sister Mary Lange—and said the Angelus. Dinner at 1:15 preceded the first recreational period of the day, necessarily brief as classes resumed at 2:15 and ended at 4:15 in the afternoon. The longest recreation period of the day occurred after class until 5:00, when study period and needlework began. At 6:00 sisters and boarding students visited the Blessed Sacrament. Spiritual reading began at 7:00; supper, at 7:30; then recreation for thirty minutes. At 8:15 night prayers preceded more spiritual reading. From the conclusion of night prayers and the day at 9:00 P.M. until 7:00 A.M. the following morning, the community observed the rule of silence. Only the absence of classes and a more generous allotment of recreation time distinguished Sundays and feast days from the normal routine. The sisters modified the devotional regimen by eliminating obligatory adoration on Sundays and feast days, "leaving the Sisters at liberty to go to chapel during the time between the services and spiritual reading, as they wished."[74]

Starting in October 1838, however, annals references to younger Oblates became increasingly critical. On 21 October 1838 Joubert lectured the community "very strongly" about their responsibilities toward the children and "spoke particularly to the young Sisters as usual." On 11 November 1838 Joubert reprimanded the sisters for the poor condition of the schoolbooks. According to the Oblate annalist, "Though he spoke to all in general, it was easy to see, however, that these reproaches were addressed above all to the poor young Sisters as they were always more guilty."[75]

On 10 February 1839 Joubert initiated the practice of reading the history of the convent at the weekly assemblies. This practice gave "much pleasure to the Sisters, except the two novices who do not understand, especially seeing everyone laugh at the account of the strange adventure of Solomon."[76] This history of the convent, evidently more popular and anecdotal than the official annals, is apparently no longer extant. It contained the recounting of the incident involving the deceased convent guard dog, Solomon, that occurred in April 1838, but the story did not appear in the annals until April 1839. Reading the history of the Oblate Sisters of Providence in a community forum effectively acculturated and integrated new members into the group. This public exercise provided younger sisters the opportunity to learn Oblate history not only from the reading but also from the spontaneous responses of the older members who had actually lived that history. Such a setting permitted the senior sisters to supplement the written record with the oral transfer of Oblate lore, traditions, and memories to the younger generation.

On 4 March 1839 the Oblate annalist reported, "The Director had the kindness not to have Assembly. He had compassion for the sorrow of the young Sisters who knew that they merited to be scolded and who were in the mean time trying to seem pleasant."[77] These reproving assessments of the younger Oblate Sisters may have resulted from a qualitatively different novice cohort as the community absorbed more immature candidates who entered as postulants, girls under sixteen years of age. Incorporating new members of Anglophone as well as Francophone ancestry also may have generated ethnic tensions in the growing Oblate community. Critical comments may have further reflected general strains and tensions accompanying the growth and bureaucratization of the community as well as the incorporation of new rules—all displaced onto the newcomers. The fact that in 1839 alone Joubert felt compelled on separate occasions to deliver "a short exhortation on mutual support," to speak "of the peace, concord, and union he desires to see reigning among us," and to speak "strongly of the defects and abuses which could exist among us" indicated the occurrence of some friction attending the Oblate community's growth.[78]

A personnel change may have contributed further to the increasingly critical assessments of the younger Oblate Sisters from 1838. Joubert himself kept the original French manuscript Oblate annals until September 1838, when declining health forced him to relinquish that responsibility. Willigman recalled that "very often Fr. Joubert would take the younger Sisters' part" against Sister Mary's severity.[79] When Sister Therese Duchemin became the Oblate annalist, she may have emulated Lange's severity more than Joubert's indulgence in her assessment of the younger Oblate members. Finally, concerns about the state of their beloved director's health, publicly articulated as early as 1835, must have further exacerbated strains and tensions within the Oblate community. In 1838 and 1839 on at least ten occasions, some as long as two months, Joubert felt too ill to officiate at Oblate functions.[80]

AS DID MOST SISTERHOODS with service ministries, the Oblate Sisters sought to reconcile frequently conflicting obligations. The arduous daily routine of household chores, teaching responsibilities, and religious observances maintained by these sisters required considerable physical stamina. But the spiritual regimen frequently advocated by many clerical directors derived from the ideal of the cloistered, contemplative religious lifestyle and consequently ignored corporeal concerns.

The health care needs of the Oblate Sisters increased proportionately as the community grew. The first Sister Stanislaus became ill in June 1832 and incapacitated in August with a malady whose "progress was extremely rapid and her sufferings excessive." The twenty-two-year-old sister died on 29 September 1832.[81] The next month, the forty-nine-year-old Sister Anthony (Betsy Duchemin) succumbed to cholera while nursing Archbishop Whitfield's housekeeper, suffering from the same disease. In August 1833 Sister Bridget (Cecile Bourgoin) began to show signs of insanity. The eighteen-year-old sister left the Oblate community in October at her family's insistence. That same month Sister Aloysius (Marie Becraft), who had suffered from a chronic chest ailment since the age of fifteen, became incapacitated and entered the Oblate infirmary, where "her sufferings were very severe and more than can be imagined." The twenty-eight-year-old sister died 16 December 1833.[82] Susan Becraft, one of the first Oblate postulants, had suffered from consumption for some time and left the community in August 1834. The teenager died at her parents' home in November of that year. In March 1837 charter Oblate Sister Marie Therese Duchemin "fell off a chair and fractured her skull," fortunately not a fatal injury. On 12 May 1837 the second Sister Aloysius (Mary Louise James), one of the first

Oblate postulants, died "after three months of illness which she bore with a patience and resignation truly edifying," at the age of eighteen.[83] In August 1837 Sister James (Jane Laurette Noel) died prematurely at the age of twenty-two. On 23 January 1838 the thirty-four-year-old Sister Magdalene (Anne Marie Barclay) died "of a malady of the chest after four or five years of almost habitual suffering."[84] Chronic and undoubtedly communicable diseases—not old age—robbed the Oblate community prematurely of the contributions of many of its youngest and potentially most talented members.[85]

In its Rule revision of 1833 the Oblate community incorporated the office of infirmarian. The Rule enjoined this sister to "breathe only charity, as much in order to serve well the sick Sisters as to support the fantasies, the sufferings, and the bad humor which sickness sometimes causes the infirmed." It further charged her to keep the infirmary "neat, proper, and well decorated with pictures, plants, and flowers according as the season permits." The Rule emphasized immediate removal of malodorous matter and "if the doctor permits," maintaining some source of pleasant fragrances. The Rule prudently mandated that "all utensils and vessels for use of the infirmary shall be absolutely separated from those for the use of the community." It further required the infirmarian to be present at all examinations of patients by the physician and to "pay scrupulous attention to the prescriptions of the doctor" and to "administer herself all the remedies, herbal tea, and other prescribed soothing medicine."[86]

Evidently, not all Oblate patients found the prescribed medications soothing. In the assembly of 27 January 1839, the infirmarian "complained of a Sister who sometimes threw away the remedies given her." Joubert reprimanded the offending sister severely, condemning her action as a sin against the vows of poverty and obedience, "of which she would repent at death." Joubert concluded by citing "the example of St. Aloysius Gonzaga who took the most disgusting remedies drop by drop to save for a longer time the bad taste."[87] Joubert's reproof provides a sobering commentary on the perceived efficacy of nineteenth-century medicines: as useful as methods of mortification, or disciplining the physical senses, as cures.

In the assembly of Oblate Sisters on 10 February 1839, Joubert explicitly addressed the perplexing issue of reconciling the physical and spiritual requirements of community members. He urged the Oblate Sisters to observe scrupulously that article of their Rule regulating exercise because of "the necessity and importance of walking when we lead a sedentary life."[88] Joubert then treated the regulations for Lenten fasting, an issue generating considerable discussion within the community. The Oblate Rule condoned no regimen of physical mortification, such as the wearing of hair shirts or self-flagellation, practiced in some contemplative orders. Nevertheless, in their spiritual fervor, some Oblate members demonstrated a tendency toward excessive self-denial.

Some sisters refused meals in the belief they were complying with Lenten fast regulations. Evidently, Joubert's assurances that such regulations did not apply to the Oblate community, "since all the Sisters are working, either in teaching or some other things," did not convince the anxious sisters: "Since in spite of these explanations they continued to question him, he asked that they bring him a loaf of bread so as to give them an example of how much for the collation in the evening and for the piece in the morning, and he said that they should not trouble their conscience for having taken a little more than was allowed."[89] In advocating moderation in keeping the Lenten fast, Joubert demonstrated the same ability to adapt regulations to accommodate the particular conditions of the Oblate mission that had characterized his approach to the Oblate Rule.

THE CHRISTIAN EDUCATION of young girls of color constituted the principal purpose of the Oblate Sisters of Providence, equal to their determination to consecrate themselves to God. Only Anglophone Oblate Sisters, or those born in America of second-generation Francophone ancestry, or those explicitly identified in Oblate sources as fluently bilingual formed the Oblate school teaching staff. As matron of the Oblate community, Sister Mary Lange probably attended more to administrative and supervisory tasks than to classroom instruction. The two-to-one ratio of Anglo to French surnames of the students listed in the student registers for 1828 to 1833 suggests that the Oblate Sisters conducted their school in English, or at least bilingually.[90]

Seven of the ten *General Observations* concluding the Oblate Rule pertained to teaching, clearly demonstrating its crucial position in the Oblate mission. Comprehensive in scope, these observations advised on proper student and teacher attitudes, teacher preparation, parent involvement, and the judicious use of home visitations. Issues of both race and gender informed the segment of the Rule addressing the prospects of the Oblate school's graduates. The following portion of Observation No. 9 served as the statement of philosophy of the school in its published prospectus and epitomized the ideal of domesticity as well:[91]

> The object of their institute is one of great importance. . . . In fact these girls will either become mothers of families or be introduced as servants into de-

cent houses. In the first case, the solid virtue, the religious and moral principles which they will have acquired when in this school will be carefully transmitted to their children; . . . instances of the happy influence which the example of virtuous parents has on their remotest lineage in this humble and naturally dutiful class of society are numerous.

As to such as are to become servants, they will be entrusted with menial offices and the care of young children in the most respectable families. How important will it not be, for those families that these girls should then have imbibed religious principles and be trained up in habits of modesty, honesty, and integrity? How valuable will such servants be to their masters.[92]

This document reflects the social caution and conservatism of James Hector Joubert, who undoubtedly authored it. He certainly financed its publication.[93] At least one nineteenth-century observer of the Oblate community took exception to this self-limiting statement of the school's objectives and remonstrated: "It is impossible to conceive of language fuller of profound and mournful import than are these humble, timid words of this little band of colored women, who thus made known the exalted scheme to which they had given themselves. Why this tone of *apology* for embarking in as noble a service as ever entered into the plans of a company of women upon the face of the earth, the attempt to lift the veil of moral and intellectual darkness which they saw everywhere resting like death upon their sex and race?"[94]

The Oblate school policy statement could have appended teacher to the career options available to their students. No fewer than eight Oblate pupils had either established or taught in schools for black girls between 1830 and 1868 in the District of Columbia and its environs alone. Given the racial climate of the period, Oblate policy formulators—chiefly Joubert—undoubtedly deemed it expedient to minimize the school's offerings and goals to avoid antagonizing the antipathetic white community.[95]

A careful review of the Oblate annals reveals another profession pursued by Oblate pupils, conspicuous in its absence from the school's publicized list of goals for its students. By 1838, within its first decade, former Oblate students formed fully one-third of Oblate community membership: seven of twenty-one sisters. This circumstance replicated a pattern prevalent among all nineteenth-century pupils educated in convent schools. The insistent glorification of virginity and the impressive example of the sisters themselves contributed to a high percentage of religious vocations among convent school girls. Furthermore, strictly enforced policies of no male and limited family contact precluded competing models of satisfying family life for the students. For a black Oblate pupil and her white convent school counterpart alike, choosing religious life, recognizing and responding to a religious vocation, involved the exercise of personal choice to participate in a divinely sanctioned lifestyle characterized by reduced male interference and control. The limited socially approved alternatives for black women could only have enhanced the intrinsic appeal of religious life for Oblate students.[96]

The Oblate Rule of 1829 provides instructive insights regarding the pedagogical principles informing Oblate instruction. It mandated that teachers "possess a sufficient knowledge of the different branches of education over which they preside." Although the Rule indicated that "an extensive knowledge, it is true, is not necessary for the school of the Oblates: reading, writing, and the first rules of arithmetic are sufficient," it nonetheless advised, "but at least these must be well known that the teacher may be able to impart them to others." In the weekly assemblies instituted in 1838, Oblate director Joubert occasionally "spoke very strongly on our duties toward the children" and lectured the sisters from "an instruction of Father Eudes to Religious who are employed in teaching young girls." Many of the principles informing Oblate education methods duplicated those the French teaching sisterhoods adopted in all of their missions.[97]

Modest expectations for the academic competence of sisters teaching female pupils extended beyond the Oblate school, crossing racial boundaries. Throughout the nineteenth century the church hierarchy seldom prepared sisters adequately for their parochial school work, a function of the low status ascribed to both nuns and women within ecclesial society. When, in 1830, financial exigency compelled the Carmelite Nuns to establish a female academy in Baltimore, the Carmelite mother superior expressed concern about the sisters' complete lack of training and experience as teachers. Archbishop James Whitfield hastened to assure her that she had "two or three Sisters capable of teaching" and that in the intervening year "several may learn enough to become competent teachers." He then commended the virtues of on-the-job training and the fact that the teachers "will always be in advance before the children."[98]

The Oblate Rule required the sisters to gain their students' respect, "not by a ridiculous excess of gravity, nor by a forbidding air of authority and haughtiness," nor by "a weak condescension or by an excessive indulgence which suffers everything." Instead, the sisters should employ "a grave and modest deportment" and "mildness and affability," convinced that "the surest means of succeeding in this, as well as in all other respects, is to gain the affection of the children." Achieving such equanimity in practice under real classroom conditions occasionally proved elusive. On 27 January 1839, Joubert counseled the sisters on "the means to inspire the respect due to us, the principal of which is to respect oneself." He urged the sisters to "remember how we were at [the children's] age and that we would gain more by using sweetness than by using too much severity."[99]

According to their Rule, Oblate teachers were to cultivate patience, "of which teachers stand in need to support the dullness and defects of their pupils." The 2 February 1839 Oblate annals entry documented this need in its report of a familiar classroom problem. Oblate Superior Lange consulted Joubert and "complained of the children who did not learn well and said that the Sisters oppressed her with continual complaints." To Lange's query "if it would not be better for the Sisters to punish the children themselves," Joubert replied that "he feared that the Sisters did not know enough about the faults of the children and that they would not punish so as to correct the cause of the offense." While Joubert stipulated that the Oblate superior retain exclusive punitive authority, he did propose as an alternative measure to read the pupils' marks aloud, as "this reading made an impression on the children."[100]

The Oblate Rule enjoined the sisters "to excite the interest of the parents for the education of their children" and to prevent parents "excus[ing] themselves from sending their children to school, under the false pretext of their poverty or the need they have of their services." The sisters should inquire of parents "concerning the character of their children, their inclinations, and the manner of correcting their defects." Oblate interaction with parents required "courteous and engaging manners," a "lively interest in their concerns," and occasional home visits when warranted.[101]

The courses of study offered at the Ladies' Academy of the Visitation and St. Joseph's Academy, Emmitsburg, for white girls in the archdiocese of Baltimore provide an instructive contrast to that of the Oblate school. In the context of antebellum education, the terms "school" and "academy" indicated two distinct courses of study. Sisters teaching in free or parochial schools offered courses including those on the fundamental tenets of Catholic belief and ritual devotional practices and in reading, writing, arithmetic, and occasionally history and geography—a curriculum equivalent to that taught in the sixth or seventh grade. Sisters teaching in select academies offered a broader range of academic subjects and social and domestic skills considered suitable for young ladies from prominent families, equivalent to those taught in high school.[102]

The 1822 prospectus of the Visitandine Academy in Georgetown listed a rather basic curriculum consisting of "Reading, Writing, Arithmetic, English Grammar and Composition, Geography with the use of maps and globes, Elements of History, plain and ornamental Needle Work."[103] The Sulpician priest

Michael Wheeler assumed the spiritual directorship of the Visitation Nuns in 1826 and immediately effected an ambitious expansion of their academy's offerings. The 1827 prospectus added the subjects "Sacred History, Profane History, ancient and modern; Chronology, Mythology and Rhetoric—French, music on the Piano Forte and Harp; Dancing, Drawing and Painting; . . . Tapestry, Lace-work, or Figuring on Bobinet, and Bead-work, etc." Wheeler outfitted the academy in 1828 with "Philosophical and Chemical Apparatus" ordered from abroad at a cost of $2,448.32 to enable the sisters "to demonstrate the theories of many useful branches of natural philosophy—such as astronomy, pneumatics, electricity, Galvanism, chemistry, Chladni's Acoustic figures, etc." His curricular emphasis and expenditures on scientific apparatus proved typical for most young ladies' select academies of the period, whose teachers considered science courses a means to improve mental discipline. Indeed, science and mathematics courses proved as prevalent in the girls' as in the boys' academies of the antebellum period.[104] Projected academic course offerings included "Algebra, Logic, Ethics, Metaphysics, Natural Philosophy in its various branches, the Spanish, Italian, and Latin languages, if required." In addition to extracurricular offerings such as "Vocal Music, the Guitar, and Painting on Velvet," the sisters planned to add "Domestic Economy, comprising the various exercises in Pastry and the Culinary art, Laundry, Pantry, and Dairy Inspection, etc. as conducted at the academy of St. Denis Banlieu de Paris."[105] Such courses in domestic economy intended to prepare young women of means to supervise the conduct of routine household chores, not primarily to perform such chores themselves.

The Sisters of Charity, Emmitsburg, also offered a basic course of study in 1822 at St. Joseph's Academy, according to their advertisement in the national Catholic directory. Subjects included "English, and if required, the French language, reading, orthography [the rules of spelling], writing, history, geography, arithmetic, music, drawing, painting, embroidery, [and] plain and fancy work."[106] In 1828 Sulpician priest John Chanche encouraged the sisters to adopt a more rigorous academic course of study including "the higher branches of Rhetoric, Philosophy, Chemistry, Botany, Algebra, Astronomy, etc." By 1833 the expanded curriculum included "the English, French, and Spanish languages, Orthography, Grammar, Composition, Writing, Practical and Rational Arithmetic, Bookkeeping, Geography, History, Moral and Natural Philosophy, Astronomy, Chemistry, Music, Drawing, Painting on Velvet, Embroidery, Plain and Fancy Needle-work."[107]

The Oblate curriculum, advertised in the national Catholic directory for the first time in 1834, offered courses in religion, "English, French, Cyphering and

Ten-year-old Oblate pupil Mary Pets completed this needlework sampler, "Virtue," at the Oblate School for Colored Girls on 4 December 1831 (Courtesy of Archives of the Oblate Sisters of Providence, Baltimore, Md.)

Writing, Sewing in all its branches, Embroidery, Washing and Ironing." The in-clusion of washing and ironing as basic courses and the notable omission of liberal subjects such as history, geography, moral and natural philosophy, as-tronomy, and chemistry as well as music, painting, and drawing distinguished the Oblate curriculum from those of the white convent academies. Practical considerations, such as the skills and abilities of the Oblate teaching staff, may have influenced the modest offerings of the original Oblate curriculum. How-ever, prosaic references in the Oblate Rule to the inferior social position of Oblate pupils as "persons of the lower order" and "this humble and naturally dutiful class of society" indicate the equally plausible intrusion of race and caste considerations in formulating the Oblate school's course offerings.[108]

The Rule of 1812 of the Sisters of Charity specified the appropriate course of study for promising white orphans and poor girls, whom the sisters educated without charge at their academy on a work-study basis. The sisters segregated poorer pupils from the more elite boarding clientele "to prevent them from contracting habits of idleness, pride, and forming notions above the sphere of life in which they may have to live should they one day return to the world." Only "reading, writing, and the principal rules of arithmetic" and "all the details of housekeeping" proved suitable subjects for this lower class of society. In general, the sisters specifically proscribed as "useless for them and calculated only to take up their attention from the useful branches" pursuits such as "embroidery, grammar, foreign or dead languages, geography and history."[109] Significantly, the black Oblate pupils studied the same curriculum stipulated for poor white girls, except for the Oblate inclusion of French and embroidery. Class and race distinctions maintained the status quo and delimited the liberating potential of education as a means of social mobility.

In addition to common school and domestic instruction, the Oblate teaching ministry obligated the sisters to instill in their pupils "certain principles of virtue becoming their situation: the love of labor and of order . . . a careful attention to avoid the frequentation of persons of a different sex, that innocent bashfulness which is the principal ornament of their sex, and that exterior modesty which is the surest preservative of virtue."[110] The decided emphasis on desirable gender traits in three of the four listed principles of virtue typifies the philosophy informing not only convent school but also all nineteenth-century education for women. Significantly, the Oblate Sisters inculcated these values of respectability in black girls, in defiance of antebellum American society's exclusion of black women from its social construction of gender. No extant evidence suggests that the Oblate school curriculum explicitly acknowledged or addressed the racial identity of its clientele. The Oblate school offered its black students a solid Catholic education. Yet, in offering a standard common school curriculum to black girls, the Oblate Sisters taught their students values, skills, and ideals beyond those ascribed for black women by white society.

From 1830 the Oblate Sisters conformed to the conventional pedagogical practice of their day and concluded the school year with a public examination of their students. Several outside examiners, usually Sulpician priests, conducted the annual evaluations. The Oblate annalist noted the satisfaction of the examiners with the exemplary performances of the Oblate pupils every year.[111]

EARLY IN THEIR EXISTENCE the Oblate Sisters confronted the need to establish their own identity as a religious sisterhood apart from the black lay community they served. As a new, indigenous society of sisters functionally independent of European religious congregations, the Oblate Sisters initially lacked precedents, traditions, and established policies defining relationships with the laity. Before the foundation of the Oblate Sisters of Providence, black Roman Catholics in general had experienced no viable opportunity to become women religious; consequently, the black laity lacked both institutional and social historical memories to structure lay/religious interaction.

All of the antebellum sisterhoods serving in the archdiocese of Baltimore affiliated with European motherhouses—the Carmelite and Visitation Nuns, the School Sisters of Notre Dame, and the Sisters of Mercy and of the Holy Cross—undoubtedly addressed their relationships with the laity at their respective times and in their respective places of origin in Europe. The first American foundation, the Sisters of Charity of St. Joseph, adopted and adapted the policies of the French Daughters of Charity, even before their formal affiliation with that institute in 1850. Significant numbers of these sisters served in the United States as foreign missionaries and had either emigrated from Europe or relocated from other regions of the United States to the archdiocese of Baltimore.[112]

Unlike many white sisters, Oblate members derived recently from the very community they served in the city of Baltimore. In citing future Oblate members Elizabeth Lange, Betsy and Almaide Duchemin, Ann Marie Becraft, Ann Marie Barclay, and Eugenie LeBarth as sponsors or godmothers to several infants, pre-1829 church records of the Baltimore Cathedral documented Oblate ties of kinship and friendship with the Baltimore black Catholic laity.[113] The absence of a community tradition regarding the laity, the explicit requirements of the Oblate Sisters' teaching ministry, and the racial, ethnic, and experiential bonds linking them to the black residents of Baltimore complicated Oblate efforts as women religious to differentiate themselves from the black laity.

The original Oblate Rule explicitly acknowledged the sisters' attachments in the world. It enjoined the sisters to treat their student charges with strict impartiality, "carefully avoiding those little preferences which [they] might be naturally inclined to feel for their relations, or the children of their friends." It proscribed Oblate participation in the disputes of their relatives and friends. Candidates had to produce clerical certificates of authenticated virtue, "unless the candidate be perfectly known by the Director or the Superior." Guests for meals required only the mother superior's permission. Oblate Sisters retained the right to dispose of any legacies in favor of relatives or friends as well as the Oblate community. Although enjoining "useless visits," the Rule stipulated home visits as an important aspect of fulfilling the Oblate teaching mission.[114] Such provisions both presumed and tolerated familiarity and interaction between the Baltimore black laity and the Oblate Sisters.

In the early development of their community life the Oblate Sisters also addressed issues raised by bonds of kinship within the Oblate membership. The twenty-five candidates who entered the Oblate novitiate between 1828 and 1839 included three family groups: the Duchemins, the Bourgoins, and the Noels. In the interest of fostering communal adhesion, the Oblate Sisters and other sisterhoods discouraged the conscious affirmation of kinship ties, just as they did the formation of particular friendships within their congregations.[115]

Neither when Betsy Duchemin applied for Oblate membership in 1829 nor when she entered the community as Sister Anthony in 1831 did the Oblate Sisters note her maternal relationship to Sister Therese Duchemin. Oblate sources acknowledged Sister Therese's relationship to her mother only at Sister Anthony's death from cholera. On her deathbed, Sister Anthony asked "to see her child (Sister Therese). She seemed surprised that she was not near her, but after a few moments she said that she would make the sacrifice to God if He thought it better that she remain at school."[116] Willigman later explained that "Sister Therese could not be allowed to see her dear mother on account of the very contagious disease."[117] Yet, other Oblate Sisters attended Sister Anthony at her death. Denying mother and daughter this final meeting dramatically illustrated the requirement imposed on every member of any religious community to subordinate natural bonds of familial affection to the general interest of the community, to supplant the individual and the secular with the communal and the religious.

This mandated deathbed separation tested both sisters' surrender of self and personal loyalties and their commitment to the religious vow of obedience. The Oblate Rule stipulated that "as in all well regulated communities the Superior is regarded as holding the place of God Himself, the Sisters of Providence must entertain for her whom they shall choose the most profound respect."[118] Evidently, Sister Anthony resigned herself to the situation. No extant record reveals Sister Therese's response to her separation from her dying mother.

The Augustine Bourgoin family of Baltimore included three Oblate Sisters and one boarder among its members. Clara Bourgoin entered the Oblate community as Sister Elizabeth on 2 October 1830; her aunt Claire Bourgoin, as Sister Scholastica on 28 May 1832.[119] Yet, on 24 September 1832, Cecile Bourgoin's application for Oblate membership occasioned the first record of family resistance to an Oblate vocation. Cecile's mother, "otherwise an excellent and pious woman, very unjustly objected to it."[120] The available evidence does not reveal the reason for Madame Bourgoin's refusal. The community hoped to resolve the problem.

Although Cecile's mother remained unreconciled to her daughter's vocation, Cecile joined the Oblate Sisters as Sister Bridget on 5 May 1833 with her father's formal consent. Tragically, within four months, Sister Bridget returned to her parents' home, as "the mind of this young person was all deranged." "On August 30th," according to the annals, "she began to show signs of insanity; since then the malady has been growing worse." At the insistence of Sister Bridget and her family, she returned home, although the Oblate community fully committed themselves to her care. The annalist noted that "it was with regret that they saw her leave the house, persuaded as they were that her relatives would do all that they could to make her lose her vocation."[121]

The strain of having to defy her mother to pursue her religious vocation undoubtedly contributed to Sister Bridget's mental instability. The Oblate response to this situation reflected the sisters' vision of the Oblate community as the surrogate family of each member, responsible for their maintenance in sickness and in health and possessive as well as protective of its members. Their abiding concern for Sister Bridget's vocation in the face of her mental collapse and their impugning her family's motives in that regard derived from the Oblate conviction of the permanence of their spiritual commitment to the religious life. Significantly, the rift between the Oblate community and the Bourgoin family proved temporary. When the Oblate Sisters organized their first major fund-raising event, a fair in 1837, four Bourgoin sisters—including Cecile—participated and contributed to its substantial success.

Eugenie LeBarth also delayed entering the Oblate community because of her family's protest. Evidently, her family reconciled themselves to her vocation. On 25 March 1833, LeBarth joined the Oblate Sisters as Sister Benedict of San Philadelpho, the first sister to receive the name of the Oblate community's recently adopted African patron saint. Hilary LeBarth, her relative, contributed an interest-free loan of $129.30 to the Oblates in 1836.[122]

The Oblate community assumed an adversarial position only when families opposed a member's vocation. Otherwise, the sisters maintained cordial relations with their members' kin. They allowed Mr. and Mrs. William Becraft of Georgetown to attend the deathbed of their daughter, Sister Aloysius (Ann Marie Becraft), in December 1833. Ten days after her death the Becrafts' daughter, Susan, became one of the first Oblate postulants. When Susan contracted consumption in 1834 and returned to her parents' home to die, the annals recorded a very amicable separation.[123]

Madame Laurette Jane Noel and her daughters Jane Laurette and Marie Louise of Wilmington, Delaware, formed the third family group to join the Oblate Sisters in this period. Oblate annals recorded only one instance in which the community explicitly acknowledged Noel kinship ties. Motivated by considerations of Sister Chantal's age, virtue, and the sincerity of her vocation, Oblate Superior Lange proposed to the sisters that they abbreviate the term of

Sister Chantal's novitiate. They feared that "it must be very painful to her to be on the same footing with the other four young novices, one being her own daughter."[124]

The Noel family case constituted the most benign of the incidents of community-kin encounters in the sisterhood's first decade. Unlike the Duchemin example, the Noel case did not oppose communal interests and natural bonds of familial affection. Unlike the Bourgoin example, the Noel case did not require members to subordinate familial to communal allegiance. Issues of age and seniority figured as prominently as kin relations in the Oblate concession allowing Sister Chantal to precede her daughter into full community membership. When Sisters James and Chantal died, in 1837 and 1841, respectively, Oblate annals reported no particular Noel familial vigils at their deathbeds. The comment that they "observed all that is customary at the death of one of the Sisters" reflected the requirement that the personal cede precedence to the communal in religious life.[125]

Amendments to the Oblate Rule in 1833 reflected the institutionalization of the primacy of community allegiance over bonds of kinship and friendship. The duties of the mother superior stipulated, "If some Sister has a little too much inclination to converse with persons from outside, even with the closest relatives, she [the superior] will withdraw from her every opportunity (to do so)."[126] This revised Rule further enforced strict censorship of all incoming and outgoing mail and surveillance of all visitors, for sisters and pupils alike. Thus, five years after their inception, the Oblates codified lines of demarcation between their order and the Baltimore black laity, including "the closest relatives." On 9 September 1838 the erection of a physical barrier reinforced this regulatory separation of religious and lay communities. The community raised "a wall which would keep us from the inconvenience of being exposed to the neighbors."[127]

But as the Oblate community began to differentiate itself as black religious from the black laity in 1833, it also began that year to forge bonds of solidarity with Baltimore's black Catholics through the use of the Oblate chapel. The first Oblate residences—rented accommodations on St. Mary's Court next to St. Mary's Seminary from 13 June 1828 to 1 June 1829 and on George Street one block from the seminary from 1 June 1829 to 21 December 1829—had afforded the sisters easy access to church facilities at St. Mary's Lower Chapel. However, when the sisters moved on 21 December 1829 into their Richmond Street property, they had to walk ten blocks to St. Mary's.[128]

Joubert petitioned Archbishop Whitfield incrementally for permission to keep the Blessed Sacrament on Oblate premises beginning in 1831. Requesting it at first for a single day, then for a week, then for six months, on 26 April 1832 after learning of papal recognition of the Oblate Sisters, Joubert finally requested the permanent presence of the Blessed Sacrament in the Oblate chapel. Whitfield readily granted all of these requests.[129]

On 27 May 1833 the class preparing to receive the sacrament of Confirmation assembled in the Oblate chapel for Mass and Holy Communion "with recollection and piety," among themselves, before proceeding as a group to the "crowded condition which always exists" in the city cathedral. This pre-Confirmation observance at the Oblate chapel allowed these black Confirmation candidates, their families, and their friends the opportunity to experience the spiritual dignity appropriate to this occasion in their own sanctuary, devoid of racial discrimination. Although not explicitly stated, the "crowded condition which always exists" in the city plausibly referred to the inescapable humiliation of racial segregation—whether of seating or of sequence—that these black Catholics would have experienced at any biracial Confirmation ceremony in the Baltimore Cathedral.[130]

This specific use of the Oblate chapel to accommodate the 1833 Confirmation class constituted an unprecedented spiritual outreach to the Baltimore black Catholic laity by the Oblate Sisters. The Confirmation classes comprised both Oblate pupils and male and female participants in Sunday catechetical classes taught by the sisters. The class of 1833 formed the first Confirmation class to experience what became an Oblate chapel tradition of Mass and Communion before Confirmation at the cathedral. In obtaining the approval of the Reverends Louis Deluol and Jean-Marie Tessier, vicars-general of the Baltimore archdiocese for this practice, the Oblate Sisters institutionalized an act that asserted and affirmed the Roman Catholic spiritual identity of these black communicants.[131]

THE OBLATE SISTERS of Providence defined the essential elements of their communal charism, or spiritual identity, in the first decade of their existence. They determined and maintained their internal community life and conducted their teaching ministry within the patriarchal Roman Catholic Church and the antebellum South. As black women, the Oblate Sisters contradicted prevailing conventional views and social expectations of women of color by their institutional existence as well as by their successful forging of a positive, assertive, and empowered communal self-image. The Oblate Sisters' insistence on "the respect which is due to the state we have embraced" for themselves and their pedagogical emphasis on respectability for their pupils conformed to what historian

Evelyn Brooks Higginbotham has identified as the politics of respectability: "By claiming respectability through their manners and morals, poor black women boldly asserted the will and agency to define themselves outside the parameters of prevailing racist discourses. . . . Respectability was perceived as a weapon against such assumptions, since it was used to expose race relations as socially constructed rather than derived by evolutionary law or divine judgment."[132]

As products of the lay community that they committed themselves to serve, the sisters predicated the development of their communal identity on the corresponding attenuation of their members' identification with friends and family. The Oblate community pursued a conscious policy to supplant members' attachment to the individual and the secular—including family ties even within the community—with the communal and the religious. Once secure in their own identity as a religious entity distinct from the general black laity, the Oblate Sisters could reach out to the black laity in institutional and spiritual ways.

The Oblate School for Colored Girls offered its black patrons a decidedly liberal curriculum. Under the aegis of more effective religious instruction, Joubert and the Oblate Sisters insinuated an entire academic curriculum so that "the catechism class had evolved into a complete school for the colored child." By insisting that only literacy could facilitate religious instruction, Joubert and the Oblate Sisters implicitly challenged the almost universal reliance on rote memorization as the preferred method of religious instruction for black people among Catholics and Protestants alike.[133]

In an age of association, the institutionalization of the Oblate Sisters of Providence as a community of women religious dedicated to the education of black children proved critical. Collectively the Oblate Sisters "transformed unknown and unconfident women into leaders and agents of social service and racial self-help in their communit[y]." In the late nineteenth century, black Protestant denominations formed church-affiliated associations of women that took "quiet and obscure women who knew not their talents . . . and brought them forth, [gave] them inspiration and work, [and] developed them into some of the strongest and most resourceful women of the age, if known only among their own people."[134] The organization of the Roman Catholic Oblate Sisters of Providence in 1828 anticipated this phenomenon by half a century.

CHAPTER FOUR

Our Convent

THE OBLATE SISTERS AND THE
BALTIMORE BLACK COMMUNITY

❖ ❖

The church served as the foundation of antebellum black community life in
Baltimore. To counter the effects of the social, economic, educational, and political restrictions that white society imposed on their existence, black Baltimoreans looked to their churches to provide social and educational as well as
spiritual dimensions to their lives. Religious denominations—including Roman
Catholicism—initiated all of the permanent schools established for the black
population in Baltimore before 1830. By 1840 the schools affiliated with Baltimore's black Protestant denominations enrolled more than 600 students; by
1860, more than 2,600 students.

Black churches molded many of the effective leaders of the black community. Despite white opponents who feared their subversive potential, the number of black churches in Baltimore increased steadily after 1835. By the 1850s
black Baltimoreans supported sixteen different black churches representing five
different Protestant denominations, as well as Roman Catholicism.[1] Previous
accounts of the Oblate experience have essentially ignored the complex and nuanced interactions between this pioneering society of black women religious
and the black community they dedicated themselves to serve. This chapter ex-

amines the mutually supportive relationship the Oblate Sisters and the black laity forged during the 1830s.

In 1836 the Oblate Sisters constructed a building to serve as both an expanded school facility and a new chapel on their Richmond Street property. Most accounts of Oblate history recognize this new chapel as the first black Catholic church in Baltimore, if not in the United States. Existing evidence does not explain the specific circumstances surrounding the designation of the Oblate chapel as a black public church. Before Francophone black Catholics from the Caribbean arrived in Baltimore in the 1790s and subsequently formed a distinct congregation at St. Mary's Lower Chapel, English-speaking black Catholics had formed parts of the congregations in every Catholic church in the city.[2]

Both black and white San Domingan émigrés worshiped at St. Mary's Lower Chapel, but not as a unified community. White resentment of the black congregation at St. Mary's Lower Chapel may have propelled the black laity to the new Oblate chapel in 1836. If it did, the black Catholic experience in Baltimore merely replicated the black Protestant experience of forming separate black churches in response to prejudicial treatment in white-dominated congregations.[3] However, in 1836 black Catholics in Baltimore may have initiated the formation of their separate black Catholic congregation at the Oblates' St. Frances Chapel, perhaps inspired by the example of proliferating Protestant black congregations in the city. If so, Baltimore black Catholics both affirmed their racial consciousness and abetted the creation of the first black church within the Roman Catholic religious tradition.

The Oblate expansion occurred during the episcopacy of Samuel Eccleston, who succeeded James Whitfield as archbishop of Baltimore in 1834. Eccleston belonged to the Sulpician faction indifferent to the Oblate cause. He may have made ecclesiastical approval of the necessary Oblate expansion contingent on the use of the new chapel as a public black church. On 6 January 1837, three weeks after the dedication of the new St. Frances Chapel on 18 December 1836, the Oblate annals reported a new order of liturgical services, including a weekly Sunday Mass and the continuation of the Sunday catechetical classes for boys. Practically, if not officially, this new schedule transformed St. Frances Chapel into a public church where the black laity could fulfill their Sunday Mass obligation. Furthermore, Eccleston's transfer of the Holy Family Society—an exclusively black devotional society Joubert had formed in 1827—from St. Mary's Lower Chapel to the Oblate chapel three days after its dedication suggested that, at least informally, he considered this new chapel a public black church.[4]

No extant evidence directly documented the response of the Oblate Sisters to the new status of their chapel from 1837. Its public use could only have exacerbated for them that dynamic tension between avoiding and engaging the world common to all sisterhoods with service ministries. Indeed, annals entries document specific expressions of the sisters' concerns about the public use of their chapel. For example, the Oblate community had observed the custom of exchanging New Year's Day greetings with Joubert since 1 January 1830.[5] Clearly, the sisters cherished this ritual occasion "to testify their gratitude to him not for form's sake, as they had assembled without exception to perform a duty which was very dear to them." However, on 1 January 1838, "the visit of a large number of strangers whom they found in the house after Mass" precluded the customary exchange of greetings.[6] The sisters referred to members of the laity as strangers. Obligations consequent to the public nature of the Oblate chapel supplanted the timely observance of an esteemed Oblate tradition.

Significantly, this annals entry concluded with an extraordinary notation: "N.B. This note is one of Sister Therese's and was written here at the request of the Sisters. This is the reproach that the Sisters made in general to the Director whom they wish ever to be ready to receive the homage which they wish to render to him and which they owe to him."[7] The appended note formally registered the displeasure of the entire Oblate community with this outcome of events. The Oblate Sisters' "reproach"—simultaneously boldly self-assertive and tempered with reverential respect—affirmed the primacy of their claim as a religious community to Joubert's attention over any claim of the general public.

Other annals entries cited conditions associated with the public use of the Oblate chapel that detracted from the sisters' ideal religious environment of female exclusivity and quiet reflection. In 1837 Joubert distributed ashes on Ash Wednesday and palms on Palm Sunday to the men first. On 31 March 1839 during the evening Benediction, "the principal singers were often detained by the coughing which resounded through the whole chapel."[8] Torrential rains almost precluded singing evening vespers on the major Oblate feast day, 2 July 1839, "because the children of the choir had not yet arrived; but happily they came in at the end and consequently Vespers were sung . . . and so the feast was complete."[9]

In anticipation of the French sermon on 20 October 1839 the Oblate annalist observed, "The chapel was filled. The Father Director, who foresaw that there would be many people, had given Communion to all the Sisters before the Mass so that they could all go upstairs to leave place for the externs [laity]." Four babies baptized at the same time "made a frightful noise in the chapel" on 27 October 1839. On 2 November 1839, the annalist noted, "There was a Low Mass.

We had counted on singing a High Mass for the dead, but we could not because of the absence of the singers . . . the girls of the choir did not come. We had to say the usual prayers after Mass."[10]

The Oblate Sisters evidently reconciled themselves to the intrusion of outsiders on their New Year's Day greeting to Joubert. On 1 January 1840, Joubert "came down into the study room where the Sisters and children were gathered to wish him a Happy New Year. There were also some strangers present." The choir problem, however, persisted because "in the evening everything was ready for Vespers and a number of people were in the chapel, but we were not able to sing because the girls came too late. It was almost night."[11]

The public use of their chapel also elicited positive responses from the Oblate Sisters. They commented frequently with apparent approval on "the considerable crowd of people from the city" in attendance at Oblate chapel services.[12] The sisters worked hard to make their chapel appear "extraordinarily magnificent" for Easter services on 31 March 1839. With evident satisfaction they reported, "All these decorations contributed to render the chapel (which itself is a masterpiece) in truth beautiful, as we heard persons on opening the door cry: 'Oh, how beautiful!'"[13]

The Oblate Sisters established a complex, nuanced relationship with their chapel congregation. They remained ambivalent about their relationship with the black laity whenever public spiritual needs infringed on their prerogatives as a religious community. But, if at times they felt ambivalent about sharing their chapel with Baltimore's black Catholic laity, the Oblate Sisters expressed no doubts about their commitment to serve the black community's educational and spiritual needs.

IN THE SPRING OF 1828 James Joubert, Elizabeth Lange, and Marie Balas consulted with both black and white Catholics concerning the necessary financial arrangements for the proposed new religious community and school. Joubert noted of his third meeting with Balas and Lange: "These two good girls came to me with a Madame Charles, a colored woman, who after a long conversation on the means to take and the funds necessary to begin this work, we were convinced we should begin at once. . . . We thought of opening a subscription and securing a certain number of pupils in advance for a kind of boarding school. I interested the charity of Madame Chatard and Madame Ducatel who wished to take charge of the subscription."[14]

The wealthy and socially prominent Chatard and Ducatel families—whose contributions to the Oblate cause all modern accounts of Oblate history have duly acknowledged—formed part of the white San Domingan emigrant population that settled in Baltimore.[15] The same historical sources, however, have omitted the vital contributions of Elizabeth Charles Arieu (the "Madame Charles" whom Joubert mentioned) and of other black people to the Oblate Sisters. Later in the nineteenth century, Oblate member and historian Sister M. Theresa Catherine Willigman elaborated upon the involvement of the black community Joubert had documented: "Want of funds prevented success, but Mde. Charles Arieu, a wealthy colored lady, opened a subscription among her friends which was eagerly taken up. The colored people of the city who had means were first to aid the work. Many of the poor refugees would offer their hard-earned savings with joy, and some would lend money with little or no interest. Madame Peter Chatard, also Madame Ducatel took an active part in soliciting subscriptions."[16]

Author Grace Sherwood did include Madame Charles in her 1931 Oblate chronicle, which is still significant because it endures as the standard source cited in most references to the Oblate experience. According to Sherwood's version of the meeting with Joubert on 22 April 1828, "Elizabeth Lange and Marie Magdalene [*sic*] Balas had come, properly chaperoned, for they were French and chaperonage was natural to them. This chaperon, friend, neighbor, relative (how one wishes one knew) was a Madame Charles, colored, like themselves. . . . A Mrs. Elizabeth Charles, colored, had lived on St. Mary's Street. . . . This *might* have been she of the interview, so near the seminary, so handy to press into service as a chaperon."[17]

Sherwood's effort to reduce Madame Charles's role at this meeting from benefactor to chaperon proves as inexplicable as it is untenable. Joubert explicitly included Madame Charles in the "long conversation on the means to take and the funds necessary to begin this work." Clearly, Joubert considered Madame Charles an integral participant in and contributor to the discussion of financial arrangements for the Oblate community and school. The meeting of Joubert, Lange, and Balas on 22 April 1828 was their third conference but was the first one to include another party. As mature women of settled circumstances, Lange and Balas would not have required an additional chaperon to visit a priest. French social customs would hardly have proven more restrictive than the Oblate Rule governing the chastity of religious, which stipulated the company of one other sister or adult woman sufficed to safeguard an Oblate member's virtue in public.[18]

A case of mistaken identity might explain Sherwood's trivializing interpretation of Madame Charles's pivotal role in the Oblate foundation. Sherwood apparently assumed that "Charles" was a surname. But Madame Charles was in

fact Elizabeth Charles Arieu, a wealthy, free mulatto woman of some consequence within the black San Domingan immigrant community of Baltimore.
Between 1828 and 1840 the name of Madame Charles appeared four times in the
Oblate annals: two citations portrayed her as a benefactor to the Oblates; one
of these citations listed her as "Madame Charles Arieux."[19]

Baltimore's archdiocesan sacramental records provide additional details
about Elizabeth Charles Arieu. As early as 11 July 1799 the baptismal registers of
St. Peter's Pro-Cathedral cited "Charles Arieu and Elizabeth St. Macarie" as
sponsors at the christening of a free mulatto infant. Between 1799 and 1830 the
Arieus stood as sponsors—either separately or together—for nine baptisms,
suggesting both their prominence within the Baltimore Francophone black
community and their active participation in church life. Charles Arieu disap-
pears from the records around 1810. Elizabeth Arieu's membership in multiple
devotional societies further indicated her religious involvement.[20]

The eager assimilation of the practice of godparenting by peoples of African
descent in Roman Catholic cultures plausibly represents another example of
European forms serving African functions, a synergistic fusion of African and
European cultural patterns. The obligations and spiritual kinship implied in the
godparenting relationship replicated the expansive kinship ties and reciprocal
obligations characteristic of the extended family structure of traditional West
African societies. The Arieus had three sons baptized: Gabriel Auguste, on 29
June 1800; John James, on 30 August 1804; and John Elias, on 3 July 1806. Gabriel
Arieu, probably Charles's brother, stood as godfather and namesake for their
first born son. Baltimore city directories cite Gabriel Arieu's occupation as a
baker between 1799 and 1801. Marie Magdeleine Sanite L'Houmeau stood as
godmother for Gabriel Auguste. Documentary evidence suggests that Sanite
maintained either a familial relationship or an intimate friendship with Elizabeth Arieu.[21]

The Arieus also owned Hortense, identified in the record as a "negro slave,"
who bore two illegitimate daughters baptized in 1803 and 1806, respectively. Perhaps a majority of the small number of black slaveowners, motivated by humanitarian concerns, held their kin in bondage to keep families intact, since southern states increasingly restricted manumission after 1830. Other black slaveowners
maintained an exclusively commercial interest in their human property. No evidence indicates that the Arieus had a familial relationship with Hortense.[22]

Although mistaken identity might plausibly explain Sherwood's failure to associate Madame Charles with Elizabeth Charles Arieu, it cannot account for
another occasion when Sherwood ignored her contributions. Sixty manuscript
pages of student enrollment data record the details of tuition payments for ninety-

four pupils who registered in the Oblate school between June 1828 and April 1834 and document Arieu's continuing support of the institution. Several pupils enrolled in the school required financial assistance to meet tuition charges of $0.50 per month or $2.00 per quarter for day students and $4.00 per month for boarders.[23]

Sherwood compiled a list of first-year students from the school registers, explicitly noting that Madame Ducatel had paid for a student named Henriette. Careful scrutiny of Henriette's account revealed that Madame Ducatel paid $3 for six months' tuition in 1829. By March of 1832, however, Henriette's bill was $7.50 in arrears. The account clearly indicated that Arieu, identified in the records as Madame Charles, made seven separate payments totalling $32.75 to subsidize Henriette's education for eighteen months and to pay the balance of her account. Furthermore, she subsidized the education of two other students for eighteen months, from September 1829 through March 1831, with eight separate contributions totalling $53. Finally, she contributed $6 toward a fourth student's tuition in 1836.[24] Sherwood included none of this information in her book.

Between 1800 and 1850 the free black population of Baltimore increased by more than 22,000 people, representing a growth rate in excess of 800 percent during the first half of the nineteenth century.[25] But the numerical strength of Baltimore's free black population did not represent an equivalent accumulation of wealth: compared to the smaller free black populations in fourteen antebellum cities, Baltimore's free black inhabitants ranked in the bottom quadrant of taxable property holders in the 1850s.[26] Racial prejudice routinely restricted most of Baltimore's free black population to the least remunerative and desirable occupations as unskilled laborers and domestic servants. From the 1830s through the 1850s skilled black artisans and mechanics encountered hostile competition from white immigrants and the number of skilled occupations customarily reserved as exclusively black steadily eroded.[27] Nevertheless, Baltimore's free black population supported a small professional elite of physicians, ministers, and teachers who served the black community. A minority of black entrepreneurs prospered, servicing an exclusively white clientele as barbers and caterers; others operated shops, boardinghouses, saloons, and a variety of small businesses for black patrons.

The mission of the Oblate Sisters engaged the support of a broad spectrum of the Baltimore black community. Working-class people as well as the small elite rallied to the Oblate cause. From their beginning the sisters had housed and educated without charge a number of poor girls designated "children of the house." Black Baltimoreans considered such charity "so touching and so well appreciated that many of those good people would joyfully offer their earnings, even sometimes depriving themselves of comfort in order to help the rising Community."[28]

Fanny Montpensier belonged to this group of working-class supporters of the Oblate Sisters. A devout Catholic and widow, Montpensier apparently worked as a servant in the Arieu household in 1815. She frequently corresponded with her cousin Juliette Noel Toussaint in New York. Juliette's husband, Pierre Touissant, was a black San Domingan immigrant who reputedly led a blameless life characterized by extraordinary humility, piety, and charity toward all people, regardless of race or condition in life. In a letter of 23 October 1829, written three months after the formal installation of the Oblate Sisters of Providence, Montpensier confided to her cousin that "our convent" prospered and that she and all her friends would join the Oblate community were it not for the prohibitive $400 dowry. She expressed her elation at the very existence of such an institution for people of color. Finally, she solicited a contribution to alleviate the black sisters' poverty, assuring her cousin that God would reward charity for such a worthy cause.[29]

Montpensier revealed the depth of her commitment to the Oblate community in this letter. Self-interest did not motivate her, as she apparently had neither the children to profit directly from enrolling in the Oblate school nor the financial resources to allow her to enter the community herself. Nevertheless, Montpensier identified with the Oblate society as a member of the black Catholic community and she assumed responsibility for its survival, a generalized responsibility she considered equally incumbent on her relatives and friends in New York. From 1829 through 1852, the year of her cousin's death, Montpensier advocated the Oblate cause with zealous persistence in her correspondence. She solicited funds, goods, and services from her New York connections, "ashamed to ask but acting for God and consequently forced to brave all."[30]

Montpensier not only solicited contributions for the Oblate Sisters from others, she donated money to them herself as her circumstances permitted. Between 1831 and 1873, she made numerous contributions to the Oblate community in amounts ranging from a few cents to ten dollars. The importance of Fanny Montpensier's support of the Oblate Sisters of Providence derived less from the specific dollar amounts of her personal donations extending over forty years than from the initiative and enterprise she demonstrated in soliciting the support of others. Defying the limitations imposed by her meager personal resources, Montpensier acted on the premise that the survival of "our convent" obligated black Catholics beyond the environs of Baltimore. She was the first black woman to exploit the potential of a black interstate support network for the Oblate Sisters that eventually provided candidates for the community and students for the school as well as material support for both. No less than Elizabeth Charles Arieu, Fanny Montpensier acted definitively in support of the Oblate Sisters.[31]

BLACK FEMALE benefactors like Elizabeth Charles Arieu and Fanny Montpensier represented a small if crucial component of black community support for the Oblate Sisters of Providence. Other black women underwrote the Oblate mission as well in its crucial early years. Future Oblate member Eugenie LeBarth lent the community $300 in 1830. Individual subscribers who pledged annual donations to the sisters by 1831 included Fanny Montpensier, $3; a Mrs. Cohen, $5; Mrs. Scotty, $3; and Julie Pelletan, $6. In 1832 Julie Pelletan lent the sisters $250, which the Oblate community repaid the following year.[32]

More typically, members of the black community demonstrated their support of the Oblate mission by patronizing the school. Willigman described the first Oblate pupils as "some of the most refined children, whose parents were if not wealthy, very respectable, honest, and hard working, thinking no sacrifice too great for the welfare of the children."[33] These "very respectable, honest, and hard working" parents included Protestants as well as Catholics from both Franco- and Anglophone cultural traditions. The Oblate school, like the white convent academies in the 1830s, readily admitted non-Catholic students. The names of only a minority of the ninety-four documented enrollees in the Oblate school between 1828 and 1834 appeared in Baltimore Catholic baptismal records. This fact suggests that a significant number of these early Oblate pupils were Protestants. Although conversion to Catholicism did not constitute a requirement for admission to the school, during the 1830s seven Protestant Oblate pupils became Catholic.[34]

Ethnic as well as religious ecumenism characterized Oblate policy in accepting pupils. The extant student records reveal that twenty-nine students had French surnames; sixty-one, Anglo surnames; and four, surnames of indeterminate ethnic origin. Two of the three "children of the house" received in 1828 had Anglo surnames. Furthermore, of the fifteen pupils who "received the votes of their companions and the sisters for the prize for excellence" between 1830 and 1833, seven had Anglo surnames; six, French surnames; and two, surnames of indeterminate ethnic origin.[35] Ethnic impartiality evidently prevailed among students and teachers in recognizing superior academic achievement.

This finding proves particularly instructive, given one twentieth-century interpretation of Oblate history that distinguishes sharply between San Domingan and native Baltimorean Oblate pupils. This source maintains that "the tuition students were originally in every instance daughters of San Domingan refugees whose rightful heritage of fine classical French and Latin education" proved inaccessible to "native Baltimoreans neither prepared nor capable of this advanced study."[36] Existing evidence fails to corroborate these blatantly ethnocentric assertions. The nearly two-to-one ratio of Anglo to French surnames listed in the 1828–33 student registers renders untenable the assertion that only Francophone pupils paid tuition. The substantial number of pre-Oblate schools not only initiated by and for but also well patronized by English-speaking black Baltimoreans belies such disparagement of their intellectual abilities and ambitions. Finally, the extant evidence clearly demonstrates that the Oblate Sisters themselves neither devised nor subscribed to ethnocentric distinctions between French- and English-speaking people in their admission of Oblate members or in their treatment of students.

Disagreement about the precise nature of the antebellum clientele of the Oblate school appears in the literature. Two sources raise the issue of the Oblate Sisters' relationship to the institution of slavery in claiming that the Oblate school educated slaves.[37] The sisters assisted Joubert in providing religious instruction in the Sunday catechetical classes open to the entire black community, including slaves.[38] Preparing candidates for the sacraments of Baptism, the Holy Eucharist (Communion), and Confirmation formed the primary purpose of the catechetical classes. Oblate annals entries occasionally included the names of candidates for the sacraments. Evidence supports the conclusion that the few entries without surnames—"Desablon" on the 1831 First Communion list and "Tranquille" and "Cecile" on the 1833 list—probably identified slaves. In his diary, the Sulpician priest Louis R. Deluol identified Tranquille as a young servant. Sources have noted the social conceit of referring to slaves euphemistically as servants—undoubtedly an example of prototypical political correctness. In 1814 a cleric had proposed that the mother superior of the Sisters of Charity avoid the society's customary title "Sister Servant," because in the United States people conflated the terms servant and slave.[39]

In teaching the weekly catechetical classes the Oblate Sisters relied exclusively on instructional methods of rote memorization, recitation, and exhortation. Annals references to "the children of the school and the persons of the catechism class"[40] differentiated one group from the other as completely as did the respective purposes of the instruction given to each group and the teaching methods the sisters used and the interactions between teachers and pupils in each case. Oblate religious instruction of slaves conformed to the methods of slave catechesis sanctioned by the nineteenth-century church and Baltimore society.

However, at least three pupils in the Oblate day school during this first decade had been born slaves. According to her baptismal certificate from Baltimore's St. Peter's Pro-Cathedral, Marie Germaine, the future Oblate Sister Clotilde, was born "the natural daughter of Louisa, belonging to Wm. Montalibort." Marie Germaine entered the Oblate school as one of the first "children of the house" at twelve years of age in 1828.[41] The available evidence does not reveal when or how Marie Germaine obtained her freedom; no extant manumission papers for her appear in the manumission file in the Oblate archives.

From June 1829 through December 1832 a woman identified only as Prudence had paid the full board and tuition for her two granddaughters, Almaide and Angelica Gideon. On 25 November 1838 the Oblate community spoke of "the necessity of assuring the fate of Angelica and Almaide" by formal contract binding the community "to provide for their sustenance in health and sickness." The girls had inherited their grandmother's slave status, and Joubert had bought their freedom to avoid legal difficulties.[42]

Other sources have emphasized the planter more than the slave origins of antebellum Oblate students. Citing unspecified "data drawn from the archives of the Oblates, Baltimore," one historian maintained that the many Oblate pupils from places beyond Baltimore "were in most instances daughters of wealthy planters, the Negro blood in their veins barring them from the schools for whites."[43] A few items of "data drawn from the archives of the Oblates" document the presence of white planters' progeny in the Oblate school.

The Oblate archives have preserved an 1834 letter in which Stephen West Foreman, scion of a Virginia planter family, explained to his daughter, Virginia Ann Foreman, a pupil in the Oblate school, the details of his eleven-year liaison with her mother, Eliza, a slave. Foreman had obtained Eliza's freedom and that of their two children in 1826. Oblate archives also hold the manumission papers of Margaret Mason, a Mississippi slave, her daughter, Elizabeth Finnall, and her son, James Edward Finnall. William Finnall, the children's father, financed the children's education at Oblate schools in the 1850s. Finally, James Redpath, author of an 1884 newspaper article about the Oblate Sisters, said of their antebellum students: "In the old times of slavery the majority of the pupils were the children of planters, who themselves brought the girls of their bondwomen to receive an education here, and so, in some degree, atone for the condition in which they were compelled by the laws of their States, written and unwritten, to keep their mothers. Children also were sent from the West Indies and from Mexico. Since emancipation this class of pupils have disappeared. No white father now brings his colored child to this convent."[44]

Certainly children of white fathers formed a segment of the Oblate school student body. However, the limited evidence cited above does not corroborate

Redpath's assertion that "the majority of the pupils were children of planters." Boarding students formed only a minority of the entire student body. The extant enrollment records of ninety-four of the students in the Oblate school from 1828 to 1834 indicate that twenty-nine were boarders; fifty were day students; and twelve changed status from one to the other during their tenure at the school.[45]

Data from these student registers cross-referenced with information from the Baltimore city directories, church records, and U.S. census data provide an informative composite profile of these ninety-four Oblate students and their families. These sources establish the fact that at least thirty-six of these ninety-four girls were the legitimate issue of black men who were, in most cases, financing their education at the Oblate school. At least six black mothers maintained independent households and worked to support their daughters' education.[46] These numbers include only those individuals whose race or occupation other records verified. The student registers did not list the responsible party for twenty-nine students, and the sources consulted for purposes of racial identification did not cite all the responsible parties whom the registers did identify. Consequently, these figures represent the most conservative reckoning of the number of black parents paying tuition at the Oblate school.

Student tenure from this sample of ninety-four Oblate pupils ranged from one to sixteen academic quarters. Although thirty-eight enrollees remained for three or fewer quarters, forty-six students persevered for four quarters, or one year; twenty-two students, eight quarters, or two years; and eight students, three or more years. The marginal financial security most antebellum black Baltimoreans experienced probably prevented lengthier enrollments for many pupils. The Oblate student figures nevertheless appear consistent with the length of student enrollment characteristic of nineteenth-century white convent school pupils.[47]

Significant social diversity characterized the black community that enrolled its daughters at the Oblate school. From Baltimore, York Mills, a bootblack, sent Ann Jean for eleven quarters. John Noel, a prosperous barber who, according to the 1830 U.S. census, may have owned a slave, sent his daughter Angela for fourteen quarters. Angela joined the Oblate community as Sister Seraphina in 1851. John Pembleton, a musician, educated four daughters at the school: Sophia for six quarters, and Emilia, Rebecca, and Sarah Ann for seven quarters. Hoger Tartar, a laborer, enrolled his daughter Asteran for ten quarters. Mrs. Mary Divitier, a cook, sent Mary Marthe for ten quarters. Mrs. Henrietta Moore, a washer, sent her daughter Henrietta for four quarters. Henrietta received a prize for excellence in 1830.[48]

Peter Seguin, a cigar maker, educated two daughters, Marie Catherine and Marie Rose, at the Oblate school for at least two years. Both daughters received prizes for excellence in 1830. Significantly, the baptismal records of Marie Catherine in 1816 and of Marie Rose in 1818 reveal nothing about the racial identity of their family. However, the baptismal record of a third daughter, Marie Elizabeth, born in 1825—for whom Elizabeth Clarisse Lange stood as godmother—specifically identifies the parties to the christening as "all coloured people." The rector appended to the designation of the child as coloured the notice: "This change has been made at the testimony of the Father and by the authority of the Archbishop."[49]

Registrars of official records, compilers of city directories, and canvassers for the U.S. census did not solicit information directly from individuals about their racial identity. Instead, these white officials assumed their own ability to determine accurately another person's racial status.[50] Such official presumption would explain the capricious racial classification of certain individuals in the public record: black in some cases, white in others. Arbitrary categorization extended to classifying black people according to color as well, whether slave or free. The oxymoronic description "dark mulatto" used in advertisements for runaway slaves undoubtedly revealed little useful information about any fugitive's skin tone.[51] In 1850, census takers declared Oblate Sisters Mary Lange, Rose Boegue, Gertrude Thomas, and Scholastica Bourgoin mulatto; however, in 1860, the census takers considered these same sisters black.[52] Racial and color classification remained in the eye of the white beholder.

The Seguin family members were sufficiently light-skinned that their racial identity as people of color was not self-evident. Apparently it mattered to Peter Seguin that the formal record identify his family accurately as persons of color. As noncitizens in most local and state jurisdictions in the antebellum South, free black people enjoyed few formal opportunities beyond church records to document their existence. On 2 August 1798 Marie Magdeleine Sanite L'Houmeau —godmother to Charles and Elizabeth Arieu's son Gabriel—used the occasion of the baptism of "Jane Margaret, born 21 June 1798, natural daughter of Lisette," her Negro slave, to declare the child free. The registrar further noted, "The child declared free by word of mouth as Marie Magdeleine Sanite L'Houmeau not being able to sign her name." As did their peers in the Gulf coastal area, free black Catholics in Baltimore relied on church sacramental records to validate their identity and status and to document official transactions.[53]

The Oblate school attracted students from outside Baltimore as well. William Costin of Washington, D.C., for example, sent his daughters Martha Park and Frances to the Oblate school for three and two quarters, respectively. A descendant of a household slave held by the family of Martha Dandridge Custis Washington, Costin served as a messenger in the Bank of Washington. At his death, he enjoyed sufficient social acceptance among the white citizenry to move John Quincy Adams to remark, "The late William Costin, though he was not white, was as much respected as any man in the District."[54]

William Becraft of Georgetown, chief steward of the Union Hotel, also earned posthumous encomia from white acquaintances for being "of the old school of well bred, confidential, and intelligent domestics . . . [and for] his benevolent and venerable aspect, dignified and obliging manners, and moral excellence." His mother, a free woman, had served as housekeeper for Charles Carroll of Carrollton. Becraft enrolled his daughters Rosetta and Susan in the Oblate school for three quarters. In 1833 Susan joined the Oblate Sisters as a postulant. She later became terminally ill, withdrew from the community, and died at home in 1834. Her older sister, Anne Marie, had joined the Oblates as Sister Aloysius in 1831. She died in 1833.[55] Truly the Becraft family had invested deeply in the Oblate community.

The Oblate school's annual charges of $80—twelve months of board and tuition at $4 a month, an annual medical fee of $24, and a bed and bedding fee of $8—appeared extremely modest compared to the basic charge of $160 assessed by the Visitation Nuns for the Georgetown Academy and that of $147 set by the Sisters of Charity for St. Joseph's Academy at Emmitsburg. Few of the other parents of Oblate pupils could replicate the payment schedules established by Jean Manuel of Norfolk or Mrs. Julia Caton, who paid their entire bills in quarterly or semiannual installments of $25 to $72.[56] Many parents struggled to pay the $2 quarterly tuition charge for day students or the monthly $4 board and tuition fees. The Oblate Sisters responded sensitively and sensibly to the straitened circumstances of many of their students' parents.

The school offered multiple student discounts to certain parents enrolling more than one child. Instead of the $0.50 per month standard day student charge, Magdeleine Jean paid $1.25 for her three daughters. When two of the girls entered the school as boarders, their monthly fees totalled $5. This figure represented a 40 percent discount on the full-board and a 20 percent discount on the half-board fees. When John Pembleton enrolled three of his daughters, he paid $10, not $12, a month for board and tuition. When one of his daughters withdrew, he paid $7, not $8, a month for his two remaining scholars. A. Lecourt paid only $1 per month for Jean Chery—50 percent of the half-board and tuition fee of $2 a month—because she brought her own dinner to school and stayed the rest of the day.[57]

Some parents fell considerably in arrears in tuition payments. After making regular payments for six months in 1828, Catherine Craig defaulted and amassed a debt of $113.50, representing twenty-eight months of nonpayment before her daughter left the school in August of 1831. However, in November of 1831 Catherine Craig paid $6, evidently as a good-faith gesture. That same month her daughter Catherine, an obviously gifted student who received prizes for excellence in 1832 and 1833, reentered the school as a boarding student, free of charge.[58]

Rachel Smith's nine-quarter tenure at the Oblate school represented a case study in community effort. Her mother and uncle contributed toward her tuition as their means allowed. Elizabeth Charles Arieu and Sulpician priest Jean Tessier subsidized her studies heavily. Rachel Smith herself contributed $21.625 toward her own education.[59]

The Oblate school engaged in creative financing, tolerated sizable deficits, offered scholarships, and in general made every effort to work with the black community to make the education that was the Oblate mission as affordable and accessible as possible. In return, members of the black community both in and beyond Baltimore rallied to the support of "our convent" and proved themselves parents who were "if not wealthy, very respectable, honest, and hardworking, thinking no sacrifice too great for the welfare of the children."[60]

BLACK COMMUNITY SUPPORT of the Oblate school remained so vigorous that increased school enrollments required two expansions of its physical plant within the Oblate community's first decade, in 1830 and again in 1836. The Oblate Sisters had bought or improved property at their Richmond Street location in 1829, 1830, 1832, and 1834.[61]

Oblate records document significant black participation in financing the 1836 construction project, cited earlier in this chapter, that expanded the school and added a new chapel. Black women figured prominently among the individuals who assumed responsibility for seeking funds from the local community in the form of subscriptions for the chapel. Between August and December 1836, Elizabeth Charles Arieu collected $103.40; Antoinette Antoin, $55.06; Fanny Montpensier, $22.62; and Eliza Greatfield, $12.75. In addition, the black devotional organization, the Holy Family Society, lent the Oblate community without interest $222 toward construction of the chapel on 30 December 1836.[62]

To meet the estimated $2,600 building expenses, Joubert also negotiated personal loans with seven individuals cited in the annals. Cross-referencing these names with other data identified six of the seven lenders as black contributors: Eli Arieux [sic], son of Elizabeth Arieu, Mrs. Delatourandai, Hilary LeBarth, Oliver Concklin, Anne Clement, and Jane Russel. Together they provided

$1,701.32 of the $2,201.32 loan amount. A white contributor, Charles William-son, lent $500. Arieu, Delatourandai, and LeBarth lent $529.30 of the amount without interest.[63] Again, accounts of Oblate history have omitted the sub-stantive participation of members of the black community, documented in the Oblate annals, in the financing of the 1836 Oblate expansion.

A fair held on 5 December 1837 to help defray the expenses of outfitting the new chapel provided a signal example not only of black community support for the Oblate endeavor in general but also of black female agency in operation in particular. Throughout the country, associations of antebellum women—black and white alike—organized fairs or bazaars in support of worthy causes. Such events ranged from sales of "useful and fancy articles" handcrafted by the par-ticipating women and homemade confections featuring "all the delicacies of the season served up in the most palatable style" to elaborate affairs including con-certs, lectures, and costly foreign goods. Organizing fairs "called for managerial skills of a high order," and black women raised substantial amounts of money.[64] Scholar Mary Oates has noted that charity fairs proved the fund-raising strat-egy of choice among antebellum Catholics as well as Protestants. The wide va-riety of activities and merchandise available at most benevolent fairs, particu-larly in urban settings, guaranteed that they would attract a large cross-section of the population and provide immediate, substantial cash returns.[65]

More than three months before the event, Oblate student Angela Noel and her mother "had the first idea of this fair" and approached the sisters. Soon "they were seconded by a certain number of colored persons, who took very much interest in it." Forty-nine black women and girls conceived, planned, and executed the Oblate fair in Baltimore in 1837. Twenty-four of the forty-nine women participating had Anglo surnames, indicating the bicultural support the Oblate community enjoyed among black Baltimoreans. The four-day event fea-tured nine tables laden with handicrafts and delicacies "arranged with good taste." Sales and general admission grossed $928.78. Oblate benefactor Madame Charles Arieu had advanced $163.445 to cover expenses. Additional revenues of $120 yielded a total profit of $885.335.[66]

On 10 December 1837 the Oblate Sisters hosted a celebratory luncheon "for all those good persons who were employed at the different tables at the fair . . . to show by this how grateful they were for the services which they had ren-dered."[67] The appreciation the Oblate Sisters felt toward these forty-nine black women extended beyond gratitude for the "services which they had rendered" to an appreciation of their talents demonstrated in the three months of inten-sive collaboration on this pioneering project. During the festivities Joubert made a significant announcement to the assembled women:

[He] thanked them for this good work which they had done, more so as it was for the glory of God that they had acted. He profited by this circumstance to speak to them of the order arranged in the chapel, and the reservation that was made of the six benches in the back of the chapel for the white people who come to the services. He told them the reasons for this convenience, we might say, as gratitude which from the beginning made the Sisters take this measure of safety, in spite of the fact that they were fully persuaded that this separation, as just and as reasonable as possible, would inconvenience certain persons, but they did not hesitate. All the people present seemed pleased with the reasons.[68]

This awkward and slightly cryptic entry constitutes one of the most poignant passages in the Oblate annals. Its stilted style reflects more than the inevitable loss of semantic nuance in translating from the original French to an English text. The challenge to articulate "as just and as reasonable as possible" a policy of racial segregation exceeded Joubert's—or anyone's—verbal facility in any language.

Joubert, sensitive to the racial indignities that assailed the Oblate Sisters and the black community in general, could not have anticipated this announcement with equanimity. Undoubtedly the sisters also understood the antithetical purposes of the luncheon—intended as a celebration of the initiative, commitment, cooperation, and enterprise of these black women—and Joubert's announcement of the pew-segregation policy, disallowing human qualities in all black people. The sisters' expressed acknowledgment of the "inconvenience" racial separation would inflict on their chapel congregation suggested the turmoil the debate on this issue generated within the Oblate community.

Grace Sherwood inaccurately justified racial seating restrictions "because the first help for the [Oblate] community had been obtained by white people."[69] Such an argument would have carried little weight with these black women, who knew from personal experience what Sherwood never acknowledged—that black people also had supported the Oblate Sisters of Providence from their beginning.

On 10 December 1837 the Oblate Sisters and their guests confronted a bitter dimension of the reality of their anomalous position within nineteenth-century church and society. Oblate tradition notes the significant reversal of racial discrimination implicit in the sisters' designating the last, not the first, six pews in the Oblate chapel for white occupancy.[70] Nevertheless, the adoption of separate racial seating—regardless of position—acknowledged socially mandated racial distinctions. At the very occasion celebrating black initiative and accomplishment in raising $900 to furnish the Oblate chapel, the black community acceded to the institutionalization of their inferior status even within the premises of that chapel. It seems improbable that either the Oblate Sisters or their guests would have been genuinely "pleased with the reasons" for racial discrimination in the Oblate chapel. But, as they had in the past and would again in the future, these black women prevailed.

THE OMISSION OF THESE significant instances of lay black initiative from historical accounts of the Oblate Sisters of Providence has distorted the historical record in several ways. It has provided only a partial—in both senses of the term—and therefore inaccurate account of the base of support the Oblate Sisters enjoyed in the Baltimore community. It has disallowed a valid indicator of the seminal importance of the Oblate Sisters to the Baltimore black community: given the smaller numbers, more limited resources, and greater social, economic, and political liabilities of the black population relative to the white, the monetary contributions from black donors represented a proportionally greater financial sacrifice than corresponding contributions from white donors. Finally, the omission of black initiatives to benefit the Oblate Sisters has perpetuated the myth of black people figuring in history primarily as victims or passive recipients of white benefaction.

Whatever the omissions of other chroniclers of their history, the Oblate Sisters themselves proved both cognizant and appreciative of the nature and extent of black community support for their mission. Nineteenth-century Oblate historian Willigman duly acknowledged the essential role played by the Baltimore black community on behalf of the Oblate Sisters of Providence.

CHAPTER FIVE

The Coloured Oblates (Mr. Joubert's)

THE OBLATE SISTERS AND THE INSTITUTIONAL CHURCH

❖   ❖   ❖   ❖   ❖   ❖   ❖   ❖   ❖   ❖   ❖   ❖   ❖   ❖   ❖   ❖   ❖   ❖   ❖   ❖

The Oblate Sisters of Providence defined themselves in their Original Rule as "a religious society of Coloured women, established in Baltimore with the approbation of the Most Reverend Archbishop, [who] renounce the world to consecrate themselves to God and to the Christian education of young girls of color."[1] A nexus of relationships inhered in this apparently simple declaration. As women of color and as religious, the sisters related to each other in the routine functioning of their internal community life within the confines of the Oblate convent walls. In identifying themselves as women of color teaching girls of color, the Oblate Sisters explicitly acknowledged the primacy of race in their particular community identity. As educators of young girls of color, the Oblate Sisters established a complex, nuanced relationship with Baltimore's black community. But the Oblate Sisters did not operate exclusively in a black racial environment. As Roman Catholic religious, they functioned within the white institutional church. Considerations of race dominated Oblate interactions with and relationships to the white hierarchy, clergy, and women religious of the Roman Catholic Church.

Racism and the institution of slavery intruded on the mission of the Roman Catholic Church to black people in the antebellum United States. Although allowing that slavery as practiced in the United States constituted a social evil, church teachings maintained that in principle slavery did not constitute a sin. Insisting on the equality of all people before God, the church nevertheless interpreted such equality in its moral and spiritual dimensions exclusively, not in a social sense. The universal church historically had not perceived its role as that of social reformer. Adept at distinguishing between the respective domains of God and Caesar, the church had challenged neither serfdom nor slavery, considering them exclusively social institutions. However, because the church held that enslaved status did not deprive an individual of her or his humanity, it insisted that the owner-slave relationship entailed reciprocal obligations. Neither more nor less than did Protestant denominations, the Roman Catholic Church condemned abuses and atrocities perpetrated by slaveowners against their human property.[2]

As did their Protestant counterparts, Roman Catholic clergy and women religious not only tolerated the institution of slavery, they also actively participated in and profited from the ownership and sale of human chattel. Several distinguished prelates, including John Carroll, the first Roman Catholic bishop in the United States, and his colleagues and successors Louis DuBourg of Louisiana, Benedict Flaget of Kentucky, and Samuel Eccleston of Baltimore, owned or had owned slaves. Societies of priests including the Jesuits, the Vincentians, the Sulpicians, and the Capuchins owned slaves. At least nine congregations of women religious including the Carmelites, the Sisters of the Visitation, and the Sisters of Charity held slave property as well.[3]

American Catholic prelates John England of Charleston, John Hughes of New York, Auguste Martin of Natchitoches, Louisiana, and Augustin Verot of Florida all earned reputations as apologists for the peculiar institution. In 1840 Francis Patrick Kenrick, a future archbishop of Baltimore and a scholar widely regarded as the leading theologian in the American church, specifically addressed the issue of slavery in a text on moral theology for seminarians. Kenrick completely subordinated concern for the slaves to respect for the law, civil society, and the sacrosanct rights of property ownership. Many Roman Catholics—including some black slaveowners—wholeheartedly embraced the South's peculiar institution. Roman Catholic identification with and espousal of southern nationalism served to mitigate Protestant suspicion of and antipathy toward Catholics in the South.[4]

To accommodate the institution of slavery the Catholic Church had adopted an equivocating attitude toward its black constituency: equal to white people in

God's eyes but not in the eyes of white people themselves; capable of achieving moral and spiritual but not social equality. For Catholic clergy and white laity alike, positing in theory nuanced distinctions of racial equality proved easier than translating such distinctions into substantive policy. Yet, individual and isolated impulses toward religious egalitarianism occasionally penetrated the shroud of caste and racial distinctions through which the American Catholic Church interacted with its black membership.

In 1819 in St. Louis, Missouri, Vincentian priest missionaries asked the Propaganda Fide in Rome about admitting black men as brothers into their community. Also in Missouri that same year, Mother Philippine Duchesne of the Society of the Sacred Heart proposed to accommodate black women wishing to enter religious life by forming a third order of "commissionary sisters." The proposed black membership would associate loosely with the Religious of the Sacred Heart through a single religious promise of obedience and would enjoy extern status. The stated position on racial integration of Mother Madeleine Sophie Barat, superior of the motherhouse of the Society of the Sacred Heart in France, reflected both her priorities and her perceptive grasp of the racial situation in the United States: "Do not be so foolish as to mix the whites with the blacks: you won't have any more students. The same goes for yourselves: no one will enter the order if you accept black subjects among the novices. We'll see what we can do for them."[5] Throughout the antebellum period the Religious of the Sacred Heart accepted neither black pupils in their schools nor black members in their order. However, Duchesne raised the prospect of black religious again in 1830, and in 1852 the society facilitated the novitiates of two of the founding members of the New Orleans black religious community, the Sisters of the Holy Family.[6]

In 1824 Charles Nerinckx, the Belgian priest founder of the Sisters of Loretto in Kentucky, attempted to organize a community of black women religious around a nucleus of three black students from the Loretto school. Their dress, offices, employment, and rules remained distinct from those of the Loretto Sisters, with whom these religious of color maintained a subordinate affiliation. Nerinckx's removal and subsequent death in 1824 effectively aborted this first effort at racial integration in a religious community in the United States.[7] Although these proposals and initiatives acknowledged the reality and legitimacy of black religious vocations, none of them entailed full acceptance of black aspirants into the priesthood or the choir sister ranks.

Two antebellum attempts to form integrated sisterhoods in New Orleans also foundered on the rocks of Roman Catholic accommodation to racism in the United States. Sister Marthe Fortière, an immigrant member of the French religious order Dames Hospitalier, had organized a school for free girls of color in the French Quarter in 1823. In 1826 she attempted to form an interracial branch of her order in New Orleans with another white candidate and Juliette Gaudin, a free woman of color and future founding member of the black Sisters of the Holy Family. New Orleans episcopal authorities refused to authorize the sisterhood. In 1836 French émigré Marie Jeanne Aliquot tried to establish the interracial Sisters of the Presentation with six women of color, including Juliette Gaudin and Henriette Delille, another founding member of the Sisters of the Holy Family. Again, church authorities did not sanction this sisterhood because its nature violated state segregation laws.[8]

From early in the nineteenth century, various Roman Catholic prelates in the United States acquiesced in social conventions of racial discrimination. Archbishop Carroll of Baltimore reportedly asserted that "this [racial] prejudice would have to be maintained as the last safeguard of morality and manners in this country."[9] In 1818 French members of the Religious of the Sacred Heart raised the prospect of enrolling black pupils in their school in St. Charles, Missouri, to their bishop, Louis DuBourg. He "said positively that we may not admit them [Negroes and mulattoes] to the boarding school or free school, and he has appointed a separate day for the instruction of the colored people; otherwise, he says, we should not hold the white children in school were we to admit the others . . . [because] that prejudice against people of color cannot be overcome in this country."[10] Bishop Benedict Flaget of Kentucky remained convinced that "[t]he slaves are made contrary to other men." "I have neglected nothing to raise them to the dignity of men," he continued; "I have spoken to their spirit, to their hearts; I have tried everything and I have always failed; there are exceptions, but they are rare; for them freedom is misery. . . . Freedom has no meaning for them."[11]

The Oblate Sisters of Providence were free women of color. Archbishop James Whitfield of Baltimore approved their formation as a community of black women religious in 1829, thus infusing a racial dimension into two characteristics customarily associated with the Maryland tradition of Catholicism: ecumenism and experimentalism.[12] Yet the persistent denial of the humanity of all black people stemming from the racial basis of slavery in the United States convinced most white people in America—including the Catholic hierarchy—of universal black inferiority. Throughout the antebellum period, uncertainty about the Oblate Sisters as black women religious plagued the Catholic Church in the United States.

Having read attentively the foregoing rules formed for the Oblate Sisters of Providence, I give my entire approbation as to them being adopted by that Religious Society, and at the same time highly approve of so useful an Institution, which promises to be very beneficial to religion and the community at large.

Signed

James, Archbishop of Baltimore[13]

With these few words, James Whitfield, fourth archbishop of Baltimore, extended formal episcopal recognition to the first permanent community of black Roman Catholic sisters. Most accounts of Archbishop Whitfield and the Oblate Sisters portray Whitfield's commitment to the Oblate cause as immediate, unvarying, and irrevocable.[14] But a review of evidence beyond the Oblate annals accounts suggests a more nuanced, complex relationship between Whitfield and the Oblate community. James Joubert's reconstructions of his conversations with Archbishop Whitfield in the Oblate annals constitute the primary source of information about Whitfield's relationship with the sisters. A chronological comparison of Joubert's entries in the Oblate annals referring to Whitfield and Whitfield's external correspondence demonstrates that Whitfield's initial involvement with the Oblate Sisters proved less than compelling.

In 1829 Whitfield submitted a report on the status of the archdiocese of Baltimore to the Congregation of the Propaganda Fide, the papal office for foreign missions. In this report dated 12 June 1829—exactly one week after he had approved the Oblate foundation—he mentioned the Visitation Sisters of Georgetown and the Sisters of Charity, Emmitsburg, but did not refer to the Oblate Sisters of Providence. Five days later, on 17 June 1829, Joubert visited Whitfield to confide his concern about the coalescing opposition to the establishment of the colored religious community, scorned by some as "a profanation of the habit." According to Joubert, Whitfield maintained that he had approved the Oblate community after due reflection because he "knew and saw the finger of God" in it, whose "holy Will" they must not oppose. Asserting his "power to make foundations in my diocese, in my Episcopal City, any religious establishment whatsoever," Whitfield assured Joubert of his commitment to protect the fledgling Oblate community.[15] Yet only ten days later, on 27 June 1829, Whitfield reported at length on the archdiocese of Baltimore to the Society for the Propagation of the Faith, organized in Lyons, France, in 1822 to disburse funds to foreign missions. He included detailed profiles of three sisterhoods in his archdiocese: the Visitation Sisters of Georgetown, the Sisters of Charity, Emmits-

Archbishop James Whitfield's letter approving the formation of the Oblate Sisters of Providence, 5 June 1829 (Courtesy of Archives of the Oblate Sisters of Providence, Baltimore, Md.)

burg, and the Carmelite Nuns. Again, Whitfield made no reference to the existence of the Oblate Sisters of Providence as a community of women religious.[16]

Whitfield's failure to include the Oblate Sisters of Providence among the sisterhoods enumerated for the archdiocese unleashed historiographical repercussions in the nineteenth century. In his treatise on the Carmelite Nuns written in 1890, historian Charles Warren Currier maintained that only the Sisters of Charity had preceded the Carmelites in establishing a religious community in

Baltimore by 1831 and that Archbishop Whitfield demonstrated solicitous concern for the three sisterhoods in his archdiocese: the Carmelites, the Sisters of the Visitation, and the Sisters of Charity. Currier cited as his source John Gilmary Shea's encyclopedic *History of the Catholic Church*, published in 1890. Shea used Whitfield's letters to the Society for the Propagation of the Faith in 1829 and 1830 to document his enumeration of three communities of women religious in Baltimore. Henri De Courcy had written an earlier history of the Catholic Church in the United States, which Shea later translated from the original French and published in 1856. De Courcy, relying on Whitfield's correspondence in 1829 and 1830, had also asserted the existence of only three sisterhoods in Baltimore.[17]

Significantly, both De Courcy and Shea included sympathetic, if factually inaccurate, treatments of the Oblate Sisters of Providence in their works.[18] Consequently, these two authoritative sources—and those who followed them—relied on Whitfield's letters as documentation and inadvertently preserved the reality of the anomalous position the Oblate Sisters occupied in the archdiocesan religious community. In acknowledging the existence of the Oblate Sisters but omitting them from the list of female religious communities in the archdiocese in 1829 and 1830, De Courcy and Shea literally represented the Oblate Sisters of Providence as in, but not of, the Baltimore religious community.

In another section of his report in 1829, Whitfield described the works of charity performed by lay, not religious, societies. He concluded this discussion of lay organizations with the comment, "Different associations have also been gotten up among the colored people for the education of their children and the care of the sick. These societies are directed by various city priests."[19] Evidently Whitfield referred to the Oblate Sisters as the association "for the education of their children." The association "for the care of the sick" that Whitfield mentioned probably referred to the Tobias Society, the group of Catholic colored laywomen formed in 1828 as a multipurpose religious devotional, mutual benefit, and burial society for black people, discussed in Chapter 1.

It proves difficult to reconcile Whitfield's failure to identify the Oblate Sisters by name in this report with Joubert's account in the annals of Whitfield's impassioned defense only ten days previously of the Oblate Sisters' right to exist and of his authority to establish them. It also proves difficult to explain Whitfield's patently oblique reference to the Oblate sisterhood in a general discussion of diocesan lay organizations only three weeks after he had approved them as a society of women religious. The defining characteristic of race distinguished the Oblate Sisters from other communities of women religious previously approved by their respective ordinaries in the United States. Evidently,

Archbishop Whitfield himself remained unsure of the ecclesiastical status of the black religious community he had approved.

Personal racial prejudice apparently played no role in Whitfield's quandary. Although he left no evidence of his attitude about slavery, Whitfield owned no slaves, according to the 1830 census. Whitfield revealed a tolerance and respect for the humanity of black people uncharacteristic of his peer prelates. In his communiqué to France on 27 June 1829, Whitfield spoke of "the wretched blacks—so valuable a portion of the flock of Jesus Christ; their lives essentially more spiritual and more solitary."[20] In 1832 he wrote, "In Maryland blacks are converted every day and many of them are good Catholics and excellent Christians. At Baltimore many are frequent communicants and three hundred or four hundred receive the Blessed Sacrament the First Sunday of every month."[21]

The Whitfield privately committed to the unqualified ecclesiastical recognition of the Oblate Sisters of Providence in conversations with Joubert contradicted the Whitfield publicly remote from the Oblate community. This dichotomy may have reflected the dilemma of an individual constrained within a racist society as much as the idiosyncrasies of Whitfield's personal style of leadership. Whitfield preferred "doing what good Providence may put in our way, and publishing it as little as possible." His self-characterization as "quite averse to unnecessary agitation and excitement"[22] revealed a style of leadership ill-suited to promote or publicize novel or potentially controversial causes, such as the black Oblate Sisters of Providence in antebellum southern society.

Thus, Whitfield's behavior regarding the Oblate Sisters during the First Provincial Council, convened at Baltimore on 3 October 1829, assumes heightened significance. In these triennial assemblies the archbishop and his suffragan bishops deliberated on such issues as clerical life and discipline, administrative matters, Catholic devotional life, and education and social welfare. A combination of public and private sessions, business meetings, and religious ceremonies suffused with solemn pomp and splendor, provincial councils extended over weeks. These convocations served to insure conformity and uniformity in church discipline both within an archdiocese and with the decrees of the Holy See in Rome.[23]

After the conclusion of the formal meetings of the council, Archbishop Whitfield accompanied Bishops Benedict Flaget of Bardstown, Benedict J. Fenwick of Boston, and Joseph Rosati of St. Louis—three of the five ordinaries attending the council—and three priests on a visit to the Oblate Sisters on 21 October 1829. Joubert recalled, "They took in everything in detail; visited the house and examined some of the pupils." The bishops heartily encouraged Joubert to continue his work as "they were certain God would bless this foundation which promised to be very useful to religion and to society in general." At the bishops' departure, Joubert asked Whitfield to bless the sisters. Instead, Whitfield invited Bishop Flaget, the eldest of the visiting prelates, to bestow the blessing.[24]

Whitfield's deference to Flaget for the blessing may have signified nothing more than his according courtesy to the elder bishop. Yet, Whitfield's action significantly enhanced the Oblate position. In requesting that Flaget bless the Oblate Sisters, Whitfield essentially secured the endorsement of his episcopal colleagues for the Oblate institute he himself had approved four months before. The bishops had assured Joubert that God would bless the Oblate community; Whitfield's action insured that men would as well. Nevertheless, the formal conciliar letter submitted to Pope Pius VIII on 24 October 1829 at the conclusion of the council omitted the Oblate Sisters of Providence from its enumeration of several of the "thirty-three monasteries and houses of religious women of different orders and congregations."[25] The enumeration did include, however, all three white female religious communities in the archdiocese of Baltimore.

Intrigued by the enthusiastic reports of the other bishops about the Oblate endeavor, Bishop John England of Charleston inspected the sisters' school and convent on 3 November 1829. After closely examining the Oblate Rule and Constitutions for almost an hour, England "approved very much of the institution, that it would produce much good, and he proposed to establish one similar in his diocese as it had a large number of colored people; it was fitting that Archbishop Whitfield had set them an example."[26] Significantly, none of the ordinaries attending the First Provincial Council followed Whitfield's example. England did establish the Sisters of Our Lady of Mercy, a white community, immediately upon his return to Charleston from Baltimore, in part to minister to black Catholics. South Carolina law required that only white teachers instruct free black pupils and only in segregated facilities. In 1835 England began a school for free black children, soon denounced by Protestant sects for "its extensive literary education of blacks." Mob threats and England's preoccupying concern that he not appear pro-abolitionist convinced him to disband the school within the year. He insisted that the "sectarian" schools for black pupils in Charleston cease as well.[27]

Bishop Michael Portier of Alabama did not attend the Provincial Council. Had he visited the Oblate Sisters personally, he might have pursued his priests' initiative to secure an Oblate mission in Mobile, discussed in Chapter 3. The resistant Bishop Portier failing to approve an Oblate mission in 1830s Alabama stood in stark contrast to the enthusiastic young priest Portier in 1820s New Orleans rhapsodizing about the lay confraternity of free black youth that he had organized to catechize black people. Portier referred to a core dozen members of this society as "fervent like angels," "his consolation," and "as faithful as the seminarians in Lyon" yet residing in the "Babylon" of New Orleans.[28] His reference to seminarians suggests an exclusively male core membership. Evidently, Portier embraced black Catholic agency in a lay cadre of young, impressionable, and perhaps exclusively male members organized under his personal direction, but he rejected the prospect of the more autonomous and authoritative role for black female Catholic agency inherent in a black sisterhood. Only with the tentative approval that Archbishop Anthony Blanc of New Orleans granted the black Holy Family Sisters in 1842 did another prelate demonstrate with his actions that "it was fitting that Archbishop Whitfield had set them an example." Church authorities did not grant the Sisters of the Holy Family full religious status until 1869.[29]

Whitfield also presided over the Second Provincial Council in 1833, the first council convened after the state of Maryland passed the Act on Free Negroes and Slaves in 1831, discussed in Chapter 6. The Roman Catholic hierarchy in the United States formulated no policy to address the needs of the thousands of free black Catholics residing in the country. However, they responded to the impulse toward colonization sweeping the nation and expressed concern about the potential fate of black Catholics colonized to Liberia. No official statistics existed, but archdiocesan authorities had estimated that the 1831 state law advocating free black repatriation to Africa could involve 15,000 black Catholics in Maryland, including 5,000 free black people. The prospect of 1,000 black Catholic families abandoned in Liberia had galvanized the Second Provincial Council into action in 1833. The convening prelates petitioned the papacy to assign American Jesuits to the Liberian Mission. Their initiative produced no results during the 1830s.[30]

Three significant developments in Whitfield's relationship with the Oblate Sisters occurred in 1832. In an elaboration of his will dated 16 January 1832, Whitfield specified "my real intentions to be fulfilled and . . . to be looked upon as strictly binding in conscience" and stipulated among others the following bequests:

$1000.00 for the charitable relief society (formerly Maria-Marthian)
$500.00 for St. Mary's Orpheline Asylum of Baltimore
$100.00 to the Tobias Society (of coloured persons)
$100.00 to the coloured Oblates (Mr. Joubert's)
$500.00 towards establishing a circulating library of Catholic books.[31]

The other bequests illustrate the relative value Whitfield assigned to each beneficiary. The fact that Whitfield included the Oblate Sisters in his will at all attested to the genuineness of his later reference to the Oblate Sisters as "these good girls whom I esteem very much."[32] Yet, the manner of Oblate inclusion in Whitfield's will suggested that the archbishop noted the Oblate Sisters' "coloured" identity more rigorously than he honored their identity as women religious.

Whitfield paired the lay Tobias Society and the religious Oblate community and bequeathed identical gifts—the smallest legacies listed—to these two "coloured" beneficiaries. He relegated the Oblate Sisters to a group of recipients consisting of charitable institutions that included no other female religious community. Whitfield's will in 1832 essentially replicated the presentation of the Oblate Sisters in the *Metropolitan*, a short-lived Catholic monthly publication that began in Baltimore in 1830. The February 1830 issue of the *Metropolitan* had also isolated the Oblate Sisters from the white sisterhoods, paired them with the lay Tobias Society, and presented them under the heading "Churches, Pious and Charitable Institutions, Etc. of Baltimore."[33] Whitfield's placement of the Oblate Sisters in his will and his failure to enumerate them among the communities of women religious in his archdiocese in communications to church authorities in 1829 revealed his early doubts about the legitimacy of the Oblate Sisters of Providence as black women religious. Papal recognition of the Oblate Sisters in 1832 allayed Whitfield's doubts about their status.

In 1832 Archbishop Whitfield fell ill during the cholera epidemic that ravaged several cities, including Baltimore. Significantly, not a Sister of Charity—whose mission mandated nursing as a field of service—but Oblate Sister Anthony Duchemin, the mother of Sister Therese Duchemin and one of the Oblate Sisters who nursed cholera victims at the Baltimore almshouse, attended the ailing prelate. No source explained why Sister Anthony, and not a Sister of Charity, nursed Whitfield. Evidently Sister Anthony's nursing proved so effective that when Whitfield's housekeeper contracted the disease "they asked for Sister Anthony. . . . The same Sister Anthony had nursed the Archbishop sick with the same disease for two weeks." However, within twenty-four hours of her third exposure to the disease, Sister Anthony herself succumbed to cholera. The Oblates considered her death a grievous loss and eulogized her as "a victim of her zeal" and a "martyr to her charity for which we think she has already received her crown."[34]

This literally life-and-death encounter with the Oblate Sisters in the person of Sister Anthony Duchemin could have affected Whitfield profoundly. During his two week convalescence, Whitfield had the opportunity to recognize Sister Anthony's effective nursing ministry. He also could have come to appreciate her spirituality in the edifying manner of her own death. Whitfield's recovery from and Sister Anthony's death from cholera provided the archbishop with an opportunity to experience the Oblate charism at that level of intensity that only tragic circumstances afford. If Archbishop Whitfield experienced such an epiphany regarding the Oblate Sisters, however, he provided no evidence of that fact. On 2 September 1833, he revised his will: "I have blotted out all that I left to the charitable relief society [$1,000] or that I intended to be distributed by their direction; because there are I perceive . . . some leading members pretending to take from the Archbishop that authority which he ought to have over that and other charitable institutions. . . . In consequence I leave that society *nothing* and should wish for the sake of my successors and of the prosperity of the institution they be told the reason.

2. I leave the Carmelite nuns one thousand dollars.
3. Five hundred dollars towards building a house for the Sisters of Charity."[35]

In his revised will Whitfield punished the charitable relief society for an alleged challenge to his prerogative. He also rewarded with substantial bequests two of the three white sisterhoods within his archdiocese. However, he did not acknowledge the affirmation of the Oblate Sisters' ecclesiastical status following papal recognition of their community. Nor did he acknowledge the altruistic ministrations that Sister Anthony Duchemin rendered in his household during the cholera epidemic in 1832. In Whitfield's will the Oblate Sisters of Providence remained on a separate page, allotted the smallest legacy, inextricably paired with the lay Tobias Society by their "coloured" designation in spite of their fundamental differences, and segregated from the other communities of women religious by their race in spite of their fundamental similarities. This position reflected their status in Whitfield's perception: religious by papal sanction but existing in a parallel, segregated dimension.

The last entry in the Oblate annals concerning Archbishop Whitfield reported his celebration of the feast of St. Benedict the Moor in the Oblate chapel on 11 May 1834. Whitfield encouraged the sisters to emulate St. Benedict "so that they might have the happiness of joining this saint in Heaven, accomplishing the words of Scripture that God has no regard for the condition of persons."[36] The significance of this exhortation could not have escaped these black women religious in antebellum southern society.

Judged by late-twentieth-century standards of racial equity, James Whitfield's support of the Oblate Sisters of Providence appears tentative and qualified. Placed in its own historical context, Whitfield's approbation of the Oblate community rightly assumes noteworthy status. Although Whitfield's public espousal of the Oblate community never equaled his private encouragement of their endeavor, he bequeathed to them a priceless legacy in his conviction that the Oblate Sisters had received papal approbation.

WHEN JAMES WHITFIELD expired on 19 October 1834, his co-adjutor Samuel Eccleston assumed the episcopacy of the archdiocese of Baltimore and served in that capacity until his own death in 1851. The thirty-three-year-old Eccleston was both the youngest ordinary to head the archdiocese and the first convert to attain the rank of bishop. Not only did his youth and brief Catholic profession afford the new archbishop little preparation for this role; but also little in his nurture or personal experience had predisposed Eccleston to favor the Oblate cause in particular or black people in general.[37]

Unlike his English predecessor, Samuel Eccleston was a native of Maryland, born and bred into the ethos of slavery. According to U.S. census records, his father, Samuel Eccleston of Kent County, Maryland, had owned fourteen slaves in 1800, the year before the future archbishop's birth. Eccleston's stepfather, William Stenson of Baltimore, owned six slaves in 1810, a substantial holding in Baltimore, where, by 1798, the average slaveowner had fewer than three slaves. Significantly, the 1840 census documented the presence of a slave in Archbishop Eccleston's household. Because census records prior to 1850 listed only heads of households and Eccleston's household included two other adult white males, Eccleston may not have owned the slave personally. However, the census material supports the conclusion that Eccleston headed a household that not only tolerated but also practiced slaveholding.[38]

Samuel Eccleston's acceptance of slavery suggests his probable attitude toward free black people. Within nineteenth-century southern society, condoning, practicing, or profiting from slaveholding frequently coincided with denigrating the humanity and deploring the viciousness of the free black population. Historian Ira Berlin observed that "southern whites almost uniformly feared and despised free Negroes." Antebellum white Americans attempted to eliminate free black populations from their midst through instituting policies of violence, expulsion, colonization, social and legal proscription, and re-enslavement. Under such circumstances, Archbishop Eccleston would have demonstrated extraordinary convictions had he responded positively to the Oblate Sisters of Providence. In this matter, however, the new ordinary of Baltimore proved himself ordinary.[39]

Archbishop Eccleston's first official act ignored the very existence of the Oblate Sisters. In the formal proclamation of James Whitfield's death, which he circulated throughout the archdiocese, Eccleston specified that "the Nuns of

Mount Carmel in Baltimore, those of the Visitation at Georgetown, and the Sisters of Charity, are requested to offer three communions each, for the same end [the repose of Whitfield's soul]."[40] The Oblate Sisters of Providence were conspicuous by their absence.

Louis Deluol served as the superior of St. Mary's Seminary, mentor to Archbishop Eccleston, and vicar-general of the archdiocese. On 2 July 1835 Deluol noted in his diary that "M. Joubert had invited the Archbishop to officiate at the Oblates; but he refused, saying that he had not yet said Mass for the other religious communities."[41] The Roman Catholic Church observed the Feast of the Visitation of the Virgin Mary on 2 July. The Oblate Sisters observed this date as a major patronal feast when they renewed their annual vows of poverty, chastity, and obedience.

Although by 2 July 1835 Eccleston technically might not have celebrated Mass for the other sisterhoods, he certainly had lavished considerable attention on at least one of the Oblate Sisters' peer communities of women religious. According to Carmelite historian Charles Currier, within one month of succeeding Whitfield, Samuel Eccleston had attended the solemn Carmelite reception in his honor at which he delivered an address and had dined at their convent. On 13 February 1835, "Archbishop Eccleston spent the day at the convent and examined into the condition of the temporal and spiritual affairs of the house." On 23 March 1835 Eccleston began a five-day canonical visitation of the Carmelite convent.[42] Eccleston also favored the Visitation Nuns, on whose Georgetown property he occasionally retreated from his episcopal duties in Baltimore, in a residence reserved for that purpose. He shared with many Visitation members a privileged Maryland planter upbringing and undoubtedly understood sisters who on occasion referred to a novice mistress as "my good old Mammy."[43] Residual personal animosity toward Joubert from the earlier "Sulpician Revolution" (see Chapter 2) might have prompted Eccleston's refusal to celebrate Mass for the Oblate Sisters on their major feast day. The point of Eccleston's rebuff—that he refused to extend a courtesy to black women religious that he had not yet provided for white women religious—suggests the inferior status Eccleston ascribed to the Oblate community.

Archbishop Eccleston first visited the Oblate establishment on 18 December 1836 to celebrate High Mass in the new St. Frances Chapel. After the Mass, Joubert introduced each of the Oblate Sisters to Eccleston, who "was very kind to all and gave each his blessing." Before departing, Eccleston "promised to come visit the house more in detail and appeared wholly satisfied."[44] However satisfied Eccleston might have appeared, he did not visit the Oblate convent again for the rest of the decade. He did not return to the Oblate premises until 1849.

Historian Thomas Spalding has argued that Samuel Eccleston presided over a church propelled by and responsive to the concerns of successive waves of European immigrants for the rest of the nineteenth century. Noting that Eccleston encouraged the development of national parishes, Spalding maintained, "The German parishes were the first to be identified as such and would be accorded a special status with the arrival of the Redemptorists."[45] The Redemptorists did not establish missions in Baltimore until the 1840s.

Although no extant specific document issued over Archbishop Eccleston's signature formally designated St. Frances Chapel the black church, apparently Eccleston initiated his national church policy with black Catholics at the Oblate chapel in 1836. Significantly, in implementing a national—or in this instance, racial[46]—church policy at the Oblate chapel, Eccleston sanctioned an initiative the Oblate Sisters themselves had commenced three years earlier. The Oblate pre-Confirmation Mass tradition dating from May 1833, discussed in Chapter 3, revealed a positive self-consciousness and nascent sense of community bonding the sisters and the black Catholic laity. Eccleston's policy merely formalized the preexisting bonds between the Oblate Sisters and the Baltimore black Catholic community.

Eccleston experienced no epiphanies regarding the Oblate Sisters or black people in general in the 1830s. In his letter of 1838 to the Society for the Propagation of the Faith, Eccleston articulated his position on black evangelization. He asserted, "The slaves present a vast and rich harvest to the apostolic laborer. I do not believe that there is in this country, without excepting the Indian, a class of men among whom it is possible to do more good." But Eccleston subordinated "the salvation of the unhappy Negroes" to "the wants of the thousands of whites who, equally deprived of the succor of religion, feel all the more keenly their spiritual abandonment."[47] Eccleston's characterization of black people lacked Whitfield's sense of black and white spiritual equality. His contention that white people "feel all the more keenly" spiritual deprivation presumed greater spiritual development in white people, a presumption consonant with conventional public conviction of black moral inferiority. Eccleston's dilemma and his resolution established a pattern the church hierarchy would replicate throughout the nineteenth century: ministry to European immigrants superseded ministry to black Catholics.

Several causes contributed to the fact that the overwhelming majority of black converts to Christianity in the nineteenth century joined Protestant denominations. When American Protestantism launched interdenominational missions in the 1830s and 1840s to convert plantation slaves, American Catholicism failed to initiate a similar effort. Furthermore, black Christians, both slave and free, found the decentralized organization, congregational autonomy, ordination of black ministers, and the more spontaneous and participatory nature of Protestant liturgies conducted in English more appealing and inclusive. By contrast, a hierarchical and centralized structure, a widespread refusal among American bishops to sanction the appointment of black priests within their jurisdictions, and insufficient clerical personnel to undertake mass black evangelization characterized antebellum Roman Catholicism.[48]

OBLATE ORIGINS in Baltimore—the premier see of the Roman Catholic Church in the United States—enabled the sisters to interact with visiting prelates and church dignitaries. Oblate annalists noted the local clerics and the visiting bishops and priests who officiated at Mass and other religious services in the Oblate chapel. While visiting Baltimore in 1833 and 1834, respectively, clerics James LeDue and Mathias Loras of the Diocese of Mobile had each inquired about establishing an Oblate mission in Alabama. During the Second Provincial Council convened in Baltimore in 1833, bishops and priests who visited the Oblate convent and school encouraged the sisters to supply "the different Dioceses of the United States with Clerical Vestments of all sorts."[49]

Oblate annalists also noted individual clerics who extended to the Oblate Sisters customary courtesies and tokens of support over time. Simon Bruté, a former Sulpician priest, a brilliant scholar, and a major figure in the American church, served as a consulting theologian in both the First and Second Provincial Councils, in 1829 and 1833, respectively. Bruté formed part of the delegation of bishops and priests who visited the Oblate convent and school in 1829. During the council in 1833, Bruté celebrated Mass in the Oblate chapel. That same year, he sent the Oblate Sisters authenticated relics of the True Cross and of Benedict the Moor, the recently canonized African saint, as gifts for their chapel reliquaries. Consecrated bishop of Vincennes, Indiana, in 1834, Bishop Bruté celebrated Mass at the Oblate chapel during the Third Provincial Council in 1837.[50]

John Mary Odin of St. Louis celebrated Mass in the Oblate chapel while in Baltimore serving as a consulting theologian during the Second Provincial Council in October 1833. The next month, Odin personally delivered to the Oblates of St. Frances of Rome a note of thanks from the Baltimore Oblate community. In December 1833 the Oblate annalist specifically credited Odin with suggesting to the sisters the idea of forming a postulant class. In 1834 Odin submitted a favorable assessment of the Oblate institute to the editor of the annals of the Society for the Propagation of the Faith in Lyons, France. In his report Odin identified the community as "the Oblate Sisters of St. Frances established in Baltimore for the education of negroes and mulattoes; they are ladies of color united in community." He concluded that "already these Sisters number twelve, their school is very numerous; piety and fervor reign among them; and they are rendering a great service to religion."[51] Odin became bishop of Texas in 1841.

In addition to the sustained support of the Oblate community demonstrated by these priests, several bishops accorded the Oblate Sisters signs of ecclesiastical favor in their first decade. Benedict J. Fenwick of Boston visited the Oblate convent and school during the First Provincial Council in 1829 and celebrated Mass in the Oblate chapel during the Second Provincial Council in 1833. Joseph Rosati of St. Louis visited the sisters in 1829 and 1833. Francis Patrick Kenrick—bishop of Philadelphia, future archbishop of Baltimore, and author of the moral theology text accommodating the institution of slavery—assisted Bishop Bruté at his Mass in the Oblate chapel in 1837.[52] This honor of having a Mass co-celebrated in their chapel by two visiting prelates must have particularly gratified the Oblate Sisters as evidence of continued episcopal favor. Such signal attention compensated them in part for the indifference they encountered from their own archbishop, Samuel Eccleston.

During the 1830s priests in Maryland other than Joubert's Sulpician allies Jean Tessier, Michael Wheeler, and Jean-Baptiste Damphoux supported the Oblate community. Adolphus Williamson, son of the socially prominent and eminently wealthy banker and businessman David Williamson, figured frequently in the Oblate annals during this decade. Stationed in Rome in 1833, Williamson sent the Oblate Sisters and students rosaries blessed by Pope Gregory XVI. In 1834 Joubert asked Williamson to secure from the Oblates of St. Frances of Rome a copy of their Rule as well as images of St. Frances and St. Benedict the Moor. In 1835 Williamson contributed a relic to the Oblate chapel reliquaries. While stationed in Baltimore during 1836 and 1837, Williamson officiated at or participated in liturgical celebrations at the Oblate chapel. Oblate member and historian Willigman included Williamson with Wheeler and Kohlmann as Joubert's worthy clerical friends who "were devoted to the Founder and did all in their power to help him, by obtaining many favors from the Holy See."[53]

The Jesuit priest John McElroy had established a Sunday school that reportedly taught reading and writing as well as religion to both slave and free black children at Holy Trinity Church in Georgetown in 1818.[54] Although transferred to Frederickstown, Maryland, in 1822, McElroy remained committed to promoting black education. In 1830 he recommended Cassandra Butler of Frederickstown for admission to the Oblate sisterhood. As her spiritual director for eight years, McElroy judged Butler well suited to teaching. He wrote Joubert, "In her you will find a subject whom I trust will serve as one of the foundation stones of that spiritual edifice so eminently calculated to promote the greater glory of God."[55] Cassandra Butler entered the Oblate community as Sister Stanislaus Kostka in 1830.

Charles I. White distinguished himself in the Baltimore clerical community not only as a learned scholar but also as the indefatigable editor of several Catholic journals and newspapers. The "principal pen of the Archdiocese" after 1834, White founded and edited from 1850 until 1855 the *Catholic Mirror*, the official newspaper of the archdiocese of Baltimore. In 1838 White, at that time the assistant at the Baltimore Cathedral, recommended Charlotte Schaaf as an Oblate candidate. Schaaf entered the community on 9 June 1838 and began her novitiate as Sister Ann Constance on 2 July 1838.[56] From their inception, the Oblate Sisters of Providence enjoyed the support of several extraordinary individuals among the clergy who both affirmed and promoted their spiritual mission. However, clerical support of the Oblate Sisters never included significant financial donations equal to those that the previously established white sisterhoods in the archdiocese had received.

The Jesuit priest Charles Neale, member of a very prominent, wealthy, and old Catholic family of Maryland, served as both spiritual director and generous patron to the first Carmelite mission in America. Within three months of their arrival in Maryland in 1790, the first four American Carmelite Nuns had settled on an 800-acre plantation worth more than $6,500 given to them by Charles Neale. By 1830 the American Carmelites owned slaves valued at $9,000. They also profited from the generosity of several European patrons, including the De Villegas family of Brussels, considered the second founder of the American Carmelites because of their substantial financial support.[57]

When in 1830 economic reversals forced the Carmelites to move to Baltimore, Archbishop James Whitfield involved himself personally in the task of locating suitable accommodations for the order of cloistered nuns. On 6 June 1830, after "looking all over Baltimore," Whitfield wrote triumphantly to the Carmelite mother superior, "I have discovered a most beautiful garden, with a brick house, in a very respectable part of the city." The property, located on Aisquith Street south of Eager Street, was within a half mile of the archbishop's own residence on Charles Street between Mulberry and Franklin Streets and included "a fine green house, a bath room for warm and cold baths, a pump of good water within the lot, and close to the house, a variety of the choicest flowers, large beds of cauliflowers, and plenty of room and good soil for planting sufficient vegetables for your community."[58] The Carmelite order purchased the house in 1830 for $6,250. Whitfield personally contributed $100 toward the expenses. In 1839 a Carmelite benefactor, the Reverend Matthew Herard, bequeathed the community $5,000.[59]

The Sisters of the Visitation established their first foundation in the United States in Georgetown in 1800. Leonard Neale—Jesuit priest, brother to Charles, and future archbishop of Baltimore—made the Visitation Sisters "the principal focus of his interest and energies until the assumption of his archiepiscopal role."[60] Neale served as the sisters' spiritual director and also purchased an entire block of Georgetown real estate for $5,670, which he deeded to the Visitation Sisters in 1808 for one dollar. The French priest Joseph Clorivière, third spiritual director of the Visitation Sisters from 1819 until his death in 1826, contributed more than $9,300 of his own money to their community.[61]

Elizabeth Ann Seton founded the Sisters of Charity of St. Joseph in Baltimore in 1809. Seton and her community received significant financial support from both European patrons, including the Filicchi family in Italy, and American benefactors. Samuel Cooper, a student preparing for the priesthood at St. Mary's Seminary, generously donated $10,000 to Seton for the purchase of property suitable for a convent and school. Three months after professing her vows in March 1809, Seton and the four other charter Sisters of Charity occupied their new estate at Emmitsburg, Maryland.[62]

The only detail in which the early experiences of the Oblate Sisters of Providence resembled that of the three sisterhoods preceding them in the archdiocese of Baltimore was in the number of their respective charter members: the Carmelites, four; the Visitation Sisters, three; the Sisters of Charity, five; and the Oblate Sisters, four. Never a large community compared to their Maryland peers, in 1829 the Oblates included their original 4 members compared to membership roles of 25 for the Carmelites, 60 for the Visitation Nuns of Georgetown, and 120 for the Sisters of Charity. By 1850 the Oblates had received 29 candidates, compared to the Carmelites' 53, the Visitation Nuns' 178, and the Emmitsburg Sisters of Charity's 680 members.[63]

Such considerations as longevity, base population, and number of established missions account for the disparity between the memberships of the Oblate community and the white sisterhoods. The Oblate community began in 1829; the Carmelites, in 1790; the Visitation Nuns, in 1799; the Sisters of Charity, in 1809. In 1785 Archbishop Carroll estimated that 3,000 black Catholics lived in Maryland. By 1865 black Catholics in Maryland numbered only 16,000, and nationally, 100,000. By contrast, continuous waves of European immigration from 1830 constantly augmented the substantial white Catholic base population, which grew from 195,000 in 1815 to 3,103,000 in 1860 nationwide. The fact that during the period under review the Oblate Sisters maintained no permanent missions outside Baltimore impeded their recruitment capabilities. By contrast, the Visitation Nuns and the Sisters of Charity had established multiple foundations or missions.[64]

Significantly, Oblate school enrollments compared favorably with those of the archdiocesan white girls' academies. In 1830 Archbishop Whitfield advised the Carmelite Nuns that an enrollment of 50 to 60 pupils would constitute a viable student body capable of supporting their institution. The Oblate School for Coloured Girls enrolled 56 pupils in 1839; the Georgetown Visitation Academy, 50 in 1830; the Carmelite school, approximately 50 pupils in the early 1840s.[65]

No priest or bishop appeared as a deus ex machina, disbursing thousands of dollars in cash or property to the fledgling Oblate community. In 1831 Archbishop Whitfield pledged an annual gift of only $5 to the Oblate Sisters. In February 1833 he gave them a one-time donation of $40. The priest Adolphus Williamson repeatedly recognized the Oblate Sisters with nonpecuniary favors. Although in 1830 Williamson donated $3,000 of his personal fortune to provide cut granite for the facade of the Sulpician institution St. Charles College, some fifteen miles outside Baltimore, evidently he did not consider financial support of the Oblate Sisters a suitable investment.[66] When circumstances required the Oblate Sisters to relocate three times between June 1828 and December 1829, no priest or bishop personally interceded on their behalf or helped defray their moving expenses. Furthermore, no wealthy European benefactors subsidized the Oblate endeavor. Unlike the other archdiocesan sisterhoods, the Oblate Sisters of Providence had to rely exclusively on their own resources and the generosity of the American lay community for financial support.

In 1836 both the Oblate Sisters and the Carmelite Nuns constructed new chapels. The Oblate Sisters borrowed money to finance construction and organized a fair in 1837 to meet the expense of outfitting their new chapel. Acting on behalf of the Carmelites, their resident chaplain, Matthew Herard, not only donated $3,000 from his personal funds for the project but also engaged some "ladies of the city" to organize a fair that raised an additional $3,500 for the Carmelite chapel.[67] The discrepancy between the unencumbered $7,500 for the Carmelite chapel and the begged, borrowed, and earned total of $3,301.02 for the Oblate chapel in 1836 accurately reflected the relative positions of these two communities of women religious in Baltimore.

In describing the ceremonies consecrating the altar stone on 31 July 1836 and the one blessing the chapel cornerstone on 27 August, the Oblate annalist declared twice, "We followed exactly all the ceremonies prescribed in the ritual."[68] This repeated statement revealed the Oblate Sisters' awareness of their anomalous position as outsiders within Catholic Baltimore society. As if in response to an anticipated, if unarticulated, challenge from the white Catholic community, the Oblate Sisters explicitly noted their knowledge of and conformity to established religious ritual. They thus asserted their status as a legitimate constituency within the Baltimore religious community.

During their first decade, the Oblate Sisters of Providence received recognition from the Oblate Sisters of St. Frances of Rome. In 1833 the Roman Oblate community responded favorably to requests from the Baltimore sisters for pictures and a relic of St. Frances. The Baltimore Oblate community did not seek formal affiliation with the Roman Oblate Sisters. Maintaining their status as an autonomous community, the Baltimore Oblate Sisters solicited acknowledgment of their existence as a sister religious community, associated with the Roman sisterhood through their mutual spiritual patronage of St. Frances of Rome. In 1836 the Baltimore sisters named their new chapel in honor of "St. Frances, foundress of the Oblates of Rome and first patron of the whole institution."[69] In 1838 the Baltimore Oblates relied on their association with the Roman Oblates to resolve an issue that had apparently developed about the procedure for selecting names for new Oblate members. The community decided that postulants "should take the name of one of the Oblates who died in the odor of sanctity in Rome, that they would cast lots for the name and that the new Sister could add a name of her own choice."[70]

For the Oblate Sisters of Providence, much was in a name. The names of St. Frances and of the individual deceased Roman Oblate Sisters identified the new, indigenous community of black women religious in the southern United States with a well-established and respected European religious community within the institutional Roman Catholic Church. In responding positively to the Baltimore Oblate community's request that they "give recognition to our life,"[71] the Oblates of St. Frances of Rome welcomed the Baltimore Oblate Sisters into the spiritual sorority of communities of women religious.

Less certain is the nature of the reception accorded the Oblate Sisters of Providence by the other archdiocesan sisterhoods. When two Oblate Sisters accompanied their school's Confirmation class to the convent of the Sisters of Charity on 23 May 1832, "they were well received by the Sisters of Charity."[72] Other evidence confirmed the impression that the Sisters of Charity maintained at least an institutional tolerance toward black people conducive to cordial relations with the Oblate Sisters. When informed of her new responsibility for black religious instruction in the Emmitsburg, Maryland, area in 1809, Elizabeth Seton wrote to her spiritual director, Simon Bruté, "And I have all the Colored, all the Colored for my share to instruct—Excellentissimo!"[73] The instruction of black people by the Sisters of Charity may have exceeded the conventional rote catechetical lessons provided the community's own and neighboring slaves by including reading and writing. Black girls—including Therese Duchemin—may have attended the school of the Sisters of Charity, at least temporarily.[74]

No extant evidence consulted explicitly connects the Oblate community to the Georgetown Sisters of the Visitation or to the Carmelite Nuns in the 1830s. Available information reveals only these sisterhoods' interactions with black people in general. Certainly the sisters provided religious instruction to their slaves. No extant records document the inclusion of black pupils at the Visitandine Academy in its early years. Nevertheless, the Visitandines may have aided and abetted formal black education in the District of Columbia. A strong oral tradition within the Visitation community links them with Maria Becraft's school prior to her entering the Oblate sisterhood in 1831.[75] Moses Goodwin corroborates the Visitandine oral tradition in his 1871 government *Special Report*: "The Sisters of the Georgetown convent were the admirers of Miss Becraft, gave her instruction, and extended to her the most heartfelt aid and approbation in all her noble work, as they were in those days wont to do in behalf of the aspiring colored girls, who sought for education, withholding themselves from such work only when a depraved and degenerate public sentiment upon the subject of educating the colored people had compelled them to a more rigid line of demarcation between the races."[76]

Although historian Barbara Misner has asserted that "the work in all eight motherhouses' archives left the definite impression that the communities were willing to help one another in whatever way they could," the available evidence documented cooperation only between the Sisters of Charity and the Carmelites in 1831.[77] No extant record indicates whether this nexus of support and assistance among the antebellum Baltimore sisterhoods included the Oblate Sisters of Providence. Evidently, the unions of prayer and good works the Carmelites forged with the Sulpicians, the Visitation Sisters, and the Sisters of Charity did not include the Oblate Sisters.

THE NATIONAL CATHOLIC directories published annually from 1833 provide another source of information about the status accorded the Oblate Sisters of Providence by the Roman Catholic Church in the 1830s. Compiled from data submitted by diocesan authorities across the nation, the directories reflected official diocesan views. Although formally professed since 1829, the Oblate Sisters received no mention as a community in the 1833 edition of the *Laity's Directory*.

Each edition of the directory published material compiled the preceding year. Although the Oblate Sisters notified Archbishop Whitfield early in 1832 that the papacy had acknowledged their community, evidently diocesan authorities did not include this information in the report submitted from Baltimore for the 1833 directory.[78]

However, the obituaries in the 1833 volume included the notice: "1832 October, Sister Antonina (col'd) of the Order of Oblates of Baltimore, a victim of charity during the cholera."[79] The obituary of Sister Anthony Duchemin followed those of the two Sisters of Charity who also died nursing cholera victims. While the obituaries of the two white sisters included their respective surnames, that of Sister Anthony Duchemin did not. Although six Oblate Sisters died between 1832 and 1839, the directory published only Duchemin's obituary. Obituaries of white sisters appeared regularly in the directories.

In 1834 the publishing firms James Myres and Fielding Lucas each produced an edition of the directory. Both editions published the identical prospectus of a "School for Coloured Girls Under the Direction of the Sisters of Providence." The treatment of the Oblate Sisters and their school in the 1834 volumes compared very favorably to that of the white sisterhoods. The prospectus noted Pope Gregory XVI's recognition of the Oblate community and replicated that portion of the Oblate Rule proclaiming the social utility of moral education for black future mothers and servants. It enumerated course offerings, specified terms and conditions of enrollment, and concluded with the Oblate offer to supply the nation's clergy with vestments.[80]

However, the manner of inclusion of the Oblate Sisters in each of the 1834 editions warrants comment. In the Myres edition, the Oblate prospectus appeared not merely at the end of the listings of convents and academies for the archdiocese of Baltimore but out of order as the absolutely last listing of all convents and schools nationally. The Fielding Lucas edition inserted a secondary citation for "The Sisters of Providence (see p. 69), a religious society of colored females" among its listings of Baltimore church buildings and charitable institutions, remote from the other, white sisterhoods. This exceptional listing of the Oblate Sisters replicated the policy first seen in the 1830 publication *Metropolitan*. Such citations emphasized the uniqueness of the Oblate Sisters, predicated on their racial identity.[81]

In 1837 the directory listed "St. Frances Chapel, Rev. H. Joubert" under the heading "Churches and Clergy" for the first time.[82] This listing connoted formal diocesan approval of the use of the new Oblate chapel as a public church. But the 1837 volume listed the Oblate convent and school not only at the end of the schools established by religious communities but also after three new institutions staffed by lay teachers.[83] Neither seniority nor religious status proved effective safeguards for the Oblate Sisters. Considerations of race demanded that these black religious cede precedence to three new, lay, white schools.

The 1837 edition also cited in its recapitulation and statistics chart only three communities of women religious for Baltimore: the Carmelites, the Sisters of the Visitation, and the Sisters of Charity. The recapitulation and statistics chart in the 1838 edition continued to omit the Oblate Sisters from the complement of archdiocesan sisterhoods. Furthermore, this edition drastically reduced the Oblate prospectus to a terse statement: "Girls of color are here taught English, French, Cyphering and Writing, Sewing in all its branches, Embroidery, Washing and Ironing" and the terms of enrollment.[84]

Not until 1839, a full decade after their formal installation, did the Oblate Sisters of Providence enjoy complete and unqualified representation in the national Catholic directory. An anonymous biographical sketch of Louis DuBourg, the former Sulpician priest credited with instituting religious instruction for the black San Domingan émigrés at St. Mary's Seminary in 1796, cited "Joubert's religious association, well known under the name the Oblate Sisters of Providence."[85] The prospectus of the Oblate school, restored to its original length and format, cited a complement of fourteen professed Oblate Sisters and three novices to serve a student enrollment of fifty-six scholars: sixteen boarders and forty day students. Included for the first time under the heading "Charitable Institutions" was notice of a generic "Sunday school for colored girls, in Baltimore," possibly a reference to the cooperative Joubert-Oblate catechetical effort operative since 1829.[86] Finally, in 1839 the recapitulation and statistics chart listed five female religious institutions, a number that at last included the Oblate Sisters of Providence.[87] Even within the institutional church, moral and spiritual equality ceded precedence to considerations of race. The omissions and relegations to last place committed against the Oblate Sisters in various editions of the Catholic directory from 1833 through 1839 documented this fact.

THE ANTEBELLUM Roman Catholic Church accommodated racism and the institution of slavery. The compromised and compromising position the church assumed in antebellum society necessarily affected its attitude and policy toward black people. The church approved the establishment of the Oblate community of black women religious in 1829. Nevertheless, the secular press publicized the Oblate endeavor before any Catholic journal noted it. Benjamin Lundy and William Lloyd Garrison edited and published the abolitionist weekly *Genius of Universal Emancipation* in Baltimore. Under the title "School for Girls of Color," the 8 January 1830 issue of that paper included a more substantive and detailed report of the Oblate sisterhood and school—initialed by Garrison himself—than did either the *Metropolitan* or the *United States Catholic Miscellany* in their February 1830 Oblate articles.[88] Throughout the 1830s, the relationships between the Oblate Sisters and Archbishops James Whitfield and Samuel Eccleston, the low level of clerical financial support they enjoyed, and the treatment accorded the Oblate community in the national Catholic directories and press revealed that the church marginalized the black Oblate Sisters within the religious community.

The Oblate Sisters did not directly protest their marginal social status. Just as nineteenth-century women religious did not routinely challenge the subordinate position of women in the institutional church, the Oblate Sisters also functioned within the parameters of racial discrimination sanctioned by the church. Oblate Sister Stanislaus Kostka (Cassandra Butler) died in 1832. Without hesitation or remark, Joubert sought from the trustee of the cathedral "a lot in that part of the cemetery where they buried colored people."[89] The sisters evidently agonized over imposing the policy of pew segregation in their new chapel in 1837. Nevertheless, they implemented this racially discriminatory policy prevalent in Catholic churches.

The Oblate Sisters acceded to socially sanctioned racial discrimination. But they resisted real and potential threats to their status as women religious. In her letter to Sulpician Superior Deluol in 1835, discussed in Chapter 1, Oblate Superior Mary Lange insisted on the guaranteed integrity of the Oblate religious state as a precondition to their domestic employment at the Sulpician seminary. Oblate experience with clerical disapproval of the concept of a black sisterhood in 1829 had prompted Lange's apprehensions about full recognition and respect for the sisters' religious state at the seminary. In June 1829 the disapproval of the Oblate foundation expressed within the Baltimore Catholic community had dismayed the four charter members. James Joubert noted, "These good girls . . . admitted to me that after all they had heard said, only through obedience would they be determined to take the religious habit." He encouraged the four Oblate novices to "rest on the purity of their intentions, and . . . put their confidence in God; that until now their work seemed good, so they must not stop because of the judgment of men who often judge things through their passions and prejudices."[90] The Oblate Sisters incorporated Joubert's sage words into their communal response to all encounters with racial discrimination.

Joubert further revealed, "I had myself heard much talk. I knew already that many persons who had approved the idea of a school for pupils disapproved very strongly that of forming a religious house, and could not think of the idea of seeing these poor girls (colored girls) wearing the religious habit and constituting a religious community." The outcry against the idea of black sisters had come to the attention of even Archbishop James Whitfield, who, according to Joubert, "knew very much himself, even more than I did, and he advised me not to be in the least discouraged."[91] The "persons" who confronted the sisters, challenged Joubert, and complained to the archbishop about the concept of a community of black women religious undoubtedly included clergy—Sulpicians among them—who were more likely to have access to the sisters, Joubert, and Whitfield than the general laity.

The 1830 and 1840 U.S. censuses indicated the presence of slaves at St. Mary's Seminary. Citizens of Maryland conflated slaves and free black people so thoroughly that they institutionalized this practice and perspective in the distinctive legal phrase "Negroes and other slaves" that recurred in state legislation.[92] The Oblate Sisters might well have questioned their prospective position within the seminary household among certain individuals who conflated slaves and free black people or denigrated the idea of black sisters.

Deluol's request for Oblate domestic services worried Joubert, who "wished to remain neutral in the affair." Such sentiments indicated Joubert's own uncertainty about the racial and religious reception the seminary would afford black sisters, perhaps fueled by his personal knowledge of Sulpician opposition to their existence. He enjoined the sisters to seek God's help in their decision-making and to be respectful and humble toward Deluol as "becomes good religious."[93] Otherwise he left them at full liberty to set their conditions and requested only that he see the letter before the sisters sent it to Deluol.

In his reply to her letter, Sulpician Superior Deluol addressed Oblate Superior Lange on terms of unaccustomed equality. He denied any intention "to enter in any manner into the borders of your Community." He requested reciprocal rights of consultation about the sisters assigned to the seminary and prior notification of any changes, "as I need not tell you that a Superior can sometimes make remarks which deserve consideration." In answer to Lange's numerous stipulations, Deluol responded, "You write the paper which shall contain the conditions under which you will come and I shall sign it."[94]

Considerations of gender informed this extraordinary exchange between these superiors of male and female religious communities. Because in antebellum American society women's sphere of influence incorporated domestic household management, Lange could assert her authority in stipulating the terms under which the Oblate Sisters would function in this acknowledged field of women's expertise. Conversely, Deluol could grant the Oblate superior a free hand in setting the terms of Oblate employment at the seminary without relinquishing patriarchal male authority, precisely because well-defined parameters of women's work delimited the situation.

Deluol may have neither intended nor attached any racial significance to his request that Oblate Sisters serve in a domestic capacity at the seminary. The custom of procuring the services of women religious to perform domestic duties in seminaries and colleges originated in France. Sisters of Charity served in this capacity at Mount St. Mary's College at Emmitsburg, Maryland, from 1815 to 1852.[95] But the racial component inherent in the Lange-Deluol correspondence certainly heightened the exceptional nature of the assertiveness of the black sister and the acquiescence of the white priest within the contexts of the antebellum South and Roman Catholic Church.

The pursuit of spiritual perfection—the common, primary goal of all religious life—provided a unique perspective that viewed suffering and hardship meekly endured as purifying experiences in imitation of Jesus Christ. The Oblate Sisters of Providence experienced in common with their peer sisterhoods purifying trials of poverty, cold, hunger, and other hardships. But these black women religious utilized their spirituality to convert the racial slights, indignities, and humiliations that the institutional church as well as white American society imposed on them into purifying trials unique to their experience.

In forming a community of black women religious within the Roman Catholic Church, the Oblate Sisters of Providence had indemnified the virtue of black women in defiance of prevailing social attitudes. In challenging white society's controlling images of black women and replacing them with their own self-images, the Oblate Sisters achieved "an essential component in resisting systems of race, gender, and class oppression."[96] In responding to incidents of racial discrimination—even within the Catholic Church—as opportunities for spiritual transcendence, they transformed intended racial denigration and humiliation into spiritual benefit, in defiance of prevailing social intent. By their very existence, the Oblate Sisters of Providence challenged the American Roman Catholic Church to revise its conventional views of black moral and intellectual capacities and to accommodate a black institutional presence.

CHAPTER SIX

The Coloured Sisters

THE OBLATE SISTERS AND THE
BALTIMORE WHITE COMMUNITY

❖ ❖

Conditions peculiar to the city of Baltimore in the early nineteenth century, including its large free black population base and its status as the first seat of the Roman Catholic Church in the United States, created a socially fertile environment capable of supporting the Oblate Sisters of Providence. However, Baltimore also experienced in common with other urban areas an influx of European immigrants and economic competition between white and black workers that engendered nativist and racial antipathies. As free women of color organized as a Roman Catholic sisterhood, the Oblate Sisters of Providence proved anomalous to both the racial and religious orthodoxies of antebellum Baltimore. But Baltimore sustained the Oblate Sisters, because the city itself constituted an anomaly in southern slave society.

The reality of free black productive labor serving white economic interests formed the basis of antebellum toleration of the free black population in Maryland. The Oblate Sisters of Providence, as a black religious society formed to serve an exclusively black clientele, had little to recommend them to antebellum white Baltimore in this regard. The Oblate community appeared economically as well as socially superfluous to white society. The ancillary Oblate objective stated in the original Oblate Rule—to produce servants "trained up in habits of modesty, honesty, and integrity"[1]—may have sufficed to validate to white Baltimoreans the Oblate Sisters as economically productive.

Baltimore's preponderance of free over slave black inhabitants and its concentration on mercantile, industrial, and financial pursuits rendered the city as unique in southern slave society as the institution of slavery proved to be in the city of Baltimore. The city's casual and seasonal labor needs did not correspond to the fixed system of labor inherent in slavery. Slavery never dominated Baltimore's political economy because it proved an institution without economic necessity. Furthermore, urban slavery presented certain advantages over the plantation experience from the perspective of the slaves themselves. Frederick Douglass, perhaps the most celebrated slave inhabitant of Baltimore, observed, "A city slave is almost a free citizen, in Baltimore, compared with a slave on Col. Lloyd's plantation. . . . Slavery dislikes a dense population, in which there is a majority of non-slaveholders. The general sense of decency that must pervade such a population does much to check and prevent those outbreaks of atrocious cruelty, and those dark crimes without a name, almost openly perpetrated on the plantation."[2]

Regardless of the anomalous nature of the slave's experience in Baltimore, or of the institution of slavery itself within that city, or of the city itself within slave society, the institution of slavery intruded on the lives of free black people in both Baltimore and Maryland. Racism rendered free black people socially anomalous in the United States. Maryland state legislation consistently stipulated that free black residents did not enjoy social or legal parity with white citizens. Historically, white American society considered free black people more black than free.[3]

The racial basis of slavery in the United States allowed public discourse to debase all black people. During the 1820s in Maryland official state correspondence referred to the free black population as "a national evil," as "a people usually extremely dissolute and idle and consequently a public nuisance," and as "a vicious and degraded population." Public statements also asserted the "impossibil[ity] in the nature of things that free blacks could be amalgamated with the whites" and that free black people "must be in some ways a distinct portion of the community." Such publicly expressed sentiments indicated a climate of opinion both dismissive of the humanity of black people and receptive to the policy of colonization, or their repatriation to Africa.[4]

The state of Maryland consistently imposed laws intended to demean its free black population. As early as 1807, Maryland introduced legislation to discourage free black immigration into the state. Such laws required free black people to petition the legislature for exemptions or to pay fines, to submit to floggings, or to risk enslavement for noncompliance. Maryland's free black inhabitants enjoyed a measure of security and freedom only within their resident communities. Travel to distant counties rendered free black people "liable to annoyance and possibly to arrest and delay." For black people, "[c]olor created the presumption that a man was a slave, and the burden of proof of freedom, by certificate of freedom or otherwise, rested on the black."[5] The Maryland penal code also discriminated against free people of color. It prescribed flogging for petty offenses for which white perpetrators served jail terms. Free black repeat offenders faced expulsion from the state as well as temporary or even permanent enslavement. Myriad acts of state legislation restricted, impeded, or prohibited free black rights of suffrage, assembly and association, fields of employment, parental custody, and ownership of property. Significantly, the city of Baltimore consistently distinguished itself from the rural counties in tempering restrictions on free black rights of assembly and association, under appropriate white supervision.[6]

From the late 1820s the state of Maryland increasingly adopted the text and tenor of the racial ideologies of states in the Deep South, even as it imposed more intrusive restrictions on its free black residents. In 1830, Maryland incorporated a branch of the American Colonization Society, formed nationally in 1816 to expedite removal of free black people from the United States. By the 1830s members of prominent Maryland Catholic families such as the Carrolls, the Taneys, and the Reads had assumed leadership positions in the Maryland State Colonization Society. In 1831—the same year the papacy recognized the Oblate Sisters of Providence—the slave insurrection in Virginia that Nat Turner led unleashed a firestorm of restrictive legislation against both slave and free black inhabitants in surrounding states. Maryland passed the Act on Free Negroes and Slaves in 1831, which, among other provisions, endorsed full implementation of black colonization to Africa. The intercession of Baltimore citizens removed some of the legislation's more repressive proposals, including mandatory registration and free black taxation. Nevertheless, Baltimore found itself "swept up in the state's maelstrom of racial hostility."[7]

Maryland legislators utilized legal proscription, forcible expulsion, threat of enslavement, and voluntary colonization to marginalize free black people and to render them social, legal, and political anomalies within the state. A collective white mentality reduced free black people and slaves to one degraded entity. The Maryland State House Committee on the Colored Population Report of 1836 captured the essence of these antebellum white attitudes toward free black people in the following passage promoting the policy of colonization: "The free black, dead to every generous prompting of ambition, because debarred of ultimate aim, has ever been an incubus on society. Our deepest, warmest sympathies they have, but while they remain among us, little more can be extended. A curse to our slaves, whom they are constantly corrupting, an evil to the whites, between whom and them the laws of God and nature have drawn lines never to be effaced, they must leave our shores if they would be happy and prosperous."[8]

In reality, most free black people in Maryland simply struggled to support themselves and their families under adverse social and economic conditions. Many free black residents of Baltimore both developed and denounced colonization schemes, organized schools, built community institutions, excoriated slavery, and advocated emancipation. In 1828 the Oblate Sisters of Providence institutionalized the black female religious presence in the Roman Catholic Church and provided a Catholic education to black girls. Like most free black residents of Baltimore, the Oblate Sisters could not have recognized themselves in the 1836 Committee on the Colored Population Report's description of free black animus and activity.

THE CITY OF Baltimore differed in degree, but not in kind, in this pattern of white thought about black people. White Baltimoreans' ambivalence toward free black people interpolated their perceptions of and responses to the Oblate Sisters of Providence. Issues of race and incidents of racism affected the Oblate Sisters of Providence from their beginning. In 1829 news of the formation of the black religious community generated opposition in Baltimore among clergy and laity alike. In his early-twentieth-century account of the Oblate formation, historian Charles Herbermann cavalierly dismissed the severity of the racial problems confronting the nascent Oblate community. He maintained, "As we hear no more of opposition to the Sisterhood and as ladies of the highest rank, like Mrs. Chatard and Mrs. Ducatel and their friends, did not hesitate to become their patrons openly, we are justified in inferring that the good Sisters were frightened by idle rumors."[9] Evidence recorded in the pages of the Oblate annals fails to corroborate Herbermann's sanguine inference.

During their first decade, the Oblate Sisters encountered incidents of racism, both subtle and overt. The racial identity of the sisters and their students complicated their securing a suitable, permanent residence. Unexpectedly evicted from their first rented property in St. Mary's Court in April 1829, the Oblate Sisters experienced a discriminatory housing market familiar to minority populations in both the nineteenth and twentieth centuries. Joubert reported, "We had to search for another place at a reasonable distance from the seminary. We found several but the price asked was exorbitant; several refused absolutely to let us have them, when they were informed that is was for a school, and still more a school for colored children. I began to lose courage as these good girls [the Oblate Sisters] were all upset."[10] Fortunately for the community, within a month of their eviction notice Dr. Peter Chatard, a wealthy white San Domingan immigrant, offered them his Richmond Street property on generous terms.

In 1834 the Oblate community decided to buy the lot adjoining their Richmond Street location. Evidently the Oblate neighborhood, unlike that of the Carmelite Nuns, was not located in a very respectable part of the city. Joubert wrote that in part "the fear of seeing the small wooden house which is on the lot converted into a grocery store, or what would be still worse, a house of ill-repute" prompted the sisters to forestall such an eventuality by buying the property. Joubert noted ruefully that "the persons to whom this house belonged felt the need we had of this lot and sold it more dearly, perhaps, than they would have to anyone else but the Sisters."[11] Whether the racial identity or the religious state of the Oblate Sisters evoked such illiberality from the owners of the property remains unclear. Having to pay premium prices for inferior goods and services proved another experience familiar to minority populations in both the nineteenth and twentieth centuries.

The Oblate Sisters bought or improved property several times in the 1830s. All the antebellum white sisterhoods in Baltimore incorporated between 1817 and 1839. But the Oblate community remained unincorporated until 1867 and consequently could not hold legal title to property. Joubert held the Richmond Street property in his name. Between 1810 and 1835 at least four black Protestant denominations incorporated in Baltimore. The evidence does not clarify why— if both white Roman Catholic sisterhoods and black Protestant denominations acquired charters as early as 1810—the Oblate Sisters of Providence remained unincorporated until 1867. The marginalized status of the Oblate community within the church provides a plausible explanation.[12]

The Oblate Sisters' willing service as nurses during the cholera epidemic of 1832, discussed in Chapter 3, demonstrated their strong sense of mission and empowerment. However, significant racial dimensions inhered in this Oblate service to the city of Baltimore. Except for the letter from Archibald Stirling, secretary of the Trustees of the Bureau of the Poor, the Oblate Sisters enjoyed no public recognition for their civic service in nursing the sick. The white Sisters of Charity received significant public acknowledgment of their efforts. The existing evidence does not specify whether the Oblate Sisters nursed black or white cholera patients at the almshouse; it does suggest, however, that the cholera incident provided another opportunity for the Oblate Sisters to serve the Baltimore black community.[13]

The outbreak of cholera in Baltimore in 1832 ravaged the free black community disproportionately to its presence in the total population. In the first week in September, 254 Baltimoreans died from cholera; 104 victims were black, and of these, 92 were free. Although composing only 14 percent of the city's population, in that one week free black victims accounted for more than one-third of the cholera dead. Crowded and inadequate housing conditions for Baltimore's black residents and municipal negligence in maintaining minimum standards of public sanitation partially explain this severe black mortality from cholera.[14]

Most nineteenth-century public and private institutions, asylums, hospitals, and orphanages did not accept black inmates. Those that did—like the Baltimore City and County Almshouse—enforced a policy of strict racial segregation. A city medical report published in 1851 detailed the inferior, segregated facilities provided Baltimore's black population at the city almshouse. The report's account of "cholera as it appeared at this institution in 1832" established that these racially segregated facilities had also existed in 1832. The Trustees of the Bureau of the Poor had requested eight Sisters of Charity, evidently to minister to both black and white almshouse cholera victims. Had the Sisters of Charity provided half the number of requested nurses, expecting the "society of religious colored women" to nurse black almshouse inmates?[15]

Even as they valiantly agreed to serve the city of Baltimore as nurses, the Oblate Sisters experienced the intrusion of racial discrimination. In informing the city officials of the sisters' consent, Joubert "also told these gentlemen that I should wish these colored Sisters in a department of the hospital entirely separate from those of the Sisters of Charity, so that they would not come in contact with them. The gentlemen understood perfectly, and promised that this should be done."[16]

However much at the time "the gentlemen understood perfectly," Joubert's unexplained but explicit request to segregate the Oblate Sisters from the Sisters of Charity at the almshouse remains puzzling. Did Joubert anticipate some racial friction should "the colored Sisters . . . come in contact with" the white Sisters of Charity? Was Joubert attempting to mitigate the humiliation of publicly mandated racial segregation by insisting on such racial segregation as a condition of Oblate service? Was Joubert insuring that the colored Oblate Sisters would nurse only where the white Sisters of Charity would not—in the segregated black wards of the municipal almshouse? The lack of acknowledgment by the Baltimore public of the Oblate service in the almshouse may have reflected, in part, not only the racial identity of the Oblate Sisters themselves but also the racial identity of the beneficiaries of their care.

But circumstances beyond race may have dictated the respective public acknowledgments accorded the nursing efforts of the Sisters of Charity and the Oblate Sisters of Providence. The Sisters of Charity of St. Joseph, Emmitsburg, who taught, nursed, and cared for orphans as their mission, constituted the largest congregation of women religious within the archdiocese of Baltimore. The outbreak of cholera precipitated requests for their nursing services from civic authorities in Philadelphia and Washington, D.C., as well as in Baltimore. Before the Trustees of the Bureau of the Poor solicited assistance from the Sisters of Charity for the almshouse, the Baltimore City Board of Health had requested their services on 19 August 1832 at two provisional hospitals set up in the city. Two Sisters of Charity died nursing at these hospitals. In their annual reports in 1832 both the commissioner of health and the consulting physician called to "the attention of the City Council" the deaths of these sisters in service to the city.[17]

The Sisters of Charity nursed at more locations and in greater numbers than did the Oblate Sisters. While two Sisters of Charity died, all four Oblate Sisters survived exposure to cholera and returned to their convent. Two separate bureaucratic agencies, the Board of Health and the Bureau of the Poor, requested the services of the Sisters of Charity; only the latter approached the Oblate Sisters. The city council formally acknowledged the services of the Sisters of Charity at the specific request of two city officials. Visibility, mortality, and bureaucracy as much as issues of race may explain the different public acknowledgments of the nursing services rendered by the Sisters of Charity and the Oblate Sisters of Providence during the cholera epidemic of 1832.

THE OBLATE SISTERS of Providence endured without complaint racial discrimination in the guise of exploitation by unscrupulous businessmen and minimal civic acknowledgment of their public service. However, the racially and religiously charged atmosphere of 1830s Baltimore required Joubert and the Oblate Sisters to remain ever alert to potential threats to their physical safety as well. Convents proved particularly vulnerable targets of nativist wrath during the Jacksonian period. Nativists—descendants of earlier waves of immigrants who considered themselves "native" Americans—feared and resented the newer wave of mostly Roman Catholic immigrants as competition for scarce jobs in the port cities and as purveyors of foreign papism. As institutions that allegedly denied freedom of choice to the individual, convents appeared antithetical to American family values of marriage and motherhood. Furthermore, convents "offered a disturbingly different lifestyle that served as a role model for impressionable girls in convent schools."[18]

In 1829 the Oblate community moved to the Richmond Street property, a location ten blocks away from the seminary chapel. Concern about "the distant location and the dangers"[19] threatening the Oblate Sisters en route to and from church prompted Joubert to petition Archbishop Whitfield for permission to erect a temporary chapel for the sisters on Oblate premises. Undoubtedly the potential for racially as well as nativist-motivated attacks on the Oblate Sisters formed a part of the dangers Joubert hoped to avoid with the in-house chapel facilities.

In 1834 threats to the safety of the Oblate Sisters of Providence assumed a more definite and ominous form. Joubert noted on 8 October 1834, "Some alarming rumors had been current for some days of the ill will born to all religious houses of the city and the desire they had to renew in Baltimore the horrible scenes enacted in the Convent of the Ursulines in Charlestown near Boston." The "they" referred to nativist mobs. The "horrible scenes enacted in the Convent of the Ursulines" referred to the violence perpetrated by a nativist mob in Massachusetts that burned the exclusive Ursuline convent school to the ground on 11 August 1834. "A good Catholic of the city" had informed Joubert "of the threats that were made in particular against the Carmelite Sisters and the Colored Sisters";[20] Joubert consequently applied to the mayor of Baltimore for protection. Anxious about the safety of the Oblate Sisters, Joubert obtained permission from the archbishop to spend the night in the Oblate parlor with two other priests. The night passed without incident, to the relief of all concerned.

Although Joubert attributed this threat against the "colored Sisters" to anti-Catholic sentiment, racial animosity provides an equally plausible explanation. In 1833 the abolitionist movement had launched a frontal assault on the institution of slavery, demanding the immediate, uncompensated manumission of slaves. This movement evoked significant antiblack reactions in several urban areas. Mob violence erupted against black residents of New York, Philadelphia, and Columbia, Pennsylvania, in July and August 1834.[21] Reports of these three incidents of racial violence could have instigated the threat against the Oblate Sisters as readily as news of the convent arson in Massachusetts.

Historian Barbara Misner disputed the year reported in the Oblate annals for this threat, primarily because Carmelite sources recorded no similar threat to their order in 1834. Ascribing greater accuracy to the Carmelite than to the Oblate source, Misner concluded that the Oblate incident occurred in 1839 to correspond to mob demonstrations at the Carmelite convent that year. The flight from the Carmelite convent of the unfortunate Sister Isabella Neale, later certified as mentally deranged, occasioned the mob response. Misner presumed a monolithically nativist, anti-Catholic motivation that would have targeted both the Carmelite and the Oblate communities as religious congregations. However, Misner has ignored the defining characteristic of race distinguishing the Oblate Sisters from the Carmelites as motivation for mob action. Historian Joseph Mannard has maintained that the nativist mob in 1839 focused exclusively on the Carmelite convent, "threatened neither individual Catholics nor their churches, nor any other religious buildings . . . [and] refrained from a wholesale condemnation of the Catholic Church and its convent system."[22] Mannard's argument challenges Misner's insistence on conflating the threat to the Oblate Sisters in 1834 with the Carmelite riot in 1839. If the Oblate Sisters alone among the Baltimore sisterhoods suffered a threat of violence in 1834, racial antipathy as much as nativist anti-Catholic sentiment probably instigated it.

In 1837 the issue of safety for the Oblate Sisters reappeared in an explicitly racial context. The Baltimore community had patronized a fair that raised almost $900 for the new Oblate chapel built in 1836. The Oblate annalist gratefully acknowledged the generosity of the white wardens of Baltimore's Cathedral of the Assumption who "very willingly loaned" the use of the cathedral school on Saratoga Street as the site for the Oblate function. But the annalist also noted, "We took all precautions that everything might pass orderly."[23] This statement revealed the Oblate Sisters' awareness of their precarious position within Baltimore society. Trebly scrutinized as black, Roman Catholic, and women religious, the Oblate community enjoyed no margin for error in any of their endeavors. Their fishbowl existence in antebellum Baltimore demanded that the Oblate membership remain ever vigilant "that everything might pass orderly."

The Oblate Sisters accommodated pew segregation in their new chapel in 1837. Significantly, Joubert called the policy a "measure of safety,"[24] implying real or potential danger to black Catholics in the absence of such restrictions. In late-eighteenth-century Philadelphia white Protestants had forcibly removed black fellow worshipers Richard Allen and Absalom Jones from church premises for ignoring racial seating restrictions.[25] Had white Catholics in nineteenth-century Baltimore replicated this behavior? Had considerations of "safety" also prompted the formation of the separate black congregation at St. Frances Chapel in 1836? Concerns for safety raised to justify segregated seating in a black Catholic house of worship attested to the racially charged atmosphere of 1830s Baltimore. The long arm of racial discrimination reached even to the last six pews in the Oblate Sisters' chapel.

The 1838 story of Solomon the dog, recounted in the annals in 1839, on one level represents a humorous tale of mistaken identity, the miraculous "return" of the deceased Oblate convent guard dog. But the subtext of the Solomon story—the Oblate Sisters' need for a vicious watchdog—proved no laughing matter. The impostor Solomon, "an even better watchdog than the first," proved "terrible and does not even permit the neighbors to put their hand on the wall of separation. Anyone who dares to enter the garden or the yard during the night runs a great risk, without doubt."[26] The obvious satisfaction with which the annalist reported the new Solomon's antisocial behavior suggested the need the Oblate community felt for some form of effective physical protection. The evidence does not reveal whether the Oblate Sisters experienced explicit threats, such as the 1834 incident, or experienced a more chronic, amorphous anxiety as a function of being both a black and a religious community in nineteenth-century Baltimore. Whatever concerns for their safety the white sisterhoods may have entertained in the wake of nativist agitation, the black Oblate Sisters also experienced—in addition to their concerns for their safety derived from their racial identity.

Nativism assumed forms other than mob violence in 1830s Baltimore. Several Protestant ministers organized the Protestant Association in 1835 to defend the principles of the Reformation against the incursions of papism. Presbyterian minister Robert J. Breckinridge and Andrew B. Cross edited the association's organ, the *Baltimore Literary and Religious Magazine*, a virulently anti-Catholic publication. In a patronizing article assessing Baltimore's black community, Breckinridge and Cross acknowledged the efforts of the teachers in the Sabbath school formed at St. James First African Protestant Episcopal Church to uplift the black race. The authors cited a "Miss Cook" and a "Miss Whipper" among the school's colored female teachers. Henrietta Cook, identified in the 1833 edition of the Baltimore City Directory as a black teacher, had participated in the Oblate fair fund-raiser in 1837. Sarah Helena Whipper and her cousin, Adalina Whipper, had attended the Oblate School for Colored Girls in 1830.[27] Undoubtedly, knowledge of the Cook and Whipper Oblate connection would have surprised Breckinridge and Cross as much as it would have dismayed them.

Incendiary nativist literature also stoked the popular perception of nuns as sexual victims imprisoned behind convent walls. Editors Breckinridge and Cross solicited and published in the *Baltimore Literary and Religious Magazine* the statement of six Baltimore residents testifying they had heard female screams from the Carmelite convent on 13 March 1835. In 1836 Maria Monk alleged that celibacy allowed lecherous priests to violate helpless nuns in the patently false *Awful Disclosures of the Hotel Dieu Nunnery of Montreal*. Editors Breckinridge and Cross sanctimoniously concurred with that publication's spurious claims in their magazine: "The popish doctrine of celibacy—the unreserved obedience due to bishops and priests from all nuns and females in all the holy orders, opens the way for the corruptions that would be expected."[28]

Even nuns' attire occasionally aroused hostile comment. In their report of Sister Olivia Neale's "escape" from the Carmelite convent in 1839, Breckinridge and Cross described her clothing as "the peculiar and shocking costume of her order." On 25 November 1838 Joubert had advised "the Sisters to attach their collars in such a manner that their necks would be more covered."[29] In an environment that impugned the virtue of even white women religious, Joubert's directive to the Oblate Sisters assumes heightened significance. These black sisters could project no hint of impropriety or immodesty in their dress to a white public that customarily disallowed the virtue of black women.

THE PERVASIVE DEBASEMENT of all black people ensuing from the racial basis of slavery in the United States convinced most white Americans of universal black inferiority. The city of Baltimore proved no exception to this pattern of white thought concerning all black people. Charles Carroll of Carrollton and Roger Brooke Taney, two exemplars of the antebellum white Baltimore Catholic laity, provide contrasting illustrations of the impact of the institution of slavery on white responses to the Oblate Sisters of Providence.

Charles Carroll, cousin of John Carroll, the first Roman Catholic bishop in the United States, achieved distinction in his own right. A noted patriot and statesman, Charles Carroll was the last surviving signer of the Declaration of Independence. Although a highly successful planter who owned 316 slaves in 1790, Carroll nevertheless introduced an unsuccessful bill for the gradual abolition of slavery in the Maryland State Senate in 1797. Yet in 1830 Carroll accepted the presidency of the American Colonization Society.[30]

An intimate friend of several Sulpician priests, Carroll proved himself a generous benefactor to Sulpician projects. In 1830 he underwrote the Sulpician St. Charles College, a preparatory school for young Catholics planning to enter the priesthood. Carroll donated the land, procured the charter for the college from the Maryland state legislature, authorized the purchase of additional property up to $6,000 to subsidize the project, and contributed fifty shares of the United States Bank for the construction of the college's buildings. He also contributed $20 annually to the Oblate Sisters of Providence from their inception in 1828 until his death in 1832.[31]

Carroll's actions indicated that he opposed slavery on some level and approved of the concept and mission of the Oblate Sisters sufficiently to subsidize their community at a modest rate. But in presiding over the American Colonization Society, Carroll also endorsed that group's racist assumptions about inherent black inferiority and the necessity of black removal. The convictions allowing Carroll's prolonged and profitable participation in the institution of slavery evidently precluded his allowing the full humanity of black people, slave or free. Charles Carroll's small annual disbursements of $20 to the Oblate community compared to his munificence to St. Charles College represented his attempt to honor the Roman Catholic Church's official position on racial matters: to promote the spiritual but not the social equality of black people. Undoubtedly considerations of gender also explain the disparity between Carroll's respective disbursements to St. Charles College for men and the Oblate school for girls in the nineteenth-century society of the American South.

Roger Brooke Taney—who in 1857 would achieve notoriety as chief justice of the Supreme Court responsible for the Dred Scott decision—gave early evidence of his thinking about black people. As attorney general in 1832, Taney opined, "The African race in the United States even when free, are everywhere a degraded class. . . . They are the only class of persons who can be held as mere property, as slaves. They were never regarded as a constituent portion of the sovereignty of any state, but as a separate and degraded people. . . . Our constitutions were not formed by the assistance of that unfortunate race, nor for their benefit."[32]

Between 1816 and 1819, while living in Frederick, Maryland, Taney served as attorney for a rural branch of a Baltimore organization formed in 1816 to defend free black victims kidnapped for sale as slaves and those apprehended without their freedom papers. Taney also arranged during this period for the eventual manumission of his own slaves, effective several years later. Furthermore, in 1819 Taney defended the right of a Methodist minister to condemn the abuses of slavery in a public forum. Taney referred to the peculiar institution at that time as "a blot on our national character, and every real lover of freedom confidently hopes that it will be effectually, though it must be gradually, wiped away."[33]

Some historians have cited these actions as evidence of Taney's humanitarian regard for black people. However, Taney's biographer, Carl Swisher, maintained that "Taney, like most other sons of Maryland planters, had been brought up in the midst of slaves, with pickaninnies as playmates, and had accepted the condition of black people as normal and right." Furthermore, Taney "was never at any stage of his life an abolitionist."[34]

Taney's legal position on slavery coincided with the position assumed by the Roman Catholic Church: both accepted the fact of the institution of slavery, but both decried the abuses and atrocities inherent in the system. But Taney's acceptance and loyal support of the South's peculiar institution necessarily converted him into an implacable foe of free black people. He believed that "the presence of free negroes within a society of white people, where other negroes were held as slaves, constituted a menace to public well being."[35] In Frederick, Taney served temporarily as vice president of a local branch of the American Colonization Society.

Although Taney held various federal offices from 1831 until 1864, he maintained and frequented a residence in Baltimore from 1823 until his wife's death in 1855. A devout Catholic and an active member of the Baltimore Cathedral congregation, Taney generously availed the Sulpician priests, the Carmelite Nuns, and the First Provincial Council convened in Baltimore in 1829 of his legal skills. As legal counsel to the Society of St. Sulpice in Baltimore, Taney corresponded both officially and informally with Louis Deluol and John Chanche. Certainly these Sulpician priests apprised Taney of James Joubert's project of the black Oblate religious community and school—if Taney's own participation in the Baltimore Catholic community had not already acquainted him with the existence of the Oblate Sisters. Deluol and Chanche probably also confided their reservations about the Oblate community to Taney, who—given his convictions about the inherent inferiority of black people—undoubtedly shared their opinions.[36]

Although a respected lawyer, Taney ignored the evidence embodied in the successful existence from 1828 of the free black Oblate Sisters of Providence and their school for black girls in Baltimore. The Oblate community defied and disproved Taney's mantra of alleged free black debasement and degradation chanted in 1832 and reiterated in the Dred Scott decision of 1857. The Oblate annals and other records documented the support rendered the Oblate Sisters by several members of Baltimore's Roman Catholic white elite families. The absence of the name of Roger Brooke Taney from these Oblate records exemplified how race and the ramifications of slavery circumscribed the responses of antebellum citizens to the Oblate Sisters of Providence.

RACE FORMED THE primary filter through which antebellum white Baltimoreans perceived the Oblate Sisters of Providence. However, ethnicity also mediated white perceptions of and responses to the Oblate Sisters. In the late eighteenth and early nineteenth centuries, white Baltimoreans, in sharp contrast to their reception of the white San Domingan refugees, had received the black Francophone immigrants from the Caribbean inhospitably.[37] Racial differences superseded ethnic similarities in the perceptions of white Baltimoreans. The Oblate Sisters also claimed European immigrant roots, as a community "French in language, in sympathy, and in habit of life."[38] Ethnic categorization often resulted in discrimination against European immigrants in the United States. But cultural identification as Francophone by white Americans in Baltimore actually mitigated the negatively perceived racial status of the Oblate Sisters. Ethnic differences between Franco- and Anglophone black people superseded racial similarities for white Baltimoreans.[39] Certainly the Francophone cultural heritage of the sisters, in concert with their Roman Catholic faith, recommended these black women religious to their supporters among the French Sulpician priests and the white San Domingan émigré community.

The Chatards and Ducatels, two wealthy white families from Saint Domingue, figure prominently in accounts of Oblate history. In 1829 Dr. Pierre Chatard offered the sisters the house on Richmond Street that remained their convent until the city of Baltimore bought the property in 1870. Although he did not donate the property to them outright, as some benefactors had for some white sisterhoods, Chatard sold the house to the Oblate community for $2,000, absorbing an $800 loss. He contributed $12 annually to the Oblate mission from 1831. Dr. Chatard and his sons also provided medical care for the Oblate Sisters, as they did for the other Baltimore religious communities. Madame Ferdinand Chatard contributed $150 toward the education of an Oblate student between September 1833 and April 1836. In addition to aiding the subscription begun at the formation of the Oblate community, Madame Ducatel modestly subsidized some Oblate scholars. Besides the Chatards and the Ducatels, a Madame De Larue lent Joubert $266 in 1834 and $228 in 1836 for the Oblate community.[40]

Significantly, neither the Chatards nor the Ducatels isolated themselves in an exclusively French émigré enclave in Baltimore. At least from 1809, Madame Chatard fulfilled her Easter religious obligations of confession and communion with the Sulpician priest Jean Tessier at St. Mary's Seminary Lower Chapel, serving the French émigré congregations. From 1825 the Easter Duty Lists included the names of two Ducatel women. But Dr. Peter Chatard contributed $500 and Edward Ducatel, $600 toward the completion of the Baltimore Cathedral. Furthermore, both men numbered among the first pewholders of the cathedral in 1821, a congregation characterized as decidedly Anglo-American.[41] The Chatards and the Ducatels consequently demonstrated a certain ethnic ecumenism in maintaining a presence in both French and Anglo-American sites of worship.

No exclusive identification with the French ethnic community constrained the Oblate Sisters from soliciting support from various sources, regardless of their ethnic origins. Most accounts of early Oblate history focus exclusively on the Chatard and the Ducatel families as resources for the sisters.[42] But Oblate annals revealed that in 1829 Joubert decided "to find some charitable friend, some rich person"[43] to subsidize the purchase of a suitable Oblate convent and school. Significantly, he resolved to approach the eminent Catholic of English ancestry, Charles Carroll, first. Only the fortuitous intervention of Dr. Peter Chatard with a counterproposal of his own property dissuaded Joubert from approaching Carroll. As discussed earlier, Carroll made modest annual contributions to the Oblate community until his death. Emily Harper, Carroll's granddaughter, proved a faithful benefactor to the Oblate community throughout the antebellum years. Oblate records first noted her support on Easter Sunday, 31 March 1839, with the entry: "There were also two beautiful candlesticks which Mademoiselle Emil[y] Harper had given to the chapel."[44]

Oblate records refer frequently to benefactors with the British surname Williamson. Between 1828 and 1831 Oblate ledgers listed seven modest monthly tuition payments jointly subscribed by Mdes. Ducatel and Williamson. Joubert's Jesuit friend Anthony Kohlmann, who facilitated the 1831 papal recognition of the Oblate community, mentioned a C. Williamson on an informal note inscribed on the reverse of the papal rescript. Perhaps this C. Williamson referred to Mr. Charles Williamson, who gave the Oblate Sisters an interest-free loan of $500 toward the construction of their new chapel in 1836. Available evidence does not indicate whether Charles Williamson belonged to the very affluent and socially prominent David Williamson family. However, Charles Williamson apparently achieved substantial prominence within the Baltimore Catholic community in his own right. He held a pew in the cathedral congregation from 1835 and served as a member of the standing committee on repairs for the cathedral. Between 1843 and 1879, Charles A. Williamson served as a trustee of the Roman Catholic Congregation of the Cathedral.[45]

Evidently, neither Joubert nor the Oblate Sisters considered themselves the product, preserve, or protégés of the Francophone ethnic community exclusively. In 1827 the French and Sulpician archbishop of Baltimore Ambrose Maréchal would not implement Joubert's proposed school for colored girls. Nevertheless, in 1828 the persistent Joubert sought and gained the approval of Maréchal's English successor, James Whitfield, not only for the school but also for a black sisterhood to conduct it. Like the universal Roman Catholic Church itself, the Oblate community solicited support from a multi-ethnic constituency.[46]

The Francophone cultural heritage of the Oblate community formed only one dimension of the role ethnicity played in the antebellum experience of the Oblate Sisters of Providence. The huge influx of European immigrants between 1830 and 1860—the period in American Catholic church history frequently identified as the era of the immigrant church—so preoccupied the American hierarchy, itself staffed by an overwhelmingly immigrant clergy,[47] that the plight of black Catholics in general and the Oblate Sisters in particular received scant attention. Referring to the church's marginalization of black Catholics in the nineteenth century, one historian has noted, "The general periodization, particularly 'immigrant church,' is simply meaningless to their experience."[48] Arguably, the immigrant church periodization proved to be no more meaningless in the experience of nineteenth-century black Catholics than the institution of slavery proved to be in the experience of the antebellum free black population. Black Catholics confronted and coexisted with immigrants in their world as much as free black people confronted and coexisted with the institution of slavery in theirs. Both groups functioned within and responded to cultural milieus defined and informed by massive European immigration and the institution of slavery, respectively.

Most of the German and Irish Catholics who settled in antebellum Baltimore enjoyed the potential if not the reality of pastoral care from clergy of their same ethnic identity. The absence of a viable black Catholic clergy in the United States precluded this comfort and affirmation for nineteenth-century black Catholics.[49] In the emphatically ethnic nineteenth-century church, black Catholics depended on the kindness and ministry of strangers.

During this period the Oblate Sisters received spiritual direction from the French Sulpicians, German Redemptorists, multi-ethnic Jesuits, and English Josephite priests. The personal proclivities and personalities of the successive Oblate spiritual directors proved as critical as their respective ethnic identities and societal affiliations in influencing their interactions with the Oblate community. Individual members of these orders proved genuinely sympathetic to the Oblate Sisters and their mission. But genuine empathy based on a common racial experience in the United States eluded the Oblate Sisters in their relationships with their spiritual directors. Issues of race and ethnicity profoundly affected the interactions between the Oblate Sisters of Providence and their fundamentally European church and their predominantly white society.

THE BLOSSOMING OF THE Oblate Sisters of Providence in 1830s Baltimore proved a remarkable achievement. As black people, as women, as Roman Catholics, as a religious community, the Oblate Sisters formed the antithesis of the white, male, Protestant family patriarch who typified the empowered citizen in nineteenth-century American society. Nevertheless, this community of determined, committed black women—some seventeen members strong in 1839 —challenged racist preconceptions about black women within church and society by its very existence. The popular imagination occasionally romanticizes religious life as a pampered sinecure of seclusion from the real world. Far from an escape from harsh realities, Oblate life entailed physical deprivation, arduous labor, long hours, and straitened circumstances. Oblate Sisters, braced by their religious faith, further endured the mistrust and antipathy of white American society. Without doubt, this black sisterhood experienced life's harsh realities as much as most antebellum free black people did.

Baltimore enjoyed a reputation for its exceptionalism in southern slave society. But Baltimore proved as vulnerable to domination by the institution of slavery and its corollary convictions about the inherent inferiority of all black people as the rest of United States society. As free women of color in 1830s Baltimore, the Oblate Sisters endured the escalation of antiblack sentiment engendered by both Nat Turner's slave insurrection and the rise of the abolition movement. Throughout the 1830s the white citizenry of Baltimore countered evidence of positive support for the Oblate Sisters of Providence with equally compelling evidence of disdain toward them as both black people and as a sisterhood.

CHAPTER SEVEN

Everything Seemed to Be Progressing

THE OBLATE SISTERS AND THE
END OF AN ERA, 1840–1843

❖ ❖

The 1840s began auspiciously for the Oblate Sisters of Providence. In 1840 three individuals came to live in the community, although not as sisters. One of the new residents, Sarah Willigman, would contribute significantly to the Oblate community in the future; another one, Elizabeth Charles Arieu, had already done so in the past. Early that year five-year-old Sarah Willigman—the future Sister M. Theresa Catherine Willigman—and her younger sister Charity arrived at the convent. Their mother, a convert to Catholicism, had requested on her death bed that the Oblate Sisters raise her daughters. Evidently, her Protestant husband did not challenge her request. The sisters acceded unanimously to Mrs. Willigman's wishes, "in spite of the difficult [financial] situation of the house." On 27 February 1840 Oblate Superior Mary Lange herself accompanied the children, "who cried all the way and seemed to be of a sweet and good disposition," to the convent. Late in that year, in November, the elderly Elizabeth Charles Arieu arranged to board with the sisters.[1]

New Oblate vocations also contributed to the growth of the community in the early 1840s. Until the death of Oblate director James Hector Joubert in November 1843, the volume of candidates exceeded the number of members the Oblate community could sustain. Consequently, the sisters continued to enforce rigorous standards of piety, ability, and commitment for Oblate membership.

Georgianna Addison, manumitted from slavery at age twenty in 1832, had applied for admission to the Oblate Sisters persistently but without success, "not fulfilling all the required conditions." However, in September 1841 the sisters and Joubert concluded that "her long perseverance had proved the truth of her vocation and the Will of God," and they admitted Addison, who brought a dowry of $200. But two members expressed continued doubts and proposed that the community test Addison's vocation before she should receive the novice's habit. The rest of the community rejected this additional condition and supported Addison's cause. The two in opposition claimed that Addison's "extraordinary appearance" had prompted their proposal.[2]

No extant evidence supports one scholar's contention that "extraordinary appearance" referred to Addison's beauty. However, Addison's manumission documents described her as "of dark complexion, 5'½", has no notable marks or scars." Furthermore, U.S. census takers categorized "Ann Addison" in 1850 and "Sister Gabriel" in 1860 as black, not mulatto. These circumstances suggest that Addison's documented dark complexion may have generated concerns about her "extraordinary appearance" among some individuals within the Oblate community. As a community, the antebellum Oblate Sisters of Providence did not discriminate against candidates on the basis of color, as their vote to accept Addison indicated. On 16 January 1842 Georgianna Addison entered the Oblate community as Sister Louise Gabriel; on 13 February 1842, she received the novice's habit.[3]

On 30 January 1842, two weeks after Addison's arrival, Joubert declared that "on account of the sufficient number of Sisters with us at present," the community could not accept any of the other candidates then seeking admission, "unless they fulfill completely all the conditions exacted by the rule."[4] At that time the Oblate community comprised sixteen sisters. In August 1842 a clergyman in Washington, D.C., submitted the names of two candidates for Oblate membership and Joubert himself proposed a candidate from Baltimore. By this date Oblate financial resources "did not at all permit the taking on of a new obligation without assurance in advance of the ability of the subjects who would present themselves."[5] Consequently, financial exigency compelled the community to adopt as policy what they had rejected as contrary to Oblate custom almost a year earlier when considering Addison's application: a prenovitiate test or trial period. By August 1842 the sisters reasoned that a six-month on-site trial would benefit candidate and community mutually, because it would allow each to assess the other in the actual experience of community life. Furthermore, as the candidates were now to provide their own clothing through the year of their novitiate, the newly instituted trial period relieved the Oblate community of assuming total financial responsibility for candidates for eighteen months. Ann Johnson, a candidate from Baltimore, paid part of her dowry in October and entered the convent on trial in November 1842.

In May 1843 Joubert corresponded with two more priests in Washington, D.C., concerning "those who wish to become Sisters in the Community and whom you have in training." He reiterated the conditions that candidates be "capable of rendering great service to the institution" and that they pay the $400 dowry stipulated by the archbishop.[6] In spite of the continuing interest in Oblate membership demonstrated by black Catholic women in Baltimore and Washington, D.C., Sister Louise Gabriel Addison remained the only candidate who entered the Oblate community in the 1840s and persevered in her vocation. The limited financial resources of the Oblate community afforded them fewer opportunities to waive the dowry requirement for even the worthiest of candidates as the community grew. Furthermore, the generally straitened economic circumstances of the black lay community produced fewer candidates who could pay the full dowry requirement. Declining Oblate admissions in the 1840s proved less a function of diminishing spiritual resources in the black Catholic community than of diminished financial resources.

Deaths further depleted the ranks of the Oblate Sisters in the early 1840s. Sister Chantal (Laurette Noel), who had suffered recurring attacks of apoplexy for a year, died on 23 June 1841. Sister Philomena (Laura Johnson), after enduring confinement to the infirmary for several months, died on 15 March 1843. Finally, Oblate cofounder and spiritual director James Joubert died on 5 November 1843, after suffering from declining health for several years.[7] With Joubert's death, other forces would intrude to foreclose Oblate community growth.

BUSINESS MATTERS remained an important aspect of Oblate community life in the early 1840s. A financial statement prepared in January 1842 included a detailed account of Oblate transactions with the firm Didier Petit in Lyons, France. Making vestments for American clergy continued to be a profitable enterprise for the sisters. Between March 1836 and January 1842 the community had received almost $11,500 worth of merchandise from which they sold over $8,000 worth of vestments and had made, but not yet sold, vestments worth almost $2,000. Between January 1840 and January 1842 the Oblate Sisters had realized a net gain of $227 on their vestment venture.[8]

Yet, the sisters did not experience unalloyed profit and prosperity in their business transactions. Like other entrepreneurs, the Oblate Sisters encountered the vagaries of the market and the caprice of supply and demand. Their profit margin declined from $440 in 1836 to $227 over a two-year period from 1840 to 1842.[9] The nature of the commodity they produced in part explained this shrinking profitability. Although clothing, vestments resembled durable goods in that their owners reserved them for occasional or ceremonial use, ignored seasonal and fashion trend turnover, and replaced them only in the event of loss, damage, or wear. Prelates John Baptist Purcell of Cincinnati purchased vestments worth more than $3,000 between 1837 and 1839; Samuel Eccleston of Baltimore, more than $1,500 worth of merchandise in 1840. Carmelite correspondence in 1841 inadvertently attested the quality of Oblate handiwork. Referring to Archbishop Eccleston's vestments, the author noted that "Sister Ann Alexis, who has all the Bishop's vestments under her charge . . . requested me to mention to you also that he is well supplied with stoles, rich and beautiful."[10] Clerics undoubtedly considered vestment purchases capital investments, not annual expenses. Furthermore, many members of the clergy ministering to Catholics in the United States had outfitted themselves with vestments before they had emigrated from Europe.

The Oblate Sisters also encountered problems with their supplier. In correspondence with Didier Petit in April 1843, an irate Joubert inquired about a shipment several months overdue. He complained, "I see that I must tell you: everyday new demands are made of the Sisters. They would have sold a large amount after nearly six months, but this is impossible, not being better stocked. . . . It is no longer possible to satisfy these requests. The Sisters lose and you do too." Joubert concluded the letter by threatening "to apply to Paris, or to New York, or to some merchants who will better assist me in continuing this good work."[11]

The itemized list of vestments the Oblate Sisters offered had filled two pages in the national Catholic directory from 1836 through 1839. In the 1840 through 1844 editions of this publication, however, the drastically curtailed advertisements did not mention the Oblate Sisters at all. The notices merely advised that "vestments of different colours and of various qualities and prices may be procured by applying to Rev. H. Joubert, St. Mary's Seminary, Baltimore."[12] Such abbreviated advertising may have reflected the reduced profitability of the vestment-making venture for the Oblate Sisters as much as their reduced inventory of vestments resulting from both sales and supply problems.

The Oblate community's financial statement for January 1840 to January 1842, figured to the quarter-penny, documented the sisters' continued practice of hard work, discipline, frugal management, and self-reliance. They balanced expenditures of $6,847.8925 with an income of $6,847.8925. Budget itemizations like "Selling of small articles by Sister Therese—$65.72" and "Particular sewing made by working Sisters—$121" demonstrated Oblate self-reliance. In the 1840—42 interval the sisters managed to retire $569.30 of the principal of their debt that then totalled $1,968.375. To eliminate this debt, the community intended to sell the Noel Wilmington estate, valued at $1,600, and items they had worth $800 for a total of $2,400, leaving "a surplus in our favor."[13]

The Oblate Sisters maintained solvency only with significant help from their friends. Joubert contributed almost $200 from his account at St. Mary's College to the Oblate assets. The $287.35 loan from black contributor Oliver Concklin that Joubert had negotiated in 1836 toward funding construction of the Oblate chapel remained outstanding in 1842, although the original terms of the agreement had stipulated full repayment by 1838. Joubert's $660.67 loan from Jane Russell, with terms identical to the loan from her son-in-law Oliver Concklin, also remained unpaid. Nevertheless, Jane Russell had lent the Oblate community an additional $224 in the interim, so that Oblate indebtedness to her amounted to $884.67 by 1842. A third individual black contributor, Mr. Francis Loiseau, had lent the Oblate Sisters $200. The black Holy Family Society also continued to support "our convent." In addition to their unrepaid $222 loan made to the Oblate community in 1836, the society advanced the sisters another loan of $88, interest free, and donated gifts and products worth $192 for a total subsidy of more than $500 by 1842. Black benefactors had provided $1,682.05 of the total $1,968.375 passive debt the Oblate community carried in 1842.[14]

Certain figures the 1840—42 financial statement reported suggested the precarious nature of Oblate solvency in the early 1840s. The Noel family's Wilmington estate represented a major, nonrenewable resource. Although its intended sale would help liquidate an outstanding debt, its loss would deprive the Oblate community of an income-generating asset. Likewise, the $800 in personal property the sisters had inventoried to sell represented a liquidation of nonrenewable assets. Furthermore, Joubert may have inflated unrealistically the projected proceeds of $2,400 from the sale of this real and personal property. In 1843 an item he valued at $127 sold for only $41.[15]

Dowries, the second largest source of income for the Oblate Sisters at almost $4,500 from 1828 through 1835, had plummeted in the early 1840s to the single dowry of $200. In November 1842 the Oblate Sisters initiated collections at Masses in their chapel to augment income. Collections produced negligible amounts ranging from a high of $3.08 on the first day to a low of $0.28 on Christmas Day 1842, and averaging $0.70 for the four months the Oblate annalist recorded the amounts.[16]

The economic plight of the Oblate Sisters remained readily apparent through the 1840s. In 1847 German Redemptorist priests invited members of the recently established Bavarian order, the School Sisters of Notre Dame, to staff three parochial schools in Baltimore. Within two months of her October arrival in the city, Mother M. Theresa Gerhardinger commented perceptively on the financial conditions of two Baltimore sisterhoods: "The Carmelite sisters here, who do not own a farm and are not provided with capital, experience great difficulties. They are obliged to teach school for their livelihood. The same is true of the colored sisters, who cannot improve their situation. In fact they are in danger of dispersing, but some priests helped them by increasing the number of the school children, and entrusting more children of the poor to them for education. This is the harsh fate of religious societies that are not provided with capital, which bears a large annual interest: 6% is the lowest rate."[17] Without an endowment or substantial income-generating assets, even the most austere and frugal lifestyle, fiscal discipline, and hard work could only forestall the relentless encroachment of insolvency for the Oblate community.

THE OBLATE SISTERS continued to contend with aspects of their ethnic identity during the 1840s. In spite of its Francophone cultural beginnings, this black religious community had attracted members from Anglophone backgrounds in significant numbers from its inception. Of the several candidates who aspired to Oblate membership in the early 1840s, the three identified by name— Georgianna Addison, Ann Johnson, and Jane Somerville[18]—all bore Anglo surnames. Ethnic exclusivity frequently proved counterproductive for people of color—free or slave, Franco- or Anglophone—in a racist society. Unlike the antebellum colored populations in New Orleans and Charleston, the antebellum black community in Baltimore understood that for most white Americans, race superseded other criteria in determining social status.

Nevertheless, if in Oblate membership and student enrollment ethnic identity proved a nonissue, Francophone tendencies persisted in liturgical observances in the Oblate chapel through 1843. Charter Oblate Sister Marie Therese Duchemin assumed the duties of community annalist in 1838.[19] She shared with Lange strong Francophile predilections. It proved no coincidence that beginning with Duchemin's tenure as annalist in September 1838, Oblate annals noted every instance of French hymns or sermons at Oblate chapel services. This trend continued in the early 1840s. On Easter Sunday in April 1841, she noted, "Mass began a quarter of an hour earlier than usual, but what was more remarkable, we had a sermon in French preached by Father Director. Until now in spite of all the representation made on the subject, he had continued to preach in English; and when we had sermons in French, they were always preached by strange priests, but at last he decided to give a French sermon a month. He chose the Second Sunday to this effect. The first day there were not many people because they did not know."[20]

The monthly French sermons in the Oblate chapel occurred almost without exception until Joubert's death in 1843. In October 1842 Duchemin noted, "The usual sermon (French) was preached by the Reverend Father Fredet after the gospel and not at the end of Mass as Father Joubert ordinarily did through an excess of compliance with the Americans."[21] Joubert was not the instigator of the Francophone innovations in the Oblate chapel. He resisted instituting French sermons and accommodated Anglophone worshipers by rearranging the order of the liturgy on Sundays featuring such sermons. Evidently, Duchemin concurred with neither concession to "Americans." Although she cited "all the representation" in favor of French sermons, the available evidence does not clarify the extent of the Francophone impulse within the Oblate community beyond Duchemin and, perhaps, Lange in the early 1840s.

Duchemin referred only indirectly to her own election as mother superior in June 1841 for the customary three-year term: they "named her Superior who had received the majority of the votes."[22] Such a modest—and guarded—acknowledgment of her election to the office of Oblate superior accurately reflected the clouded circumstances under which it occurred. In the preceding election cycle, Duchemin had lost a position to Sister Chantal Noel. The annalist had noted of the 24 June 1838 election, "As there existed a division, some contentions arose among the Sisters for the election of the assistant superior. The Director, to put an end to this division, and with the advice of the superior, thought he ought to use his right and named Sister Chantal assistant superior."[23] In 1841, Noel, the assistant superior overwhelmingly favored to assume the office of superior, had died the night before the community election. Duchemin thus acquired the Oblate superiorship only after the death of the expected winner.[24]

The occasionally harsh assessments of Oblate novices first apparent in the annals in 1838 continued in the early 1840s. In June 1841 the sisters evaluated the readiness of their cohort of novices for advancement and decided to postpone their profession of vows until mid-August. In late August the community postponed the advancement of the novices twice more, causing the exasperated annalist to assert, "It is something to have to deal with silly women!"[25] Apparently this group of novices, never identified by name or number in the annals, did not persevere in their vocations. Oblate records cited no profession of vows between Sister Angelica Gideon on 9 March 1841 and Sister Louise Gabriel Addison on 9 March 1843. On 23 January 1842, one week after Sister Louise Gabriel Addison entered the community, the novices again formed the principal subject of the weekly assembly. Consequently, "Father Director spoke strongly on the reading of the rules; this did not please the Sisters very much because there was a new Sister this day."[26]

Even more tolerant members of the community occasionally concurred with Duchemin's often severe appraisals of the novices. But Duchemin trained her critical perspective on professed Oblate members with equally unrelenting intensity. In the assembly of 26 October 1840, "Father Director read only two articles of the rule which furnished him with ample means for scolding. One of these articles had been violated the day before."[27] According to Duchemin's records, vigilance against "the faults which exist in all religious communities and which naturally would exist in ours"[28] formed a recurrent theme in Joubert's instructions to the sisters. On 3 April 1842 Duchemin noted, "It has been some time since we had Assembly, but today Father Director assembled the Sisters to scold them."[29] In the assembly of 25 September 1842 Joubert warned the community against "useless visits": "He spoke heatedly of the dangers to which we would expose ourselves by neglecting our own affairs in this regard, so much so that the astonished Sisters felt that there was a snake in the grass somewhere. And they were not mistaken. Undoubtedly Father Joubert knows well what he is talking about and has some ones of us in mind, as this is his style."[30]

Duchemin's own style warrants consideration. As mother superior from 1841 to 1844, she had the power, the authority, and the responsibility to familiarize herself with all community members and events. The Oblate community, in her assessment, merited scoldings from their spiritual director. A strict adherent to the rules, Duchemin approved when Joubert "observed to the letter that which is said in *Christian Perfection* in regard to the observance of the rules, 'that the reprimand and correction should follow the faults against the rules so that one can say that the observance of the rules is in its vigor.'" She noted that the love that the sisters bore Joubert and his manner of censure "in a way so polite" effectively ameliorated the sting of the reprimand.[31] Evidently, Duchemin failed to cultivate or imitate either characteristic she noted in Joubert. She suspected "snakes in the grass" in the community, not based on evidence but on her own prejudicial predisposition.

Occasionally Duchemin found Joubert's communal scoldings insufficient and she offered her own critical observations. Of the Oblate Sisters' first effort to sing a particular liturgical passage at a High Mass in 1840 she noted, "We succeeded only in such a way as to reach the end."[32] On Palm Sunday in 1842 she commented, "That which was remarkable was that the three candles in triangle was very badly made and the bouquet badly arranged and very old and Father Director did not scold."[33] When in May 1843 visiting prelate John Baptist Purcell of Cincinnati encouraged the Oblate Sisters "to keep and increase the virtue of humility that he believes we possess already," annalist Duchemin noted gratuitously, "whereas we are still in the first degree of this adorable virtue."[34] Her response may have represented her humble deflection of a compliment on Oblate virtue—or it may have indicated her own doubts about the spiritual worthiness of her community, then fifteen years old. Oblate annalist and superior Duchemin found fault with her community where Joubert and others did not.

As the sisters attempted to resolve communal tensions caused by generational, ethnic, and personality differences, they continued to refine their relationship with the Baltimore black Catholic laity. As products of the very community that they committed themselves to serve as religious, the Oblate Sisters remained cognizant of the distinctions between the spiritual needs of the general public and their own prerogatives as a religious community. Although only a few people were present at Mass in the Oblate chapel on 6 January 1842, the priest celebrating the Mass refrained from directing an instruction to the sisters "because he did not like to speak to religious in front of worldly people."[35] That same month, according to the Oblate annalist, Joubert addressed a sermon "not only to the seculars but also to the Sisters."[36] The annalist consciously distinguished between the laity and the sisterhood.

The black Catholic community remained supportive of the Oblate Sisters during the early 1840s. It provided aspiring candidates for Oblate religious life and subsidized their convent, chapel, and school consistently. For three consecutive Sundays in December 1840 the sisters suspended services in their chapel to allow members of the congregation to paint it as a "means to make reparation, which made the chapel very nice." When services reconvened on Christmas Day 1840, the sisters acknowledged the gift of two handsome reliquaries for their chapel donated by a parishioner, Mr. Dorsey, "so that the Sisters would not forget to pray for him, above all after his death."[37] The Dorsey family did not forget the Oblate Sisters either. The Dorseys would remain steadfast supporters of the Oblate community well into the twentieth century.[38] The Oblate Sisters and the black Catholic community maintained their affirming and supportive relationship established at the formation of the sisterhood in 1828.

The Oblate school appeared infrequently in Oblate records between 1840 and 1843. On 8 September 1840, Joubert discussed with Oblate Superior Lange "the means to take to reorganize the school and take care of the children,"[39] including appointing a sister as prefect, or head teacher. When on 10 January 1841 Lange informed Joubert that the community had not yet accomplished his proposed reorganization, specifically "naming one Sister head teacher whose duty it would be to maintain as good order as possible . . . so that it might be well understood, he explained how he intended it to be, etc."[40] Joubert apparently urged the appointment of a head teacher in order to align Oblate school administration more closely with that of the other convent academies in the archdiocese. The Sisters of Charity had stipulated the office of head school mistress in their Constitutions of 1812. School reopened in September 1841 "with so few children that it was not necessary to have a change of classes."[41] The sisters considered small enrollments at the beginning of the year a normal occurrence.

Joubert's illness and unspecified other reasons prevented the customary public examination and distribution of prizes at the close of the school year in 1842. Instead, the Oblate Sisters feted the students and their parents at a luncheon. This event made parents and children alike "much more pleased than usual, because they are always dissatisfied when their children do not get a prize."[42] At the conclusion of the 1843 school year, four Sulpician priests conducted the public examinations, but no prize distribution occurred, "for the same reasons as the preceding year."[43]

THE 1840S ALSO BEGAN auspiciously for the Oblate Sisters in terms of their participation in the activities of the Roman Catholic Church on the local, national, and international levels. In February 1840 vandals broke into Baltimore's Cathedral of the Assumption, stole the ciborium—a covered container for storing consecrated communion wafers—and discarded the communion hosts in the process. This sacrilegious act incensed the entire Baltimore Catholic community, including the Oblate Sisters and the black congregation at St. Frances Chapel. In response, the Oblate annalist reported that "Father Director made the Stations of the Cross publicly, in order to unite with the other churches in trying to repair in some way the outrage done to Our Lord in the Sacrament of His Love at the Cathedral by the miserable thieves."[44] A popular religious devotion commemorating Christ's journey to Calvary, his death, and burial, the Stations of the Cross utilize fourteen pictures or crosses representing each station or event along the way on the walls of Catholic churches.

In March 1842, on Holy Thursday, four Oblate Sisters and the older students renewed the custom, unobserved for several years, of visiting local churches to venerate the Blessed Sacrament. They visited the cathedral at the corner of Mulberry and Cathedral Streets, St. Mary's Seminary Lower Chapel on Paca Street, and the chapel of the Visitation Sisters at the corner of Park and Centre Streets.[45]

In June 1842 the Pope proclaimed a solemn jubilee with plenary indulgences and graces to induce the faithful worldwide to pray for the relief of the beleaguered church in Spain. The Oblate chapel congregation participated in this international unified prayer effort. In the printed circular announcing this jubilee in all public churches in Baltimore, Archbishop Samuel Eccleston added a parenthetical note: "the Chapels of St. Mary's, the two convents, the Coloured Sisters, and St. Vincent's Retreat are considered 'Public Churches' in the sense above contemplated."[46] Eccleston segregated the Oblate community in the circular from the two convents of white sisters and called them only "the Coloured Sisters." Furthermore, the black sisters appeared in the document literally as an afterthought—written in above the text, a caret indicating the point for their insertion. Nevertheless, in this notice in June 1842, Eccleston had at least acknowledged the Oblate Sisters as a legitimate constituency in the church.

In December 1842 Joubert read another circular letter from Eccleston concerning a request from the governor of Maryland to observe a day of thanksgiving. In compliance with this request from a public authority, sanctioned by episcopal authority, the Oblate community and St. Frances Chapel congregation attended a High Mass in the chapel on the appointed day. In January 1843 the Oblate members enrolled in another devotional society, the Archconfraternity of the Most Holy and Immaculate Heart of Mary.[47] In participating in these church-sanctioned activities and organizations, the Oblate Sisters of Providence and the black Catholic congregation that worshiped in their chapel united with other Catholics worldwide. They transcended racial and national distinctions to function in the universal realm of the Roman Catholic Church and to experience spiritual, if not social, equality.

The fact that, starting in the early 1840s, several white sisterhoods expanded their educational ministry to include black pupils further substantiated the impression that "everything seemed to be progressing" for black Catholics nationwide. The Sisters of Mount Carmel continued to direct the St. Claude Street School for Colored in New Orleans through the antebellum period. The Sisters of Our Lady of Mercy in Charleston, South Carolina, reopened the segregated black school so hastily abandoned in 1835 and succeeded in maintaining the school until 1848. The Sisters of Charity in Mobile, Alabama, conducted a school for free girls of color for a few years during the 1840s.[48]

The Sisters of St. Joseph of Carondelet proved very persistent in their efforts to educate black children. On 5 February 1845, three sisters opened St. Joseph's School for the Colored in St. Louis, Missouri. The school enrolled "about eighty children all good and well behaved (there were about twenty little boys) and they were already making fine progress." In addition to their school, the sisters "also prepared slaves for the reception of the sacraments, and this displeased the whites very much."[49] After a mob repeatedly attacked the school in one night in 1846, the mayor advised Bishop Peter Richard Kenrick to close the school. The Missouri state legislature passed a law in 1847 prohibiting any school for the instruction of black people, under penalty of fine and imprisonment. Nevertheless, the Sisters of St. Joseph conducted a school for free black girls in St. Louis from 1853 to 1863. Sisters of Mercy also opened a school for children of color in St. Louis in 1856.[50] These white sisters often demonstrated great personal courage in their efforts to maintain schools for a black clientele during the antebellum period. Nevertheless, with few exceptions, after a brief existence these schools routinely succumbed to the animosity of a white public unwilling to tolerate the extension of educational opportunities— even in segregated settings—to the black population in their midst.

IN 1840 AND 1843 the Fourth and Fifth Provincial Councils convened in Baltimore. As had occurred during the preceding three councils, visiting prelates extended customary courtesies and favors to the Oblate Sisters while in town. On 28 May 1840 Mathias Loras, now bishop of Dubuque, sang a Pontifical Mass and preached in French in the Oblate chapel. Before leaving, the bishop breakfasted, conversed cordially with the sisters, and blessed the community. That evening, cleric Peter Paul Lefevre of Detroit "sang Vespers, after which he visited the house and left singing the praises of our establishment."[51] On 19 May 1843, during the Fifth Provincial Council, Lefevre, now bishop of Detroit, said Mass in the Oblate chapel and visited their school. The second visit occurred during the administration of Sister Marie Therese Duchemin. Francis Patrick Kenrick, bishop of Philadelphia and future archbishop of Baltimore, celebrated three Masses in as many days in the Oblate chapel. The Oblate annalist remarked of Kenrick that "he has lived up to all that he has said regarding his affection for our endeavor."[52]

John Baptist Purcell, bishop of Cincinnati, prefaced his Mass in the Oblate chapel on 16 May 1843 with "some words to us to share with us the satisfaction that he felt in celebrating Mass in the Chapel of St. Frances." After breakfast Purcell requested that the children sing and then he quizzed them on their religious knowledge. The students "responded rather well, undoubtedly his kindness had encouraged them to overcome their ordinary shyness."[53] In the 1860s Purcell would distinguish himself as the first American Roman Catholic bishop to advocate publicly emancipation of the slaves.[54]

Clerics visited the Oblate community for reasons and on occasions other than provincial councils in the early 1840s. On 10 December 1941 Joseph Rosati, the bishop of St. Louis newly assigned as apostolic delegate to Haiti, came to the Oblate convent accompanied by Joubert. Extant evidence does not indicate whether the Oblate Sisters ever knew that in July 1841 the papacy had issued apostolic briefs appointing Joubert vicar-apostolic to the Republic of Haiti and elevating him to the rank of bishop. The Propaganda Fide, or papal office for foreign missions, had enjoined Archbishop Eccleston to consent to the appointment and to urge Joubert to accept it. That December, Rosati came to Baltimore specifically to recruit Joubert for Haiti. Joubert's debilitating illness ultimately prevented his departure from Baltimore. Rosati's initial negotiations with Haitian president Jean Pierre Boyer appeared promising. A Baltimore Catholic publication reported in 1842, "President Boyer was much pleased to learn [of] the existence of the society of colored sisters in Baltimore, and has directed the secretary of state to write to Rev. H. Joubert, their superior, for the purposes of procuring their services in Hayti."[55] In spite of these propitious preliminaries, Haiti and the papacy did not formalize diplomatic relations until 1860.

In 1841 the papacy directed Bishops Francis Patrick Kenrick of Philadelphia and John Hughes of New York to send priests to Liberia, activating the initiative the Second Provincial Council had passed in 1833. Kenrick pursued the matter vigorously, first approaching the American Colonization Society unsuccessfully and then the Maryland State Colonization Society, which granted assurances of cooperation, support, and land for a Catholic mission in Maryland-in-Liberia at Cape Palmas. In October 1841 Eccleston joined the effort and encouraged pastors in counties in southern Maryland to advocate colonization among their black parishioners. The Diocese of Philadelphia collected $2,400, including a personal donation of $900 from Kenrick, to support this first American foreign mission; the Archdiocese of Baltimore contributed $265.

Between 10 and 20 December 1841, Jesuit priests Edward Barron from Philadelphia and John Kelly from New York celebrated Mass in the Oblate chapel and conversed with the sisters frequently before embarking on their mission to Liberia. Barron was "very fond of our house in hopes of one day having a colony of Sisters for his country." On 20 December 1841 Barron and Kelly sailed for Cape Palmas. When the two missionaries departed, the Oblate Sisters "prayed with all our heart for the success of their enterprise."[56]

In spite of the heartfelt prayers of the Oblate Sisters of Providence for the

Liberian Mission, the project proved abortive. In 1842 fewer than twenty black Catholics lived in Liberia. American black people remained intransigent in their opposition to colonization schemes. Disease, cultural misunderstandings, religious denominational rivalries, and international politics further hampered the earnest efforts of Barron and Kelly, who abandoned the Cape Palmas Mission in 1844.[57]

Between 1840 and 1843 the Oblate Sisters of Providence experienced continued community growth, solvency, and a secure relationship with the Baltimore black Catholic laity. The sisters further defined their bicultural ethnic identity, survived communal tensions created by generational, ethnic, and personality differences, and participated more completely as an acknowledged constituency in the life of the Catholic Church. Yet, like their cherished acquaintances Barron and Kelly in Liberia, by 1844 the Oblate Sisters were encountering a series of crises that threatened the very survival of their community in Baltimore.

FROM THE LATE 1830s the declining health of their beloved spiritual director haunted the Oblate community like some inexorable specter. Joubert's bouts of sickness caused him to relinquish his responsibilities as Oblate spiritual director to Sulpician colleagues Edward Damphoux or John Hickey, often for weeks at a time.[58] Oblate historian Willigman recalled, "Everything seemed to be progressing, but a cloud was beginning to lower, which made the Sisters feel very sad. Reverend Father Joubert was now failing in health, and although for a long time he continued to watch over the Community, yet it was plainly visible that he was suffering; still he did not wish to give up. Sister Mary [Lange] and the other Sisters were troubled, but all joined in earnest prayer and in resignation."[59]

By July 1842 Joubert's illnesses had become so frequent that the annalist commented, "Father Director was very sick, as he always is at this time."[60] Sometime in 1842 Oblate cofounder Sister Mary Lange joined the Oblate Sisters serving at the Sulpician St. Mary's Seminary, "as the Sisters there needed help." "Besides," she continued, "at this time it was necessary to give some special care to the Reverend Founder, who was critically ill."[61] Lange would remain at the seminary until 1850. While devotion to cofounder Joubert undoubtedly summoned Lange to attend his final days at the seminary, financial concerns kept her there after his death in 1843. The sisters expected the promised compensation for their household management at the seminary to provide a dependable source of income for their community during the 1840s.

On 15 June 1843 Joubert came to the Oblate convent for a ten-day visit that extended until 4 July. At his departure, the sisters noted anxiously, "We do not know when we will have the pleasure of seeing him again."[62] Joubert, "too sick and too feeble to leave his room," did not return to the Oblate premises until 8 September 1843. Too incapacitated to participate in the planned activities, he greeted the sisters but had to return to the seminary prematurely. The sisters presciently concluded, "We were much saddened too by the firm conviction that this would be the last time we would ever see him here again."[63] By 29 October Joubert was "ever between life and death."[64] On 5 November 1843 James Hector Joubert died, mourned by the entire Oblate community. On 7 November, the day of his funeral, the sisters and the school children stood at the cemetery in the bitter cold "until they had entirely finished covering the grave." They observed that "the weather was gloomy and seemed in some way to share our affliction."[65]

The Oblate Sisters had realized the newly precarious nature of their position within the Baltimore religious community even before Joubert's death. On 24 July 1842, with Joubert sick and no other priest available to celebrate Mass in their chapel, all the Oblate Sisters had had to go out to Mass, a portent of things to come. On 14 and 21 July 1843, Louis Gillet, a Redemptorist priest, said Mass in the Oblate chapel. Although founded by Alphonsus Liguori in Naples, Italy in 1732, the Congregation of the Most Holy Redeemer had flourished in German-speaking countries. The order followed German emigrants to America and established a mission in Baltimore in 1840.[66] Several Redemptorist priests would play vital roles in Oblate history in the next several years, but in July 1843 the Oblate Sisters particularly appreciated Gillet's two Masses and instructions, given the relative inattention from local clergy they were experiencing.

On 20 August 1843 the Oblate annalist noted, "Since July 30th until today there has been nothing in the chapel because of the absence of Father Hickey."[67] By 3 September 1843, diocesan authorities assigned John Hickey, who had essentially functioned as Joubert's surrogate in ministering to the Oblate community since 1841, to the Baltimore Cathedral as assistant rector. On 10 September 1843 the Oblate annalist reported, "There is still nothing in the Chapel, and we may well believe that this will continue, since we have not the same confessor. May God's will be done."[68] Two days later a priest celebrated Mass in the chapel "in order to consume the Host of the Monstrance," a receptacle used to display a Communion host or wafer for public adoration.[69] Between 12 September and the end of the year—5 December excepted—priests said Mass in the Oblate chapel, not to accommodate the sisters or their needs as a religious community but only as required by church law to maintain the Blessed Sacrament in authorized houses of worship.

On 8 October 1843 the church observed the feast of St. Benedict the Moor.

Traditionally, the Oblate community had celebrated the feast of St. Benedict, their one patron saint of African descent, with appropriate pomp and solemnity. The sisters, who had had no Mass in their chapel since 12 September, observed that "today, the feast of St. Benedict, Father Superior of the Seminary [Deluol] had the goodness to procure a Mass for us, but it was said, not so much for St. Benedict, as to renew the consecrated Host."[70] That the local clergy neglected this feast in 1843 boded ill for the Oblate community and Baltimore's black Catholics, who venerated St. Benedict as one of their own. From 1835 through 1842 Deluol himself had sung a High Mass in the Oblate chapel on St. Benedict's feast day; in 1843 he did not even attend the modest observance of this major patronal feast day for black Catholics.

When on 29 October 1843 the Sulpician priest Augustin Verot said Mass in the Oblate chapel, again "in order to renew the Host," the sisters requested that Verot have "the goodness to give a little instruction after the Gospel."[71] They thus asserted their legitimate claim as a religious community to customary pastoral care, a right recently withheld from them by Baltimore's clergy.

On 8 November 1843, the day following Joubert's funeral, Louis Deluol, superior of St. Mary's Seminary and vicar-general of the Archdiocese of Baltimore, met with the Oblate Sisters of Providence. The Oblate annalist reported that after conferring privately with Oblate Superior Duchemin, Deluol "assured us of his protection and that he was ready to do everything that depended on him for our welfare." "He also recommended us to pray to the Good God that He would make it clear as to what he would have to do," the report continued. "All the Sisters were very grateful to him, for they had been very uneasy in the belief that he would not consent to take care of the house. They thanked him for his goodness and felt more at ease." The sisters maintained, "His visit was for us as would be that of a consoling angel."[72]

However, little in Deluol's remarks provided substantive grounds for rejoicing. His cryptic request that the sisters entreat God to inform Deluol of "what he would have to do" for their benefit hardly reflected conviction and a clear sense of purpose or commitment on Deluol's part. Only in the context of the clerical neglect they had recently experienced could the Oblate Sisters find comfort in this interview. In contrast to their detailed and hopeful account of this meeting on 8 November 1843, Deluol reported simply, "At 4:30 I went to the Providence convent, where I had not gone since 9 March. Saw all the professed Sisters."[73]

On 5 December 1843, the month anniversary of Joubert's death, Deluol celebrated a commemorative Mass in the Oblate chapel that many people attended. After Mass, Deluol, whom the sisters called "our present superior and protector,"[74] attended to some affairs of the convent. Evidently Deluol noted neither the Mass nor the meeting in his diary.

On 27 November 1843 Ann Johnson, the Oblate candidate from Baltimore who had entered the community on 21 November 1842, left the convent "feeling that she did not have the strength to bear the kind of life that she wished to embrace."[75] The Oblate annalist recorded Johnson's departure belatedly, sometime in December. With this entry, the Oblate annals ceased for all of 1844, all of 1845—save three isolated entries—and all of 1846. In effect, in the words of Oblate historian Willigman, "Of the sorrow and deep distress of the Sisters in the years following we draw a veil."[76]

CHAPTER EIGHT

Of the Sorrow and Deep Distress of the Sisters . . . We Draw a Veil

THE OBLATE SISTERS IN THE CRUCIBLE,
1844–1847

❖ ❖

From late 1843 through 1847 the Oblate Sisters of Providence confronted a series of crises—the death of cofounder James Joubert, the first departures and dismissal of professed members, and apparent desertion by church authorities. The sisters persevered in their observance of religious life and the conduct of their school without benefit of official clerical sponsorship. Few contemporary sources counteract the vacuum of information about the Oblate Sisters created by the discontinuation of the Oblate annals during the critical middle years of the 1840s. However, some glimmers of the Oblate experience penetrate the veil of silence in which the sisters enveloped themselves.

An untitled and unremarked ledger housed in the Oblate Archives preserves accounts of Oblate business transactions from January 1844 through December 1854. The very existence of the ledger bears silent witness to the remarkable stability and continuity of the Oblate experience during the crisis of 1844–47, as the sisters accomplished the routine requirements of conducting their community and school life without benefit of male guidance. Ledger entries reveal that the sisters continued the practice established under Joubert's directorship of depositing sums on a regular basis in an account with Louis Deluol at St. Mary's Seminary. Between January 1844 and October 1849, the sisters had deposited $1,556.81 with Deluol in amounts as small as $3 and as large as $177 on an almost monthly basis. These deposits frequently represented 30–75 percent of monthly Oblate expenses and, not infrequently, an even larger percentage of their monthly income.[1]

Significantly, Oblate income exceeded expenses by $170.45 January 1844 through December 1847. This fact challenges the conventional portrayal of the Oblate condition as exclusively one of dire need during this period. The only unencumbered income cited in the ledger for the entire decade 1844–54 appeared in January 1844: a New Year's gift of $10 from Louis Deluol and an anonymous donation of $50. Oblate income consisted almost exclusively of board and tuition fees, compensation for goods and services provided by the Oblate Sisters, and occasional loans.[2]

Ledger information also challenges the contention of several sources that the sisters derived "no income except washing and mending for the Seminary and Cathedral."[3] Although a dependable source of income, laundering the cathedral altar linens earned the Oblate Sisters only $3 to $4 a month through 1847. Sewing clerical vestments remained a more lucrative enterprise for the sisters, accounting for an income of $483.67 during the 1844–47 period alone.[4]

This ledger proves as informative for its contents as for entries it did not include. It duly recorded four separate entries of $5.00, $2.60, $2.31, and $4.375 as "Cash of Sister Mary for making preserves for Seminary."[5] However, the ledger cited no receipts of the annual $120 the Sulpician priests had contracted to pay for Oblate household managers, although Oblate sisters Mary Lange and Rose Boegue filled these positions at the seminary until 1850.

The 1844–54 Oblate ledger sheds new light on other aspects of the Oblate community and school during this critical period. It reveals the names of several of the families who continued to subsidize the school with substantial, regular payments for board and tuition. A Mr. Charleville remitted $50 and $93.38 in August 1844 and March 1845, respectively, for his daughter Adelaide. Mr. and Mrs. Small paid their daughter Mary Ann's fees eight times in amounts ranging from $13 to $40 between January 1844 and July 1845. These pupils may have attended the Oblate school prior to the extant record of their enrollment starting in January 1844 and consequently completed the course of study by the time of their departures.[6]

Mr. J. Smith made five payments of $30 for his daughter Laurenda's board and tuition between April 1844 and February 1846. Evidently, the Oblate Sisters had expanded their curriculum to offer music lessons by 1844 for a quarterly fee of $10. Mr. Smith paid for three quarters of piano lessons for Laurenda, under the tutelage of Oblate student Angela Noel. An individual variously identified as Mr. or Dr. Stinecki remitted five payments averaging $20 for the board and tuition of Emily Galloway between June 1845 and December 1846.[7]

Oblate pupil Charlotte Manganos first appeared in the ledger in 1845. Her father, Joseph Manganos, paid her fees either directly or through agents in eight installments ranging from $8 to $81 between August 1845 and September 1848. A convert to Roman Catholicism, Charlotte received baptism on 26 June 1846. She still resided at the Oblate school in 1850, when census information identified her as a thirteen-year-old black orphan from Virginia.[8] This selective listing of long-term boarders represents the larger body of pupils—including the significant number of day students cited in the ledger—who continued to patronize the Oblate school during this period.

Entries in the 1844–54 Oblate ledger corroborate that significant racial integration characterized residential patterns in antebellum Baltimore. One Oblate ledger entry in 1844 reported receipt "of an Irish woman for 1 Week boarding—$1.50."[9] Evidently, Baltimore accommodated interracial households, both in the conventional pattern of black servants or slaves incorporated into white households as well as white people boarding in black homes. The neighborhood of the Oblate property on Richmond Street remained integrated through the antebellum period.

Since June 1834 the sisters had received a modest income of $3 per month from each of two rental houses on convent property. From February 1844 through August 1848, the German immigrant Rutherton Wernerth family occupied one of these Oblate houses. The ledger documents how consistently, if on occasion belatedly, the Wernerths paid their rent. It further documents the unexpected finding that the Wernerth's ten-year-old daughter, Rosine, attended the Oblate school as a day student between April 1844 and November 1847. This enrollment of a white student in the Oblate School for Colored Girls proved no isolated phenomenon. Five entries in an early Oblate student ledger noted monthly payments for the board of a student identified only as "la petite blanche," the little white one, in 1832 and 1833.[10] Oblate action in consensually admitting white students to their school for black pupils and the Wernerth family's action in entrusting their daughter to the Oblate school proved equally defiant of the dictates of prevailing racial etiquette.

The 1844–54 Oblate ledger further reveals that John and Margaret Eschbach, another German immigrant family and the sisters' immediate neighbors, occasionally paid the Oblate school tuition for Rosine Wernerth. More than physical proximity connected the Wernerth and Eschbach families. John and Margaret had stood as godparents for John, a Wernerth son, in 1838 at the immigrant German community's St. John's Roman Catholic Church. This fact establishes Baltimore residence for both families at least six years before their documented interaction with the Oblate community—sufficient time for them to have adopted prevailing white racist attitudes toward black people, had they chosen to do so. Both men also listed their occupations as pavers in the 1850 census.

Bonds of cordiality and cooperation existed between the Oblate Sisters and the Eschbach family as well. The sisters regularly purchased milk from Mrs. Eschbach, who, on at least one occasion, donated their supply. The Eschbachs also paid the sisters for laundry and sewing services. The positive experiences of the black Oblate Sisters with these two German immigrant families in their neighborhood during the 1840s proved consistent with Frederick Douglass's assessment of German immigrants as "our active allies in the struggle against oppression and prejudice." In stark contrast, Douglass characterized Irish immigrants, who wrapped themselves in the mantle of white privilege, as "the enemies of Human Freedom, so far, at least, as *our* humanity is concerned."[11]

LOUIS DELUOL MENTIONED the Oblate Sisters in his diary throughout the 1840s. Furthermore, several later nineteenth-century sources, including the Oblate Sisters themselves, reconstructed various aspects of the critical 1844–47 period in Oblate history and both elaborated upon and corroborated Deluol's limited information.

Deluol documented the occurrence of two episodes of constitutional deliberations within the Oblate community, the first of which precipitated the major internal crisis the sisters experienced during this period. On 28 December 1843, Deluol presided at the convent over "a long session there concerning the Rule."[12] Although the Oblate community has preserved no record of it, Sister Therese Duchemin revealed later in conversations that, as Oblate superior, she had proposed Rule revisions that included changing the name of the community to the Oblates of St. Charles, "because of Charles Carroll whose [grand]daughter she hoped to interest in the financial troubles of the Community . . . , but she always referred to these Sisters as Oblates of Saint Charles or Charlottines."[13] Duchemin proposed to exchange financial security in the form of an endowment, similar to those enjoyed by many European communities of women religious, for the original Oblate identity and patronal allegiance to St. Frances of Rome. The Oblate Sisters considered and then rejected Duchemin's proposals on 28 December 1843. As future events proved, Duchemin did not reconcile herself to the community's rejection of her proposed Rule revisions. Oblate sources referred only obliquely to the community's response to Duchemin's proposals. In a rare annals entry in 1845, the annalist noted that on 9 September Sister Marie Therese left the Oblate community for a religious community in Monroe, Michigan, "finding it inconvenient to make a reform in the one she had left."[14]

On 15 July 1844, seven months after his first constitutional session, Deluol "went to the Providence to publish a few rules."[15] The Oblate archives have preserved copies of an undated French document entitled "Notes on the Constitutions of the Oblate Sisters of Providence established in Baltimore June 1829," attributed to Deluol. Three characteristics distinguished Deluol's proposals from previous revisions of the Oblate Rule. Explicit assertions of the archbishop's authority over the community appeared for the first time: "The Community is governed by a Director appointed by the Most Reverend Archbishop of Baltimore, Superior of all the Religious Communities of his Diocese and who has an unerring right to visit them at his discretion, also to examine if they conduct themselves according to the Rules and the spirit of the Church."[16] Deluol's Rule also enjoined the mother superior to lead by her example, not only in the observance of the Rule but also in "retreat from the world, having no communication with Seculars, only by grave and indispensable necessity."[17] While antithetical to the original Oblate Rule that tolerated significant interaction between the sisters and the black laity, this provision aligned the Oblate community more closely with other congregations of women religious in discouraging extraneous secular-religious communication. Finally, Deluol's Rule revisions assumed a highly proscriptive quality, detailing the procedure for dismissing members from the community and intoning a litany of offenses punishable by dismissal. They also delineated the procedure for deposing the mother superior for mental illness and "willful intoxication," among other offenses.[18]

Issues of mental competence, intoxication, and fitness for office undoubtedly preoccupied Deluol as vicar-general of the archdiocese and intimate of Archbishop Samuel Eccleston at this time. However, these conditions Deluol stipulated for the Oblate Sisters reflected not the putative potential for problems in these areas within that sisterhood but the reality of the problems Deluol experienced with Samuel Eccleston between 1843 and 1846. Deluol projected onto the Oblate community his concerns about Eccleston's mental fitness as archbishop. While traveling with Eccleston in 1843, Deluol had witnessed such bizarre behavior on the archbishop's part that he had enjoined the prelate to refrain from strong drink. But Eccleston's hallucinations and paranoia persisted, along with rumors of his intemperance. In 1843 and 1844 news of Eccleston's erratic behavior prompted papal authorities in Rome to initiate inquiries about his mental condition. The papacy refrained from naming a successor for Eccleston after Francis Patrick Kenrick, bishop of Philadelphia, attested Eccleston's competence. In 1845 Eccleston withdrew from performing his official duties as ordinary for several weeks, under physicians' orders. In 1846 the papacy urged Eccleston to name a co-adjutor or co-ordinary, but Eccleston successfully eluded compliance.[19]

On 21 June 1844 Deluol noted that he had held a meeting at "the Providence." On 5 July, the three Oblate Sisters serving at the seminary—charter members Balas, Boegue, and Lange—had accompanied him to the Oblate convent. These two meetings in close succession prior to the publication of the "few rules" on 15 July 1844 provided an opportunity for the Oblate Sisters to exercise the collaborative governance operative during Joubert's tenure as their spiritual director. Certainly the proposed Rule revision changing the date of triennial Oblate elections from 24 June to the October feast of St. Benedict the Moor, Oblate patron of African descent, would have originated more plausibly in the sisters' articulated racial consciousness than in any initiative from Deluol.[20]

Louis Deluol remained indifferent to the interests and concerns of black people. He owned, or had owned, slaves. In a letter to Charles Carroll's granddaughter, Deluol equivocated on the issue of slavery. He proclaimed his personal feelings "most violently opposed" to slavery, yet he cautioned that "if we want to be right we must act from principle and not from feeling."[21] He then repeated the American church's official position accommodating the institution of slavery.

In 1839 Deluol corresponded with Sister Margaret George, treasurer of the Sisters of Charity of St. Joseph, Emmitsburg. Cynically casting his directions as "a nubbin of theology for you," he advised her that she could sell two of her community's slaves at a premium, "without doing an injustice to anybody." In another reference to the sale of the "yellow boys" (mulattoes), Deluol opined, "Pity that you did not send them down ten or twelve days sooner—They would have brought $75 to $100 more."[22] Neither principle nor feeling, but racism and profit-seeking prompted Deluol to conclude that the sale of black children as chattel property produced no "injustice to anybody." The institution of slavery, not a conviction of the humanity of black people, informed the American cultural values Deluol so eagerly embraced.

The extant evidence does not explicitly document the Oblate community's disposition of Deluol's Rule revisions. Some sources have maintained that the Oblate Sisters rejected Deluol's proposals.[23] However, certain considerations militate against this interpretation. The Oblate archives would not have preserved the Rule, nor would nineteenth-century Oblate member and historian Willigman have expended the time and effort to translate them from the original French had the Oblate community rejected them. Furthermore, rejecting Rule revisions touting the archbishop's authority over religious communities within his archdiocese would have risked certain and immediate dissolution of their community by a prelate already indifferent to the Oblate cause. Finally, in 1848 Oblate elections occurred on the feast of St. Benedict the Moor, the date stipulated in Deluol's Rule revisions. Consequently, this study contends that the Oblate Sisters accepted Deluol's Rule proposals in 1844. However, the absence of a duly appointed spiritual director between November 1843 and October 1847 delayed implementation of these Rule revisions until 1848.

Even as the Oblate Sisters deliberated Deluol's Rule revisions in July 1844, the term of office of the serving mother superior, Sister Marie Therese Duchemin, had expired the month before. Historically, the Oblate community had adhered very strictly to the election date of 24 June stipulated in their original Rule. On the occasion of her own election on 24 June 1841, Oblate Superior and annalist Duchemin had noted that the community proceeded with the election on the date mandated in the Rule "in spite of the fact that there was a Sister dead in the house."[24] Failure to conduct elections on 24 June 1844 reflected not disarray within the Oblate community but the neglect the Oblate community endured at the hands of the Baltimore clergy. From their inception, the Oblate Sisters had conducted their elections at the summons and in the presence of their spiritual director, James Joubert. Louis Deluol, superior of St. Mary's Seminary and vicar-general of the archdiocese, had customarily verified the Oblate election results.[25]

Not until 26 December 1844 did Deluol call for Oblate elections. The members chose Sisters Mary Louise Noel as superior, Marie Therese Duchemin as assistant, and Scholastica Bourgoin as counselor. Willigman later recalled the reaction of Sister Mary Louise Noel to her unanimous election as mother superior: "It was a terrible and sudden shock to her; for a time she lost consciousness, and very Reverend Father Deluol had to use his fatherly influence to make her accept the heavy arm."[26] As superior, the twenty-seven-year-old Noel confronted daunting problems. Teaching remained the primary Oblate ministry; nevertheless, the Oblate annals during these four years mentioned the school only once, to acknowledge falling enrollment. Their survival as a religious community and those Oblate members "fearing that the community would not be able to hold out [who] were losing courage" preoccupied the sisters during these years.[27] Charter Oblate member Marie Therese Duchemin, former superior and serving assistant, numbered among the latter. Persistent doubts about her religious status tormented Duchemin.

THE AMBIVALENCE OF THE Roman Catholic Church toward sisterhoods with service, not contemplative, ministries informed with particular intensity in the 1840s the experience of the Oblate Sisters of Providence and other communities of women religious in the United States who engaged in teaching or care of the sick, indigent, or orphaned. The wave of European immigrants arriving in the United States in the 1840s included priests who "required time and experience before they could balance ascetic practices with the needs of the American sisters whom they directed." Under the influence of immigrant spiritual directors who were following "the practice of looking to Europe for models of excellence while despising native creations," several individual members of American communities of women religious, like Oblate Sister Therese Duchemin, "wanted to be genuine religious rather than members of a half-caste group which was neither religious nor lay." Such sisters "sometimes endured crises of conscience when living in communities in which it was impossible to carry out cloister rules."[28]

James Joubert, a longtime Baltimore resident, had personally favored a service ministry for women religious and had also accommodated the realities of the Oblate southern American milieu. As spiritual director of the Oblate Sisters of Providence, Joubert had secured the Oblate Sisters in their active orientation. But Joubert's declining health, especially after 1841, had circumscribed his effective functioning as Oblate spiritual director. His death in 1843 and the subsequent alienation of the Sulpician priests from the Oblate community exposed the Oblate Sisters to the guidance of the Redemptorist priests, an order established in Baltimore only since 1840 and unfamiliar with American culture.

Limited to Masses in their chapel only "once a month for renewal of the Sacred Species and also when a stranger pass[ed] through the city who[m] charity would induce to offer the Holy Sacrifice for us,"[29] the Oblate Sisters increasingly went out for Mass. Between 1842 and 1845 they frequented St. James Church, located at Aisquith and Eager Streets, more than a half-hour walk from their convent and in the charge of Redemptorist priests. When the Redemptorist order first arrived in Baltimore in 1840, Archbishop Eccleston had assigned them to St. John's Church, located directly down the street from the Oblate convent. Baltimore's burgeoning German Catholic community soon required a larger building, and in 1842 construction of the spacious St. Alphonsus Church began on the site of the former St. John's, razed in 1841. During the construction of St. Alphonsus Church from 1842 until 1845, the Redemptorist priests relocated their headquarters to St. James Church. In 1845 the Redemptorists returned to their original site, now St. Alphonsus Church, conveniently located near the Oblate convent. In incorrectly asserting that the sisters attended St. Alphonsus Church from 1843, Oblate chronicler Grace Sherwood underrepresented the sisters' spiritual commitment in making the distant trek to St. James Church for three years.[30]

Later, Duchemin would recall that as an Oblate Sister she attended St. James Church as often as possible, "as everything was so fervent, some pious exercise seemed to be going on whenever one went. Though all the Fathers were German, some of them could hear confession in French and some in English."[31] Duchemin's recollection revealed two salient characteristics of Redemptorist ministry that appealed to her immediately and personally: spiritual fervor and the French language. As the Redemptorist priests undertook their pioneering mission in the United States, reconciling the spiritual with the temporal, the service with the contemplative dimensions of their ministry formed an abiding concern of the order. In 1844 Joseph Passerat, the vicar-general of the Redemptorist order in Vienna, issued a circular letter to the American Redemptorists in which he enjoined them to nurture their inner spiritual lives even as they devoted themselves to their external missionary activities.[32]

Initial Oblate contact with the Redemptorists occurred in July 1843, when Louis Gillet, a Belgian Redemptorist and gifted preacher who spoke French exclusively, celebrated two Masses in the Oblate chapel. Gillet preached for an hour to the sisters on the obligations of the religious profession. Oblate Superior and annalist Duchemin noted, "He explained to us very well what a spouse of Jesus Christ must do in order to remain faithful to her divine Spouse."[33] Years later, her confidant in the community of the Sisters of the Immaculate Heart of Mary recalled that Duchemin "used to tell of her joy in hearing a sermon in real French from Father Gillet when he first came to America. . . . She had been for several years under the direction of the Redemptorists, and she never lost a chance to mention that fact when speaking of them."[34]

In the 1890s Louis Gillet recalled his interaction with the Oblate Sisters during the critical mid-1840s. Briefly stationed at St. James Church in Baltimore upon arriving in the United States in 1843, Gillet left Baltimore almost immediately for a mission in Monroe, Michigan, where he decided to establish a girls' school and a community of women religious to staff it. Significantly, Gillet—Joubert's analogue in the formation of the Sisters, Servants of the Immaculate Heart of Mary—initially named the sisterhood he established in Monroe in 1845 the "Sisters of Providence." On a return visit to Baltimore in 1844 to solicit aid from Redemptorist headquarters for his project, Gillet "gave a retreat to the 'Sisters of St. Charles,' then entirely abandoned, living still in community, but whose vows had not been renewed for a long time. Two of them [Duchemin and Schaaf] expressed the desire to be admitted into a regular congregation. One was sufficiently educated to accomplish the object which I was considering."[35]

A source generally considered Duchemin herself later recorded a personal, if third-person, account of her spiritual struggle: "Although belonging already to a religious Society, she had for a long time felt the desire of consecrating herself to God in a religious order of strict observance. . . . She placed herself under the guidance of a religious, the Reverend Father Schackert.[36] . . . It was therefore, that she discovered to him everything that passed in her soul. . . . Her Director, instead of sending her to a convent already established, as she wished, decided upon sending her to the Reverend Father Gillet, another Redemptorist who had charge of the parish of Monroe."[37] On 9 September 1845 Sister Marie Therese Duchemin left the Oblate community for Michigan, armed with the permission, the blessings, and the letters of introduction from her confessor, the Redemptorist Superior Peter Czackert, and the Sulpician Superior Louis Deluol.[38]

Duchemin's departure precipitated two other defections from the Oblate community in 1845: Sisters Ann Constance (Charlotte Schaaf) and Stanislaus (Josephine Amanda).[39] Writing later, Willigman revealed the reactions of the Oblate Sisters to this unanticipated rupture in their community:

In 1845 Sister Therese made known that she intended to sever her connection with the Order, as from the state of affairs she did not know what the result would be. It must be said to the credit of the Sisters that they were willing to put up with all their trials, and it was far from their intention to give up. The Community numbered then fourteen Sisters, but only three were of the same opinion. Sisters Therese, Ann Constance, and Stanislaus had their plans fixed in secret, and only at the last minute did they make them known. Everything had been arranged and the place of their next establishment decided upon. There was a mantle of good feeling and charity shown by the Superior, Sister Louisa [Noel], who said Sister Therese's motives were to serve God in greater perfection than in the present Community. But all had not the same opinion of her leaving. Superiority had a great share in the separation. . . . A few weeks later according to the arrangement made between them, Sister Ann Constance left for the same destination. The third member, Sister Stanislaus who was to have followed, received word from Sister Therese not to come as

Sister Marie Therese Maxis Duchemin, wearing the habit of the Sisters, Servants of the Immaculate Heart of Mary, ca. 1885 (Courtesy of Sisters, Servants of the Immaculate Heart of Mary Monroe Archives).

her color was too dark, but by the advice of Ecclesiastical Superiors she received her dismissal from the Community.[40]

Issues of ethnicity, religion, and race inhered in this internal rupture in the Oblate community in 1845. Certainly the withdrawal of French Sulpician support for their community compounded the problems, stresses, and uncertainties confronting the Oblate Sisters after Joubert's death in 1843. Duchemin left the Oblate community in part because "as from the state of affairs she did not know what the outcome would be."[41] The German Redemptorist priests had arrived in Baltimore only in 1840, their mandate directed them to provide pastoral care for immigrant European populations, and the Redemptorist contingent in Baltimore comprised immigrant priests exclusively. Redemptorist unfamiliarity with U.S. culture from a racial perspective benefited the Oblate Sisters: not yet acculturated to racist influences, the newly immigrant priests perceived people of color as human beings fully deserving of pastoral care.

Nevertheless, evidence suggests that not all members of the Oblate community may have viewed the substitution of Redemptorist for Sulpician guidance as an unalloyed blessing. In 1868 Ann Constance Schaaf, former Oblate and current Sister of the Immaculate Heart of Mary, would write Oblate Superior Mary Louise Noel, entreating her to receive exiled Immaculate Heart of Mary Sister Theresa Maxis Duchemin, "now growing old and childish," back into the Oblate community. To excuse Duchemin's defection from the Oblate community in 1845, Schaaf asserted, "As you know, she permitted herself to be led away from you by foreigners."[42] Schaaf's reference to the Redemptorist priests as "foreigners" invoked negative nativist images of immigrants that may have resonated more broadly in the Oblate community she knew, in spite of its own immigrant heritage. Conversely, her statement may represent nothing more than a manipulative ploy to plead her cause. In either case, Schaaf evidently believed that raising the specter of nativism would prove beneficial. The Oblate Sisters took no formal action on Schaaf's unauthorized request because Duchemin herself never contacted her former community.

Issues of religion compounded the impact of this ethnic transition in clerical guidance on Oblate Sister Therese Duchemin individually. Duchemin had become personally conflicted about her status as a "true religious" in the Oblate community and individually more militantly Francophile than the other Oblate Sisters, even before her initial contact with the Redemptorists. The vulnerable Duchemin evidently inferred from the spiritual guidance of Redemptorists Louis Gillet and Peter Czackert—who delivered messages of spiritual discipline through the medium of the French language—encouragement to pursue a different religious experience. Initially, she sought membership in a "regular" religious congregation in Europe before agreeing to join a new service sisterhood. No extant information explains the personal motivations of Oblate Sisters Ann Constance and Stanislaus for defecting from the Oblate community, beyond the fact that they had allied with Duchemin in the unsuccessful reform attempt in 1843.[43]

Issues of race intruded in the form of the racism of diocesan authorities Eccleston and Deluol, who were indifferent to the fate of the Oblate Sisters of Providence as a religious community because of the racial identity of its members. Their lack of confidence and support for the Oblate Sisters served as a catalyst rupturing the Oblate community. On 13 October 1844 Deluol had noted in his diary that "someone had written to Belgium to have Sister Therese, an Oblate, taken in at a convent of Religious Sisters." On 22 November 1844 he reported, "Sister Therese, an Oblate, told me that she saw Father Louis [Gillet], but she did not get much satisfaction from him."[44] These entries in Deluol's diary documented Sister Therese Duchemin's increasing alienation from the Oblate community, her determination to sever her ties to it, and Deluol's awareness of both. Had Deluol felt genuinely protective of the integrity and welfare of the Oblate community, he certainly would have informed the sisters of Duchemin's disaffection and attempted to mediate their differences, rather than merely expedite Duchemin's departure in 1845.

Race—or more specifically, color—also informed the post-Oblate experiences of the three departed members. Duchemin and Schaaf, both light-skinned mulattoes, passed for white in their new religious community, the Sisters, Servants of the Immaculate Heart of Mary in Michigan. Sources differ about the impact of Duchemin's rupture with the Oblate community on the integrity of her French cultural identity. Several secondary sources maintain that Duchemin "from now on became another entity. No longer was she the French-speaking Mere [*sic*] Marie Therese but Mary Maxis, later Sister and then Mother Mary Theresa, who used English exclusively, and who wished apparently to break completely with the past, especially with the Oblates."[45] Although resonant with dramatic potential in their implication of a total identity crisis on Duchemin's part, these undocumented assertions prove inconsistent with the evidence. The area of Michigan where Duchemin relocated supported a sizable Francophone population. Duchemin could not have communicated with her cofounder, the exclusively Francophone Louis Gillet, in English. Furthermore, in 1851 French was still the language of the Immaculate Heart of Mary Sisters, as well as that of their original Motherhouse Chronicles.[46] Duchemin remained bilingual for the rest of her life. Duchemin did indeed "break completely with the past, especially with the Oblates" by divesting herself of her former racial identity in 1845. However, she clung steadfastly to her status as a Roman Catholic woman religious and her French cultural heritage.

Sister Stanislaus represented the true victim in this series of critical events. The annals account cited her "desire of being the third of the *reform*" and the perceived "singularity and a (something)[,] which was a word that the definition could or would not be given[,]"[47] of her manner as cause for her dismissal from the Oblate community. Historian Patricia Byrne has noted that "singularity," or the appearance of standing out in any way, violated religious community goals of self-effacement and humility and constituted "a considerable transgression of good convent manners."[48] The Oblate Sisters disagreed with the reform initiative but harbored no ill will toward its three perpetrators. They had elected Sister Therese Duchemin assistant superior in 1844. The following cryptic passage from the annals account implicates the forceful exercise of Deluol's prerogative as director in causing Sister Stanislaus' dismissal "by the advice of Ecclesiastical Superiors": "As Directors have to or are generally mentioned as a cloak to cover all disorder (that is in religious matters) all was imputed to him, but as no one probably attempted to ascertain from him the reasons, no one in the order knew so everyone was at liberty to pass their opinion on the subject."[49]

Alienated from the Oblate community because of her allegiance to the failed reform effort motivated in part by religious concerns, but barred from religious fellowship with her former allies because of her dark skin color, Sister Stanislaus faced no alternative except to leave communal religious life completely. Although people of color had established another community of women religious, the Sisters of the Holy Family in New Orleans in 1842, this community imposed strict requirements of wealth, free-born status, and fair skin on its membership, precluding it as a viable option for ex-Oblate Sister Stanislaus.[50]

This circumstance highlights the broadly inclusive nature of antebellum Oblate membership. As a community, the Oblate Sisters of Providence had not discriminated against candidates based on their ethnicity, color, or previous condition of servitude. The antebellum membership of the Oblate Sisters of Providence included women from both Franco- and Anglophone cultural traditions, mulatto and black women, the free-born, and those born into slavery. Such ecumenical inclusiveness distinguished the Oblate Sisters from many of their contemporary associations of people of color—both secular and religious— throughout the antebellum South.

THE OBLATE SISTERS faced another crisis in the withdrawal of support for their continued existence by Baltimore's diocesan authorities and clergy in the middle years of the 1840s. The sisters characterized their condition during these years as "in a pitiable state." Keenly feeling the spiritual "deprivation of all the consolations they had enjoyed," the sisters "resigned their cares to God and his Divine Providence."[51] Several twentieth-century sources partial to the Sulpician perspective have attributed clerical abandonment of the Oblate community between 1844 and 1847 to Sulpician retrenchment and consequent withdrawal from all external ministries in the 1840s. But the impetus from Sulpician headquarters in France for the American Sulpicians to restrict themselves to their original mission to train seminarians did not arise until 1845; actual implementation of the retrenchment policy did not occur until the spring of 1849.[52]

The indifference and inaction with which Baltimore's episcopal authorities—the Sulpician archbishop Samuel Eccleston and his Sulpician vicar-general Louis Deluol—responded to the black Oblate community's loss of their spiritual director in 1843 contrasted starkly to their expressed concern and sense of obligation toward the communities of white women religious as late as 1849. Eccleston maintained to French Sulpician authorities that the traditional Sulpician direction of the Sisters of Charity obligated the order to continue this relationship until appropriately replaced.[53] No extant evidence indicates that either Eccleston or Deluol expressed such concern or initiated such efforts on the Oblate Sisters' behalf between 1844 and 1847. Sulpician retrenchment does not explain the Baltimore clergy's abandonment of the Oblate Sisters of Providence in the middle years of the 1840s.

Another source has explained the Oblate community's four years of clerical neglect as a function of "the lack of motivation on the part of the few priests in the city to transcend racial barriers by making a long-term pastoral commitment to the Oblates."[54] However, individual priests had demonstrated their personal interest in the spiritual welfare of the Oblate community during this period. Joubert's fellow Sulpician John Hickey had functioned as surrogate director of the Oblate Sisters from 1841 until assigned to the assistant rectorship of the cathedral in September 1843. One of only three Oblate annals entries dated 1845 maintained that a priest identified only as Reverend Carroll convalesced at St. Mary's Seminary under the care of an Oblate Sister, "during which time he spoke of the interest he felt for the salvation of persons of color, consequently of our little community." Carroll celebrated Mass "in our little chapel on Sundays, Thursdays, and great festivals," until his declining health obliged him to return to his native Canada shortly before his death.[55]

In 1845 several Redemptorist priests acted on their concern for the Oblate Sisters. Peter Czackert, Redemptorist superior in America from 1845 until 1847 and personal confessor to former Oblate Sister Therese Duchemin, had prepared for the Oblate community "a series of devotions to keep aflame their fervor."[56] Furthermore, in the fall of 1845 Czackert permitted fellow Redemptorist Giles Smulders to conduct for the Oblate community a spiritual retreat, as the sisters noted, "the first we had the happiness to make since the death or rather the bad health of our Reverend Founder." To the Oblate Sisters, Smulders "was as a messenger sent from heaven to bring comfort to the abandoned." He "spared no pains" in providing them with a meaningful spiritual experience.[57] On 5 October 1845 Deluol noted that Smulders had conferred with him "about the Oblates, to whom he is giving a retreat."[58] The 1844–54 Oblate ledger reveals that the Oblate Sisters and the Redemptorist priests assumed a business relationship as well from 1845. The Reverends Peter Czackert, Thaddeus Anwander, and Alexander Czvitkovicz purchased various vestments and church furnishings from the sisters on at least six occasions between 1845 and 1847.[59]

Thaddeus Anwander, a Redemptorist seminarian in 1845, remembered that

Giles Smulders had first introduced him to the Oblate Sisters; consequently, "then I made up my mind to learn English at least so much as to enable me to help the poor colored people."[60] Willigman wrote that while Anwander "was a student, Reverend Father Smulders frequently brought him to our Convent on his way to say Mass at Mount Hope."[61] In December 1845 Czackert implemented the renewal of the Oblate Sisters' vows.[62] At least from 1845, the putative unwillingness of priests to transcend racial barriers on behalf of the Oblate Sisters does not explain the Baltimore clergy's abandonment of the Oblate Sisters of Providence in the middle years of the 1840s.

Writing in 1900, chronicler L. W. Reilly presented a Redemptorist perspective on the clerical neglect of the Oblate community between 1843 and 1847:

> But a storm was gathering that threatened the very existence of the Institute [Oblate community]. Archbishop Eccleston was not well disposed to it. Several other clergymen who had formerly viewed the formation of the society with approval now entertained doubts of its utility. Some even expressed the opinion that "good servants were needed," hinting at the dissolution of the community. The death of the founder they thought available as an opportunity to destroy his work. If no one else would take it up, it must perish.
>
> The Sulpitians [*sic*] did not care to keep up the responsibility of the Sisterhood in view of the disfavor with the diocesan authorities into which it had fallen. They accordingly withdrew from its direction.[63]

Although Reilly identified only Samuel Eccleston by name, Louis Deluol could well have numbered among the unnamed "several other clergymen" opposed to the Oblate community. Sulpicians Samuel Eccleston and Louis Deluol constituted "the diocesan authorities" at this time. As Eccleston's former professor, confessor, and current confidant, Deluol exerted so much influence over the archbishop that at times "it was never really clear which of the two was running the archdiocese."[64]

From the beginning of the Oblate Sisters in 1828, both Eccleston and Deluol had remained personally indifferent, if not hostile, to this community of black women religious. Between his elevation to the episcopacy of Baltimore in 1834 and the year 1848, Eccleston had visited the Oblate premises only once, when his obligations as presiding prelate of the archdiocese undoubtedly required that he dedicate the new Oblate chapel in 1836. Louis Deluol's semi-annual celebrations of Mass in the Oblate chapel likewise may have reflected less any personal interest in the Oblate community than an obligatory performance of his duties as vicar-general. After Joubert's death, the Oblate Sisters "had been very uneasy in the belief that he [Deluol] would not consent to take care of the house."[65] The sisters had undoubtedly intuited Deluol's ambivalence toward them. Consequently, Deluol's mere titular prerogative as vicar-general of the archdiocese, not Oblate conviction of his genuine interest in their welfare, probably explains occasional Oblate references to Deluol as "our present Superior and protector."[66]

Some sources have interpreted Deluol's presence at Eccleston's reception of Oblate Sisters Therese Duchemin, Louise Addison, and Gertrude Thomas on 2 January 1844 as his attempt to interest Eccleston in the Oblate cause. However, the date of their audience and Deluol's words indicate the ceremonial nature of the sisters' visit, to extend New Year's greetings, rather than to discuss any substantive matters. After Joubert's death, Deluol's ministrations to the Oblate community did not perceptibly increase beyond the semi-annual Masses he had said previously in their chapel on the feasts of St. Frances of Rome and St. Benedict the Moor. In correspondence in 1858 Deluol would identify Oblate Sister Mary Louise Noel as a girl of color and Oblate member who, "if my memory doesn't fool me, her name in the world was Angela Noel, which she changed in religion to that of Sister Mary Louisa Noel."[67] Sister Mary Louise Noel had served as Oblate superior during the final five years of Deluol's tenure in Baltimore and consequently represented the Oblate member with whom he would have experienced the most recent and substantive contact; nevertheless, Deluol confused Mary Louise Noel of Delaware with Angela Noel of Baltimore, who did not even enter the Oblate community until 1851, after Deluol's departure for France. An understandable memory lapse or case of mistaken identity may explain Deluol's confusion/conflation of the two Oblate Noels; however, Deluol's error just as plausibly reflected his fundamental ignorance of and unfamiliarity with the colored Oblate membership, corroborating this study's thesis of his basic indifference to the Oblate sisterhood. From 1844 until 1847, Deluol presided at two Oblate constitutional sessions and an Oblate election, visited gravely ill sisters, assigned Oblate Sister Catherine Rock to conduct cooking classes for the Sisters of Charity at their Emmitsburg and Frederick locations, attended two Oblate vow renewal ceremonies, and said the funeral Mass for charter Oblate Sister Frances Balas in March 1845.[68] But he did not conduct weekly assemblies, organize annual retreats, or provide the customary spiritual ministrations to enhance religious fervor or to fortify the bonds of community life; nor did he appoint an official spiritual director for the Oblate community who would perform these functions.

The "disfavor with the diocesan authorities" afflicting the Oblate community assumed several forms. Thaddeus Anwander later maintained that "after the death of Rev. James Joubert, they [the Oblate Sisters] were forbidden to receive any more candidates."[69] Diocesan authorities reduced the number of Masses celebrated in the Oblate chapel to one a month for renewal of the Host, thus effectively eliminating the functional status of the Oblate chapel as the primary place of worship for this community of women religious and the black St. Frances congregation.[70] Willigman also alluded to the restrictions imposed on the Oblate community by diocesan authorities in several of her accounts. The Redemptorist Giles Smulders "could not say Mass" at the Oblate convent but distributed Holy Communion to the sisters. Willigman stated that Redemptorist priests gave the Oblate Sisters "all the encouragement in their power, but having no direct approval, feared to go too far" and "felt for, but could not help the Oblates."[71] This evidence suggests that diocesan authorities did indeed determine to prevent clergy from taking up Joubert's work with the Oblate community to insure that it would perish.

The Oblate Sisters of Providence responded to their twin crises of internal community rupture and of external alienation by diocesan authorities with commendable fortitude. In 1845 the sisters themselves characterized what had been their condition since 1843 and would remain so until October 1847 as "abandoned or apparently so, if the world was consulted, but not by God, for since the establishment of the community not once has Almighty God ceased to bestow His gifts and graces, not withstanding our unworthiness."[72] Although "by degrees it appeared that everything was falling, the school decreased, sad was it to think on the future state of the community," still the sisters were "willing to put up with all their trials and it was far from their intention to give up."[73] Willigman recalled, "One great consolation was left them . . . namely the presence of Our Lord in the Blessed Sacrament in the Tabernacle. Their dear Chapel was their refuge in trial."[74]

After 9 September 1845 the Oblate community functioned without benefit of the personal presence and potentially steadying influence in crisis of the four charter Oblate members. Since 1835 Sisters Rose Boegue and Frances Balas had served at St. Mary's Seminary, where Sister Frances had died on 14 March 1845. Oblate cofounder Sister Mary Lange had also resided at the seminary since 1842, where she remained until 1850.[75] Sister Therese Duchemin had just deserted the Oblate community. Nevertheless, in these dual crises of internal communal rupture and external clerical abandonment, the Oblate Sisters sustained themselves through their own agency and faith. They demonstrated their communal internalization of the positive conviction of the Oblate religious vocation, clear sense of mission, and strong spiritual commitment characteristic of Oblate cofounder Sister Mary Lange.

Contemporary observers verified the Oblate community's spiritual integrity during this critical period. On 19 April 1844 Deluol himself reported, "I went to the Oblates and for five hours examined them; I found them better disposed than I had expected."[76] The Redemptorist priest Louis Gillet recalled that in 1844 the Oblate Sisters, "then entirely abandoned" and "whose vows had not been renewed for a long time," were nevertheless "living still in community."[77] Before departing for New Orleans in 1847, former Redemptorist Superior Peter Czackert enjoined fellow Redemptorist Thaddeus Anwander to do all in his power to help the Oblate Sisters, "for they were good, holy, simple souls and good religious."[78] The spiritual worthiness of the Oblate Sisters of Providence had manifested itself clearly to those who would see it.

DIOCESAN INDIFFERENCE toward the Oblate community between 1843 and 1847 affected not only the sisters but also the black Catholic laity who had congregated at the Oblate chapel since January 1837. The exact size of this congregation remains unknown; but five hundred people had attended the Mass blessing the Oblate chapel in December 1836, a figure that may have included white supporters of the Oblate community as well as clerical and civic dignitaries.[79] When liturgical functions in the Oblate chapel ceased, its black congregation evidently dispersed among other Catholic churches.

Clerical abandonment of the Oblate community in particular and the black Catholic laity as a distinct racial entity in general represented in microcosm the deteriorating status of the free black population in Maryland in the 1840s. In 1841 a convention of slaveholders prepared a series of legislative proposals for the Maryland State Assembly to safeguard the institution of slavery and to control the burgeoning free black population, whose presence was "deemed an evil by almost everyone." These proposals included prohibition of manumission, except on condition of immediate expulsion from the state; continued support for colonization schemes; prohibition of ownership of real estate or slaves by free black people; and mandatory annual free black registration and payment of a bond guaranteeing good behavior. Other measures proposed mandatory apprenticing of free black children between the ages of eight and twenty, and their subsequent expulsion from the state; out-of-state sale or expulsion as punishment of all free black criminals for noncapital crimes; and the prohibition of "meetings of negroes for any purposes whatever after sunset."[80]

Throughout the 1840s either the House Committee on Colored Population or one of the chambers of the state assembly introduced variations on the anti–free black legislative themes presented by the convened slaveholders in 1841. What the House passed, the Senate rejected. Furthermore, special memorials or the delegation from the city of Baltimore occasionally protested the draconian measures proposed and their potentially pernicious consequences "on many honest and industrious blacks."[81] However, the persistent consideration—and occasional successful passage—of ever more restrictive legislation against free black people indicated their worsening position within Maryland society during the 1840s.

As increasing numbers of German and Irish immigrants settled in Baltimore during the 1840s, free black workers found themselves excluded from occupations they had previously dominated. Immigrant replaced free black laborers as domestic servants in homes and as workers on the docks, in the warehouses, and in the factories so inexorably that in 1851 an observer commented, "The white man stands in the black man's shoes, or else is fast getting into them."[82] The diminishing economic options for free black people in Baltimore may explain in part the reduced student enrollment at the Oblate school during the 1840s.

Little extant evidence describes the range of individual and group responses of free black people in Maryland to their worsening legal and economic positions during the 1840s. However, an extraordinary document reveals how a segment of the black Catholic laity in Baltimore responded to the restrictions imposed on the Oblate Sisters' chapel by diocesan authorities. Within a month of Joubert's death in November 1843, between 150 and 200 black Catholic men and women formed the Society of Coloured People, which met weekly on Sundays from 3 December 1843 until 21 October 1845 at Calvert Hall, on the site of the razed Old St. Peter's Pro-Cathedral. Eccleston intended Calvert Hall for use as a boys' school for the cathedral parish and as a meeting hall. John Hickey, Joubert's Sulpician colleague, served as director of this Society of Coloured People and recorded its journal. Hickey's presence at the weekly meetings of this black society conformed to Maryland's legal requirement that responsible white witnesses attend or authorize black religious gatherings. Of course, with no black priests, black Catholics complied a priori with regulations mandating white supervision at their worship services. The national Catholic directory acknowledged the existence of this black Catholic association with the notice, "The colored people meet at Calvert Hall, on Sunday, for religious purposes."[83]

At their first meeting on 3 December 1843, the members defined their purpose as "the affording of the coloured people an opportunity of attending more particularly to their salvation and spiritual concerns [and] the adopting of such regulations as may tend to render the society useful." At the second weekly meeting, seventy-five people present voted to name the group the Holy Family Society; seventy preferred the name St. Benedict's Society, in honor of St. Benedict the Moor. The membership elected as its president John Noel—San

Domingan native, prominent Baltimore barber, and father of Oblate student and future Oblate member Angela Noel. Miss Mary Holland, one of the forty-nine black women organizers of the Oblate fair in December 1837, served as first counselor.[84] The available evidence does not clarify whether this organization represented a continuation of the Holy Family Society established in 1827 at St. Mary's Lower Chapel by James Joubert and transferred to the new Oblate chapel in 1837. The membership of Joubert's society may have participated in this later society as well. But the proceedings at the first meetings—statement of purpose, selecting a name, and election of officers—indicate that this group considered itself forming a new constituency.

The membership roster listed 285 names over the two-year existence of the Holy Family Society: 82 members were male; 203, female. The membership was overwhelmingly Anglophone, as only 31 French surnames appeared in the enumeration. The Holy Family roster listed many family names closely associated with the Oblate community, including Berry (Oblate students, future member); Brisco (Oblate students, fair organizers); Concklin (substantial underwriter of Oblate expansion, 1836); Divertier (Oblate student); Dorsey (Oblate donors); Greatfield (Oblate students and fair organizer); Hammond, Holland, and Powell (Oblate students, fair organizers); LaTourrandais (substantial underwriter of Oblate expansion, 1836); LeBarth (Oblate member, substantial underwriter of Oblate expansion, 1836); Moquette (Oblate student, server at Mass in Oblate chapel, 12 December 1832); and Noel (Oblate student, member, fair organizer).[85]

The format of the weekly meetings consisted of prayer, a religious instruction by Hickey, hymn singing, and the opportunity for members to express ideas or to give remarks relevant to matters before the society. Evidently, members occasionally interpreted this license rather freely: on 5 May 1844, "Jane Thompson came out with the Gospel of St. John by heart"; on 16 June, "Jane came out with something about the rock of Peter." On 13 October, "Jane Thompson disturbed the meeting at the close by coming out with her singing."[86]

Jane Thompson's enrollment in the devotional society Confrérie du Scapulaire as recently as 16 April 1842 suggests that she may have been an adult convert to Catholicism. Her spontaneous and exuberant outbursts, an accustomed and basic component of several Protestant worship styles, proved alien and unwelcome in the Eurocentric Roman Catholic religious tradition. The next meeting of the Holy Family Society featured "some remarks by the President about order and some remarks by the Director about what is out of order." Undoubtedly, cradle Catholic president John Noel and Sulpician director Hickey urged restraint on the indomitable Jane Thompson. In spite of their conservative views of appropriate deportment at their religious services, the Holy Family Society demonstrated an ecumenical spirit: Hickey noted of the 8 September 1844 meeting, "Pretty full meeting—many Protestants."[87]

At the 25 August 1844 meeting Holy Family Society member Caroline Thomas proposed that the group consider "providing for poor children clothes in order to attend church and Sunday school." The next evening the society's executive council considered Thomas's proposal, judged it "a laudable concern," but declined to adopt it "as a business of the society of the H[oly] F[amily] any more than any other charitable work."[88]

The Holy Family Society accepted its financial obligations as a functioning unit within the archdiocese of Baltimore. Contributing monthly to the Cathedral Fund Association—a group authorized by Archbishop Eccleston in 1839 to liquidate the debt incurred by the construction of Baltimore's Cathedral of the Assumption—formed the Holy Family Society's principal financial objective. Officers of the society—four men and four women—agreed to contribute the difference between $5 and the collection proceeds to guarantee a $5 monthly contribution to the Cathedral Fund from the Holy Family Society. At times contributions to the Cathedral Fund proved so insignificant that President Noel remarked that "the collection for the Cathedral Fund last month was very small, smaller than he wished to see it, and [he] exhorted the people to be more liberal." In her will, Holy Family Society member Lucy Butler bequeathed legacies of $21 each to the Holy Family Society and the Cathedral Fund.[89]

Between January 1844 and August 1845 the Holy Family Society consistently contributed $5 every month to the Cathedral Fund; just as consistently the collection shortfall required the society's officers to contribute, often more than half of the society's donation. It evidently proved a point of honor and racial pride that the members of the Holy Family Society meet their monthly subscription to the Cathedral Fund, for President Noel personally presented the society's contribution to the Cathedral Fund Association at their monthly meetings.[90] Even as diocesan authorities withdrew clerical ministrations from the Baltimore black Catholic laity as a distinct racial entity, the religious Society of Coloured People who called themselves the Holy Family Society expended extraordinary effort to participate in and support financially the life of the Baltimore Roman Catholic community.

At two consecutive meetings in June 1845, Director Hickey noted that he "mentioned the subject of the Free School for Girls, etc" and "mentioned the invitation to Supper for the purpose of raising funds for the Free School—."[91] That the journal records neither the society's response to Hickey's two "mentions" nor evidence of a contribution warrants consideration. One source interprets this passage as evidence of the society's financial support of the Oblate

School for Colored Girls. However, the Oblate Sisters did not establish a free school until the 1860s. Furthermore, as rector of the cathedral, Hickey would have promoted the cause of the St. Mary's Orphan Asylum and Free School for Girls, staffed by the Sisters of Charity and considered the parish school for the cathedral.[92] Both the orphan asylum and free school admitted a white clientele exclusively. Hickey thus solicited funds from black Catholics for an institution that would not serve them.

This situation proved no more incongruous in the climate of racial exclusion prevalent in antebellum Baltimore than the municipal authorities' presumption of the legitimacy of taxing black residents for a public school system that excluded their participation. Maryland had authorized a public primary school system for white pupils in 1826. In 1839 black Baltimoreans petitioned the city government for exemption from paying the public school tax; in 1844 and again in 1850 they sought financial support from the city to establish black primary schools. All these organized black initiatives seeking public support for black education failed.[93] Both religious and secular white society regularly imposed obligations and responsibilities on free black people without admitting them to full privileges of membership in the polity.

Because of an apparent misunderstanding in September 1845, the Holy Family Society could "no longer occupy the basement of Calvert Hall, as the Brothers of the Christian Doctrine have taken possession of it." The expansion of the teaching function of Calvert Hall evidently infringed on its meeting function. The problem proved irresolvable, and the society's officers "unanimously determined that we would not ask for or accept of the Cathedral as a place of meeting of the Holy Family Society," despite their faithful contributions to the Cathedral Fund. The following month the officers voted to dissolve the society for lack of a meeting place. When Edward McColgan, the pastor of St. Peter's Church at Poppleton and Hollins Streets, "intimated a willingness to give room in the basement of his Church or in his school house for the colored people," the society agreed to transfer its library and effects to St. Peter's for that purpose. The officers also proposed to sell all the society's possessions and apply the profits "to the relief of poor colored people." Finally, the officers designated any remaining funds in the treasury for "the relief of the poor and in particular those who were members of said society."[94]

Even as they disbanded their organization, the members of the Holy Family Society asserted their racial identity within the Catholic Church. They recognized the priest willing to accommodate black people and insured that black people would benefit from the liquidation of their resources. Like the Oblate Sisters of Providence, this segment of Baltimore's black Catholic laity embraced its dual identity as both black and Catholic. Consequently, it found itself still in, but not of, the larger Baltimore Catholic community in the critical middle years of the 1840s.

HOWEVER MUCH diocesan authorities may have concluded that the Oblate community must perish after Joubert's death if no one else would take it up, the Oblate Sisters themselves refused to give up. Because the sisters constituted a diocesan community of women religious, their archbishop retained the authority to disband them. Archbishop Samuel Eccleston had withheld ministerial support from the Oblate community between Joubert's death in November 1843 and October 1847; however, he had not mandated their dissolution. Unconvinced of the spiritual fervor and commitment of these black women religious, Eccleston may have assumed that a policy of neglect alone could effect Oblate disintegration. Furthermore, the publicized papal recognition of the Oblate community probably stayed Eccleston's hand.[95] Between 1843 and 1846, as Eccleston contended with papal inquiries about his own mental competence and fitness for office, he may have refrained from provoking Roman authorities further by initiating the dissolution of a presumed papally recognized diocesan community.

However, by October 1847 the Oblate Sisters of Providence still persisted and diocesan authorities evidently determined to proceed against them. No extant official correspondence or proclamation documented this decision, but on 7 October 1847 Louis Deluol maintained to Father Alexander, a Redemptorist priest, that the Oblate Sisters' "purpose has failed, and we can't hope to preserve it."[96]

Oblate historian Willigman's persistent portrayal of Deluol as actively sympathetic to the Oblate cause provides the only instance of her historical accounts varying substantively from the evidence. Willigman claimed that "the good Father Deluol did all in his power, but no one dared come forward to take up the work." She characterized Deluol as the sisters' "consoling angel" who was "not able to do all his heart prompted." She incorrectly maintained that not John Tessier but Deluol, "lifelong friend to Father Joubert," had introduced Joubert to James Whitfield to facilitate the formation of the Oblate community.[97]

Antagonism and formality characterized the relationship between Joubert and Deluol more accurately than the compatibility and intimacy Willigman asserted. Her personal contact with Deluol had consisted of nothing more than his semiannual celebrations of Mass in the Oblate chapel between 1840, when

Willigman came to live with the sisters as a five-year-old child, and 1849, when Sulpician authorities recalled Deluol to France permanently. Willigman reconstructed Deluol's role in Oblate history, obviously unaware of Joubert's and Deluol's adversarial positions in the "Sulpician Revolution" from 1827 to 1829—or of Deluol's incriminating diary entry of 7 October 1847, proclaiming the failure of the Oblate mission.

Three days later, on 10 October, John Neumann, who had replaced Peter Czackert as Redemptorist superior in America early in 1847, delegated Thaddeus Anwander "to take charge of the Oblate Sisters, then in a very bad condition of abandonment, for it was unfortunately the wish of high Ecclesiastical authority that the Sisters should dissolve and disband."[98] Anwander immediately sought appointment as spiritual director of the Oblate Sisters from Archbishop Eccleston, who initially refused the young priest's request. Had Eccleston resolved to disband the Oblate community only because he could find no cleric willing to direct them, as some sources maintain, he would not have refused the very offer of what he allegedly sought.[99] Anwander responded to Eccleston's laconic refusal, "Cui bono?" ("To whose good?"), by dropping to his knees and pleading with the archbishop for his blessing and permission to try. Eccleston relented and Anwander left his audience with the archbishop the newly appointed spiritual director of the Oblate Sisters of Providence.[100] Therefore, the sequence of events that portended the dissolution of the Oblate community in October 1847 accomplished its preservation instead.

Several agents shared the credit for the propitious resolution of the Oblate Sisters' position. Most accounts of Oblate history duly recognize that John Neumann, future bishop of Philadelphia and canonized saint, played a critical role in Oblate survival. As superior of the Redemptorist priests in 1847, he courageously risked the displeasure of high ecclesiastical authority in committing his order to the formal spiritual direction of the Oblate Sisters, when confronted with their imminent disbandment.

No account has acknowledged Father Alexander's contribution. Alexander Czvitkovicz, Redemptorist superior in America from 1841 until 1845, had become sufficiently familiar and involved with the Oblate community since his arrival in the United States in 1841 to have assisted at Joubert's funeral on 7 November 1843. As Redemptorist superior he had approved all Redemptorist ministrations to the Oblate Sisters through August 1845.[101] Czvitkovicz served as the crucial conduit through which the Redemptorist priests learned of the diocesan authorities' conviction of Oblate failure and determination to disband the black religious community. It proved no mere coincidence that within three days of

Czvitkovicz's conversation with Deluol about the Oblate community, Neumann had authorized Anwander to seek the directorship of the Oblate Sisters from Eccleston.

Born in 1823, Thaddeus Anwander had enjoyed a privileged youth in a wealthy farm family in Bavaria. He entered the Redemptorist Novitiate in Freiburg in 1841, responded favorably to Father Alexander Czvitkovicz's recruitment efforts for the American missions in 1843, arrived in New York in 1845, and immediately set out for Baltimore.[102] Ordained a priest in December 1846, Anwander already served as pastor of St. James Church in Baltimore when Neumann proposed that he assume the additional responsibility of directing the Oblate Sisters. Extraordinary powers of persuasion, if not divine inspiration, enabled Anwander to convert Eccleston from his determination to disband the Oblate Sisters. Perhaps just once, in the earnest, pleading eyes of the young priest on his knees before him, Eccleston fathomed the spiritual worth of the first permanent community of African American women religious.

Finally, the Oblate Sisters of Providence had acted on their own behalf. Between 1843 and 1847 they steadfastly observed religious community life, strictly adhered to their vows and community Rule, and faithfully attended Mass and confession—no longer in the security and convenience of their own chapel but out in distant, public churches. The Oblate commitment to their religious state first attracted the notice, then the interest, and finally the admiration of individual priests of the Redemptorist order, who observed the sisters at St. James and St. Alphonsus Churches. In successfully sustaining their internal spiritual integrity during the critical middle years of the 1840s, the Oblate Sisters of Providence precipitated the series of events that effected their revalidation as a legitimate religious constituency by diocesan authorities in Baltimore.

In the crucible of the years 1844 to 1847, the Oblate Sisters of Providence had encountered and prevailed over a series of events that tested both their faith and their viability as a community of women religious. They steadfastly lived as committed women religious, in compliance with their own spiritual vocations and in defiance of clerical antipathy, indifference, and neglect. Oblate action and perseverance during this period fully conformed to what historian Rosalyn Terborg-Penn has identified as "perhaps the two most dominant values in the African feminist theory . . . developing survival strategies and encouraging self-reliance through female networks."[103]

On 7 October 1847 Louis Deluol had accurately informed Redemptorist priest Alexander Czvitkovicz that something had failed. But the failure resided neither with the Oblate Sisters, as Deluol asserted, nor with the lay black Catholic community. The failure of the years 1844 through 1847 proved that of diocesan authorities to attend the spiritual needs of the Oblate community and the black Catholic laity because of their racial identity. In reflecting on the critical middle years of the 1840s in the Oblate experience, author Grace Sherwood observed, "It had been a wearying, soul trying four years since Father Joubert's death, endured with not only patience but honor! All the doubt, all the disagreement about the Oblates were from without. Within were steadfastness, devotion to the community life, quiet hope that all was not lost. It is a superb story."[104]

CHAPTER NINE

Happy Daughters of Divine Providence

THE MATURATION OF THE OBLATE COMMUNITY, 1847–1860

❖ ❖

For three years the Oblate Sisters of Providence had known that 10 October 1847 would be a significant date for their community: the Oblate Rule revisions of 1844 had designated the feast of St. Benedict the Moor, celebrated the second Sunday in October, for the triennial elections of Oblate community officers.[1] No election of a new Oblate mother superior occurred on 10 October 1847, however, and serving Superior Mary Louise Noel remained in office. Instead, sources external to the Oblate community decided the sisters' fate. On 10 October 1847 Archbishop Eccleston consented to appoint Thaddeus Anwander spiritual director of the Oblate Sisters of Providence.

Anwander began his spiritual ministrations to the Oblate community immediately. He heard confessions and celebrated Mass in the Oblate chapel on 15 October 1847. When he assumed its direction, the Oblate community comprised twelve sisters; but within a month the death of Sister Catherine (Rose Rock) reduced their number to eleven. Anwander's first goal was "to get as many children into their school as I could get."[2] The black community responded very enthusiastically to Anwander's appointment as Oblate spiritual director, interpreting it as evidence of revalidation of the Oblate community by diocesan authorities. Within one year student enrollment in the Oblate school had increased from under twenty to sixty or seventy students. On 4 September 1848 the Oblate Sisters "commenced the scholastic year with a sufficient number of scholars, which gave hopes of a future increase which has continued until now and which, trusting to Providence, we hope will not cease."[3]

Having a spiritual director revitalized the Oblate community. On 8 December 1847 the Oblate Sisters renewed their vows. Oblate book purchases such as *World and Cloister, Rome and the Abbey*, a Latin tract on the Immaculate Conception, *Life of St. Ligouri, Life of the Companions of St. Ligouri, and Ligouri on the Religious State* represented some of the sources that informed the ever evolving Oblate charism, or spiritual identity, under Redemptorist influence during the 1850s.[4] The resumption of school examinations and prize distributions on 27 July 1848 preceded an eight-day retreat for the Oblate Sisters, their first opportunity for such spiritual affirmation since the retreat Giles Smulders had arranged for them in 1845. On 8 October 1848, the feast of St. Benedict the Moor, in accordance with their rule revisions of 1844, the Oblate Sisters held an election, re-electing Sister Mary Louise Noel as mother superior.[5]

The new Oblate spiritual director also reestablished St. Frances Chapel as a black Catholic church. Anwander's purposeful restoration of the celebration of the feast of St. Benedict the Moor deeply gratified both black Catholic religious and laity. Like his predecessor, James Hector Joubert, Anwander recognized the crucial importance for black Catholics of identifying with a fellow black saint. He always celebrated St. Benedict's Feast "very solemnly to attract the people."[6] For St. Benedict's Feast on 14 October 1849, "the chapel was crowded, it was truly a happy day reminding us of our founder who also celebrated the festival with great solemnity."[7] On that same day, the Oblate Sisters registered their restored accreditation as a religious community by accepting their first new candidate in six years, Sarah Willigman, the future Oblate historian Sister M. Theresa Catherine Willigman.

On her deathbed a scant two weeks after Anwander had assumed direction of the Oblate community, Sister Catherine Rock allegedly said of the new young director, "His name is Wonder. May he do wonders for the poor Oblates."[8] The story may be apocryphal, but Anwander's accomplishments were not. Given the clerical abandonment they had experienced between November 1843 and October 1847, the Oblate Sisters might well have considered the diocesan authorities' reconciliation to their continued existence miraculous. On Christmas Day 1849, Anwander presented the Oblate Sisters with a dove, whose virtues he enjoined them to emulate.[9] Perhaps the sisters also appreciated the

Sister Mary Theresa Catherine Willigman, O.S.P., Oblate historian and superior, 1885–97 (Archives of the Oblate Sisters of Providence, Baltimore, Md.)

further connotation of the dove as the symbol of peace after the turmoil they had experienced during the decade of the 1840s.

RELYING ON THEIR OWN agency and convictions, the Oblate Sisters of Providence had successfully withstood crises in the mid-1840s. Under the nurturing spiritual directorship of Thaddeus Anwander from 1847 until 1855, the Oblate community expanded both its membership and the scope of its mission. Anwander received and professed nine new Oblate Sisters of Providence from approximately a dozen aspiring candidates. In receiving Sarah Willigman and siblings Franciette and Henriette Messonier, the Oblate community continued its tradition of admitting to its ranks "children of the house," orphans or poor girls raised within the Oblate community since childhood.[10]

Sarah Elizabeth Willigman had first applied for Oblate membership in 1848 "but was told to wait" until the Feast of St. Benedict the Moor, 14 October 1849. Willigman entered the community on 15 October and received the postulant's habit four days later, "with a promise to receive the habit of a novice on the eighth of December."[11] Anwander later recalled that when the Oblate community resumed admitting candidates, "Sister Theresa applied first; about her we had a lawsuit (a habeas corpus case) pleaded by the good lawyer [T.] P[arkin] Scott and decided in our favor."[12] In a rare instance of personal disclosure, Willigman herself later revealed some details of this case. Her father, misled "by the writings of a very vile woman," believed the Oblate Sisters had pressured his daughter to join their order and initiated a lawsuit to prevent it. Even after the favorable resolution of the case, Willigman postponed receiving the habit of a novice, "as it was judged more prudent to delay."[13]

This experience proved a trial to Willigman in more than a legal sense. It generated reproval against her within the Oblate community and strained her relationship with Anwander. Because of the trial and attendant delays in Willigman's progression toward Oblate membership, another Oblate candidate, Frances (Franciette) Messonier, received the name Sister Mary Alphonsa on 7 June 1850, in honor of St. Alphonsus Liguori, founder of the order of Redemptorist priests. Custom dictated that the first candidate admitted by the spiritual director of a community of women religious receive the name of his special patron. Writing in another context in the third person, Willigman concluded her own story: "Sarah Willigman, who had been a postulant eight months, was to have been invested at the same time, but some remarks coming to her ears, that she had caused the community trouble enough, and it might be the cause of serious insult to the Sisters, she preferred to wait. It was a source of great mortification to Reverend Father Anwander as she had been the first he had received and he at once thought she wavered. But in time he overlooked it."[14] Sarah Willigman finally began her novitiate as Sister Theresa Catherine on 15 August 1850.

Frances (Franciette) and Henriette Messonier came to the Oblate Sisters almost in tandem with Sarah Willigman and her younger sister, Charity Grant Willigman, in 1839 or 1840 and under similar circumstances. Sources identified the Messonier girls' parents only as "French, both Catholics." They remained at the Oblate school several years. Upon leaving the convent, however, they lived and worked in turn in the John Noel household and then in the white Chatard and Van Bibber households. The younger sister, Franciette, applied for Oblate membership on 13 May 1850, began her novitiate as Sister Mary Alphonsa on 7 June 1850, and with her fellow novice, Sister Theresa Catherine, pronounced her vows on 8 December 1851. Her older sister, Henriette, entered the Oblate community on 8 January 1853, began her novitiate as Sister Theresa Victoria on 2 February 1853, and pronounced her vows on 2 February 1854.[15]

Another Oblate school alumna, Angela Noel, began her Oblate novitiate as Sister Mary Seraphina on the Feast of St. Benedict the Moor, 12 October 1851.

Daughter of the prosperous barber John Noel, Angela had been an active supporter of the Oblate community even as a pupil, when she and her mother had suggested and organized the first Oblate fair in 1837. Although Mrs. Noel had died in February 1851, her daughter persisted in her religious vocation. When Sister Seraphina pronounced her vows the following year on the Feast of St. Benedict the Moor, 10 October 1852, family friend Fanny Montpensier wrote that the ceremony was beautiful and the sacrifice on the part of the father as well as the daughter admirable.[16]

Three of the candidates who applied for Oblate membership during the 1850s had reached their maturity in slavery. Ann Harker began her novitiate as Sister Anna Theresa on 18 August 1852 and pronounced her vows on 9 September 1853. Manumitted on 18 June 1849 at "about sixteen" years of age, Harker lived at the Oblate convent classified as an orphan in 1850.[17] Maria (Mary) Johnson, manumitted on 12 September 1840 at "about thirty" years of age, entered the Oblate community on 28 November 1853, received the habit of a novice as Sister Frances Catherine on 2 February 1854, and pronounced her vows on 2 February 1855.[18]

Harriet Reynolds pronounced her vows as Sister Celestine on 29 April 1855. Available evidence does not indicate when Reynolds entered the community or began her novitiate. The 1844–54 Oblate ledger included at least one entry documenting that Harriet's owner, Emily Harper, granddaughter of Charles Carroll of Carrollton, had paid tuition for her at the Oblate school. Reynolds received her freedom on 24 May 1856 at "about twenty-five" years of age. If the dates of Reynolds's profession as an Oblate Sister in 1855 and of her manumission in 1856 are accurate as recorded, then Reynolds would have professed vows as an Oblate Sister while still a slave.[19] Reynolds's manumission during the turbulent 1850s, a decade characterized by an accelerated repression of the free black population and several state initiatives—including Maryland—to re-enslave them, proved remarkable in itself. The social prominence of her owner, Emily Harper, undoubtedly facilitated Reynolds's manumission. Furthermore, the fact of Reynolds's professed membership in a religious community would have strengthened the case for her freedom. It provided evidence of her permanent gainful employment and eliminated the possibility that as a free person Reynolds would either threaten municipal security or drain municipal resources.

The estimated ages on the manumission documents of these former slaves reflected the demeaning casualness with which white antebellum society recorded the vital statistics of all black people, slave or free. In accepting these former slaves as members in the 1850s, the Oblate Sisters of Providence continued to observe their broadly inclusive membership policy established in the 1830s.

Merit—unencumbered by worldly considerations of color, class, or previous condition of servitude—still prevailed as the defining criterion of Oblate membership during the 1850s.

Two final candidates completed the group professed during Thaddeus Anwander's directorship. Charlotte Donaldson began her novitiate as Sister Agnes on 9 March 1854 and pronounced her vows the following March. Susan Riley, an Oblate school alumna, entered as novice Sister Theodora on 15 August 1854. The Oblate Sisters shortened her year of novitiate by almost four months to 29 April 1855, enabling her to pronounce her vows before Anwander's departure as Oblate spiritual director on 2 May 1855.[20]

The Redemptorist priests remained the spiritual directors of the Oblate Sisters until November 1860. Anwander's successors in the position professed four more Oblate Sisters from the seven candidates who applied for membership between 1855 and 1860. Two members identified only as Sister Clara and Sister Dóminica Thomas began their novitiates on 4 April 1858 and pronounced their vows on 1 May 1859. Margaret Waters, an Oblate school alumna from Frederick, Maryland, entered the community on 9 January 1860 and began her novitiate as Sister Agatha on 19 February. Agnes Boyd entered the community as a postulant on 1 June 1860 and began her novitiate as Sister Martha on 9 September 1860.[21]

By 1857 the Oblate community numbered twenty sisters. Between 1850 and 1860 only two Oblate Sisters died: Sister Benedict (Eugenie LeBarth) on 14 May 1857 and Sister Angelica (Angelica Gideon) on 20 February 1860. Dismissals also depleted the ranks of the Oblate Sisters during the 1850s. Anwander recalled that during his tenure as spiritual director, "only two Sisters were refused renewal of their vows and then dismissed, viz. Sisters Clotilde [Marie Germaine] and Elizabeth [Clara Bourgoin]."[22] On 30 April 1859, "Sister Magdalen was dismissed, she having for some time appeared as unfit for the religious life; she accordingly left the same evening."[23] Oblate annals and other sources contain no previous reference to Sister Magdalen concerning her identity, date of entrance, or status in the community as novice or professed sister. In spite of attrition from death and dismissals, Oblate membership experienced a consistent net gain during the 1850s.

The Oblate Sisters developed in other areas of their community life beyond size in the 1850s. During their first three decades, the Oblate Sisters maintained relationships with their respective spiritual directors that varied with time and circumstance. While a nascent community, they had maintained a filial relationship with Oblate cofounder James Joubert. They functioned with increasing autonomy during Joubert's incapacitating illness from 1842 until his death on 5 November 1843.[24] Abandoned by the Baltimore clergy from 1843 until 1847, the Oblate Sisters of Providence maintained themselves as a religious community without benefit of regular clerical spiritual direction.

When Thaddeus Anwander undertook the spiritual direction of their community in 1847, the sisters formed a close, collaborative bond with the youthful Redemptorist priest. On more than one occasion the sisters referred to themselves as "truly happy Daughters of Divine Providence" as a consequence of Anwander's ministrations to them. The terms "zealous" and "indefatigable" most frequently described Anwander in Oblate accounts. Whether describing Anwander as Oblate spiritual director or as pastor of the St. Frances Chapel congregation, the sisters repeatedly referred to him as both friend and benefactor.[25]

The feast of St. Benedict the Moor in 1850 provided the occasion for the Oblate Sisters to make an assessment of Thaddeus Anwander as poignant as it was perceptive: "Accordingly at 4 o'clock the instruction took place and our Reverend Father [Anwander] gave way to his fervor and zeal on the virtues of St. Benedict. We can here say that out of his mouth we could judge the sentiments of his heart towards that saint, and that prejudice finds no place in him. . . . Thus ended the happy feast of St. Benedict, which afforded happiness to all the inmates of St. Frances, or rather to the daughters of Divine Providence."[26] The Oblate Sisters of Providence rarely dignified racial prejudice with explicit references in their records. Oblate celebration of Anwander's lack of racial prejudice toward St. Benedict—applicable by extension to themselves and to black people in general—spoke volumes in its silence about the racial prejudice they had endured.

When five years later on 29 April 1855 Anwander announced to the assembled Oblate community and St. Frances congregation his transfer to New Orleans, "there was no need of saying (it can be well understood) the great surprise and general feelings of sorrow of those present."[27] The Redemptorist Order assigned Anwander to New Orleans in a customary rotation. Oblate member and historian Willigman corresponded with Anwander for several decades after his reassignment. In assessing his impact on the Oblate community, Willigman stated, "The day of his taking leave of the congregation, his dear Oblates, and the children was like a solemn funeral. He never lost his fatherly solicitude and love for the Sisters and until his death, left nothing undone that was in his power to benefit the community. His memory will always be alive in the hearts of the Oblates."[28]

James Poirier succeeded Anwander as Oblate spiritual director from 7 May 1855 until 18 March 1857. Poirier's imprint on the Oblate experience concerned their communal regulations. On 1 January 1856 Poirier did not observe the Oblate tradition of the sisters and children greeting the director with the compliments of the season. The sisters reported, "On the contrary we were obliged to settle ourselves to prepare for confession, which cleared away all our cheerfulness for the moment. But still we offered our annual present, as we formerly had been accustomed."[29]

Except for the triennial elections of officers in 1848, 1851, and 1854, no mention of weekly Oblate assemblies appeared in the annals during Anwander's tenure as director. On 24 February 1856 Poirier convened an assembly to reconcile "in our Rule some points taken from the Rule of St. Frances, our Patroness" concerning the practice of abstinence, or food restrictions on certain days, that proved dysfunctional in the context of Oblate life in Baltimore. Poirier resolved the issue "with the entire satisfaction of all."[30] The next month he again assembled the community to modify their observance of the rule of silence. Although the sisters deferred to Poirier on these issues, they did not always accept his initiatives. An undated copy of the Oblate Rule included a table of virtues "inserted (1856 by our worthy director, Reverend Father Poirier) in this book to serve as direction to Sisters in their efforts to attain perfection. But it belongs not to our Rules."[31] On the feast of St. Frances of Rome, 9 March 1857, Poirier "enforced particularly on the esteem we should have of our institute being approved by the Holy See."[32] This proved to be his last address to the Oblate Sisters. James Poirier died on 18 March 1857 after a brief illness.

Nicholas Van Emstede may have served as Oblate spiritual director between March and June 1857. John B. Vogien followed as Oblate spiritual director, but ill health forced him to resign after only three months, on 20 September 1857. Dominic Kraus undertook Oblate spiritual direction from 1 October 1857 until the Redemptorist priests relinquished this responsibility on 5 November 1860.[33] Oblate sources made few personal references to or observations about their Redemptorist directors following Anwander. Certainly the relatively brief tenures of these priests in this position and their respective infirmities inhibited the development of relationships with the sisters comparable to those enjoyed by Joubert and Anwander. When the Oblate Sisters established two new schools in south Baltimore in 1857 and Fells Point in 1858, discussed in Chapters 10 and 11, Redemptorist priest Dominic Kraus received no mention in Oblate accounts of the initiatives or the negotiations conducted by Oblate Superior Gertrude Thomas.[34] The antebellum experience of the Oblate community demonstrated that the agency, conviction, and faith of its members determined the efficacy of the group more than the personalities of priest directors Poirier, Van Emstede, Vogien, and Kraus.

Between 1851 and 1860 the Oblate Sisters of Providence elected Sister Gertrude (Helen) Thomas to three consecutive triennial terms as mother superior of the community.[35] Evidently a skilled administrator whose leadership ability the other Oblate Sisters recognized, Thomas also embodied both the Oblate past and present. As a former Oblate school honor student and a member of the first class of postulants organized in 1833, she identified strongly with Oblate traditions. As a convert to Roman Catholicism in her youth, Sister Gertrude could appreciate the Redemptorist missionary efforts in the black community during the 1850s and facilitate Oblate involvement in the process.[36]

The death of Thomas's brother in New York in late December 1856 revealed that reconciling blood kin and religious communal family obligations remained a challenge for Oblate members. Thomas's departure for New York to attend her ailing brother saddened the entire Oblate community "as the head of the community being afflicted, the other members of course partook." Immediately after her brother's death, Thomas requested that the sisters consent to accept her mother as a resident in the community, as they had Oblate Superior Lange's mother some twenty years previously. The sisters agreed unanimously, although "it was an exception that for approved of reasons it could be done, but not without the approbation of the Director." When Thomas returned with her mother on New Year's Day 1857 the sisters "were happy at the return of our beloved mother, for her absence appeared much longer than it was."[37]

Oblate Superior Thomas corresponded with Bishop John Purcell of Cincinnati in December 1857 concerning the prospect of an Oblate school in his diocese, discussed in Chapter 11. White sisterhoods like the Daughters of Charity often negotiated favorable terms with clerical and civic leaders competing for their services in staffing schools, hospitals, and asylums because of the general shortage of sisters available for such work.[38] In contrast, the black Oblate Sisters of Providence virtually pleaded with prelates to allow Oblate missions in their jurisdictions. In response to Purcell's inquiry, Thomas consulted with and secured the approval of Archbishop Francis Patrick Kenrick for the project, selected three or four sisters for Cincinnati, and wrote Purcell twice in three weeks, because having "not received any answer I concluded perhaps you did not get my letter." She assured Purcell both that "the Sister [sic] are all desirous of the same as I wrote to you immediately" and that "as to the Condition I have made none on the Contrary I have left this to you and I am waiting for your own arrangements whatever they may be and if possible I will acquiesce to your good pleasure in every respect as far as lies in my power [sic]."[39] Thomas demonstrated that Oblate commitment to promoting education for black children beyond Baltimore remained constant, whether or not others chose to employ it.

Oblate cofounder Sister Mary Elizabeth Lange had returned from service at St. Mary's Seminary in 1850 to resume an active role in the leadership of the community. She served as novice mistress from 1851 until 1855, assistant superior from 1857, and as superior of the Oblate mission at St. Benedict's School in Fells Point from September 1858.[40] The strong female leadership of Thomas and Lange provided direction and stability for the Oblate community as it undertook new or expanded responsibilities.

WHILE ENJOYING NEWFOUND security in several crucial aspects of their lives during the late 1840s and 1850s, the Oblate Sisters still struggled to maintain solvency. Anwander later noted that when he became Oblate spiritual director in 1847, the sisters had "orphan and school children about 10, some $700 debt, and no income except taking in washing and mending for the Seminary and the Cathedral."[41] Oblate chronicler Grace Sherwood elaborated upon Anwander's account—dramatically, if inaccurately—asserting, "There were but twenty children under their care, ten scholars and ten orphans. . . . The ten scholars were taught free of charge, evidently. The mind goes back to Father Anwander's words, arrested by them—'no income'—but they managed to shelter and to teach some twenty children!"[42]

The 1844–54 Oblate ledger and other financial records challenge both Anwander's terse summary and Sherwood's elaboration of the Oblate financial picture in 1847. For the month of September—the customary beginning of the Oblate school year—immediately preceding Anwander's assumption of the Oblate directorship, Oblate receipts of $150.44 exceeded Oblate expenses of $132.59. Furthermore, at least fifteen parents paid monthly board and tuition or day scholar fees, a figure excluding pupils paying on an annual or semiannual basis, or those actually educated free of charge.[43] Such evidence negates assertions of no income, a pupil enrollment of only ten girls, and an entire student body educated free of charge.

In January 1842, Oblate records cited a debt burden of $1,968.375.[44] Anwander's prosaic statement that the sisters carried a $700 debt in 1847 masked their extraordinary achievement in significantly reducing their debt, under the less than propitious circumstances ensuing from Joubert's death in 1843. Between 1844 and 1861, the Oblate Sisters realized more than $2,000 in income from sewing vestments.[45] Oblate tuition, vestment income, and funds deposited at St. Mary's Seminary enabled the sisters to retire more than $1,400 of their debt between 1842 and 1847.

Only two months after Sulpician authorities appointed Francis Lhomme superior of St. Mary's Seminary in Baltimore and recalled Louis Deluol to France permanently in November 1849, an Oblate ledger entry under date 1 February

1850 noted, "Cash given for to save to the Redemptorist fathers from Rev. Mr. Lhomme, on the 31st of January $500, when [sic] $200."[46] However, this transfer of the balance of Oblate deposits at the Sulpicians to the Redemptorists did not settle all accounts. No Oblate ledger documented receipt of the $720 contracted compensation for Oblate household management at the Sulpician seminary for the six-year period 1844–49. Furthermore, Louis Deluol in France, Baltimore Sulpician Superior Lhomme, and Oblate Assistant Superior Mary Louise Noel corresponded in 1858 about the location of a bank book for an Oblate account at the Baltimore Savings Bank in the amount of $50. At Lhomme's urging, Deluol searched for and discovered the bank book in question in his room. He disclaimed, "I don't believe that I had the least idea of it" and deferred the matter to Lhomme's best judgment.[47]

Between 1849 and 1860 Oblate annual expenses exceeded annual receipts every year. The sisters continued to supplement their income from the board and tuition of their students with sewing for both the public and local religious institutions. Board and tuition from all pupils represented $1,975.44 and sewing, $247.28 of the total cash amount of $2,911.59 the sisters received in 1859.[48] The community assumed a more public profile in fund-raising efforts, soliciting contributions in person either from other parishes in the archdiocese or by canvassing the households of St. Frances parishioners. In 1857 the Oblate community solicited "for the benefit of the institution, also for payments of curtains for the Church."[49] Sisters Louise Gabriel Addison and Celestine Reynolds collected $8.00; Sisters Louise Gabriel and Theresa Catherine Willigman, $3.25; Sisters Alphonsa Messonier and Theresa Catherine, $5.78; and Sisters Celestine and Helen Joseph West, $7.13. In 1860 Sister Louise Gabriel collected $10.00; Sister Angelica Gideon, $10.21; and Sister Scholastica Bourgoin, $19.75. Sister Gabriel also took charge of selling articles from the display case in the Oblate parlour. Between March 1857 and October 1861 she added $232.44 in sales to Oblate income.[50]

At regular intervals between 1857 and 1861 the Oblate community noted items such as "By cash of Sister Scholastica from the produce of her Store" in amounts ranging from $10 to $100. Several members of the Bourgoin family had earned their living as confectioners since the 1830s.[51] Evidently, Sister Scholastica had retained or inherited an interest in or income from her family's business. Oblate candidates applying in the 1850s lacked the financial resources with which Oblate cofounder Sister Mary Elizabeth Lange and Sisters James, Chantal, and Marie Louise Noel had endowed the community. Most candidates brought little or no dowry. Thus the Oblate Sisters especially appreciated the sums Sister Scholastica contributed from her sales. As they had since their foundation in 1829, the Oblate Sisters of Providence continued to maintain themselves materially through hard work, discipline, frugal management, and prayer.

THE ORIGINAL OBLATE MISSION of the School for Colored Girls developed significantly during the 1850s. Enrollment in 1850 totalled sixty-seven pupils, including ten boarders and an additional seven orphans.[52] By 1853 the Oblate school—now known as St. Frances School for Colored Girls—enrolled ninety-one students: sixty day scholars and thirty-one boarders, who enjoyed "advantages for education in this institution to be had no where else in this country for their color, and several of them are Protestants."[53] In 1854 school enrollment grew to 135 pupils "and several orphans."[54] Oblate ledger entries reveal that between 1856 and 1859 Protestant pupils in the Oblate school included the daughter of at least one Protestant clergyman, variously identified as Mr. or Rev. Henry Price. The program of the exhibition concluding the 1859 school year prominently featured Johnanna Price, who participated in the dialogue on "Truthtelling" and performed piano and vocal selections.[55]

The Oblate Sisters advertised their School for Colored Girls in Baltimore's *Catholic Mirror* for six months in 1853, undoubtedly contributing to the school's steadily increasing enrollment. The sisters had made significant changes in their school's original statement of purpose, as the modified one presented in these advertisements clearly indicated. They had deleted the original assertion that "in fact these girls will either become mothers of families or household servants"; the obsequious reference to "this humble and naturally dutiful class of society"; and the gratuitous comment, "How valuable will such servants be to their masters."[56] Instead the sisters used less servile language, referring to their pupils only as "a numerous portion of society." Furthermore, the sisters allowed for less restrictive and potentially more numerous options for their pupils in their new statement. The sisters maintained, "Thus whether destined to the care of families or to be otherwise employed in the service of their fellow creatures, the pupils of this Institution will be found fully competent for the discharge of their respective duties."[57] The tenor of the advertisement for their school reflected the sisters' genuine aspirations for their pupils.

The Oblate community revised and expanded the curriculum of St. Frances School for Colored Girls in the 1850s. The original course offerings advertised in the 1830s besides religious instruction included "English, French, Cyphering and Writing, Sewing in all its branches, Embroidery, Washing and Ironing." By 1853 the Oblate curriculum added geography to its core offerings constituting "the ordinary branches of an English education" and music lessons.[58] In eliminating washing and ironing from the curriculum and offering optional music lessons, the Oblate Sisters conformed more closely to the standard offerings of contemporary white girls' schools. By 1859 basic Oblate course offerings included catechism, reading, history, geography, arithmetic, and writing. The incremental inclusion of music, geography, and history in the Oblate curriculum— subjects earlier deemed useless to "persons of the lower order"—demonstrated the Oblate Sisters' implicit challenge to antebellum white society's efforts to circumscribe black life. It proved significant that the Oblate school offered its black clientele French and music, "popular and considered desirable cultural subjects for young ladies from good families" and staple offerings of white select academies.[59]

The Oblate Sisters had removed French from the standard curriculum and offered it as an optional course like music, for a fee. This development reflected the "English education" the Oblate Sisters offered their pupils as much as an attempt to increase revenues by charging additional fees for less basic courses. The Catholic academies for white girls in Baltimore had charged additional fees for foreign language courses—including French—from the 1830s.[60]

No extant evidence suggests that the decision to eliminate the French language from the basic curriculum generated debate within the Oblate community. Several circumstances may explain the status of this decision as a nonissue. By the late 1850s the ethnic composition of the Oblate community itself had changed significantly. Although in its first decade the Oblate community had accepted nine women not of Francophone ancestry among its thirty candidates for membership, between 1840 and 1860, of the fifteen sisters professed in the Oblate community only three bore identifiably French surnames—Franciette and Henriette Messonier and Angela Noel. From the beginning of the school the day scholars had always constituted the majority of the student body. Those with Anglo surnames had always outnumbered the students with French surnames. Although Oblate Sister Marie Therese Duchemin had championed the cause of monthly French-language sermons in the Oblate chapel during the early 1840s, the practice evidently did not continue with the resumption of the public use of the Oblate chapel in 1847. The Oblate annals never referred to French-language sermons in the 1850s, if the practice persisted.

Neither the mostly German Redemptorist priests pastoring the St. Frances Chapel congregation nor the hundreds of converts to Catholicism who increasingly formed that congregation during the 1850s and lacked a Francophone ethnic identity felt allegiance to the French language. By 1859, for most members of the Oblate community, the black St. Frances Chapel congregation, and Oblate pupils alike, the French language represented an academic subject, not an aspect of ethnic identity. When in 1866 the Oblate Sisters established a mission in New Orleans, their Jesuit director Peter Miller assured the bishop of New Orleans that Sister Victoria Messonier, "the one we intend to send as Superior[,] speaks French very well, and will only require some practice to speak it fluently."[61] Miller's observation indicated how foreign the French language had become to the life of the Oblate Baltimore community.

From 1829 the Oblate Sisters had concluded the school year with a public examination of their students conducted by several outside examiners, usually priests. The sisters especially appreciated clerics who made the public examinations "interesting both to the children and parents and all those present, also rendering it easy to the children, who on such occasions get confused."[62] The public examination usually occurred either the day before or the morning of the annual exhibition and distribution of awards. Anwander noted that these events "helped a great deal to attract the people and [convince them to] send their children to the school."[63]

The Oblate pupils' needlework displays drew much attention at these annual exercises. Needlework classes remained popular even after the sisters had removed embroidery and ornamental work from the basic curriculum in 1860, designating them optional courses like French and music, available at additional charge. Oblate pupil needlework received praise in the black New York City newspaper, *The Weekly Anglo-African*, which first appeared in July 1859. This publication would later earn recognition as "the most influential black newspaper of its time."[64] The Reverend John Mifflin Brown, the newspaper's Baltimore correspondent, reported on the Oblate exhibition concluding the 1859 school year: "I witnessed their exhibition of needlework, wife and other lady judges better qualified than myself in such matters, say that their efforts had been climaxed. Miss Lake, of Annapolis, worked 'The Father of His Country,' in full size. The judges at the National Fair pronounced it the best they had ever seen; but as there was no premium for colored girls, Miss L. had to content herself with mere praise. Well, it is some satisfaction to be praised, for we so seldom get even that."[65]

Although Brown noted the Oblate student's deft needlework, the motif she worked warrants notice as well. In assigning their students such a patently patriotic theme as "The Father of His Country," the Oblate Sisters demonstrated their promotion of American values in a highly visible manner. Undoubtedly, the theme Mary Lake depicted, as much as the skill with which she accomplished her task, elicited warm praise from the judges at the National Fair. Such palpable proof of the promotion of patriotism within a black and Roman

Sarah. Solomon, worked at the Sisters of Providence School May 30ᵗʰ 1849 Baltimore.

Oblate pupil Sarah Solomon worked this sampler of St. John at the Oblate School for Colored Girls in 1849 (Archives of the Oblate Sisters of Providence, Baltimore, Md.).

Catholic school surely demonstrated the social worth of the Oblate educational mission.

The Baltimore correspondent continued, "There were worked chairs, vests, shirts, etc., but none excelled those representing the blessed Savior receiving the tribute money and 'The Holy Night.' They were charming."[66] These images of God and country, painstakingly worked in millions of brilliant, tiny stitches by hundreds of antebellum Oblate pupils bore vivid, if silent, testimony to the Oblate Sisters' patient inculcation into their charges of American as well as Roman Catholic values.

In addition to their needlework displays, Oblate students annually demonstrated their other talents and accomplishments in performances of instrumental and vocal music and recitations during the premium distribution ceremonies. The themes of several of the dialogues and speeches recited at these exercises revealed the broad common ground occupied by American and Roman Catholic values. Oblate pupils declaimed on such topics as "Kindness Recommended," "Truthfulness and Honesty," "On Pride," "Truthtelling," and "Generosity."[67]

Oblate account books with the Baltimore publishing firm John Murphy and Co. itemized book and school supply purchases between 1852 and 1861. Student textbooks ordered annually in multiples of a dozen during this decade included *Kerney's Catechism History of the United States*, evidently a book in question-and-answer form, *Kerney's First Class Book of History*, *Kerney's Introduction to Columbian Arithmetic*, *Pike's Arithmetic*, and *Kerney's Grammar*. *Comly's Spelling Book, Carpenter's, Canon's and Webster's Elementary Spellers*, First, Second, and Third *Book of Reading Lessons*, *McGuffey's Second Reader*, *Hazen's* and *Webster's Definers*, *Mitchell's Primary Geography and Atlas*, and *Mitchell's School Geography* contributed to the "ordinary branches of an English education" the Oblate Sisters offered their pupils.

Texts addressing the religious component of Oblate student education consisted of an assortment of catechisms, *Reeves'* and *Challoner's Bible Histories*, *A Catholic Primer*, *Gems of Devotion*, and children's prayer books. Works like *Porney's Syllabaire Français*, *Collott's Interlinear French Readers*, *Lhommond's French Grammar*, *Histoire Sainte*, and *Choquet's French Conversations* supplied the needs of the Oblate French curriculum.

Choral music with a Catholic imprint formed a part of the Oblate school experience, as such purchases as chapel choir books, *Peter's Catholic Harmonist, Lyra Catolica, Organist Gregorian,* and *Catholic Harp* indicate. The sisters also taught public speaking, using *Marshall's Oratory, The Natural Orator, Northend's Little Speaker,* and *Entertaining Dialogues*. Unlike the white girls' academies in the archdiocese, the Oblate school did not offer science at this time, so purchase of *Comstock's Botany* most plausibly provided floral patterns for use in drawing or needlework designs.

Single-copy purchases of numerous titles suggest that the Oblate Sisters read to their students. Selection of Cardinal Nicholas Wiseman's 1854 historical novel *Fabiola*—an enduring classic that prevailed on parochial school reading lists a century later—and Henry Wadsworth Longfellow's Acadian idyll *Evangeline* among less renowned works of fiction like *The Governess, Poor Scholar, Miner's Daughter,* and *The Miser* demonstrated Oblate inclusion of contemporary works in their didactic use of edifying fiction and moralizing tales to reinforce their overall educational program. Titles like *Roman Catacombs, Young Savoyard, War of the Peasants,* and *Curse of the Village* reveal a historical predilection in the selection of discretionary reading material. Books such as *Sick Calls* and *Christian Mother* instilled ideals of womanly duty and responsibility. *Lily of Israel, Legends of Mary,*

Graces of Mary, Mary Star of the Sea, and biographies of Saints Margaret of Cortona, Frances of Rome, Agnes of Rome, Rose, and Angela inculcated virtues and values through the inspiring examples of female role models. Selections such as *Sacred Heart of Jesus, Child of Mary, All for Jesus, Hours before the Altar,* and *Tales of the Sacraments* addressed Oblate student spiritual formation. Collections and series like *Mrs. Tuthill's Juvenile Library, McGrath's Parochial Library,* and nine- and twelve-volume sets of *Schmid's Tales* completed the Oblate pupils' options for reading.

Other Oblate purchases provide revealing insights about the sisters' approach to teaching. Several hundred certificates of "Reward for Merit" and "For Diligence" suggest that the Oblate Sisters employed techniques of positive reinforcement. Purchases of a dozen toy books from Murphy and five dozen oranges, one dozen coconuts, and seven and one-half pounds of candy from William Bridges, purveyor of "foreign fruits, confectionary of all kinds, oranges, lemons, filberts, walnuts, palm nuts, pecans, Havana segars, Havana and refined sugars, Bordeaux and Marseilles almonds, sardines, preserved ginger, firecrackers, etc., etc. etc." indicate that the Oblate Sisters always remembered that they ministered to children.[68]

IN 1849 THE Oblate Sisters marked their twentieth year as a corporate entity. An evolving consciousness of their group history emerged as one consequence of Oblate community maturation. On 5 November 1849, "being the Anniversary of the death of our reverend founder Father Joubert," the Oblate community attended a requiem Mass in their chapel, "being six years since his death."[69] On 5 November 1851 the Oblate community again observed Joubert's anniversary with a requiem Mass. In addition, "on the following Friday the same ceremony was performed for the deceased Sisters."[70] By 1854 the statement "the Mass of Requiem for Reverend Father Joubert and the Sisters was as usual"[71] indicated that the Oblate community had institutionalized commemoration of their deceased significant others and combined it into one service. By 1855 the ceremony commemorated "our lamented Father Joubert, our holy founder, and the deceased Sisters of the community."[72] In 1859 James Poirier and John Vogien joined Joubert in the ranks of deceased Oblate spiritual directors and the community again commemorated their deceased directors and members in separate ceremonies.[73]

These annual commemorative requiem Masses allowed the sisters to reflect on past communal experiences and to assess the development of the community as a religious institution. The reference to Joubert in 1854 as "our lamented

Father Joubert, our holy founder" marked the transition of the Oblate community from one whose entire membership had known Joubert personally to one whose most recent members would have known Joubert only as a historical figure. The Oblate community commissioned a portrait of Joubert in January 1860.[74]

When the Redemptorist priests relinquished the spiritual direction of the Oblate community on 5 November 1860, the sisters' reaction revealed an appreciation of significant dates in Oblate history. In response to the departure of the Redemptorists and the closing of their chapel to the public, the sisters observed, "It was remarkable that it was the anniversary of the death of our beloved Founder that this sudden change took place."[75]

Not merely time but growth had marked the progress of the Oblate Sisters of Providence since their organization in 1828. As a community of women religious, they had matured into a self-empowered, self-confident, and historically conscious corporate entity. The Oblate School for Colored Girls reflected this development in its expanded curriculum and bolder statement of purpose. On 16 January 1861 Thaddeus Anwander, "our old father and benefactor," visited the Oblate Sisters for the first time since his departure as their spiritual director six years before. Anwander attempted to comfort the Oblate Sisters during their potentially anxious and unsettling transition occasioned by "this sudden change" of both their spiritual direction and the closing of the Oblate chapel, "our beloved Church," to the public.[76] The Oblate annalist reported that "he encouraged us to do all in our power to please God and not to lose courage if we had some portion of the Cross, for it was a true sign that God loved us."[77] Anwander's advice merely reflected what the Oblate Sisters of Providence themselves had believed and practiced since their inception in 1828.

CHAPTER TEN

Our Beloved Church

THE OBLATE SISTERS AND THE
BLACK COMMUNITY, 1847–1860

❖ ❖

By the 1850s a nexus of circumstances enabled the Oblate Sisters of Providence to resolve their ambivalence about the public use of their chapel evident in the 1830s. The conviction and confidence accompanying their corporate maturation as a community of women religious allowed the sisters to maintain their discrete religious identity, even in close association with the black laity. Furthermore, the departures of Sisters Therese Duchemin, Ann Constance Schaaf, and Stanislaus Amanda in 1845 may have purged the Oblate community of those members most concerned with preserving their status as "true religious" by distancing themselves from the black laity.

When in the mid-1840s the Baltimore clergy had virtually abandoned the Oblate Sisters, the black community had continued to support "our convent" as its means allowed through the crisis. This experience undoubtedly demonstrated to the Oblate Sisters not only the primacy of considerations of race over religion in defining their status within white antebellum Baltimore society but also the extent of the black laity's identification with the Oblate mission. Finally, the pastoral orientation of the Redemptorist priests, the sisters' spiritual directors from 1847 until 1860, facilitated Oblate interaction with broader segments of the black community.

Nothing illustrated the Oblate community's reconciliation to its vital role in the parish life of St. Frances Chapel more than the sisters' reaction when that association ceased in 1860, with the departure of the Redemptorist priests. The sisters observed, "On this day we received the sad although not unexpected news that our worthy and kind Director was to leave us and that our beloved Church was to be closed. It is impossible to describe our feelings at such an event."[1] The Oblate attachment to the St. Frances Chapel congregation expressed in this statement demonstrated the sisters' acknowledgment of their symbiotic relationship to their black laity. The diversification the Oblate Sisters experienced as a community during the 1850s occurred in conjunction with the expanded services they offered the black Baltimore community. The St. Frances Chapel congregation provided both impetus and occasion for much of the Oblate expansion.

FROM THEIR INCEPTION the Oblate Sisters had assisted their spiritual directors in providing weekly religious instruction to the black laity.[2] The Sulpician priests had considered training seminarians their primary mission and had viewed pastoral care as an extraneous, temporary ministry. James Joubert had focused his efforts at religious instruction rather narrowly on children. By contrast, the mission of the Redemptorist priests in the United States required them to provide pastoral care to their congregations as their primary ministry.

Within ten months of assuming the spiritual directorship of the Oblate Sisters of Providence in October 1847, Thaddeus Anwander had established weekly Sunday religious lessons "for the first time expressly for the coloured congregation in the chapel."[3] The Oblate Sisters assisted Anwander in this weekly ministry. In preparation for First Communion on 30 June 1848, Anwander conducted a three-day retreat for the first communicants. He performed a First Communion service commemorated as "truly an imposing and solemn ceremony which ought to be deeply imprinted in the hearts of all present."[4] In spite of his service there as part-time pastor, Anwander offered a variety of spiritual services for the black Catholics again congregating at the Oblate chapel. He held vespers, instruction, and Benediction in the Oblate chapel on Sunday afternoons, to which "the colored people came in crowds."[5]

Anwander's pastoral outreach to the black community bore bountiful fruit. Before he assumed direction of the Oblate community and pastoral responsibility for the black Catholic laity, only three children had made their First Holy Communion on 3 June 1847. But his vigorous ministry produced twenty-one first communicants on 30 June 1848 and thirty on 24 March 1849.[6] Anwander achieved his goals as spiritual director of the Oblate Sisters and minister to the black Catholic laity swiftly and thoroughly. This accomplishment reflected not only the self-sustained integrity of the Oblate community's religious life and the resilience and durability of the black Catholic laity despite years of clerical neglect, but also Anwander's earnest commitment to his tasks.

On 29 April 1849 Archbishop Samuel Eccleston confirmed fifty-six candidates in the Oblate chapel. This event symbolized the rehabilitation of the Oblate community in the estimation of diocesan authorities. Both children and adults composed this Confirmation class, the culmination of Anwander's catechetical efforts begun 27 August 1848. Redemptorists Louis Gillet, in town for the Seventh Provincial Council, and Thaddeus Anwander assisted the archbishop at the Confirmation ceremony. Afterward Eccleston observed that "in twelve years he had never at one time in any parish confirmed so many colored people as on that day."[7] Archbishop Eccleston confirmed "a large class of children, converts, even some old men and women" in the Oblate chapel in 1850.[8] The thirty-nine candidates confirmed in the Oblate chapel in 1851 included fourteen slaves. Of the twenty recipients of First Communion on 7 May 1852, "several were converts." Francis Patrick Kenrick, Eccleston's successor as archbishop of Baltimore in 1851, confirmed a class containing "several adult converts" on 28 May 1852. Kenrick confirmed "47 colored persons, 22 of whom were converts" on 21 May 1853.[9] That same year the Oblate Sisters had assisted with "a Sunday school for colored children in the basement of St. Frances Church, Richmond street, for girls from 10 to 12M., for boys from 2 to 4 P.M. Number of scholars, about 65."[10]

During his tenure as pastor of the black congregation at St. Frances Chapel, Anwander received some 300 adult converts into the Roman Catholic faith. He encouraged these adult converts to participate completely and immediately in all facets of Catholic life. On 1 February 1850 he baptized Henrietta Gibbs; on 15 February she "entered the house as a candidate," receiving the postulant's habit on 9 March 1850.[11] Evidently, Gibbs later left religious life. Anwander's evangelizing efforts among adults increased the size of the congregation worshiping at St. Frances Chapel significantly. Consequently, the Oblate community enlarged its chapel in 1851. Renovations required four months, and the chapel reopened on the feast of St. Benedict the Moor on 10 October 1851.

The little extant information concerning the financing of this construction project indicates that, as they had done in 1836, the black St. Frances congregation met the expenses of the chapel expansion, totalling $2,500. Anwander later recalled that construction "was paid for by the generous contributions of the people. A colored girl (now a Sister) gave me the first money, a little gold dol-

The Reverend Thaddeus Anwander, C.SS.R., Oblate director, 1847–55, photographed in his later years (Archives of the Oblate Sisters of Providence, Baltimore, Md.)

lar, which I put in the tabernacle and left it there until the Church was paid for."[12] Future Oblate member Henriette Messonier—probably the "colored girl" Anwander mentioned—collected subscriptions for the chapel totalling $29.30. Mde. Antoinette Antoin reprised her role in 1836 and solicited funds totalling $37.50. St. Frances parishioners organized a Sinking Fund Society to retire outstanding debts; it donated $75.00 between 1852 and 1857.[13] On 3 October 1852 James Powell, George Holley, A. Gibbs, J. Holley, John Colbert, and J. H. Darnall assumed responsibility for payment for the chapel organ. By 20 May 1853, in installments ranging from $10 to $100, they completed "payment cash in *full* for the new organ of St. Frances Church, $250."[14]

Numerous entries in the Oblate ledger record anonymous donations for the church in amounts ranging from $1 to $5 "from different persons to Fr. Anwander—$5" as well as donations "from Mr. John Noel for Chapel—$5" and "of Mrs. Madison for the Church—$5."[15] The small amounts of individual donations reflected the modest circumstances of the black St. Frances congregation; the many entries reflected the wide participation of the black community in support of the project. The newly enlarged chapel accommodated 400 persons. By 1855 the black congregation worshiping at the Oblate chapel increased to 500 members; by 1857, 600.[16] Redemptorist evangelization among black Baltimoreans produced significant results through the 1850s.

Black Catholics worshiping at the Oblate chapel experienced an almost complete parish life. Baptismal and Confirmation Registers documented the sacramental ministrations provided members of the Oblate chapel congregation during the 1850s.[17] In 1852 Anwander established a chapter of the Holy Family Society and organized different classes for married men and women.[18] While Anwander was pastor, "the chapel was filled. Pews were rented and Societies of the Holy Family, St. Frances of Rome, and St. Benedict had a large membership."[19] Members of these various devotional societies wore distinctive garb. They added pageantry to the parochial experience of St. Frances congregation by attending High Masses commemorating the major patronal feast days of the Oblate Sisters—St. Frances of Rome and St. Benedict the Moor—as well as Christmas and Forty Hours Devotions in full dress regalia.[20] These devotional societies subsidized the Oblate community with hall rental fees, donations, and legacies. Between 1855 and 1861 the Holy Family Society contributed $6.00; St. John's Society, $43.00; St. Benedict's Society, $71.25; the Good Samaritan Society, $100.25; and St. Frances of Rome Society, $120.50 to the Oblate community's revenue.[21]

In 1850 Anwander inaugurated what became an annual parish social event—a picnic excursion to a local park or wood where the schoolchildren, the Oblate Sisters, and members of St. Frances congregation all "spent the day in innocent amusement."[22] In addition to the opportunity to bond socially that these picnics provided the participants, they evidently served as fund-raising events. Picnic receipts included $29 from a "Pic-Nic Collection on Sunday," $15 from "Produce for the Picnic," and $39 from "Ladies of the Pic-Nic."[23]

Pew rental fees formed an important component of Oblate community income. Scholar Mary Oates has explained that the pew rental system originated in Germany, became commonplace in America by the 1840s in areas of heavy German settlement, and served to stabilize parish finances, augmenting the unpredictable Sunday collections. Although some prelates objected to the inherently undemocratic nature of the system, financial exigency prevailed. Through the antebellum period, pew rents remained a vital source of parish revenue, frequently representing half of a parish's income. Pew allocations occurred at annual auctions where front seats commanded higher prices.[24] Annual pew rents in St. Frances Chapel ranged from $9.00 to $12.50. Members of the congregation frequently rented individual seats in pews for fees ranging from $0.62 to $2.50. In October 1857 a Mrs. Emily paid $1 "for six months of a seat in #7."[25]

Oblate financial ledgers from this period documented the full participation in and financial support of St. Frances parish community life by the Uncles family. Lorenzo Uncles paid room and board expenses for his daughter, Georgianna, while she attended the Oblate school from 1854 through 1858. He also rented a pew in St. Frances Chapel, purchased several devotional articles, and made donations to the Oblate community during this time. Georgianna Uncles participated in and submitted revenues from an Oblate fair in 1860.[26] The black Catholic activism apparent in the Uncles family's involvement in the St. Frances Chapel congregation in the 1850s would nurture the religious vocation of Charles Randolph Uncles. Born in 1859, he would become the first black Roman Catholic priest ordained in the United States in 1891.[27]

Another family association evident in the 1850s extended back to Oblate origins and continued into the twentieth century. Magdeleine Jean Deshais enrolled her daughters, Adine (Adeine), Ursula, and Hospiliene—who would join the first Oblate postulant class in 1833—among the first pupils in the Oblate school in June 1828. The eldest, Adine, married Emile Joseph Dubois, a barber, in the 1830s. Barbering proved a lucrative trade for black men in antebellum cities and remained one of the few occupations they successfully defended against the onslaught of European immigrant competition.[28] Black barbers provided much of the antebellum financial support the Oblate community and school received. Baptismal records of two Dubois daughters at St. Patrick's Church in Fells Point in 1837 and 1838 document that Mary J. Deshais stood as godmother to one child and Nelson Moquette, discussed below, as godfather to another, thus superimposing spiritual kin ties on their blood relationships to these girls. When the Oblate community sponsored its first fund-raising fair in 1837, "Adeine Dubois and her two sisters" monitored Table number 7.[29]

The Oblate Sisters were teaching the Dubois's daughter Philomena by 1850, when the census identified her as an eight-year-old boarder at the school. A member of the Confirmation class of 1851, Philomena recited the dialogue on "truthtelling" with Mary Lake at the exhibition closing the school year in 1854.[30] Some seventy-five years later, in 1929, Oblate chronicler Grace Sherwood interviewed "the oldest living pupil of the Oblates, Mrs. William Deaver, now eighty-seven years old." While not disclosing her subject's given name, Sherwood identified Mrs. Deaver as "the granddaughter of a San Domingan colored physician named Moquette [who] was named Dubois herself before her marriage."[31] Kin ties, names, and age corroborate the identity of Mrs. William Deaver as the former Philomena Dubois. Her family's association with the Oblate Sisters spanned a century.

Between 1850 and 1855 the Oblate Sisters of Providence and the St. Frances black Catholic congregation undertook two additions to the Oblate convent, enlarged the chapel and classroom building, and constructed a boys' school and meeting hall at a cost of over $10,000. By the time of Anwander's departure in 1855, the congregation had liquidated this debt.[32] Oblate ledgers document several loans to the Oblate community from black contributors during this period. Mr. Emile Joseph Dubois, Philomena's father, lent the Oblate Sisters $400 on 16 November 1852 through John Noel. Noel himself continued his staunch support of the Oblate community during the 1850s. The sisters repaid John Noel a $115 loan in May 1855. In 1858 John Noel purchased the only real estate the sisters acquired during the 1850s, the house for St. Benedict's School in the Fells Point area of Baltimore. Ruth Hopp, a member of the Holy Family Society in 1844, a boarder in the Oblate convent, and a pew renter in St. Frances Chapel, provided a $100 loan in October 1854.[33]

Patrons beyond Baltimore subsidized the sisters as well. Mrs. Mary Augustus of Philadelphia lent the sisters $200 in April 1853. Her daughter Mary earned individual notice in a report in the *Catholic Mirror*, the official organ of the archdiocese of Baltimore, on the closing exercises at St. Frances School in 1853 "for her proficiencies both on the piano and in vocal music, singing both in French and English."[34] Mrs. Mary Jackson of Boston paid her daughter's board and tuition at the Oblate school in annual sums of $80 to $95 between 1852 and 1857. She received repayment of a $100 loan to the sisters in August 1855. Oblate records verify repayment of all these loans except for the $200 Augustus loan by 1858.[35]

The *Catholic Mirror* reported in 1850 that "an old colored man, John Jones," left an estate valued at $10,000. He bequeathed $1,000 to James Dolan, pastor of St. Patrick's Church, for the parish.[36] The precedent existed for black Baltimoreans of means to endow Catholic institutions. Marie Noel evidently bequeathed the Oblate Sisters a small legacy at her death in 1851. An Oblate ledger entry noted, "By cash of Mr. J. Noel from what was allowed by Orphans Court 2 years ½, $75."[37] On 10 January 1859 the Oblate Sisters rejoiced that "a worthy old gentleman of our country" had bequeathed them "a legacy of $340 which was really a God-send, for the Community was much embarrassed with debts." The sisters asserted, "This was a great relief and only convinces us we must never repine under wants. As this good old man was so liberal to us, we have reserved $5 for Masses for the repose of his soul."[38] Providential legacies proved a rare experience for the Oblate community during the 1850s. Nevertheless, black Catholics supported the Oblate community and St. Frances parish life to the fullest extent their means allowed.

But the black congregation at St. Frances Chapel did not enjoy exclusive pastoral attention. The large German congregations, first at St. James's Church and later at St. Michael's Church in Fells Point, constituted Thaddeus Anwander's primary assignment.[39] Ministering to the German parishes prevented his celebrating Masses in the Oblate chapel on Sundays and major feast days. Consequently, the black Catholic congregation at the Oblate St. Frances Chapel attended other churches to fulfill their Sunday Mass and feast day obligations. As the *Catholic Mirror* observed in 1853, "It is to be regretted that the great scarcity of priests precludes more particular attention being given to the Catholic people of color."[40] The chronic shortage of priests in the archdiocese affected white Catholics as well. Throughout the antebellum period, several parishes in the outlying districts of Baltimore depended on services from priests assigned primarily to city parishes, according to information printed in the *Laity's Directory*.

Thaddeus Anwander, about whom the Oblate Sisters had noted "that prejudice finds no place by him,"[41] initiated a bold, even radical solution to the problem of insufficient numbers of priests ministering to black Catholics. Perhaps inspired by his six years of experience with the Oblate Sisters of Providence as exemplary women religious, Anwander proposed a black man, William Augustine Williams, for admission to the Propaganda Fide College in Rome to study for the priesthood in 1853.

Anwander must have had some personal knowledge of Williams in terms of his character, ability, and religious convictions to propose him as a candidate for such a pioneering venture. Raised as a Baptist in Virginia, Williams had converted to Roman Catholicism in Baltimore, where he had earned a living as a barber for three years prior to beginning his seminary studies in Rome in 1855.[42] Plying his trade in Baltimore probably brought Williams in contact with established barber John Noel. Presumably Williams had participated actively in the parish life of the black Catholic congregation worshiping at the Oblate chapel under Anwander's care. According to Anwander's records, Williams, along with thirty other candidates, received the sacrament of Confirmation in St. Frances Chapel on 28 May 1852.[43] Williams had definitely established contact with the Oblate Sisters of Providence in Baltimore prior to leaving for Rome. While studying in Rome in 1856, Williams sought and received a papal blessing for John Noel's daughter, Oblate Sister "Maria Seraphina, a Baltimore nun of the Order of St. Frances of Rome."[44]

Anwander obtained the requisite endorsements for Williams from two prelates, Bishop Louis Amadeus Rappe of Cleveland and Archbishop Francis Patrick Kenrick of Baltimore. However, neither bishop shared Anwander's conviction of the viability of Williams's priestly profession in the United States.

From 1853 until 1860, both Rappe and Kenrick corresponded at length with the Propaganda Fide, the papal bureaucracy supervising foreign missions, insisting that racial prejudice precluded assigning Williams to the United States. They suggested instead that Williams serve in Haiti, Liberia, or any mission outside the United States.[45] In the vacuum of support from the U.S. Catholic hierarchy, in 1862 Williams, "after mature deliberation, on the advice of his teachers . . . concluded he has no calling to the clerical state."[46] When Williams returned to the United States, he resided in Baltimore, where he continued to work actively in the black Catholic community as an educator, publisher, and clerical brother— but not as a priest—until the 1880s.[47]

Knowledge of Thaddeus Anwander's genuine concern for the welfare of antebellum black Catholics spread beyond the boundaries of the archdiocese of Baltimore to New York City, where, in 1853, a black Catholic woman named Harriet Thompson wrote a personal letter to the reigning pontiff, Pope Pius IX. No extant evidence documents the details of Harriet Thompson's life. Thompson's own words indicated that she knew the Baltimore priests Edward McColgan—the pastor of St. Peter's Church sympathetic to the Holy Family Society when they disbanded in 1845—and Thaddeus Anwander personally, suggesting a prior Baltimore connection. A Baltimore confraternity register included as a member a Harriet Thompson in 1829.[48] Thompson may have encountered Oblate influence directly as a student in their school or in weekly classes in religious instruction, or perhaps more obliquely through the Oblate presence resonating in the active parish life of the St. Frances Chapel congregation, or perhaps not at all. Yet Harriet Thompson's action in 1853 replicated the self-definition and empowerment increasingly associated with the Oblate Sisters of Providence in the antebellum era.

Concern "for the salvation of the black race in the United States who is going astray from neglect on the part of those who have care of souls" prompted Thompson to write her letter to Pope Pius IX in October 1853, shortly before the anticipated visit of the papal representative to the United States. Disclaiming any disrespect of clergy, she nevertheless asserted that most bishops and clergy in the United States were ethnic Irish or Irish descent, "and not being accustom [sic] to the black race in Ireland, they can't think enough of them to take charge of their souls." Thompson continued, "Hence it is a great mistake [sic] to say that the church watches with equal care over every race and color, for how can it be said they teach all nations when they will not let the Black race mixt with the white?"[49]

Thompson objected that black Catholics in the archdiocese of New York had no access to a Catholic education to counter the influence of the blatant anti-Catholic bias of public school education. She contended that "the Catholics teach the pure word of god [sic] and gave learning at the same time; the protestants gave learning and teach the word of god adulterated." Thompson then exposed the racist double standard of education operative in the archdiocese of New York. She asserted that "the church does remedy these evils for the white children by providing schools where they can learn the pure word of god and how to keep it and be educated at the same time, but the church do [sic] leave the colored children a prey to the wolf."[50]

In protest, "the colored people of the cathedral congregation of the city of new york [sic]" had approached John Loughlin, vicar-general of the archdiocese of New York. Although sympathetic to the black petitioners' cause, Loughlin lacked the authority to require the Sisters of Charity to integrate their schools. Thompson understood that "in new york nothing cannot [sic] be done because the Most Rev. Archbishop Hughes does not recognize the Black race to be a part of his flock ... moreover it is well known by both white and black that the Most Reverend Archbishop Hughes do [sic] hate the black Race so much that he cannot bear them to come near him." Thompson appealed directly to the pope to intercede: "I only write to pray your Holiness to take charge of our souls in your Holy Authority. I never knew but 4 priests in this country that tried to bring the black Race to god, namely Reverend Fathers McColgan and Anwander baltimore and the Reverend Father Lafont, new york and the Right Reverend Father Loughlin ... is the only ones I ever knew to take notice of African race [sic]."[51]

Occasional misspellings and peculiarities of grammar and capitalization notwithstanding, Harriet Thompson's letter proved the work of a knowledgeable and perceptive community-oriented activist. She bluntly accused the American Catholic hierarchy of racism toward black Catholics. Issues of ethnicity and racism informed the problem Thompson identified, embodied in the attitudes of Archbishop John Hughes of New York. Hughes's racist views merely reflected the more general Irish-black antipathies pervasive in antebellum New York City and grounded in social, political, and economic causes.[52] Thompson fully comprehended the seriousness of her indictment of ecclesial racism in the United States. Impelled by her strong commitment to her Roman Catholic faith, she denied motivations of disrespect or scandal, "for which I would deserve punishment From god [sic] and From your Holiness."[53]

Thompson analyzed in nuanced fashion the educational dilemma confronting black Catholic families in New York, a problem that the existence and mission of the Oblate Sisters of Providence had solved for the Baltimore black Catholic community. In 1849 Rev. Annet Lafont, pastor of St. Vincent de Paul's parish in New York, had attempted to establish a school for black Catholic children, but Archbishop Hughes had refused to endorse it. Both racial consciousness and a strong Catholic identity motivated the black members of the cathedral congregation of New York to mobilize and petition the sympathetic Loughlin. But the black Catholic phalanx foundered on the rock of Archbishop Hughes's obdurate racism. Thompson observed of Hughes's attitude, "This is very Hurtful indeed to think that the greatest Light the church has in America should dislike any creature Because it is the will of god that we should be of a darke Hue [sic]."[54]

Undeterred, Harriet Thompson sought from Pope Pius IX a just resolution of the ecclesially sanctioned racial discrimination confronting "the colored Catholics in most of the United States." Her close identification with and loyalty to the larger group reflected a sense of nationalism in her appeal to the pope on behalf of all black Catholics in the United States. As if to verify that her personal voice represented more than an individual position, Thompson submitted to the pontiff the names of the seven married couples and thirteen individuals—eleven of them women—who had signed the petition to Rev. Loughlin. Politically astute, Thompson further emphasized the critical condition of New York City's black Catholics by raising the specter to the pope of "many Familis [sic] with the parents Catholics and the children protestants—overwhelmed with the belief that the name of Catholic amongst the black race will in a few years pass away." She also provided examples of the protestant "word of God adulterated" inculcated in black Catholic children in public schools: "the BLESSED EUCHARIST is nothing but a wafer; that the priest drinks the wine Himself [sic] and gives the bread to us; and that the Divine institution of confession is only to make money; and that the Roman Pontiff is Antichrist." Vatican authorities submitted Thompson's letter to the pope with the note, "will be kept in mind when writing to American bishops."[55] Harriet Thompson's singular act in 1853 epitomized the exercise of black female Catholic agency in the antebellum United States.

Black Catholic allegiance to St. Frances Chapel in the 1850s reflected the long tradition in Baltimore of acknowledgment of and pride in the dual identities of being both black and Roman Catholic. Only a racially conscious, assertive, and confident black Catholic community—like the one in antebellum Baltimore—would have sustained the Oblate Sisters of Providence during the critical decade of the 1840s. Only such a fully realized black Catholic community could have nurtured such extraordinary individuals as William Augustine Williams and Harriet Thompson in the 1850s.

THE REDEMPTORIST PRIESTS as a matter of policy opened parochial schools immediately to anchor their parishes. Time had not eroded the original zealous commitment of the Oblate Sisters of Providence "to contribute all the means in their power for the glory of God and the religious education of the girls of their race."[56] During the 1850s under Redemptorist direction, they expanded their educational mission to include boys of their race as well. The Oblate Sisters instructed boys from 1850.[57] Sisters Angelica Gideon and Theresa Victoria Messonier staffed the boys' school in the 1850s. While no extant information reveals the content of the male school curriculum, the sisters evidently employed gender-appropriate materials: at the annual exhibitions and distribution of awards ceremonies, male pupils declaimed on topics such as the one titled "The Good Boy and Truant."[58]

By 1852 male student enrollment warranted construction of a separate school building. The community built St. Frances Male School at the rear of convent property on Tyson Alley in 1852.[59] Oblate historian Willigman recalled that the modest building consisted of "two stories, one used for a schoolroom, the other as a hall for the Societies to meet. A deep cellar under the schoolroom was used for storing fuel, as there was no cellar in the other part of the convent. Over the hall was the attic, which was filled with pupils' trunks, etc."[60] The multiple purposes this one building served for convent storage, schoolhouse, and society meeting hall physically symbolized the increasing interconnection of the Oblate community, the boys' and girls' schools, and the St. Frances Chapel congregation as a parochial or parish unit during the 1850s. As they had in the past, black people assumed the major financial responsibility for the boys' school construction. The item "donation for the boys' school $1.00" appeared among the charges listed on Philadelphia resident Mrs. Mary A. Jackson's account for her goddaughter at the Oblate school in 1852.[61] That the Oblate Sisters solicited and received support for their mission of male education from the families of their female boarders demonstrates the level of black community responsibility beyond one's immediate interests that the Oblate Sisters expected of their patrons.

St. Frances Male School, conducted by the Oblate Sisters of Providence, proved exceptional among the Catholic schools in the archdiocese of Baltimore. Various orders of priests directed the white male literary institutions. The Brothers of Christian Schools staffed several of the male pay and free schools associated with parishes throughout Baltimore. Several male parish schools and obviously coeducational establishments such as the School for Boys and Girls and the School for German Children employed lay teachers. Only one community of white women religious in the entire archdiocese of Baltimore, the Sisters of the Holy Cross in Washington, D.C., staffed a school for young boys in the late 1850s.[62]

In general, clerical authorities disapproved of women religious teaching boys, condoning the practice only in cases of exceptional need.[63] Considerations of race clearly contributed to the exceptional need allowing the Oblate Sisters to educate boys. St. Frances Male School represented the first effort to provide a formal Catholic education for black males in the archdiocese. In 1853 the *Catholic Mirror* endorsed this outreach of the mission of the Oblate Sisters of Providence. In a feature article devoted to the topic of colored schools, the writer opined, "We are pleased to hear that the wants of the large Catholic colored population of Baltimore in the matter of education, are likely to be further ministered to by the establishment of a day-school for boys to be under the charge of the colored 'Sisters of Providence.'"[64]

References to the two Oblate schools in the national Catholic directories soon reflected parochial school aspirations. From 1834 until 1852 the national directory had listed the Oblate school for girls sui generis as "School for Colored Girls." The directory cited the Oblate school for girls as "St. Francis [*sic*] School for Colored Girls" for the first time in 1853. In 1854, immediately following the listing of "St. Frances School for Colored Girls," the directory inserted the first notice of "St. Frances Male School," which charged $1.50 quarterly tuition, although "very poor children are taught gratuitously."[65] Both schools had assumed the name of the Oblate St. Frances Chapel, indicating the parochial association among them and the chapel.

By 1853 the Oblate Sisters revised their tuition charges. From its inception in 1828 the Oblate School for Colored Girls had charged fees of $4 monthly for board and tuition and $2 quarterly for day scholars. The 1853 fee schedule charged $6 monthly for board and tuition and $1.50 quarterly for day scholars. The sisters responded to the deteriorating economic conditions confronting black people during the 1850s by adopting a policy long implemented by the white teaching sisterhoods: subsidizing services to the poorer students through higher fees assessed wealthier patrons. The select academies of the white sisterhoods subsidized their parish and free schools.[66] The Oblate Sisters made education more widely available to the black community by lowering the fees for day pupils at the expense of their more elite clientele.

Oblate ledgers from the 1850s record that several pupils came from families of sufficient means to pay their fees on a quarterly, semiannual, or even annual basis and to enroll their daughters for several years. Mrs. H. Simpson of West Point, New York, enrolled her daughter in the Oblate school from 1853 through at least 1858, paid her fees in amounts ranging from $50 to $150, and twice

Oblate pupil Mary Goodridge posed for this photograph in 1865. Her family numbered among the first black professional photographers (Archives of the Oblate Sisters of Providence, Baltimore, Md.).

boarded at the Oblate convent when visiting the school.[67] Mr. and Mrs. G. W. Apperson of Richmond, Virginia, enrolled their daughters, Tarquina and Leonede, as Oblate pupils from 1857 through 1860, paying their fees quarterly. Tarquina played a prominent role in the program closing the school year in 1859.[68] Mrs. Charlotte Thomson of Washington, D.C., enrolled her daughter, Isa, from 1855 through 1860. Isa performed a prodigious seven vocal and piano selections on the 1859 school exhibition program. In 1860 she entered the Oblate community and began her novitiate as Sister Mary Laura.[69] She did not, however, persevere in her religious vocation.

William C. Goodridge, a successful barber, merchant, and entrepreneur in York, Pennsylvania, began life as a slave of Charles Carroll of Carrollton in Maryland in 1806, according to Goodridge family tradition. An associate of black businessman and activist William Whipper, Goodridge himself engaged in abolitionist activities, including the Underground Railroad in the 1850s. Goodridge enrolled his daughter, Mary, in the Oblate school in 1855 and 1856.[70]

Henry Jakes, a barber numbering among the wealthiest black property owners in antebellum Baltimore, with holdings valued at $16,000, enrolled three children—Anastasia, Mary, and Henry—as day scholars in the Oblate schools between 1852 and 1861. His wife, Mary, had belonged to the Holy Family Society in 1844. His children Mary and Henry joined the Oblate Confirmation class of 1860. The participation of all three Jakes children, as well as others identifiable as day scholars, in the 1859 school exhibition program indicated that Oblate day scholars suffered no disadvantage in access to public recognition.[71]

St. Frances Male School enrolled "over 50 boys" annually between 1854 and 1859. Evidently, the Oblate Sisters educated a significant number of male students either at a reduced rate or free of charge. Fifty students paying $1.50 for four quarters would have yielded $300 annual tuition from the boys' school. However, Oblate records listed revenues averaging $121 from the boys' school in each of the years 1857, 1858, and 1859.[72]

St. Frances School for Colored Girls and St. Frances Male School on the Oblate Richmond Street property served the needs of black students residing in the vicinity of the Oblate convent in the northwestern section of Baltimore. In October 1857 Jesuit priest William F. Clarke, pastor of St. Joseph Church in south Baltimore, invited the Oblate Sisters to conduct a school for black children in his parish. The community assigned Sisters Mary Louisa Noel, Ellen Joseph West, and Frances Johnson to staff the school.[73] Nativist sentiment aroused by the city elections held that week caused civil disturbances, and assailants targeted the new Oblate site. The sisters demonstrated characteristic Oblate courage in withstanding the attacks. Nevertheless, Oblate Superior Gertrude Thomas recalled them home, "as by all appearance it was not possible for them to remain and commence a school in a place where they apparently would be continually attacked."[74]

When Clarke procured another dwelling for the Oblate Sisters the following May, the community did not hesitate to accept the post, noting that "as this was the second attempt to open a school, the news was gladly received."[75] As they had done in the 1830s, the intrepid Oblate Sisters of Providence again demonstrated their apostolic enthusiasm in the 1850s by conducting this school for people of their race in a hostile environment. Their agency reflected the "courage in order that, like strong young women, they might do good works with a solid and powerful perfection" mandated by the Oblate Rule.[76]

In April 1858 the Oblate Sisters established another school for black children in Fells Point. Encouraged by "a fine prospect of having a good school," Oblate Sisters Seraphina Noel and Celestine Reynolds began the school on 5 April 1858 and soon enrolled thirty-five pupils. In May the sisters obtained a residence in the area, "which was very much needed, as they had to return home every week which was very inconvenient."[77] In September Sister Mary Elizabeth Lange became superior of the Oblate mission at Fells Point.

These two Baltimore schools under Oblate direction served as adjuncts of St. Joseph's and St. Michael's parishes. However, in both cases the Oblate schools distinguished themselves from the parish schools for white students with names that identified them as black as well as Catholic. The sisters named their school in St. Joseph's parish for St. Peter Claver, a seventeenth-century Spanish Jesuit priest celebrated for his spiritual and corporal ministry to African slaves in Colombia. Popular custom acclaimed him the patron saint of Negro missions.[78] The sisters named their school in St. Michael's parish for St. Benedict the Moor to honor this saint of both African and slave descent. A prospectus for St. Benedict's School referred to it as "a branch of the School of St. Frances for Colored Children, Richmond street" and assured prospective patrons that "the same plan of Instruction is pursued as taught at St. Frances." St. Benedict's School accepted male and female pupils and offered a boarding- as well as a day-scholar program. The prospectus also stipulated that "tuition must be paid invariably in advance, or within the first ten days."[79] In instructing male students and in establishing sites in other areas of Baltimore, the Oblate Sisters of Providence provided the opportunity for a Catholic education with the Oblate imprint to a significantly larger number of black children in the 1850s.

Nevertheless, all four Oblate schools differed from the free parish schools for both boys and girls established in the archdiocese of Baltimore for white pupils in the 1850s.[80] The Oblate Sisters depended on tuition to operate their schools. Since 1828 they had engaged in creative financing, tolerated debts, and offered scholarships to make education as affordable and as accessible as possible to children in the black community. That black pupils had to pay for the Catholic education many white pupils received free constituted another example of the disadvantaged position accorded black people within the Baltimore Catholic community. The willingness of black people—the segment of the population with the least discretionary income—to support the Oblate schools demonstrated their commitment both to the promise of a Catholic education and to its agents in Baltimore, the Oblate Sisters of Providence. Oblate involvement with the boys' school and the sisters' later involvement with schools in south and east Baltimore did not compromise the continued growth of the sisters' original mission of the School for Colored Girls in the 1850s. Combined enrollments for the Oblate male and female schools reached 120 in 1850. By 1855 the Oblate Sisters instructed between 250 and 300 pupils in their schools, a figure which may also include pupils in the Sunday religious instruction classes.[81]

During the 1850s, alumnae of the original Oblate School for Colored Girls continued to exceed the conventional expectations for black women as mothers or domestic servants proposed for them in the original Oblate prospectus. Indeed, little information documents the antebellum experience of Oblate school alumnae in domestic service. An undated note in the Oblate Archives addressed impersonally "To the Sister Superior" from a John D. Boland introduced a "Mrs. E. Pyle—who wishes to secure a girl from your house." This note suggests an established procedure by which the sisters referred girls for domestic service. Oblate ledger entries "Of Mrs. Devourge for one month's wages of A.M.F.—$2," "Of Mrs. Servary for one mo. wages of Anna M.—$3," "Of Mrs. Servary for Anna M.—$9" three months later, and "By cash of Mrs. Lake for the service of A.J.—$5.25" document the practice.[82]

That segment of the Oblate student body consisting of orphans and the "children of the house," those girls the sisters were "educating free of charge and [who] help to keep up the chapel and the house,"[83] formed the more probable source of domestic servants. Almira Gideon, sibling of Oblate Sister Angelica Gideon, remains one of the few Oblate students for whom information about her post-Oblate student life in domestic service exists. Gideon and her sister attended the Oblate school from 1829 until well into the 1830s. Almira completed her Oblate schooling at eighteen years of age and found employment in St. Louis around 1841 in service to the socially prominent Pierre Chouteau family for over sixty years and four generations. Almira Gideon proved loyal to more than her employers. Beginning in the late 1860s through the 1880s, she contributed modest sums of money to the Oblate Sisters of Providence. At her death Almira Gideon bequeathed $6,000 to the Oblate community.[84]

Most Oblate students from families who enjoyed sufficient financial security to afford their Oblate school education undoubtedly found employment— when sought—in teaching or skilled needlework before marriage. Many Oblate school alumnae continued to pursue religious vocations and teaching careers, roles more consonant with the revised expectations for their students the Oblate Sisters articulated in their 1853–54 school advertisement.

Beginning in December 1852 through September 1856 Oblate ledgers recorded twelve entries totalling $2,165.67 for six children. Alexius J. Elder, pastor of St. Mary's Chapel at the Sulpician seminary, apparently acted as trustee of a Riley account or executor of a Riley estate in disbursing funds semiannually "for the Rileys and D. Cage."[85] Little extant information elucidates the family background of the children, beyond the fact that their racial identity qualified them for enrollment in the Oblate school. Oblate sacramental records identified Agnes, Mary Ann, Eliza, and Mary Rose Riley among the members of the 1853

Confirmation class. Susan Riley began her novitiate as Sister Theodora on 15 August 1854 and professed her vows as an Oblate Sister on 29 April 1855.[86]

The Lake family of Annapolis associated with and supported the Oblate school from 1844. On 8 November 1838 Louis Deluol had officiated at the marriage of Moses Lake and Mary Effy Peterson. Mary Lake belonged to the Holy Family Society in 1844. Between 1845 and 1847, in addition to paying for her daughter, also named Mary, Mrs. Lake subsidized the tuition of a pupil identified only as Margaret at the Oblate school. The 1850 census listed a nineteen-year-old Margaret Chew living in the Lake household. Between 1845 and 1852 the Lakes made several donations to the Oblate community and contributed toward the purchase of the organ for the Oblate chapel. By 1850 Moses Lake, a barber, had acquired real estate worth $1,500.[87]

In 1850 Mary Lake was a nine-year-old boarding student at the Oblate school. She evinced more than the extraordinary needlework skills, discussed in Chapter 9. In 1854 she recited part of a dialogue on "truthtelling" at the school's closing exercises. During such exercises in 1856, Lake and an unidentified partner delivered an address in both French and English honoring Archbishop Francis Patrick Kenrick, who was present at the ceremony. She also studied music at the Oblate school between 1854 and 1857. Mary Lake entered the Oblate community as a postulant on 9 January 1860 and began her novitiate as Sister Mary Lucy on 19 February 1860.[88] Evidently, Lake did not persevere in her religious vocation.

On Christmas Day 1853, "Arabella Jones, one of our former pupils, came from Washington, D.C., to make her First Communion."[89] Although the District of Columbia boasted several Roman Catholic churches noted for their tolerant treatment of black Catholics, the nineteen-year-old Jones demonstrated her allegiance to the Oblate school by returning there to make her First Communion. Like the Costins and the Becrafts in the 1830s, the Jones family in the 1850s belonged to the black elite in the District with service ties to the most socially and politically prominent white families in Washington. Arabella's mother had been "from her youth through many years a favorite servant in the family of John Quincy Adams, commencing when he was Secretary of State."[90] While the Becrafts professed the Roman Catholic faith, the Costins and the Joneses did not. Eliza Ann Cook, niece of noted Presbyterian minister and educator John F. Cook, also attended the Oblate school for two years as part of her education before pursuing a teaching career.[91] Like several other families in the Washington, D.C., black community, the Jones family sought to provide their daughter with the best education available, regardless of their religious affiliations. Consequently, Arabella Jones attended the Oblate school in Baltimore, where she converted to Catholicism.

Moses Goodwin, a Reconstruction era federal official, wrote the expansive essay "Schools and Education of the Colored Population" as part of the *Special Report* on education in Washington, D.C., submitted to Congress by Commissioner of Education Henry Bernard in 1871. In his report Goodwin discussed Arabella Jones in such detail and with sufficient familiarity to suggest he was personally acquainted with her. In fact, Moses Goodwin proved exceptionally knowledgeable about the personal lives and family histories of most of the black individuals he discussed in his report. Canvassers for the Georgetown City Directory did not identify Goodwin as a person of color—whether correctly or incorrectly.[92] Goodwin's thorough familiarity with many members of the black educational elite in Washington, D.C., and his overwhelmingly positive and explicit portrayal of black agency in providing educational opportunities in his report documented his bonds of sympathy, if not of blood, with the black community he studied.

According to Goodwin, Jones "had a good English education, wrote and spoke with ease and propriety the French tongue, was proficient in music and in all the useful and ornamental needlework branches." Her father had bought Jones "a piano and a well selected library including a full set of the British poets in a handsome binding, bought in London expressly to his order, among which was a specially handsome edition of Shakespeare, the favorite author of the daughter."[93] Jones herself gained local recognition for her published poetic works.

The multitalented Arabella Jones demonstrated more than a sacramental affinity for her alma mater. Jones established St. Agnes Academy for girls of her race in Washington, D.C., in 1852. The prospectus Jones circulated advertising St. Agnes Academy recalled the Oblate school's original philosophy in its statement that "females in this age are naturally destined to become either mothers of families or household servants." However, former Oblate student Jones envisioned a further purpose her institution would serve that reflected the temper of the 1850s: "Last, though not least, many of our citizens of color are emigrating to Liberia, and it is necessary, as well wishers of our race, that our children be well educated, in order to impart their knowledge to the illiterate. Shall we, my friends, go there to teach or be taught? As emigrants from a land of intelligence, I answer, to teach."[94] Moses Goodwin considered Jones's prospectus illustrative of "the praiseworthy and honorable ambition of many of the colored people."[95] Jones's statement proved equally remarkable as evidence of this former Oblate student's belief in black female agency and empowerment and of her nationalistic conviction of the ordained role for black women in the construction of a black nation-state in Liberia.

Emigration to Liberia remained a viable alternative to some antebellum free black people. Although voiced in Washington, D.C., Jones's interest in emigration echoed the sentiments of some of Maryland's black residents, who convened in Baltimore in 1852. This group angrily denounced their deteriorating position within Maryland society and proposed emigration to Liberia as the most plausible solution to the problem.[96] Henry and Maria Dorsey, members of the Holy Family Society that had met in Calvert Hall from 1843 until 1845, emigrated to Liberia in 1852 with their four children, ten-year-old Mary, eight-year-old Henry, five-year-old Martha, and one-year-old Ellen.[97] Espousing emigration represented a minority position among free black people in Maryland, as the hostile black protesters threatening the Baltimore convention amply demonstrated. Nevertheless, for a significant number of black Baltimoreans and Marylanders, departure from the state—whether to Africa or northern states—remained the most feasible response to the increasingly restrictive conditions threatened and imposed on their lives in the state of Maryland during the 1850s.[98]

In spite of her vision and ambition and the fact that "she taught with great delight and success," Arabella Jones maintained her school for only a few years. She found greater financial security in her skilled needlework. Jones married in 1857 and received an appointment to a government clerkship before her death at age thirty-four in 1868.[99]

Two other Oblate students from this period pursued first religious and then teaching professions. Julia Smith entered the Oblate community as a candidate for membership on 29 November 1859. She brought no dowry, although she had $180 to commit, "if she remains in the house."[100] Smith, however, left religious life. In 1866 she served as assistant director of St. Martin's School for Colored Girls in Washington, D.C.[101]

Elizabeth Brown, a native of Philadelphia, enrolled at St. Frances School for five years. She entered the Oblate community as a postulant on 9 November 1860, began her novitiate as Sister Anastasia on 15 May 1861, and professed her vows on 15 August 1862. Nevertheless, in 1867 Elizabeth Brown would serve as assistant director in St. Aloysius School in Washington, D.C., "well educated, and competent to teach Latin, French, and music as well as primary branches."[102] Inspired by the personal example of their teachers, the Oblate Sisters of Providence, the students enrolled at St. Frances School for Colored Girls in the 1850s made career choices that served the needs of the black community—some potentially on a global scale—even as some of their cohort served as domestic servants to others.

MULTIDIRECTIONAL GROWTH in the services they provided the black community characterized the development of the Oblate Sisters of Providence between 1847 and 1860. Transcending its Francophone cultural origins, the black community of women religious fully assimilated the African American cultural identities forming most of the Oblate membership, their pupil population, and the Oblate chapel congregation during the 1850s. The resolution of their early ambivalence toward the public use of their chapel with an unqualified embrace of the St. Frances lay congregation further characterized the maturation of the Oblate Sisters of Providence.

As the teaching staff of both St. Frances School for Colored Girls and St. Frances Male School, the Oblate Sisters played a pivotal role in the evolution of the Oblate chapel congregation from the first black church within the Roman Catholic religious tradition since 1836 to the first black parish in the Catholic tradition during the 1850s. By 1860 the Oblate education mission encompassed male pupils as well as two coeducational Oblate schools in different areas of Baltimore. The significance of St. Frances School for Colored Girls, the original Oblate mission, had surpassed its immediate impact on its student body and alumnae. In 1859 the Reverend John Mifflin Brown, pastor of Baltimore's Bethel African Methodist Episcopal Church and the Baltimore correspondent to New York's *Weekly Anglo-African*,[103] said of St. Frances School for Colored Girls:

> The "Sisters of Providence" (Catholic) gave a grand demonstration at the close of their school. I did not witness the literary exercises, but all are abundant in their laudations of these faithful "Sisters." Their pupils number 160. I witnessed their exhibition of needlework. . . . When I left the room I felt deeply impressed that the man who could go there and gaze upon such work from the hands of *colored girls*, and they entirely under the control of *colored teachers*, and hear their sweet music and charming voices, must be either a madman or a fool, if he adopt such silly and uncalled-for sentiments as those published by that Republican paper in Philadelphia and republished by the editor of the New York "Herald" with his remarks. If these Northern editors will come "down South," we will teach them that some of us live otherwise than by *blacking their boots, shaving their faces, and waiting upon their tables*.[104]

Significantly, the same dispatch to the *Weekly Anglo-African* extolling the virtues of the Oblate enterprise at great length briefly acknowledged, "Mrs.

Maria Stewart, formerly of your city, had also an exhibition and examination at the Presbyterian Church. Mrs. S. is a veteran at teaching, and of course she gave general satisfaction."[105] Stewart had achieved fame as America's first black woman political writer and public speaker in Boston in the early 1830s. When the Boston black community proved unreceptive to her public exhortations suffused with religious piety and jeremiads, Stewart relocated to New York, where she embarked on a teaching career. In 1852 she moved to Baltimore and for almost a decade attempted to earn a viable living as a teacher. She described her Baltimore tenure as an unending trial in which black individuals and churches alike abandoned or exploited her before she left the city for Washington, D.C.[106] The individual, not communal, nature of Stewart's endeavor and the absence of institutional support undoubtedly contributed to Stewart's problems as a teacher in Baltimore. As a corporate entity professing piety and virtue and as an institution within the Roman Catholic Church, the Oblate Sisters of Providence legitimized their claim to public recognition and support to an extent unrealizable by many individual, secular black women in antebellum southern society.

In responding to the call of their teaching mission the Oblate Sisters of Providence nurtured the minds and souls of black folk, the very elements of black existence white society routinely disallowed in its monolithic focus on the profitable exploitation of black servile labor. Protestant minister John Mifflin Brown's glowing tribute to these Catholic sisters' efforts in the *Weekly Anglo-African* reflected how broadly the Baltimore black community recognized this Oblate contribution. The school's established reputation and the competence and commitment of its dedicated staff of teachers, the Oblate Sisters of Providence, came to symbolize for many black people—regardless of their religious affiliation—both an affirmation of black humanity and the standard of excellence achievable in an increasingly hostile environment.

CHAPTER ELEVEN

The Oblates Do Well Here, Although I Presume Their Acquirements Are Limited

THE OBLATE SISTERS AND THE WHITE COMMUNITY, 1847–1860

❖ ❖

Between 1847 and 1860 the Oblate Sisters of Providence functioned as an anomalous constituency within both the American Roman Catholic Church and antebellum southern society. Issues of race, gender, and religion continued to dominate the interaction between the black and Roman Catholic Oblate Sisters of Providence and their white church and southern society.

During the 1850s the Roman Catholic Church in the United States convened three councils in Baltimore: the national First Plenary Council in 1852, the Eighth Provincial Council in 1855, and the Ninth Provincial Council in 1858. Several bishops attending these councils continued the tradition of visiting the Oblate convent and celebrating Mass in the Oblate chapel during their stay in Baltimore. In 1852 visiting prelates Bishop John Neumann of Philadelphia, the former Redemptorist superior in Baltimore, and Archbishop Peter Richard Kenrick of St. Louis celebrated "two or three Masses for two weeks every day" in the Oblate chapel. In 1858 Richard Vincent Whelan, bishop of Wheeling, Virginia, said Mass daily in St. Frances Chapel.[1]

The Oblate Sisters continued to correspond with bishops from other dioceses in the 1850s concerning potential Oblate proliferation. Since 1833 they had received inquiries from clergymen in other states interested in establishing Oblate missions in their dioceses. Although the sisters had responded affirmatively to such inquiries, all such antebellum initiatives proved abortive. Seeking an Oblate mission in 1850, Bishop John Baptist Purcell of Cincinnati had approached both Archbishop Eccleston of Baltimore and the Oblate community. On 30 March 1850 Eccleston responded to Purcell: "Father Anwander . . . has, at present, charge of the Coloured Sisters and knows more about their affairs than I do. So far as I am concerned, I would be much pleased to second your wish to have a colony. In fact, I believe that they could do a great deal more good in a Free State than here. I have requested Father Anwander to exert himself to carry out your views. On him mainly will depend the direction given to the minds and wishes of those good Oblates. A favorite spiritual Director is all powerful with female communities."[2]

Considerations of gender and race informed Eccleston's reply to Purcell. Eccleston's conviction that male directors dictated policy to communities of women religious patronized these sisterhoods. At least it acknowledged female instrumentality in restricting such male influence to "favorite" directors, those the sisters themselves so designated. The histories of nineteenth-century American sisterhoods include numerous examples of these women challenging and occasionally prevailing over the demands of priest directors and even prelates.[3] In Eccleston's own experience the Oblate Sisters had successfully withstood his pressures on them to disband.

Some sources maintained that Eccleston had experienced a conversion regarding the Oblate Sisters and had become "their interested friend."[4] However, in his reply to Purcell, Eccleston demonstrated his continued ambivalence about and ignorance of—if not indifference toward—the Oblate Sisters. His stated preference for permanent removal of the Oblate Sisters from Maryland indicated that Eccleston remained unconvinced of the positive good they had accomplished for the black community, in spite of their anomalous position within a slaveholding state. The racial identity of the Oblate Sisters remained their most salient characteristic for Eccleston, a fact reflected in an exchange with the Visitation Sisters in 1848. Coal dust and soot polluted the air where the Visitandines established a foundation in Wheeling, Virginia. On visiting the new convent, Eccleston pronounced the nuns "as dark as the Oblates" and called one of them, Sister Clare Agnes Jenkins, Sambo. She reported, "We are determined to be white ladies—although the Archbishop expects to find us colored ones! He said I could now sing 'Coal Black Rose' without much altering in my dress."[5]

Purcell replied to Eccleston that Oblate Superior Mary Louise Noel had informed him the sisters could come to Ohio, but not until the following year. In 1850 Oblate membership had declined to eleven sisters, their smallest complement since the 1830s. This fact may explain the uncharacteristic Oblate postponement of establishing a new mission. The sisters had resumed receiving new candidates only in 1849. Purcell further observed, "The Superior seems, if I may judge from her letter, to have an imperfect knowledge of English Grammar. She tells, or asks me to 'pray for I.' Many of our blacks here could beat that."[6] Purcell focused on one example of a very common, if regrettable, grammatical error in Noel's letter, evidently no longer extant. An example of Noel's later correspondence revealed no "imperfect knowledge of English Grammar" beyond infrequent use of punctuation.[7]

In 1857 Purcell enacted a reprise of this 1850 scene with Oblate Superior Gertrude Helen Thomas and Archbishop Francis Patrick Kenrick. He sought an Oblate mission through an emissary, Rev. Peter Senez, a Cincinnati priest visiting Baltimore. A Purcell scholar has concluded that Purcell did "not seem to have been very sincere in this application, because when the [Oblate] superior agreed to come he did not answer her letter."[8] Purcell did communicate with Archbishop Kenrick about the Oblate Sisters: "I tried, many years ago, to get a branch of yr. Oblates for Cincinnati. I was then refused—and not sorry, as the Letter of the Superioress showed the want of knowledge of English. They now propose to grant the colony I asked for by Rev. Mr. Senez—But the Letter they write is fresh proof of their want of the English language, which many of our Colored folks read and write correctly. Still I hope I can find a place for them. We lately baptized twenty four colored children in Mercer County, where there is a large settlement of that race, and many adults are there preparing for baptism."[9]

Regardless of Purcell's expressed hope to find a place for the Oblate Sisters, no Oblate mission materialized in Cincinnati. Oblate Superior Thomas's second letter to Purcell, discussed in Chapter 9, did indeed contain spelling and punctuation irregularities and word omissions, displaying a level of literacy skill commensurate with the essentially elementary education available at the Oblate school. However, Purcell's punctilious embrace of the principles of grammar as cause for rejecting an Oblate mission belied his fundamental lack of commitment to bringing the black sisters to his diocese. He denied the black members of his pastoral flock an educational opportunity offered unconditionally, in compliance with his "own arrangements whatever they may be."[10] Although he twice vaunted the superior literacy skills of Cincinnati black Catholics to those of the Oblate Sisters and noted their significant number, Purcell never considered establishing his own diocesan black sisterhood to serve the needs of his black constituency. By 1858 the Oblate community responded to inquiries about establishing new missions circumspectly. On 23 September Bishop John Timon of Buffalo visited the Oblate convent and declared that he wanted an Oblate mission in his city. The sisters observed that "these offers so often have been proposed and ended with the same."[11]

During their early years the Oblate Sisters had cherished every customary courtesy and ecclesiastical favor extended to them by visiting clergy and prelates. Such occasions had affirmed and validated the Oblate community's status as a society of women religious and had furnished proof of continued episcopal favor. Attention from visiting bishops had partially compensated the sisters for the indifference they encountered from their own archbishop, Samuel Eccleston. However, in the 1850s the Oblate community had come to regard both the customary courtesies from visiting prelates and inquiries about establishing out-of-state Oblate missions with greater reserve. In part, this development reflected the aplomb associated with Oblate corporate maturation as a religious community. In part, the Oblate community's diminished dependence on validation from other bishops reflected the transformation in their relationship with their own diocesan superior. Samuel Eccleston died on 22 April 1851. His successor, Francis Patrick Kenrick, proved a supporter of the Oblate cause.

Before accepting the episcopacy of Baltimore, Francis Patrick Kenrick had served as a missionary priest and seminary teacher in Kentucky, had guided the diocese of Philadelphia through troubled times, and had earned a reputation as a published scholar and theologian fluent in four modern and three ancient languages. Although a native of Dublin, Ireland, Kenrick did not personally identify with the Irish immigrant masses, nor did he advance their cause in Baltimore. The dignified, aloof Kenrick aligned more naturally with the Catholic elite of Baltimore, shunned pomp and public display, and retreated into his scholarly pursuits and administrative tasks.[12]

Kenrick's positions on slavery and black people epitomized that duality plaguing the Roman Catholic Church in the United States on these issues. In 1840 Kenrick had defended the institution of slavery as sanctioned by law in his textbook on moral theology.[13] As archbishop of Baltimore, Kenrick presided over the three church councils convened there during the 1850s. Although the moral as well as the social, political, and economic ramifications of the issue of slavery increasingly preoccupied all segments of American society during the decade, at Kenrick's direction these hierarchical councils assiduously avoided any consideration of the problem. Church scholars disagree whether the hierarchy's official silence on the problem of slavery in the 1850s constituted a noble position, or an example of Kenrick's "modesty and prudence [that] were, perhaps, a mask for timidity and his diffidence [that was] a shield from criticism."[14]

Kenrick had also temporized on the issue of black priests serving in the United States. In spite of Thaddeus Anwander's proactive initiatives in 1853, no black Roman Catholic priest, recognized as such, would minister to black Catholics in the United States until 1886. James Augustine Healy, Patrick Francis Healy, and Alexander Sherwood Healy, the mulatto progeny of an Irish planter who settled in Georgia and his slave mistress, were ordained in Europe in 1854, 1858, and 1864, respectively. Because these priests did not publicly identify themselves as people of color or advocate for, associate with, or minister to black Catholics in any capacity, they do not qualify as black priests in any nationalistic sense.[15]

The aversion expressed by Bishop Rappe of Cleveland and Kenrick to accepting a black priest in the United States in the 1850s proved a pervasive response among the Catholic hierarchy in the United States.[16] That antebellum Catholic bishops in the United States could tolerate black sisterhoods, but not black priests, demonstrated the interaction of racial and gender considerations in defining opportunities within the antebellum American church. Because the hierarchical church ascribed women religious a subordinate status delimited by gender, male clerics could allow black sisters, while remaining immune to encroachments on their own authoritative preserve within the church establishment. Black priests threatened to penetrate the racial exclusiveness of the previously all white male control of power, authority, and prestige within the American church. Although African priests served in other domains of the universal Roman Catholic Church, the assignment of black priests in the racist United States proved a challenge too sensitive and threatening to antebellum U.S. clergy. Racism, not religious principle, prevailed.

Louis R. Deluol's reception of black seminarian candidate William A. Williams in Paris in 1855 en route to Rome illustrated the problem. Deluol registered his astonishment that "a young Negro . . . was being sent to Rome to become a priest!!! 'Will wonders never cease?'" Among his letters of reference, Williams carried one personally to Deluol from Redemptorist priest Francis Krutil, pastor of Baltimore's St. James Church. Krutil had advised Williams that Deluol would lodge him at the Paris seminary. According to Deluol, "Big was [Williams's] disappointment when I told him that he could not stay over at the seminary. 'Father Krutil,' he said, 'ought to have known better.'" Deluol pronounced Williams very intelligent and "well behaved"; nevertheless, Deluol mused, "But what will he do in Baltimore as a priest? Perhaps God has an eye on him—'Time will tell.'"[17] As did most antebellum American clerics and prelates who even considered the prospect of black priests, Deluol refused to assume any agency in forming a black American priesthood; rather he acted as a passive observer upholding the racial status quo and relied on divine intervention to resolve the problem.

In spite of his equivocal position on black priests, Archbishop Kenrick believed in the humanity of black people and their spiritual equality in God's— if not white people's—eyes. Concern for the salvation of black Catholics emigrating to Liberia had prompted Kenrick to participate actively in establishing an American Catholic mission there in 1841. Even before his tenure as archbishop of Baltimore from 1851 until 1863 had begun, Kenrick had demonstrated his positive disposition toward the Oblate Sisters of Providence by his attentions to them during the Fifth Provincial Council in 1843.[18]

As archbishop of Baltimore, Kenrick continued to provide the Oblate community with evidence of his affection for their endeavor. Between 1852 and 1860 Kenrick confirmed classes of black Catholics at the Oblate St. Frances Chapel at least six times.[19] He attended every annual ceremony concluding the Oblate school years between 1853 and 1857.[20] In 1853 Kenrick authorized Oblate spiritual director Thaddeus Anwander to solicit contributions in the archdiocese to complete the construction of the Oblate St. Frances Male School. Between 1852 and 1858 Kenrick made seven $10 donations to the Oblate community.[21] In 1857 Kenrick responded to Purcell's impugning Oblate competence, "The Oblates do well here, although I presume their acquirements are limited."[22] In correspondence in 1860 Kenrick asserted that under the auspices of "about twenty Sisters here . . . two schools are taught and much good is done among persons of color." About the sisters themselves he maintained, "The conduct of the inmates has been uniformly edifying."[23]

Kenrick's personal knowledge of the Oblate Sisters' history and activities appeared superficial. He identified the male St. Francis of Assisi rather than the female St. Frances of Rome as the major Oblate patron saint. He erroneously credited the Oblate community with conducting only two schools when in fact they operated four.[24] Nevertheless, Kenrick's sanction of the Oblate St. Frances Male School project and subsequent authorization of Oblate solicitation to fund it in January 1853 provided the community with more than official permission to canvass the diocese for financial support. Kenrick's actions forcefully reminded the archdiocesan establishment of the status of the Oblate Sisters of Providence as a legitimate constituency within the Baltimore religious community. With the archbishop's patronage the Oblate community experienced the warmest reception accorded them by the Baltimore ecclesiastical establishment in the antebellum era.

Not only individual clerics but also religious orders interacted with the Oblate Sisters during the 1850s. Like the Redemptorist priests, the Jesuits actively ministered to Baltimore's black Catholics and involved themselves with the Oblate community in the latter part of the decade. In 1851 Archbishop Kenrick authorized the Jesuit order to establish Loyola College in Baltimore and to found St. Ignatius parish next to it, on the corner of Calvert and Madison Streets. The priests occupied the newly constructed college building in 1855; the new church, in 1857.[25]

On 20 September 1857 the Jesuits dedicated "their beautiful chapel for the special benefit of the colored population of the city . . . under the patronage of the Blessed Peter Claver." Located in the basement of St. Ignatius Church, the Claver Chapel offered Baltimore's black Catholics a 9:00 A.M. Mass "on all Sundays and holydays."[26] The Redemptorist priests did not provide this service to the black congregation at the Oblate St. Frances Chapel because of their primary pastoral commitments to German parishes. Services for black Catholics at St. Frances and Claver Chapels may have complemented each other. Oblate sources made no reference to the Jesuit Claver Chapel between 1857 and 1860. Continued full attendance at Oblate chapel services suggested that the St. Frances congregation experienced little attrition as a consequence of the Jesuit endeavor.[27]

That the Jesuits felt compelled to provide Baltimore black Catholics with their exclusive place of worship Sunday mornings indicated that black Catholics encountered increasing intolerance in white churches on Sundays in the racially charged atmosphere of Baltimore in the late 1850s. If native-born white Catholic pewholders resented the European immigrant presence in their churches as "counterfeits of humanity" crowding the aisles by the hundreds and contributing nothing to the upkeep of the building,[28] a black Catholic presence in "white" churches undoubtedly engendered even more antipathy in the 1850s.

In early October 1857, as previously mentioned, the Jesuit priest William F. Clarke, pastor of St. Joseph Church in south Baltimore, engaged the Oblate Sisters to conduct a school in his parish to serve the black children in the area. That month, Oblate ledgers cited: "By cash of Reverend Father Clarke from Collection in his parish, $2."[29] The sum collected proved modest; nevertheless, it indicated a measure of support for the Oblate mission in a predominantly Irish immigrant parish. Nativist attacks disrupted the first attempt to open the school. The first attack, which took place at 1:00 A.M. on 13 October 1857, dislodged a panel of the front door "leaving a place large enough for a person to enter." The three sisters kept a vigil themselves that night, "not seeing or knowing anyone to come to their assistance." When the Oblate Sisters informed Clarke of the disturbance the next morning, "he appeared somewhat surprised, but perhaps not [to] alarm the Sisters, he did not seem alarmed. He, not withstanding his apparent tranquility, took measures to have the house guarded by applying to the Mayor, as it was the day of the election." A second attack later that evening removed the entire front door. This time the sisters sought refuge with a black Catholic family, the Queens, across the street.[30] In May 1858 the Oblate Sisters succeeded in opening the school.

The cooperative bond formed between the Oblate Sisters of Providence and the Jesuit priests in the 1850s strengthened in 1860. When the Redemptorist priests relinquished the spiritual direction of the Oblate community in November 1860, Archbishop Kenrick prevailed upon the Jesuits to assume this responsibility. At that time the Jesuits closed the Oblate St. Frances Chapel to public use and transferred its black lay congregation to their Peter Claver Chapel in the basement of St. Ignatius Church.[31]

In the 1850s several members of the white Catholic lay community interacted with black Catholics on terms of respect and supported the efforts of the Oblate Sisters of Providence. On the Feast of St. Benedict the Moor in 1851 four singers from St. Joseph Church "played and sang the High Mass, also Vespers" and "showed great zeal in singing the praises of God" at the Oblate St. Frances Chapel.[32] This guest performance by white choir members from St. Joseph Church honored the Oblate Sisters and the black congregation of St. Frances Chapel on the major patronal feast day acknowledging their black Catholic identity.

On several occasions throughout the 1850s white musicians and singers from Immaculate Conception, St. Joseph, and St. Alphonsus parishes performed at the Oblate chapel on the feast days of St. Benedict the Moor and St. Frances of Rome as well as on general liturgical occasions like the Forty Hours Devotion and First Communion ceremonies. The Oblate Sisters responded with refreshments for the guests after the services.[33] Such gestures of recognition and respect offered by white to black Catholics suggested an inchoate consciousness of their common brotherhood in Christ across the racial barriers imposed by antebellum white society.

White Catholics continued to support the Oblate community and its work financially through the 1850s. Kenrick's authorization of an Oblate subscription in January 1853 in support of the boys' school construction prompted Baltimore's *Catholic Mirror* to publicize the cause in a feature article in March 1853.

Significantly, the Oblate Sisters, the St. Frances congregation, and Father Anwander had secured most of the estimated construction costs before the newspaper appeal, because the reporter maintained, "The Reverend Anwander . . . has not yet realized by about $250 as much as will be required to cover the expenses he has directed." Noting the archbishop's "liberal donation" to the subscription, the reporter enjoined "our Catholic fellow citizens" to follow suit. With evident complacency he enthused, "Quite a number has [sic] contributed even ten and twenty dollars each." Several clerics contributed to the Oblate subscription "even ten and twenty dollars": the Most Reverend Francis Patrick Kenrick, $20; the Very Reverend H. B. Coskery, vicar-general and rector of the Cathedral, $5; Rev. Thomas Foley, the archbishop's secretary, $5; Rev. Bernard Hafgenschied, provincial of the Redemptorists, $25; Rev. Francis Lhomme for St. Mary's Seminary, $10; Rev. John G. Ruland, rector of St. Alphonsus Church, $10; and Rev. Bernard J. McManus of Ellicot Mills, $5.

Prominent Catholic merchants, manufacturers, and bankers contributing to the Oblate subscription included C. Oliver O'Donnell, $10; Mathias Benzinger, $15; Patrick McKanna, $20; and John Murphy, $10. The Oblate Sisters conducted a substantial volume of business with Benzinger, McKanna, and Murphy, according to Oblate ledgers. Civic-minded Emily Harper, a granddaughter and heir of Charles Carroll of Carrollton who had occasionally subsidized Oblate students at a modest level since 1844, distinguished herself by making the largest single donation—$130—listed in Anwander's subscription book. Catholic activist lawyer T. Parkin Scott, who had represented the Oblate Sisters in the habeas corpus case involving Sarah Willigman in 1850, gave $5; the wife of prominent public figure William George Read gave $20; and Mr. Crey of Crey's Chapel gave $15.

Significantly, the names Chatard and Ducatel do not appear among the contributors listed in Anwander's subscription book. Furthermore, Oblate ledgers from 1844 through 1861 document the fact that these two families gave money to the sisters solely in exchange for goods or services during this period. In a pattern atypical of touted benefactors, the Chatards and the Ducatels paid for shirts and chemises sewn by the Oblate Sisters on a regular basis; they did not, however, disburse any monetary gifts, donations, or even loans to the Oblate community during these years, according to the extant records. Black Catholic John Noel contributed $13 to the subscription. Several tradespeople—noted as such in the list—donated $10 each. The subscription secured a total of $498 for the Oblate boys' school building.[34]

Nevertheless, the level of support white Catholics provided the Oblate Sisters during the 1850s remained low relative to their support of white religious communities. The Sisters of Mercy established a mission in Baltimore in 1852. Mrs. Emily McTavish, another granddaughter of and heir to the Charles Carroll fortune and a generous patron of Catholic causes, purchased a residence for the community sufficiently spacious to house both their novitiate and an academy for girls.[35] In 1862 wealthy donor Charles M. Dougherty presented the Sisters of Charity with a Baltimore mansion in which they established St. Agnes Hospital.[36]

By contrast, when the Jesuit William F. Clarke secured a house in St. Joseph parish for an Oblate school in 1858, he "kindly allowed us to pay no rent until there be a sufficient number of scholars, and then the Sisters will pay only half of the rent."[37] But in 1855 the *Catholic Mirror* had reported that the free, white parochial St. Joseph's Female School, conducted by the Sisters of Charity, "is pleasantly situated in a commodious house on Barre street, which we are gratified to learn, has been purchased and paid for by the zealous Pastor, Rev. Wm. F. Clark [*sic*], S.J."[38] Just as Oblate pupils paid for a Catholic education provided free by the archdiocese of Baltimore to most white pupils, so the Oblate Sisters ministered to the black community with the least support from white Baltimoreans. The differential levels of support white Catholic Baltimore provided the Oblate Sisters of Providence and communities of white sisters in the 1850s continued to reflect the subordinate position ascribed the Oblate Sisters in the Catholic community, predicated on their racial identity.

THE FIRST ISSUE of the *Catholic Mirror* appeared in January 1850. This publication quickly identified with the southern nationalist position on the divisive issue of slavery. An article titled "Slavery and Abolitionism" appearing in its fourth issue defended the former and condemned the latter.[39] In 1851 the newspaper recounted in detail the substance of the commencement speeches delivered at two Baltimore-area Catholic colleges for men. These articles revealed not only the southern nationalist proclivities of the archdiocesan newspaper but also those of the educated Catholic elite and, by extension, of the clerical faculty directing these colleges. At Mount St. Mary's College, Emmitsburg, Luke Tiernan Chatard, a member of the white San Domingan émigré family historically associated with the Oblate Sisters, discussed the church's role in the abolition of slavery in Europe. Chatard emphasized the church's historic recognition of the rights of property and condemnation of servile insubordination. He asserted that "in these two points the Church presented a bright contrast to modern abolitionists, who seek the destruction of the American Government in their idle fanaticism and appeals to 'Higher Law.'" The reporter noted that the speaker "closed to universal applause."[40]

The commencement speakers at the Sulpician St. Mary's College addressed the issue of domestic slavery. The reporter deemed the speaker proving slavery compatible with religion "very successful." The opponents of slavery experienced "severe but deserved condemnation for the unchristian-like language which they apply to the Southern slave holder."[41] Such sentiments demonstrated how thoroughly white Roman Catholics in Baltimore embraced the South's peculiar institution and concomitant racial caste system.

The treatment accorded the Oblate Sisters in Catholic publications in Baltimore in the 1850s reflected their marginal status within the Baltimore religious community. Between 1850 and 1852 the *Catholic Mirror* included no coverage of the Oblate Sisters or their work, except to note the annual administration of the sacrament of Confirmation in the Oblate St. Frances Chapel.[42] Thaddeus Anwander had restored annual public examinations and award ceremonies to conclude the Oblate school year from 1848. However, the *Catholic Mirror* did not include the Oblate school in its detailed coverage of Baltimore-area school, academy, and college commencements. The Oblate community had resumed admitting candidates for membership in 1849. But the *Catholic Mirror* failed to acknowledge the reception of any of the Oblate Sisters who professed their vows between 1850 and 1860, even as it regularly reported the receptions of members into the white sisterhoods. The 1850, 1851, and 1852 editions of the national Catholic directory allowed the Oblate Sisters and their school minimal notice. They listed the Oblate chapel simply as "St. Frances Chapel, (colored Sisters of Providence, Richmond st.) occasionally attended from St. Alphonsus Church."[43]

However, in 1853 the coverage the *Catholic Mirror* and the national Catholic directory allotted the Oblate Sisters of Providence increased significantly, coincident with Archbishop Kenrick's sanction of the Oblate male school project. Kenrick's endorsement effected wider acknowledgment of and receptivity toward the Oblate community within the consciousness of the archdiocesan establishment. Accordingly, in the 1853 edition of the national Catholic directory, a significantly expanded notice reported of St. Frances Chapel, "attended every Friday from St. Alphonsus. Every Sunday at 4 o'clock P.M., Vespers, Instruction, and Benediction for the colored people. The church has been enlarged and will accommodate more than 400 persons."[44]

Similarly, in the March 1853 *Catholic Mirror* feature article "Colored Schools," the writer championed the worthiness not only of the cause, the Catholic education of black youth, but also of the agents of black Catholic education, the

Oblate Sisters of Providence. The author allowed that black Baltimoreans "share in a more eminent degree than the whites in the injustice committed by our laws on education. For while they are taxed for school purposes, there is not even the poor pretense held out to them, with which some portions of the white population are attempted to be cajoled, that there are public schools open to them."[45]

Furthermore, the writer unequivocally endorsed the Oblate community, asserting that "the Sisters of Providence have long enjoyed the esteem of those who are acquainted with their pious and self-denying manner of life, and as teachers are thoroughly qualified for the task they have undertaken in behalf of the people of color. Their house is maintained with the order and neatness characteristic of Catholic conventual establishments."[46] The extant evidence does not reveal the reactions of the Oblate Sisters to such lavish praise of their institution. Certainly the older Oblate Sisters must have appreciated the radical difference in the opinions diocesan authorities entertained about the Oblate community in 1853 and those the previous diocesan authorities had expressed about them in 1843.

In 1853 and again in 1855 the newspaper reported on two of the five exercises concluding the year at the Oblate schools that Archbishop Kenrick attended. In 1853 the reporter characterized the audiences at both the public examination and the prize distribution as "highly gratified by the different performances, the evidence of the progress made by the pupils, the skill of the good Sisters in teaching, and by the admirable system pursued in St. Francis [sic] Female Colored School."[47] In 1855 the reporter again wrote approvingly of the Oblate school enterprise: "The examination was conducted by disinterested persons, and in the presence of numerous spectators. The pupils were examined in the various branches of their studies, and the clearness and promptness with which they answered the numerous questions propounded were sufficient to prove that the good Sisters had bestowed much labor on those who had the happiness of being confided to their care. Indeed, the examination did much credit to both teachers and pupils, and was highly gratifying to all present, as well as satisfactory to those by whom it was conducted."[48]

The three articles in the *Catholic Mirror* in the 1850s focusing on the Oblate Sisters of Providence or some aspect of their mission consistently portrayed the Oblate community in a highly positive manner. At this level of specificity the Catholic newspaper definitely acknowledged the Oblate Sisters as a functioning component of the Baltimore religious community. However, these isolated, self-contained assessments of the Oblate community and mission provided only a partial perspective of the position accorded these black women religious and black Catholics in general within the archdiocese of Baltimore. Even as Baltimore's Catholic publications explicitly recognized the valuable services of the Oblate Sisters during the 1850s, they also revealed the subordinate position assigned to both the Oblate community and the black Catholic laity in their general coverage of events within the archdiocese.

Archbishop Samuel Eccleston of Baltimore died at the Episcopal Residence in Georgetown on 22 April 1851. The *Catholic Mirror* reported the order of the procession accompanying Eccleston's corpse to the railroad station in Washington, D.C., for transport to Baltimore. "Citizens and Strangers" preceded the "St. Tobias Society (Colored)" as the last two groups in formation.[49] Black Catholics had organized the Tobias Society, a mutual benefit and burial organization, in 1827. The archdiocese of Baltimore had recognized the group as an official diocesan organization since 1830.[50] But because of their racial identity, members of the Tobias Society had to cede precedence in a Catholic procession to the white general public.

Even the positive reports on Oblate endeavors appearing in the *Catholic Mirror* from 1853 contained both subtle and explicit evidence of the circumscribed status of Baltimore's black Catholic community. In urging white Catholics to support the Oblate boys' school project, the reporter appealed to the white sense of noblesse oblige toward "a much neglected race." He also appealed to white self-interest when he reminded his readers of the vital social and economic services provided by Baltimore's "Catholic people of color, many of whom among those at service have endeared themselves to their employers by their fidelity and good conduct, and in other employments are well and favorably known."[51]

The reporter assured the newspaper's white readership of the modest scale of the Oblate boys' school building. He described it as "a well, but plainly constructed building of two stories in height, with an attic . . . dimensions thirty-nine feet by nineteen."[52] Such information allayed potential white concern that black Catholics might flout racial etiquette in erecting for themselves a physical structure inappropriately grand in any aspect.

By contrast, the same year, the newspaper announced the latest improvements to the campus of St. Joseph's Academy for Young Ladies, conducted by the Sisters of Charity at Emmitsburg. The installation of the most modern plumbing conveniences, including wash basins and water closets "in every story above stairs, and also in the Sisters' building" rendered "the supply of water the most extensive we have ever seen in any public establishment." The Oblate buildings boasted no indoor plumbing, as privies still standing on convent property in 1870 attested.[53]

When Archbishop Kenrick attended the exercises concluding the school year at St. Frances Female Colored School for the first time on 29 July 1853, the *Catholic Mirror* covered the annual Oblate event for the first time. Although Kenrick attended every Oblate school closing ceremony between 1853 and 1857, the *Catholic Mirror* reported these visits only in 1853 and 1855. Even the presence of the archbishop proved insufficient to guarantee the Oblate schools the annual coverage of their commencements this newspaper granted the white institutions as a matter of course.

The reporter ascribed undertones of racial paternalism and an implicit acknowledgment of the racial status quo to the occasion. According to his account, an unidentified senior Oblate student delivered "a very appropriate and well conceived little address" to the archbishop, "supplicating him to continue to extend his protection over them, and finally, begging him to impart his paternal blessing to them, 'the humblest of his spiritual children.'" The entire black congregation then knelt spontaneously to receive Kenrick's blessing. The reporter observed the archbishop visibly moved "by the touching scene before him."[54]

Humility had formed an essential component of the Oblate charism, or spiritual identity, from the beginning of the Oblate community. Oblate historian Sister Theresa Catherine Willigman recalled that spiritual director James Joubert had "always made Charity, Obedience, and above all, Humility the prominent virtues to be observed by one consecrated to God and never tired of repeating to them [the Oblate Sisters], 'Be meek and humble of heart.'"[55] In the tradition of Roman Catholic asceticism, humility represented an ideal that all aspirants—men and women, black and white alike—strove to achieve in their pursuit of spiritual perfection. However, the characterization "the humblest of his spiritual children" contained in the *Catholic Mirror* article referred not to the Oblate Sisters specifically but to the black lay student body and the entire assembled lay black congregation. In the context of the racial caste system operative in southern antebellum society, describing the black population as "the humblest" corroborated an ascribed trait of the inferior group in support of the existing racial status quo.

Kenrick's remarks to the Oblate pupils at the premium distribution exercise in 1855 also affirmed the social circumscriptions on black aspirations inherent in American society's racial caste system. As reported in the *Catholic Mirror*, Kenrick enjoined the Oblate pupils "to persevere in their desire to acquire knowledge and virtue, and that by so doing the reward they would receive in a future world would far surpass what they then received as acknowledgment of their good conduct and attention to studies during the past year."[56] As Kenrick accurately observed, recognition of academic achievement for black pupils occurred within the confines of the Oblate school, a metaphor for the black community, and in heaven. Unlike their white counterparts, black students could expect few prospects of upward mobility or equal access to opportunities in their racially riven world. Racism remanded even educated black people to a subordinate status in antebellum society.

In 1856 a news item in the *Catholic Mirror*, "Edifying Death of an Indian Sister," provided further evidence of the marginal position of black Catholics within the institutional religious community. Communities of white women religious accepted Native American women as members, but not black women. The writer eulogized Sister Mary Christina, a member of the Ottawa tribe and a School Sister of Notre Dame, as "this swarthy child of a race now fading from the earth," whose conversion and religious vocation represented "one of the triumphs of Christianity."[57] Did, then, the refusal of the American institutional church either to integrate women of African descent into white sisterhoods or to accept duly constituted communities of black women religious on a basis of complete equality not constitute one of the failures of Christianity?

Frenchman Henri De Courcy included the Oblate Sisters of Providence in his work on the Catholic Church in the United States, published in 1856. De Courcy applauded the existence of the Oblate community and cited John Odin's 1834 laudatory appraisal of Oblate accomplishments but cautioned, "This is but a small development, and the good to be done among the blacks would need a very large community."[58] In comparing the Baltimore Oblate community to the Oblates of St. Frances of Rome, De Courcy said of the latter, "Their numbers are generally filled up from the most distinguished classes of society, and many princesses have been members of the order, while their sisters in America are taken in the humblest condition. Such is the equality of the great Christian family before God."[59]

De Courcy's observation accurately reflected the status of "the colored Sisters" in antebellum Baltimore. He noted the socially ascribed "humblest condition" of the American Oblate Sisters predicated on their racial identity that "the equality of the great Christian family before God" accommodated. However, the responses of both the institutional church and secular Baltimore society to the Oblate Sisters revealed that these black women religious enjoyed no corresponding "equality of the great Christian family" before white people.

Sins of omission as well as sins of commission in the treatment of the Oblate Sisters of Providence in Baltimore's Catholic publications indicated their exceptional status within the antebellum religious community. In October 1857 nativist opposition erupted against the new Oblate mission in south Baltimore. The *Catholic Mirror* neither reported the incident nor expressed any editorial condemnation of the attack. However, in April and September 1857 the editor of the *Catholic Mirror* had reprinted vigorous defenses of Supreme Court chief justice Roger B. Taney and condemnations of his detractors in the aftermath of the Dred Scott decision.[60] In the landmark court case *Dred Scott v. Sanford* the Roman Catholic Taney had characterized black people as "beings of an inferior order [who] had no rights which white men were bound to respect." Taney designated all black people noncitizens, deprived of both legal status and protection. Taney thus enshrined in federal law "the sentiment that the negro cannot be the political or social equal of the white,"[61] the legitimizing principle of the racial caste system imposed throughout the South and acknowledged throughout the nation. In 1857 moral outrage bellowed forth twice from the pages of the *Catholic Mirror* to defend the honor of Roger B. Taney as he simultaneously upheld a fundamental tenet of the institution of slavery and legally debased an entire race of people. In contrast, moral outrage found no voice in the *Catholic Mirror* to condemn attacks on the Oblate Sisters of Providence as they endeavored to educate more children of their race.

From 1858 the Oblate Sisters of Providence conducted four schools in Baltimore: St. Frances School for Colored Girls and St. Frances Male School at the Oblate Richmond Street property, St. Peter Claver School in St. Joseph's parish, and St. Benedict School in St. Michael's parish. But the *Catholic Mirror* never mentioned the Oblate schools associated with St. Joseph's and St. Michael's parishes. Furthermore, the national Catholic directory eliminated mention of any Oblate school from its enumeration of educational establishments in the archdiocese of Baltimore between 1859 and 1861. It did list "St. Frances Chapel (colored Sisters of Providence)" last under "Churches and Clergy" and "Oblate Sisters of Providence (colored)" last under "Convents" during these years. However, no Oblate citation appeared under either "Female Literary Institutions" or "Pay and Free Schools."[62] Although the 1861 edition of the directory noted as the last entry under "Charitable and Beneficial Societies" the existence of "schools for colored children in St. Joseph's parish and in St. Michael's," it did not credit the Oblate Sisters with conducting these schools.[63]

Such omissions of substantive Oblate activity from the pages of official Catholic publications proved habitual in the 1850s. In spite of its title, the *Catholic Mirror*, Baltimore's official archdiocesan organ failed to reflect accurately the entire constituency of the Baltimore Catholic community. The antebellum institutional church in Baltimore relegated black religious and laity alike to a marginal position where they remained in but not of the Baltimore Catholic community.

THE RACIALLY DELIMITED acceptance and recognition within the institutional church that the Oblate Sisters experienced during the 1850s did not extend to Oblate interaction with the larger Baltimore white community. Conditions for free black people throughout the United States worsened, as both abolitionists and apologists for slavery ossified in their respective positions during the decade. Furthermore, a resurgence of nativism in Maryland again focused on Roman Catholic convents as institutions antithetical to contemporary family values of marriage and motherhood. As both women of color and institutionalized religious, the Oblate Sisters of Providence proved doubly vulnerable to the racially and religiously charged atmosphere of Baltimore in the 1850s.

The two chambers and several committees of the Maryland state legislature proposed increasingly restrictive measures to combat "free negroism" in the state during the decade. The constitutional convention in 1850–51 considered "the vice and ignorance of the blacks" and recommended that Maryland enact legislation to rid the state of its free black residents through wholesale colonization to Africa.[64] The legislature chanted the mantra of free black idleness, dissipation, criminal proclivities, and incapacity for self-government to justify the exceptional civic status accorded free black people as statutory, not constitutional, citizens. Manumission did not grant citizenship to the manumitted, who "merely ceases to belong to one man and really becomes the property of the whole state."[65] In 1857 Chief Justice Taney stripped the free black population of any citizenship in the *Dred Scott v. Sanford* case. The *Dred Scott* decision fanned the flames of hostility toward free black people and reinvigorated the movement to expel them from southern states, including Maryland.[66]

However, economic realities prevailed over political polemics. Even the majority report of the slaveholders' convention meeting in Baltimore in June 1859 allowed, "It is highly inexpedient to try to remove all the free blacks. They are indeed an evil in a slaveholding community, but the majority of them are not idle, unproductive, and vicious. Their removal would be a greater evil than all the harm ever suffered. In Baltimore they number twenty-five thousand, mostly servants and laborers. Much of our soil could not be tilled without them."[67]

In 1860 the House Committee on Colored Population recommended total elimination of future manumissions and "the grant to free blacks under fifty-five years of the privilege of choosing masters and going into slavery at any time." A minority of this committee "wished to put free blacks back into slavery—complete and at once."[68] In November 1860 the Maryland State Assembly submitted to popular referendum a Negro code that included provisions for voluntary reenslavement and unconditional abrogation of manumissions. The Maryland electorate overwhelmingly rejected the code.[69] The strident ideologues advocating reenslavement of free people or wholesale expulsion had misinterpreted the equivocal sentiments of most Marylanders regarding the free black population. Although determined to relegate free black people to a permanently inferior position socially, politically, and economically, Maryland citizens nevertheless considered the measures proposed by the apologists for slavery beyond the pale of justice and decency, as well as economically unfeasible.[70]

The crucial economic role free black people played in Baltimore brought them into conflict increasingly with white native and immigrant labor. The trend begun in the 1840s of white encroachment on historically black fields of labor, like the caulking trade, continued unabated in the 1850s.[71] But white labor considered black labor the problem. Economic competition formed a major component of nativist antipathy toward the immigrant Catholic population in the 1850s. Nativists contended that immigrant workers accepted substandard wages, poorer working conditions, and a lower standard of living than native-born workers sought. This argument proved identical to the charges white labor leveled against free black and slave hired-out labor in cities like Baltimore.[72] Baltimore's exceptional position as the antebellum free black capital within a slaveholding state presented its native white labor force with the compounded problem of economic competition not only from immigrant white labor but from black free and slave labor as well. White labor's prominent opposition to free black people throughout the decade suggests that the nativism that erupted in Baltimore during the 1850s incorporated elements of racism toward Baltimore's significant black population, both slave and free, as well as the anti-Catholic and anti-immigrant impulses traditionally associated with nativist movements.

As the site of the premier see of the Roman Catholic Church in the United States, Baltimore participated fully in what one source has termed "the most violent outbreak of nativism in the history of Maryland" during the 1850s.[73] Nationwide, the Catholic Church initiated campaigns in 1852 and 1853 to eliminate Protestant Bible readings in public schools and to divert a portion of general school taxes to support the Catholic parochial school system. Such unseemly assertiveness by the Roman Catholic hierarchy not only proved unproductive, it also served to increase memberships in Know-Nothing clubs in Baltimore and other cities.[74] In 1854 incensed nativist mobs responded to the visit of a papal ambassador to Baltimore by burning him in effigy near the Baltimore Cathedral and terrorizing Archbishop Kenrick's residence, St. Mary's Seminary, a Catholic orphan asylum, and the convent of the Visitation Sisters of Georgetown "with firing of pistols and hellish yells."[75] The political embodiment of nativism, the Know-Nothing, or American, Party, controlled the administration of the city of Baltimore between 1854 and 1860. It dominated the state assembly from 1855 to 1859 and seized the state governorship in 1857.[76]

In 1854 Baltimore nativists targeted Roman Catholic sisterhoods when the Reverend Andrew B. Cross published *Priests' Prisons for Women*, an anthology of letters to Catholic attorney T. Parkin Scott. In the 1830s Presbyterian ministers Robert J. Breckinridge and Andrew B. Cross had coedited the *Baltimore Literary and Religious Magazine*, a compendium of virulently anti-Catholic sentiment. In 1856 Cross escalated his anticonvent crusade by petitioning the state legislature for statutes to protect persons unlawfully confined in convents and nunneries. On 4 March 1856 the Maryland State House Select Committee on Convents and Nunneries, composed "of regular, sworn-in Know-Nothings," reported that none of the allegations of illegal confinements in convents had basis in fact. A reporter for the *Baltimore Republican* derided the Know-Nothing press for its failure to publicize the committee's findings as assiduously as it had reported "the whole charge of imprisonment and other monstrous horrors depicted by Mr. Cross and his brother scribblers."[77] Such sensational excesses committed by nativist ministers and the press embarrassed the Know-Nothing Party as much as the havoc wreaked by the mobs who acted in their name. Lawless nativist gangs roamed the city of Baltimore at election time so that "mayhem and murder, unchecked by the police, came to be expected each election day."[78] These circumstances provided the context for the nativist attack on the Oblate Sisters of Providence in south Baltimore in 1857.

Evidently, the area around St. Joseph's parish constituted a Know-Nothing stronghold. Oblate efforts to establish not only another Catholic school there —the Sisters of Charity and lay teachers already conducted free parish schools for white girls and boys respectively in the area—but also one for black children during the week of city elections provoked a violent reaction. Nativist agitation during the 1857 city election resulted in one murder, numerous injuries, and significant property damage.[79] However, the Oblate Sisters of Providence remained the only Catholic institution attacked at that time.

On 28 November 1857 Archbishop Kenrick, writing to Bishop Purcell in Cincinnati of the incident, said that the Oblate Sisters had "prepared to open a school in another part of the city, but were deterred, their doors having been broken in by rowdies on the day before the city election." Kenrick also informed Purcell that the Oblate Sisters formed a particular target of the Know-Nothing city administration because "an attempt was twice made to pass a city ordinance to open Park St., apparently with a view to break up their establishment. It happily failed."[80] Again, no other convent came under political assault at this time.

Nevertheless, in their own neighborhood where they had resided since 1829, the Oblate Sisters enjoyed civil and even cordial relations with their white neighbors and tradespeople with whom they interacted. In May 1853 the sisters borrowed $30 from their neighbor, Mr. Eschbach, that they repaid "in due time." In June 1857 Mrs. Eschbach reimbursed the sisters "for sundry little debts—$1.125 and for sewing, $13.75."[81]

In 1851 craftsman George T. Rosensteel contracted with the Oblate Sisters to work on the St. Frances Chapel renovations. Wonderfully descriptive invoices from Rosensteel's work through the 1850s partially recreate details of the chapel's structure, otherwise irretrievably lost to posterity. The St. Frances Chapel measured 27'5¾" by 57'4⅝". Rosensteel itemized "painting, marbleing, varnishing, and gilding the alter [sic]," "painting tabernackle [sic] polish white and gilding the door," "furnishing and glazing 310 lights [panes] in new sash," and "painting, graining, and varnishing new pews, pew doors, and outside of confessional." An inscription lettered in gold hung above the grained wood front door. Venetian shutters covered the five rear windows. "Piecing the stained light in front of the Church" referred to one of three front windows. The sisters paid all Rosensteel's invoices in full. Rosensteel in turn demonstrated his appreciation of the Oblate Sisters and their mission with donations of $7.50 in January 1854 and $1 in January 1857.[82]

During the 1850s the Oblate Sisters' account with Patrick McKanna for meat and groceries constituted one of their biggest monthly expenses, ranging from $80 to $150. In addition to his $20 subscription for the Oblate boys' school, McKanna lent the sisters $300, a sum they repaid on 6 April 1853 "in the presence of Sister Mary." If some merchants and tradespeople with whom the Oblate Sisters conducted business remained shackled by racial considerations in their perceptions of the Oblate community as primarily or even exclusively the "Cullord Sisters of Charity" or simply "the Colored Sisters," the Oblate sisters also experienced relationships with antebellum white Baltimoreans that transcended limitations of race and addressed them as human beings.[83]

By the 1850s, time and growth had eroded the original Francophone cultural identity of the Oblate Sisters of Providence—for the Oblate as well as the lay black and white communities. Because the Oblate Sisters alone among the Baltimore sisterhoods experienced violence and political threats in October 1857, racism as much as anti-Catholic or anti-immigrant sentiment probably motivated them. The challenges the Oblate Sisters of Providence had encountered in the 1830s as a function of their being both black women and a formal religious community in Baltimore had only intensified in the city during the 1850s. Whatever concerns for their safety the white sisterhoods continued to entertain in the wake of nativist agitation, the black Oblate Sisters also still experienced, in addition to their concerns for their safety derived from their racial identity.

THE BALTIMORE WHITE community in general at times harassed, when it did not ignore, the Oblate Sisters, doubly disdained and consequently doubly vulnerable as a black and Roman Catholic sisterhood. Nevertheless, in musical ministry, business transactions, or financial and legal contributions, white antebellum Baltimoreans who interacted personally with the Oblate community occasionally overstepped the barriers of racial caste to support the work of the Oblate Sisters of Providence.

Nineteenth-century white Catholics in the United States recognized their status as Catholics in a non-Catholic world. Their responses ranged from insularity and a beleaguered defensiveness to a heightened sense of religious nationalism, an articulated pride in their Catholic identity, and defiance of their socially ascribed minority status. Yet, American society's subjection of white Catholics to public suspicion, derogation, and discrimination predicated on religious affiliation rarely elicited their empathy or tolerance for black people, another group subjected to social proscription, predicated on their racial identity.

The experiences of the Oblate Sisters of Providence in antebellum Baltimore provided a unique counterpoint to the course of mainstream American Catholic history. Antebellum white Catholics did indeed experience critical scrutiny and oppression. However, as black Roman Catholic women religious, the Oblate Sisters endured the double jeopardy of external scrutiny by an essentially white, Protestant, and antipathetic nation as well as internal scrutiny by a white and essentially ambivalent institutional church and laity.

It is axiomatic that if we do not define ourselves, we will be defined by others —
for their use and to our detriment. —*Audre Lorde, 1984*

Black and free in a slave society that privileged only whiteness, female in a patriarchal society, Roman Catholic in a Protestant society, committed to celibacy instead of social expectations of matrimony and motherhood, the Oblate Sisters of Providence constituted an anomaly in antebellum southern society. They aspired to and realized religious vocations in a slaveholding society that denigrated the virtue of all black women—slave or free. Refusing to internalize such social disparagement, these extraordinary black women demonstrated self-definition, self-possession, and self-empowerment instead.

In institutionalizing the Oblate Sisters of Providence as a religious community within the Roman Catholic Church, cofounders Sister Mary Elizabeth Lange and the Reverend James Hector Joubert claimed for pious black women "the respect which is due to the state we have embraced and the holy habit which we have the honor to wear."[1] The critical imprint of the individual charism and personality of Sister Mary Elizabeth Lange guided the nascent community during its formative years in the decade of the 1830s. Her commitment to virtue and the disciplined pursuit of spiritual perfection as a formal religious constituency within the institutional church defied racist stereotypes of black people as inveterate wantons. Lange's executive skills, authority, positive conviction of the Oblate religious vocation, example, and leadership fortified the community in its encounters with trials, challenges, and rejection throughout its first half century.

Humility formed an essential component of the Oblate spiritual identity. In a worldly context, humility connotes a demeanor of deference from an inferior toward a superior, a socially hierarchical relationship between people. However, in a religious sense, humility means a voluntary submission of self to God, a spiritual relationship between the individual and the divine. In practice, the moral virtue of humility "avoids inflation of one's worth or talents on the one hand, and avoids excessive devaluation of oneself on the other. Humility requires a dispassionate and honest appreciation of the self in relationship to others and to God."[2]

While distinctions between the secular and spiritual connotations of humility applied generally to all religious congregations, they acquired particular racial significance for the black Oblate Sisters in the antebellum South. Embracing the religious state and rejecting secular concerns and status could prove both liberating and empowering to black women debased by the worldly social order. In renouncing the world to consecrate themselves to God, the Oblate Sisters of Providence achieved symbolic release from socially ascribed derogation based on their identities as black women. As the Oblate Sisters of Providence, women of color in the antebellum South utilized their piety and spiritual fervor to defy their socially ascribed inferior status and to act assertively in service to others.

In their lucid analysis of the role of nuns in shaping Catholic culture and American life, historians Carol Coburn and Martha Smith have argued that the parameters of the moral virtue of humility restricted female assertiveness so that "sisters could assert themselves only on behalf of others—an acceptable 'feminine' trait that women have historically utilized in efforts to gain agency in a patriarchal society."[3] This ideology of "maternal feminism" allowed women to "utilize their power as mothers to actively take on abuses of patriarchy and at times of capitalism in defense of their concern for children, not necessarily their own self-interest."[4]

In contrast, this study contends that the racial identity of the Oblate Sisters of Providence required them to identify and to assert themselves as "people of color and religious at the same time"[5] and to promote their self-interest as a sisterhood, functioning in a society that disallowed their identity as moral women and nurturing mothers a priori because of their color. Only by acting in their own self-interest and establishing themselves as genuine religious—women of virtue—did the black Oblate Sisters wring from white society acknowledgment of the legitimacy of their status and white support of their efforts to exert agency, like white sisterhoods, within the parameters of "maternal feminism."

As a religious constituency within the institutional church, this black sisterhood adhered to church policy of nonintervention in social and political issues. However, the explicit statement of their racial identity in their constitutions documented their racial self-consciousness. Furthermore, the mandate of the

Oblate mission to educate black girls insured that the Oblate community contributed substantively to the nurture and support of the antebellum black Baltimore community. The black lay community both supported and appreciated Oblate educational and spiritual efforts on their behalf. In financial contributions, patronage of Oblate schools, or in volunteering time, labor, and resources to benefit the Oblate cause, members of the antebellum black community amply demonstrated their conviction of the seminal importance of "our convent."

During the 1840s the Oblate Sisters of Providence encountered and prevailed over a series of events that tested both their faith and their viability as a community of women religious. Issues of ethnicity, religion, and race inhered in the internal rupture in their community and the external clerical neglect they experienced in the middle years of the 1840s. To resolve their critical situation, the Oblate Sisters steadfastly lived as committed women religious, in compliance with their own spiritual convictions and in defiance of clerical antipathy, indifference, and neglect. In successfully sustaining their internal spiritual integrity, the Oblate Sisters of Providence precipitated the series of events that effected their revalidation as a legitimate religious constituency by diocesan authorities in Baltimore.

Multidirectional growth in the services they provided the black community characterized the maturation of the Oblate Sisters of Providence during the 1850s. Through assisting in weekly religious instruction classes, the sisters facilitated the growth of their chapel congregation by 300 converts and interacted with broader segments of the black community, including slave and free adults as well as more children. By 1860 the Oblate education mission included four schools. During the 1850s, as the teaching staff of both St. Frances School for Colored Girls and St. Frances Male School, the Oblate Sisters played a pivotal role in the evolution of the Oblate chapel congregation as the first black parish in the Catholic tradition. By providing educational and social as well as spiritual dimensions to their lives through their church, the black St. Frances congregation countered the effects of the restrictions white society imposed on their existence. Oblate presence and participation facilitated this process. Oblate efforts in antebellum Baltimore insured that not only within the Protestant religious tradition did church and school prevail as the preeminent cultural institutions for the black community.

BALTIMORE ENJOYED a reputation for its exceptionalism in southern slave society. Nevertheless, Baltimore proved as vulnerable to domination by the institution of slavery and its corollary convictions about the inherent inferiority of all black people as the rest of southern society. The white South imposed more prejudices and proscriptions than it demonstrated positive support for these black women religious. Yet the Oblate Sisters utilized their religious status to assert and to insert themselves in antebellum Baltimore as a legitimate constituency empowered to serve the black community. Oblate provenance in Baltimore proved to be a defining feature of their antebellum experience; reciprocally, the Oblate presence helped to define life in antebellum Baltimore.

Throughout the antebellum era the Roman Catholic Church provided modest support for the Oblate community. Few clerics matched the unstinting zeal and total commitment to the Oblate cause evinced by their cofounder James Joubert. The Redemptorist priest Thaddeus Anwander proved a worthy successor to Joubert as Oblate spiritual director from 1847 until 1855 in his exceptional lack of prejudice toward black people, his zealous efforts to strengthen and expand the Oblate mission, and his determination to enhance the quality of black Catholic life in Baltimore. Several priests and prelates demonstrated varying degrees of support for the Oblate Sisters throughout the antebellum period. But clerical support of the black Oblate Sisters never equalled that bestowed on the white sisterhoods in the archdiocese of Baltimore. Issues of race and the grip of the institution of slavery on social mores intruded on the response of the institutional church to this community of black women religious.

Considerations of race, gender, ethnicity, and religion informed antebellum white perceptions of and responses to the Oblate Sisters of Providence. Gender, ethnicity, or religion intervened in white attitudes toward the Oblate community in the absence of racial factors or in a capacity subsidiary to race. White Baltimoreans favorably regarded the Francophone ethnic identity of the original Oblate community only when comparing them to other black people. But white Baltimoreans had discriminated against black San Domingan émigrés compared to their reception of the white refugees. The subordinate position ascribed to women religious in the hierarchy of the institutional church allowed the American clergy to tolerate the existence of black sisterhoods decades before they accepted the reality of identifiably black priests.

Race superseded gender, ethnicity, and religion in defining the status of the Oblate Sisters within both church and southern society. The dominance of race over other issues proved consistent in a society that both predicated the legal enslavement of a people and delimited a tertium quid of free black people — neither slave nor citizen in the polity — exclusively based on racial identity. Antebellum white society and the church alike referred to the Oblate community exclusively as "the colored Sisters," repeatedly demonstrating the primacy of race in forming their perceptions of this religious community.

Considerations of race and ethnicity also informed the Oblate Sisters' perceptions of themselves and sense of community identity. They had explicitly defined themselves as "a Religious society of Coloured Women" in their original Rule and Constitutions. But no Francophone ethnic exclusivity figured in the Oblate communal identity. While acknowledging their Francophone cultural origins, the Oblate Sisters fully assimilated the African American cultural identities forming most of their membership, their pupil population, and the St. Frances Chapel congregation in the 1850s.

THE OBLATE SISTERS determined and maintained their internal community life and conducted their teaching ministry within the patriarchal Roman Catholic Church and the antebellum South. As black women, the Oblate Sisters contradicted prevailing conventional views and social expectations of women of color by their institutional existence as well as by their successful forging of a positive, assertive, and empowered communal self-image. They distinguished themselves as black women in the Roman Catholic tradition by their collective profession and practice of spirituality formalized in the pursuit of religious communal life. As did all religious sisterhoods, the Oblate Sisters defied the narrow conventional social concept of voluntary female association. In religious life women functioned in permanent association in an exclusively female environment and claimed spirituality—not marriage and maternity—as the primary determinant of their identity. The Oblate Sisters first claimed for black women the traditional entitlements of respectability and societal exemption inherent in the religious state. In this pioneering incarnation, black women felt empowered to transcend mere social opposition to their divinely mandated mission: their own personal spiritual perfection and the education of black children.

In forming a community of women religious, the Oblate Sisters demonstrated that moral virtue and spiritual fervor among black people occurred not in isolation but permeated the population sufficiently to motivate a group of black women to claim religious piety as their primary identity. As an institution, the Oblate Sisters bore witness to the virtue and spirituality of black women. They utilized their communal profession of piety as currency to validate and legitimize their claim to public recognition and support to an extent unrealizable by individual, secular black women in antebellum society. White support of the black sisters never equalled that bestowed on the white sisterhoods in the archdiocese of Baltimore. Nevertheless, the fact that the institutional church and individual white benefactors among both clergy and laity recognized, promoted, and subsidized the Oblate enterprise at all attested the viability of Oblate virtue as currency in antebellum society.

Black female agency proved the hallmark of the antebellum Oblate experience. In the signal act of institutionalizing themselves as a community of women religious within the Roman Catholic Church, the Oblate Sisters of Providence converted their religious status into an effective counteridentity with which to resist, to defy, and ultimately to transcend the restrictions and social controls white antebellum society sought to impose on them, predicated on their identity as black women. No extant evidence suggests that the Oblate Sisters of Providence either articulated or subscribed to any prototypical black feminist agenda; nevertheless, as Scripture advises, "By their works shall you know them." In her perceptive analysis of the career of early-twentieth-century black womanist activist Maggie Lena Walker, historian Elsa Barkley Brown concluded, "The clearest articulation of her theoretical perspective lies in the organization she helped to create and in her own activities. Her theory and her action are not distinct and separate parts of some whole; they are often synonymous, and it is only through her actions that we clearly hear her theory. The same is true for the lives of many other black women who had limited time and resources and maintained a holistic view of life and struggle."[6]

Brown's cogent argument applies with equal validity to the antebellum experiences of the Oblate Sisters of Providence. In their actions the Oblate Sisters of Providence had conformed to the black feminist model of empowerment by "rejecting the dimensions of knowledge, whether personal, cultural, or institutional, that perpetuate objectification and dehumanization."[7] They nurtured and inculcated into their communal consciousness positive senses of themselves as black women and as committed religious. In their actions, especially during the crisis of the 1840s, this black sisterhood accomplished what historian Rosalyn Terborg-Penn has identified as "perhaps the two most dominant values in the African feminist theory . . . developing survival strategies and encouraging self-reliance through female networks."[8]

Throughout their antebellum existence the Oblate Sisters of Providence accomplished their mission as they had from their foundation: independently of and, not infrequently, in defiance of prevailing social attitudes and intentions. A community of women of faith, the Oblate Sisters adopted as their motto "Providence will provide." However, in their pursuit of spiritual perfection and in their vigorous execution of their teaching ministry, the Oblate Sisters of Providence acted on what could have served as the essential subtext of their motto: "God helps those who help themselves."

NOTES

Abbreviations

AAB	Archives of the Archdiocese of Baltimore, Baltimore, Md.
Annals	Translation of "The Original Diary of the Oblate Sisters of Providence," typescript and manuscript copies, vols. 1 and 2, Box 47, Archives of the Oblate Sisters of Providence, Baltimore, Md.
AOSP	Archives of the Oblate Sisters of Providence, Baltimore, Md.
CACI	Archdiocese of Cincinnati Collection, University of Notre Dame Archives, Notre Dame, Ind.
Calendar	Finbar Kenneally, O.F.M., et al., eds., *United States Documents in the Propaganda Fide Archives: A Calendar*, 1st ser., 7 vols. (Washington, D.C.: Academy of American Franciscan History, 1966–)
"Deluol's Diary"	"Excerpts from Louis R. Deluol's Diary Concerning the Oblate Sisters of Providence," compiled by John W. Bowen, S.S., Sulpician Archives, Baltimore, Md.
"Easter Duty Lists"	"Fr. Tessier's Easter Duty Lists" (1809–33), RG 1, Box 17, Sulpician Archives, Baltimore, Md.
1844–54 Ledger	Oblate Ledger, 1844–54 (unpaged), Box 51, Archives of the Oblate Sisters of Providence, Baltimore, Md.
1855–61 Ledger	Oblate Ledger, 1855–61 (unpaged), marked "Box 10 Ledger #1," Box 1, Archives of the Oblate Sisters of Providence, Baltimore, Md.
"A Few Facts"	M. Theresa Catherine Willigman, O.S.P., "A Few Facts Relating to the Oblate Sisters of Providence of Baltimore, Md.," typescript copy, n.d., Archives of the Oblate Sisters of Providence, Baltimore, Md.
"First Foundress"	M. Theresa Catherine Willigman, O.S.P., "First Foundress of the Oblates," typescript copy, n.d., Archives of the Oblate Sisters of Providence, Baltimore, Md.
JFA	Josephite Archives, Baltimore, Md.

"Journal"	"Journal of the Commencement of the Proceedings of the Society of Coloured People [Holy Family Society]," 1843–45, Record Group 42, Box 2, Sulpician Archives, Baltimore, Md.
Laity's Directory	*Metropolitan Catholic Calendar and Laity's Directory* (Baltimore: James Myres, 1833–37; Fielding Lucas, 1834–57; John Murphy, 1859–61)
MdHR	Maryland Hall of Records, State Archives
"Memories"	M. Theresa Catherine Willigman, O.S.P., "Memories of Sister Theresa Duchemin," typescript copy, n.d., Archives of the Oblate Sisters of Providence, Baltimore, Md.
MPRF	Propaganda Fide Archives Microfilm, University of Notre Dame Archives, Notre Dame, Ind.
"Notes"	"Notes on the Constitutions of the Oblate Sisters of Providence, Established in Baltimore, June 1829, by Very Rev. L. R. Deluol, Superior of St. Mary's Seminary," partially translated from the original French by M. Theresa Catherine Willigman, O.S.P., manuscript copy, n.d., Box 52, Archives of the Oblate Sisters of Providence, Baltimore, Md.
Original Ledger	Original Oblate Ledger Sheets, 1828–30 (unpaged), 1829–36, Eagle File Box 44, Archives of the Oblate Sisters of Providence, Baltimore, Md.
Original Rule	The Original Rule and Constitutions of the Oblate Sisters of Providence, English manuscript copy, Box 41, Archives of the Oblate Sisters of Providence, Baltimore, Md.
Revision of 1833	The Original Rule of the Oblate Sisters of Providence, Revision of 1833, as amended by Fr. Jacques Joubert, translated from the French text by Cyprian Davis, O.S.B., cited in Thaddeus Posey, "An Unwanted Commitment: The Spirituality of the Early Oblate Sisters of Providence, 1829–1890" (Ph.D. diss., St. Louis University, 1993), appendix 2.
RG	Record Group
SAB	Sulpician Archives, Baltimore, Md.
"Souvenir of Love"	M. Theresa Catherine Willigman, O.S.P., "Souvenir of Love and Grateful Remembrance of the Foundress of the Oblate Sisters of Providence, Sister Mary, Established in Baltimore, June 5th, 1828, Made Their Vows July 2nd, 1829, Celebrated Her Golden Jubilee July 2nd, 1879, Died February 3rd, 1882, First Superior of the Oblate Sisters," manuscript copy, n.d., Archives of the Oblate Sisters of Providence
Student Registers	Early Student Registers (1828–33), Eagle File Box 44 and Box 95, Archives of the Oblate Sisters of Providence
West Chester Notes	The West Chester Notes: "Mother M. Theresa," dictated by Sister Mary James to Sister Maria Alma, 22 February 1920, typescript copy, Villa Maria House of Studies, West Chester Motherhouse Archives, Sisters, Servants of the Immaculate Heart of Mary, Immaculata, Pa.

Introduction

1. "Women without Virtue" broadcast program no. 305 of *Sound and Spirit* series, hosted by Ellen Kushner, aired on Public Radio International, 8 February 1998.

2. Sherwood, *Oblates' Hundred and One Years*, 118; Gillard, *Colored Catholics*, 118. Historians Carol Coburn and Martha Smith have provided an effective clarification of certain religious terms that applies to their use in this book as well: "The term 'religious' when used in reference to a member of a religious community (i.e., a group of individuals who live together as sisters or brothers and publicly profess religious vows) is a *noun* and 'women' would designate the gender of the group. Although the term 'nun' specifically refers to a member of a religious order whose chief purpose and work is to worship in a cloistered setting, it is popularly used to refer to any woman religious. Therefore, throughout this book we will use the terms 'sister,' 'nun,' and 'woman/women religious' interchangeably" (Coburn and Smith, *Spirited Lives*, 288 n. 3).

3. Original Rule.

4. Christopher J. Kauffman to Elaine Maisner, 6 April 2001, The University of North Carolina Press Reader's Report on this manuscript. I thank Professor Kauffman for his insights on a more expansive conceptualization of the term "spirituality" as "derived from contexts and not [as] simply ahistorical holiness" (Kauffman to Morrow, 16 April 2001).

5. Collins, *Black Feminist Thought*, 224.

6. Ibid., 230.

7. Terborg-Penn, "African Feminism," 25.

8. Kauffman, *Tradition and Transformation*, 38–43.

9. Color designations such as "black," "mulatto," or "colored" used in reference to people of African descent throughout Caribbean, Central American, and South American societies often denoted substantive social, legal, and economic differences in status, as I explain in Chapter 1. However, white U.S. mainland society recognized no social or legal distinctions between "black" and "mulatto." Consequently, throughout this work I use these terms interchangeably.

10. Gillard, *Colored Catholics*, 76–80; Glenn O. Phillips, "Maryland and the Caribbean," 202–5; Posey, "Unwanted Commitment," 39–40; Rouse, *Study of the Development of Negro Education*, 32; Gregory, "Education of Blacks," 78–79; Misner, *"Highly Respectable and Accomplished Ladies,"* 45.

11. Annals, 1:1–2.

12. Ibid.

13. Collins, *Black Feminist Thought*, 4.

14. *Laity's Directory* (1839), 96; Thaddeus Anwander to E. J. Sourin, 27 March 1876, and Anwander letter fragment, December 1886, Thaddeus Anwander Director File, AOSP.

15. *Metropolitan* 1 (January 1830): 31. I thank Professor Christopher J. Kauffman for this reference.

16. Misner, *"Highly Respected and Accomplished Ladies,"* 257, 259–63, 268; Spalding, *Premier See*, 142, 168–69.

17. Berlin, *Slaves without Masters*, 15–20, 23–26, 45–48, 54–55; Posey, "Unwanted Commitment," 54; Graham, *Baltimore*; Curry, *Free Black*, 6–8; Gillard, *Colored Catholics*, 76–80.

18. Gillard, *Catholic Church*, 14–15, and *Colored Catholics*, 63, 88, 99, 76–79.

19. Hunt, *Haiti's Influence on Antebellum America*, 74; Gregory, "Education of Blacks," 80.

20. Herbermann, *Sulpicians*, 233; Sherwood, *Oblates' Hundred and One Years*, 7; Gillard, *Catholic Church*, 28.

21. For thorough treatments of antebellum black communal institutions in Baltimore see Woodson, *Education of the Negro*, 138–44; Wright, *Free Negro*, 200–238; Gardner, "Free Blacks in Baltimore," 49–127; Collier-Thomas, "Baltimore Black Community," 17–39, 57–61, 74–80; Gregory, "Education of Blacks," 64–103, 131–36; Curry, *Free Black*, 154–59, 181; Graham, *Baltimore*, 63–85, 93–135, 216; and Christopher Phillips, *Freedom's Port*, 117–76.

22. Fields, *Slavery and Freedom*, 57.

23. Ibid., 7–8; Brackett, *Negro in Maryland*, 204, 246.

24. Fields, *Slavery and Freedom*, 3, 83, 86–88; Berlin, *Slaves without Masters*, 192, 207–8.

25. Misner, *"Highly Respected and Accomplished Ladies,"* 5; Miller and Wakelyn, eds. *Catholics in the Old South*, 6; Schmandt, "Overview of Institutional Establishments," 55; Duncan, "Catholics and the Church," 87–90; Ochs, *Desegregating the Altar*, 15; Spalding, *Premier See*, 160.

26. Miller, "Church in Cultural Captivity," 14–17; Steins, "Mission of the Josephites," 2–3; Cyprian Davis, *History of Black Catholics*, 39–57.

27. Brewer, *Nuns and the Education of American Catholic Women*, 123–24, 136; Thompson, "Women and American Catholicism," 127, and "Philemon's Dilemma," 90; Mannard, "'Maternity of the Spirit,'" 147; Ewens, "Leadership of Nuns," 105–7; Thompson, "Women, Feminism, and the New Religious History," 143–53; Donovan, "Spirit and Structure," 6; Woods, "Congregations of Religious Women," 102–7.

28. Sherwood, *Oblates' Hundred and One Years*, 5.

29. Cott, *Bonds of Womanhood*, 15–17.

30. Mannard, "'Maternity of the Spirit,'" 218; Dries, "Americanization of Religious Life," 18; Revision of 1833, 329.

31. Boston, *Blossoms Gathered from the Lower Branches*.

32. Gloria Hull et al., eds., *All the Women Are White, All the Blacks Are Men, But Some of Us Are Brave* (New York: Feminist Press, 1982).

33. Cyprian Davis, *History of Black Catholics*, 115.

34. This omission proves particularly puzzling, as several of the secondary sources Phillips cites substantively note Oblate contributions to Baltimore's antebellum black community life. See citations in note 21, above, Phillips excepted.

Chapter One

1. *New Catholic Encyclopedia*, 1967 ed., s.v. "Charism"; John A. Hardon, SJ, *Modern Catholic Dictionary*, 1980 ed., s.v. "Charisms"; Wolfgang Beinart and Francis Schüssler Fiorenza, eds., *Handbook of Catholic Theology*, 1995 ed., s.v. "Charism/Charisms."

2. Donovan, "Spirit and Structure," 2–3; Jarrell, "Development of Legal Structures," 25–26; Misner, *"Highly Respectable and Accomplished Ladies,"* 13, 53–54; Annals, 1:1, 4.

3. Jarrell, "Development of Legal Structures," 25; Misner, *"Highly Respectable and Accomplished Ladies,"* 46; Spalding, *Premier See*, 501 n. 32; "A Few Facts"; Boston, *Blossoms Gathered from the Lower Branches*, 7–8.

4. Thompson, "Women and American Catholicism," 125, "Discovering Foremothers," 74, and "Women, Feminism, and the New Religious History," 137; Cosgrove, "Mother Mary Elizabeth Lange," 3–6; Annals, 1:1.

5. *Catholic Church*, 3:75.

6. "First Foundress," 1.

7. Annals, 1:1; Misner, *"Highly Respectable and Accomplished Ladies,"* 45; Gregory, "Education of Blacks," 79; Sherwood, *Oblates' Hundred and One Years,* 4; Rouse, *Study of the Development of Negro Education,* 32; Gillard, *Colored Catholics,* 79.

8. Annals, 1:1. The use of the term "free school" here appears contradictory, since, according to Willigman's recollections, Lange charged her pupils tuition. The term "free" may refer to the fact that Lange's endeavor was an independent or private school, not affiliated with any church denomination.

9. Ibid.

10. *New Catholic Encyclopedia,* 1967 ed., s.v. "Charism."

11. Cyprian Davis, *History of Black Catholics,* 100; *New Catholic Encyclopedia,* 1967 ed., s.v. "Oblates".

12. *New Catholic Encyclopedia,* 1967 ed., s.v. "Frances of Rome, St." In accounts of the foundations of both the Visitation Nuns, originally conceived as an apostolic community, and the Daughters of Charity, the roles of their respective male cofounders completely supersede those of their respective female cofounders. See Donovan, *Sisterhood as Power,* 17, and Cain, *Influence of the Cloister,* 15–16, 30–37.

13. Posey, "Unwanted Commitment," 116–17; Annals, 1:2, 5–6; Sherwood, *Oblates' Hundred and One Years,* 16, 20–21.

14. Cosgrove, "Mother Mary Elizabeth Lange," 4.

15. Misner, *"Highly Respectable and Accomplished Ladies,"* 8–11; Wright, *Free Negro,* 200–202; Rouse, *Study of the Development of Negro Education,* 10–11, 16–17, 102.

16. Current historical evidence identifying Lange's country of origin proves inconsistent. Information from the U.S. Census Population Schedules lists her birthplace variably as the West Indies (1850), San Domingo (1860), and Cuba (1870 and 1880) (Seventh through Tenth United States Censuses [1850–80], Population Schedules, State of Maryland, Baltimore City, Ward 12 [1850], Ward 11 [1860–80]).

17. Jean Fouchard, *Les Marrons du Syllabaire: Quelques aspects du problème de l'instruction et de l'éducation des esclaves et affranchis de Saint-Domingue* (Port-au-Prince, Haiti: Editions Henri Deschamps, 1988), 67–70. I thank Professor Doris Kadish for providing this reference.

18. Lange obituaries in the *Baltimore Sun,* 4 February 1882, and the *Catholic Mirror,* 11 February 1882; "First Foundress," 1; Lannon, *Response to Love,* 3–4; "Where He Leads I Will Follow" (pamphlet, n.d.), 3, AOSP; Records of Confraternities: "Registre, Confrerie du Rosaire," 30 May 1813, "Elizabeth Clarisse," RG 1, Box 17, SAB.

19. "First Foundress," 8; Annals, 1:20, 23.

20. Records of Confraternities: "Confrérie du Scapulaire" (1796–1855), 17 July 1815; "Confrérie de Notre Dame du Rosaire" (1802–56), 30 May 1813; "Confrérie de Notre Dame Auxiliatrice" (1815–45), 8 November 1815, RG 1, Box 17, SAB; *Laity's Directory* (1845), 19–42. The spelling of "Magdelaine" varies in the sources. For purposes of consistency, I use "Magdelaine" throughout the text for Magdelaine Balas.

21. Annals, 1:1.

22. Records of Confraternities: Duchemin: "Auxiliatrice," 9 June 1822; "Scapulaire," 17 September 1826; Boegue: "Auxiliatrice," 15 August 1823; "Rosaire," 15 August 1823, RG 1, Box 17, SAB; Annals, 1:4.

23. "Easter Duty Lists."

24. Goodwin, "Schools and Education," 217–19; Woodson, *Education of the Negro,* 135 n. 2; quote taken from Rouse, *Study of the Development of Negro Education,* 35.

25. Information on St. Mary's Lower Chapel segregation provided in a conversation with John W. Bowen, S.S., current Oblate chaplain and Sulpician archivist emeritus, on 27 June 1994.

26. Information provided in a telephone conversation with John W. Bowen, S.S., on 28 February 2001.

27. For excellent treatments of these trends developing among white women around this time see Cott, *Bonds of Womanhood*, and Ginzberg, *Women and the Work of Benevolence*. For a treatment of southern women see Friedman, *Enclosed Garden*.

28. "The Condition of the Colored Population of the City of Baltimore," *Baltimore Literary and Religious Magazine* 4 (April 1838): 174; Gardner, "Free Blacks in Baltimore," 171, 325–26; Christopher Phillips, *Freedom's Port*, 171; quotes taken from *Metropolitan* 1 (February 1830): 67.

29. All quotes taken from "Rules and Regulations of the Coloured Female Roman Catholic Beneficial Society of Washington City, Instituted July 1828," Dorothy Sterling Papers Collection, *We Are Your Sisters* Series, Additional Papers, Box 3, "Black Female Literary and Mutual Benefit Societies, 1828–1860" Folder, Amistad Research Center, Tulane University, New Orleans.

30. "First Foundress," 4, 5, 9, 11–12; Posey, "Unwanted Commitment," 21, 338–39; Misner, *"Highly Respectable and Accomplished Ladies,"* 297; Sherwood, *Oblates' Hundred and One Years*, 120–21, 183–85, 238.

31. All quotes taken from "First Foundress," 9, 10, 12; Annals, 1:16.

32. "First Foundress," 8–10.

33. Ibid., 12, 9.

34. Posey, "Unwanted Commitment," 139, 187; quote taken from Revision of 1833, 329–30.

35. Revision of 1833, 326.

36. Annals, 1:61.

37. "First Foundress," 12; Anwander to E. J. Sourin, 27 March 1876, Thaddeus Anwander Director File, AOSP.

38. "First Foundress," 12–13, 16.

39. See Meier and Rudwick, *From Plantation to Ghetto*, 69–71, 74–75; David Brion Davis, *Problem of Slavery*, 273–86.

40. James, *Black Jacobins*, 36–44; Berlin, *Slaves without Masters*, 57; David Brion Davis, *Problem of Slavery*, 280–88.

41. Meier and Rudwick, *From Plantation to Ghetto*, 89–90; Gatewood, *Aristocrats of Color*, 157–58; Christopher Phillips, "'Negroes and Other Slaves,'" 36, 80–82, 126–27, and *Freedom's Port*, 156.

42. "First Foundress," 13, 15.

43. Annals, 1:42.

44. Ibid., 38–39.

45. Ibid.

46. Sherwood, *Oblates' Hundred and One Years*, 75.

47. Annals, 1:15.

48. Ibid., 27–28, 31.

49. Posey, "Unwanted Commitment," 10; Records of Confraternities: "Auxiliatrice," 15 August 1823; "Rosaire," 15 August 1823, RG 1, Box 17, SAB; first quote taken from Annals, 1:60; second quote taken from "First Foundress," 15.

50. Sherwood, *Oblates' Hundred and One Years*, 30–31, 108; Lannon, *Response to Love*, 28–29; Gillespie, *Mother M. Theresa*, 13–24; Kelly, *No Greater Service*, 37–46; Alma, *Thou, Lord, Art My Hope!*, 1–33; Code, "Mother Theresa," 317–19; Shea and Supan, "Apostolate of the Archives," 10–13.

51. Annals, 1:4; "Memories"; Sherwood, *Oblates' Hundred and One Years*, 21, 108; Lannon, *Response to Love*, 28–29.

52. Gillespie, *Mother M. Theresa*, 14.

53. Alma, *Thou, Lord, Art my Hope*, 7–8; quote taken from Gillespie, *Mother M. Theresa*, 15.

54. Annals, 1:4.

55. Records of Confraternities: "Rosaire," 4 October 1812; "Auxiliatrice," 15 August 1815, RG 1, Box 17, SAB; "Easter Duty Lists"; Kelly, *No Greater Service*, 39; Shea and Supan, "Apostolate of the Archives," 10; Gillespie, *Mother M. Theresa*, 14; Alma, *Thou, Lord, Art My Hope*, 10; Code, "Mother Theresa," 317; Annals, 1:6, 12, 19–20.

56. The manuscript notes, known as the "West Chester Notes," dictated by Sister Mary James to Sister Maria Alma, 22 February 1920, recalled these conversations. Mother Theresa to Joos, Palm Sunday, 1861, Monroe Motherhouse Archives, and an unidentified letter to a Sister Genevieve, cited in Kelly, *No Greater Service*, 762–63 n. 10, 39–40, 762–63 nn. 8 and 10; Alma, *Thou, Lord, Art My Hope*, 10–11 n. 4; Marita-Constance Supan, I.H.M., "Dangerous Memory: Mother M. Theresa Maxis Duchemin and the Michigan Congregation of the Sisters, I.H.M.," in Sisters, *Building Sisterhood*, 34 n. 10.

57. *Heads of Families at the First Census of the United States Taken in the Year 1790, Maryland* (Washington, D.C.: Government Printing Office, 1907), 18–22.

58. Baptismal Registers of St. Peter's Pro-Cathedral, 1809–11, 403, 413, 365, AAB microfilm, M1510–11, MdHR; "Deluol's Diary," 24 June 1841.

59. West Chester Notes, 2.

60. Ibid., 3; "Memories," 2.

61. West Chester Notes, 3. See Chapter 8 for an explanation of this reference to the Oblate Sisters of Providence as the Oblates of Saint Charles.

62. Goodwin, "Schools and Education," 205.

63. Alma, *Thou, Lord, Art My Hope*, 13; Gillespie, *Mother M. Theresa*, 15; "Memories," 1–2.

64. Records of Confraternities: "Auxiliatrice," 9 June 1822; "Scapulaire," 17 September 1826, RG 1, Box 17, SAB; quote taken from Alma, *Thou, Lord, Art My Hope*, 1–2.

65. Colin Palmer, "Defining and Studying the Modern African Diaspora," *Perspectives: American Historical Association Newsletter* 36, no. 6 (September 1998): 22.

66. Sherwood, *Oblates' Hundred and One Years*, 5.

67. Raboteau, *Slave Religion*, 22–27, 87–89; Herskovits, *Myth of the Negro Past*, 50; Law, "Slave-Raiders and Middlemen," 48; Geggus, "French Slave Trade."

68. Frey and Wood, *Come Shouting to Zion*, 12.

69. Gomez, *Exchanging Our Country Marks*, 98; quote within quote from Anita J. Glaze, *Art and Death in a Senufo Village* (Bloomington: The University of Indiana Press, 1981), 45, cited in ibid., 96.

70. Raboteau, *Slave Religion*, 9–11; Herskovits, *Myth of the Negro Past*, 61–77; Meier and Rudwick, *From Plantation to Ghetto*, 12–19.

71. Blassingame, *Slave Community*, 20.

72. See the works of Oblate Sisters Mary of Good Counsel Baptiste, M. Liberata Dedeaux, M. Wilhelmina Lancaster, and M. Reginald Gerdes, listed in the Bibliography; Cyprian Davis, *History of Black Catholics*, 114–15; and Posey, "Unwanted Commitment," 168.

73. Higginbotham, "African-American Women's History," 264.

74. For thoughtful treatments of white society's derogation of black women's morality see Angela Y. Davis, "Reflections on the Black Woman's Role," 3–15; Deborah Gray White, *Ar'n't I a Woman?*, 27–61; Fox-Genovese, *Within the Plantation Household*, 192–241; Morton, *Disfigured Images*, 1–25; Lerner, ed. *Black Women in White America*, 47–53, 150–71; Darlene Clark Hine, "Rape and the Inner Lives of Black Women: Thoughts on the Culture of Dissemblance," in Hine, *HineSight*, 37–47; Giddings, *When and Where I Enter*, 31–55; and Higginbotham, "African-American Women's History," 256–66.

75. Cooper, *Voice from the South*, 31.

76. The author speaks metaphorically here, since the Oblates did not replace their distinctive bonnets with veils until 1906. See Sherwood, *Oblates' Hundred and One Years*, 190.

77. Du Bois, *Souls of Black Folk*, 138–39.

78. Herbert Aptheker, ed., *The Correspondence of W. E. B. Du Bois*, vol. 3 (Amherst: University of Massachusetts Press, 1973), 27. Dr. Cecilia Moore graciously brought this concrete Lange/Du Bois connection to my attention and provided the reference.

Chapter Two

1. Herbermann, *Sulpicians*, 232–33; Sherwood, *Oblates' Hundred and One Years*, 6–7; Kauffman, *Tradition and Transformation*, 113–14; Joubert obituary, *Baltimore American*, 15 November 1843, SAB.

2. For a thorough discussion of the antebellum church's position on slavery see Hennesey, *American Catholics*, 143–49; Duncan, "Catholics and the Church," 77–98; Miller, "Church in Cultural Captivity," 11–52, and "Failed Mission," 149–70; J. C. Murphy, *Analysis of the Attitudes*, 33–51, 76–79, 136–44; and Cyprian Davis, *History of Black Catholics*, 35–57.

3. Quote taken from Herbermann, *Sulpicians*, 232–33; Sherwood, *Oblates' Hundred and One Years*, 7; Kauffman, *Tradition and Transformation*, 113–14.

4. Indemnities, RG 41, Box 2, SAB; "Deluol's Diary," 27 August 1832, 1, 8 December 1841; *Calendar* 1, section xi, 1489, section xiii, 2059; 3:799–800, 809; 4:586, 597, 665.

5. Kauffman, *Tradition and Transformation*, 115.

6. Posey, "Unwanted Commitment," 212, 183.

7. Annals, 1:68.

8. Ibid., 1, 2, 5.

9. Ibid., 59, 60, 62, 68, 70; Herbermann, *Sulpicians*, 236; for the Visitation Nuns see Misner, *"Highly Respectable and Accomplished Ladies,"* 74; for the Dominican Sisters of St. Catharine see Thompson, "Women, Feminism, and the New Religious History," 147, and Ewens, *Role of the Nun*, 60–61.

10. Kauffman, *Tradition and Transformation*, 120.

11. Ibid., 116, 119, 120.

12. Ibid., 117.

13. Ibid., 117–18, 120–21; quote taken from Spalding, *Premier See*, 106.

14. Spalding, *Premier See*, 128.

15. *Calendar* 1, section xi, 1489.

16. For a discussion of the Catholic Church's position on slavery see Chapter 5.

17. Baptismal Registers of St. Peter's Pro-Cathedral, 1802–11, 427, AAB microfilm, M1510–11, MdHR; for evidence of other Tessier slaves see also RG 1, Boxes 9 and 10, SAB,

cited in Butler, *History of Black Catholics*, 7. See also Kauffman, *Tradition and Transformation*, 113, 118, 121; Annals, 1:1–2, 4, 8–10, 12–13, 15, 25, 29–30, 67; Original Ledger and Student Registers, 1828–36, Box 44; and Original Ledger, 1828–30, 19 June, 30 November 1829, 27 August 1830.

18. "Deluol's Diary," 20 June 1829.

19. [Daughters of Charity], *1809–1959*, 16.

20. Currier, *Carmel in America*, 208.

21. Baudier, *Catholic Church in Louisiana*, 105.

22. Charles Nolan, "New Wine in Old Wineskins: Women Religious and the Revitalization of Louisiana Catholicism, 1803–1836," unpublished paper delivered at the Conference on the History of Women Religious, Chicago, 21–24 June 1998, p. 5.

23. Baudier, *Catholic Church in Louisiana*, 103–5; Emily J. Clark, "A New World Community: The New Orleans Ursulines and Colonial Society, 1727–1803" (Ph.D. diss., Tulane University, 1998), 73, 80, 93–94. I thank Professor Clark for providing me relevant passages of her dissertation.

24. Baudier, *Catholic Church in Louisiana*, 364–65, 392; Bell, *Revolution, Romanticism*, 123–25, 128–29; Cyprian Davis, *History of Black Catholics*, 105–6.

25. Cyprian Davis, *History of Black Catholics*, 90; Goodwin, "Schools and Education," 195–200, 218; Dabney, *History of Schools for Negroes*, 6–7, 20; Woodson, *Education of the Negro*, 131–32; Rouse, *Study of the Development of Negro Education*, 29–30, 36.

26. Gregory, "Education of Blacks," 66–76; Gardner, "Free Blacks in Baltimore," 53–54, 94–96, 113–23; Christopher Phillips, *Freedom's Port*, 163–69, 226–28; Woodson, *Education of the Negro*, 140–41; Brackett, *Negro in Maryland*, 198; Wright, *Free Negro*, 200–208; Rouse, *Study of the Development of Negro Education*, 34–35; Collier-Thomas, "Baltimore Black Community," 298–300; Graham, *Baltimore*, 63–85, 93–135; Curry, *Free Black*, 154.

27. Annals, 1:1.

28. "Easter Duty Lists"; Berlin, *Slaves without Masters*, 150–51, 177; Curry, *Free Black*, 8–11, 253–54.

29. Brackett, *Negro in Maryland*, 197; Rouse, *Study of the Development of Negro Education*, 16–17, 102; Goodwin, "Schools and Education," 308; Wright, *Free Negro*, 201–2 n. 4, 200–220; Dabney, *History of Schools for Negroes*, 19; Posey, "Unwanted Commitment," 255–56.

30. Goodwin, "Schools and Education," 205–6.

31. Posey, "Unwanted Commitment," 117.

32. Donovan, "Spirit and Structure," 6; Ewens, "Leadership of Nuns," 105–6; Woods, "Congregations of Religious Women," 102–7.

33. For insightful treatments of this issue of the ecclesial status of women religious see especially Cain, *Influence of the Cloister*; Ewens, *Role of the Nun* and "Double Standard of the American Sister"; and Donovan, *Sisterhood as Power*, the sources for the following discussion.

34. Ewens, *Role of the Nun*, 14–21, 87–91, 253–57 (quote from 254); Cain, *Influence of the Cloister*, 48–62; Donovan, *Sisterhood as Power*, 16–20, 35–45.

35. *Catholic Church*, 2:457–63; Ewens, *Role of the Nun*, 36–44, 61–64; Misner, *"Highly Respectable and Accomplished Ladies,"* 14–28; Mannard, "'Maternity of the Spirit,'" 51–91.

36. Misner, *"Highly Respectable and Accomplished Ladies,"* 59.

37. Ellin M. Kelly, ed., *Numerous Choirs*, 1:268.

38. Misner, *"Highly Respectable and Accomplished Ladies,"* 28–32, 37–41, 57–62, 264; Ewens, *Role of the Nun*, 44–49.

39. Misner, *"Highly Respectable and Accomplished Ladies,"* 41–42.

40. Ibid., 33–37, 41–45, 62–67; Ewens, *Role of the Nun*, 49–61.

41. All quotes taken from Misner, *"Highly Respectable and Accomplished Ladies,"* 67–69, 45–49.

42. Kauffman, *Tradition and Transformation*, 114; Spalding, *Premier See*, 108; Misner, *"Highly Respectable and Accomplished Ladies,"* 62; Posey, "Unwanted Commitment," 117.

43. Ellin M. Kelly, ed., *Numerous Choirs*, 1:243–80, 277; Original Rule.

44. Original Rule.

45. Ibid.

46. Annals, 1:34–35.

47. Sherwood, *Oblates' Hundred and One Years*, 38; Annals, 1:1; Misner, *"Highly Respectable and Accomplished Ladies,"* 70, 252, 255. See the discussion of Oblate dowries in Chapter 3.

48. Original Rule.

49. Quote taken from *United States Catholic Miscellany* (12 February 1830), Charleston, South Carolina, cited in Misner, *"Highly Respectable and Accomplished Ladies,"* 85; Spalding, *Premier See*, 93, 102. Misner characterizes this editorial comment as an example of racial bias. However, Bishop England had visited the Oblate establishment on 3 November 1829, closely scrutinized their Rule and Constitutions, and enthusiastically approved of their endeavor (Annals, 1:7). England's editorial correction proved nothing more than a statement of fact.

50. "Deluol's Diary," 28 October 1828.

51. Annals, 1:1, 2, 4 (quote from 5).

52. For the fact that throughout the period under consideration the approbation of the bishop or the ordinary of the diocese in which they resided sufficed to validate congregations of sisters—as opposed to orders of nuns—see Cain, *Influence of the Cloister*, 54; Thompson, "Women, Feminism, and the New Religious History," 143; and Misner, *"Highly Respectable and Accomplished Ladies,"* 53.

53. Whitfield to England, 27 December 1831, cited in Spalding, *Premier See*, 118–19.

54. Posey, "Unwanted Commitment," 131; M. S. Wheeler to Prop. Fide, 10 November 1829, MPRF 15, *Calendar 6*, no. 64, vol. 945, fols. 118rv and 119r. Translation from the original French courtesy of Professor John H. Morrow Jr.

55. Prop. Fide to Michael Wheeler, 9 January 1830, MPRF Lettere, *Calendar 3*, no. 2231, vol. 311, fols. 20v and 21r. Translation from the original Latin courtesy of Joseph R. Berrigan, professor emeritus.

56. *Calendar* 1:xi–xvi; Ewens, *Role of the Nun*, 14; Guilday, *History of the Councils*, 10; Ochs, *Desegregating the Altar*, 19, 30.

57. *Catholic Church*, 2:492; Posey, "Unwanted Commitment," 131.

58. Cyprian Davis, *History of Black Catholics*, 39–40.

59. All quotes from "Beatissime Pater" of Michael Wheeler, 2 October 1831, File Box 44, AOSP; see also Annals, 1:13–14; Sherwood, *Oblates' Hundred and One Years*, 52–53.

60. "Beatissime Pater," AOSP.

61. Ibid.

62. Annals, 1:14.

63. *Laity's Directory* (1834), 69–70.

64. "Brief History of the Oblates," unpublished memorandum, n.d., AOSP.

65. See the illustrative experience of the Sisters of St. Joseph of Carondelet in Savage, "Congregation of Saint Joseph," 118–22, and Coburn and Smith, *Spirited Lives*, 61–62.

66. Ewens, *Role of the Nun*, 40; *Catholic Church*, 2:492; Misner, *"Highly Respectable and Accomplished Ladies,"* 259; Mannard, "'Maternity of the Spirit,'" 249.

67. "Rescript" defined in *Calendar*, glossary in index to volumes 1–7.

68. Wissel to Mother Magdalen Cratin, 12 November 1903, no. 2, "Cratin Superior Files," AOSP. See also *Catholic Church*, 3:60, 68, and "Wissel to Willigman" and "Wissel to Cratin" Correspondence, AOSP.

69. Annals, 1:7.

70. Ibid., 15.

71. Joubert to Kohlmann, 10 March 1833, *Calendar* 3, no. 742, Congressi: America-Antille, 1820–34, vol. 4, fols. 490r to 493r, MPRF.

72. Cyprian Davis, *History of Black Catholics*, 19; Annals, 1:26–27, 32, 45, 46, 59.

73. Records of Confraternities: "Registre, Confrairie du Scapulaire," 17 July 1808, "Marie Magdelaine—N—Joubert," RG 1, Box 17, SAB; Annals, 1:18, 70.

74. Joubert to Kohlmann, 10 March 1833, MPRF; Annals, 1:47; Posey, "Unwanted Commitment," 72–73, 78.

75. Kauffman, *Tradition and Transformation*, xiv, xvi, 31, 55, 58–66, 71–72, 110–11, 157.

Chapter Three

1. Brewer, *Nuns and the Education of American Catholic Women*, 18–23; Mannard, "'Maternity of the Spirit,'" 216–25; Coburn and Smith, *Spirited Lives*, 67–76.

2. Original Rule; Sherwood, *Oblates' Hundred and One Years*, 190.

3. Annals, 1:6–7, 12; Goodwin, "Schools and Education," 204–5. The spelling of LeBarth varies widely in the sources. For purposes of consistency, I use LeBarth throughout the text.

4. Annals, 1:2–20; quote from 30.

5. Student Registers, 21.

6. Annals, 1:9, 10, 15, 22, 25, 30; *Population Schedules of the Seventh (1850) and Eighth (1860) United States Censuses*, State of Maryland, Baltimore City, Ward 11; Posey, "Unwanted Commitment," 338.

7. Boston, *Blossoms Gathered from the Lower Branches*, 24; Sherwood, *Oblates' Hundred and One Years*, 33; Annals, 1:31, 40, 45.

8. Annals, 1:2–70; Posey, "Unwanted Commitment," 143, 342–43, 346–50; McNamara, *Sisters in Arms*, 581.

9. Annals, 1:4, 6, 7, 8, 31, 35.

10. Quote taken from Annals, 1:7. The five were: Anne Marie Barclay (ibid., 7); Athanaise DuMourier (ibid., 35); Marie Germaine (ibid., 40); and Laura Johnson and Mary West (ibid., 54).

11. "Where He Leads," unpublished pamphlet, 11, AOSP; Herbermann, *Sulpicians*, 74; *Morning News* (Wilmington, Del.), 22 February 1975; Jessie M. Milbourn to Sister Ignatius Toodle, O.S.P., July 1949 and 19 January 1950, typescript copies, Mother Louisa Noel Papers, AOSP.

12. Sherwood, *Oblates' Hundred and One Years*, 180–81.

13. "Souvenir of Love," 53; Sherwood, *Oblates' Hundred and One Years*, 73; Misner, *"Highly Respectable and Accomplished Ladies,"* 119.

14. Annals, 1:22.

15. Ibid., 36.

16. "Souvenir of Love," 57.

17. Annals, 1:45; "First Foundress," 13; Lannon, *Response to Love*, 30–31.

18. Annals, 1:20.

19. Ibid., 6, 52.

20. Annals, 1:26. The Oblate annals' translation identifies Mary Tritt as Marie Trite.

21. Ewens, *Role of the Nun*, 16–20; Original Ledger, 1829–36, 97, 98.

22. Annals, 1:40.

23. Annals, 1:40–41, 42, 44 (quote from 68); "Recette," 5 May 1834, Original Ledger, 100.

24. Reilly, "Famous Convent," 106.

25. Annals, 1:5, 38.

26. Ibid., 31, 62–63.

27. *Harper Collins Encyclopedia of Catholicism*, 1995 ed., s.v. "humility."

28. Annals, 1:38.

29. Ibid., 26, 32, 45, 46, 59.

30. Cyprian Davis, *History of Black Catholics*, 101.

31. Annals, 1:9; Cyprian Davis, *History of Black Catholics*, 100; Posey, "Praying in the Shadows," 25.

32. "Where He Leads," commemorative pamphlet, n.d., 11, AOSP; Manumission Documents, Box 21, AOSP; Marie Germaine: Baptismal Registers of St. Peter's Pro-Cathedral, 1812–19, 230, AAB microfilm, M1511, MdHR.

33. Original Rule.

34. Ibid.

35. For thorough discussions of the anomalous position of communities of women religious in patriarchal nineteenth-century American society and their relationship to the cult of domesticity, see Brewer, *Nuns and the Education of American Catholic Women*, 123–24, 136; Baumgarten, "Education and Democracy"; Thompson, "Women and American Catholicism," "Women, Feminism, and the New Religious History," and "Philemon's Dilemma"; Ewens, "Leadership of Nuns"; and Mannard, "Maternity . . . of the Spirit," 322–24. For specific examples of nineteenth-century gender-charged disputes between various communities of sisters and clerical authorities, see James K. Kenneally, *History of American Catholic Women*, 43, 46–51, 53–54; Thompson, "Women, Feminism, and the New Religious History," 143–53, and "Women and American Catholicism," 126–28; Misner, *"Highly Respectable and Accomplished Ladies,"* 74, 153–67, 253; and Ewens, *Role of the Nun*, 60–61, 105–6, 123–34, 212–15, 284–87.

36. All quotes taken from Revision of 1833, cited in Posey, "Unwanted Commitment," 331.

37. All quotes taken from Annals, 1:16–18.

38. Ibid., 25, 33.

39. Misner, *"Highly Respectable and Accomplished Ladies,"* 264; [Daughters of Charity], *1809–1959*, 33, 266.

40. Misner, *"Highly Respectable and Accomplished Ladies,"* 110–11, 113–15, 120.

41. Ibid., 70; Annals, 1:41, 6; Dowry List of Nineteenth-Century Oblates, AOSP.

42. Annals, 1:6.

43. "Recette," 9 September 1829, Original Ledger.

44. Misner, *"Highly Respectable and Accomplished Ladies,"* 119; Annals, 1:41, 6; Dowry List of Nineteenth-Century Oblates, AOSP. Also see Chapter 4.

45. Misner, *"Highly Respectable and Accomplished Ladies,"* 71, 115; Spalding, *Premier See*, 57; Ellin M. Kelly, ed., *Numerous Choirs*, 1:157.

46. Annals, 1:2, 6.

47. Ibid., 22.

48. Ibid., 2, 12, 19, 21, 24–26.

49. Ibid., 53.

50. Ibid., 22–23.

51. Ibid., 61.

52. Ibid., 23, 50; "First Foundress," 8–9; Buckler, *History of Epidemic Cholera*, 7.

53. *Laity's Directory* (1834), 71.

54. Annals, 1:34–35; Sherwood, *Oblates' Hundred and One Years*, 73; Misner, *"Highly Respectable and Accomplished Ladies,"* 47.

55. "First Foundress," 11.

56. *Laity's Directory* (Myres, 1836), 169–70; (1838), 146–48; (1839), 183–85.

57. Annals, 1:42; "Rule and Constitution" (undated), English manuscript copy, 1, Box 41, AOSP.

58. Annals, 1:41–42.

59. Sherwood, *Oblates' Hundred and One Years*, 5.

60. Annals, 1:18; "First Foundress," 10; Annals, 1:15; *Laity's Directory* (1834), 70.

61. Herbermann, *Sulpicians*, 233; Misner, *"Highly Respectable and Accomplished Ladies,"* 67; "First Foundress," 13.

62. Annals, 1:18.

63. Ibid., 13, 31 59, 66, 70, 23, 49 (quote from 56).

64. Ibid., 71.

65. Ibid., 72.

66. Herbermann, *Sulpicians*, 233.

67. Spalding, *Premier See*, 123–24, 132–35; Blassingame, *Slave Community*, 105.

68. Annals, 15, 37, 54 (quote from 7).

69. Thompson, "Sisterhood and Power," 151–52; Ewens, "Leadership of Nuns," 103, and *Role of the Nun*, 92; Mannard, "'Maternity of the Spirit,'" 143–51.

70. Misner, *"Highly Respectable and Accomplished Ladies,"* 75–88; Cyprian Davis, *History of Black Catholics*, 38–39; *New York Sun*, 28 September 1884; James Redpath, "The Colored Nuns of Baltimore," typescript, 3–4, AOSP. Quote taken from "Souvenir of Love," 57.

71. Quote taken from Annals, 1:45. See also Thompson, "Women, Feminism, and the New Religious History," 142, and "Sisterhood and Power," 151–54; and Ewens, "Leadership of Nuns," 103, and *Role of the Nun*, 92–95.

72. Joubert to Kohlmann, 10 March 1833, *Calendar 3*, no. 742, Congressi: America-Antille, 1820–34, vol. 4, fols. 490r to 493r, MPRF. Quotes taken from Annals, 1:60, 62, 53, 35.

73. Annals, 1:55.

74. Original Rule; Annals, 1:55.

75. Annals, 1:59.

76. Ibid., 62.

77. Ibid.

78. Ibid., 58, 61, 70.

79. "First Foundress," 9.

80. Spalding, *Premier See*, 501 n. 32; "First Foundress," 9, 13; "Memories," 2; Sherwood, *Oblates' Hundred and One Years*, 108, Misner, *"Highly Respected and Accomplished Ladies,"* 48; Annals, 1:57, 58, 62, 67, 68, 70, 71, 72, 73.

81. Annals, 1:18.

82. Ibid., 28.

83. Ibid., 49.

84. Ibid., 54.

85. Annals, 1:19, 33–34, 35, 51; "Deluol's Diary," 6 March 1837.

86. Revision of 1833, cited in Posey, "Unwanted Commitment," 334–35.

87. Annals, 1:61.

88. Ibid., 62.

89. Ibid.

90. Annals, 1:45, 58; "First Foundress," 13; "Memories," 2; Student Registers, File Box 44.

91. Mannard, "Maternity . . . of the Spirit," 321.

92. Original Rule.

93. Financial Register no. 37, p. 414, under date 22 September 1831: "Prospectus for School," SAB.

94. Goodwin, "Schools and Education," 206 (emphasis his).

95. Ibid. The former Oblate students who taught included Arabella Jones (ibid., 211, 222); Martha Costin (ibid., 203–4); Eliza Ann Cook (ibid., 216); Elizabeth Brown (ibid., 239); Angela Noel and Julia Smith (ibid., 240); and Jane Crouch and Sarah A. Gray (ibid., 285–86). See also Baptiste, "Study of the Foundation and Educational Objectives," 28, and Dedeaux, "Influence of St. Frances Academy," 17–18.

96. Annals, 1:4 (Duchemin), 10 (Bourgoin), 30 (James), 40 (Thomas and Amanda), 44 (Germaine), 54 (Johnson); Brewer, *Nuns and the Education of American Catholic Women*, 123–24, 136.

97. Original Rule; Annals, 1:59–60; see also Frances, *Convent School of French Origin*.

98. Mannard, "'Maternity of the Spirit,'" 22; quotes taken from Currier, *Carmel in America*, 187.

99. Original Rule; Annals, 1:60–61.

100. Annals, 1:61.

101. Original Rule.

102. Stewart, *Marvels of Charity*, 112.

103. Misner, *"Highly Respectable and Accomplished Ladies,"* 272–73.

104. Coburn and Smith, *Spirited Lives*, 165–66.

105. All quotes taken from Sullivan, *Georgetown Visitation since 1799*, 74–75.

106. Misner, *"Highly Respectable and Accomplished Ladies,"* 273.

107. [Daughters of Charity], *1809–1959*, 16.

108. *Laity's Directory* (Lucas, 1834), 65–71; Original Rule.

109. Ellin M. Kelly, ed., *Numerous Choirs*, 1:264.

110. Original Rule.

111. Annals, 1:15–16, 25, 37, 44, 51, 70.

112. Mannard, "'Maternity of the Spirit,'" 175–77, Tables 6, 6a, 7; see also Misner, *"Highly Respectable and Accomplished Ladies,"* and Ewens, *Role of the Nun*.

113. Baptismal Registers of St. Peter's Pro-Cathedral, 1812–19, 55, 230; 1819–27, 136, 245, 251, 306, 379, 394; 1827–37, 64, 76, AAB microfilm, M1511, MdHR.

114. Original Rule.

115. Posey, "Unwanted Commitment," app. 7, 346–50.

116. Annals, 1:19.

117. Ibid., 6, 12, 19; "Memories," 2.

118. Original Rule.

119. Annals, 1:10, 12, 14, 22.

120. Ibid., 17, 21.

121. Ibid., 26.

122. Ibid., 6, 21, 43.

123. Ibid., 33.

124. Ibid., 40.

125. Ibid., 85, 51.

126. Revision of 1833, cited in Posey, "Unwanted Commitment," 329.

127. Ibid., 336; Annals, 1:58.

128. Posey, "Unwanted Commitment," 122; Annals, 1:2, 4, 7.

129. Annals, 1:10, 11, 12, 14.

130. Ibid., 22.

131. Ibid., 22, 36–37, 57.

132. Higginbotham, *Righteous Discontent*, 192.

133. Blassingame, *Slave Community*, 84–88; Raboteau, *Slave Religion*, 152–62; Levine, *Black Culture*, 44–45. Quote taken from Rouse, *Study of the Development of Negro Education*, 33.

134. Higginbotham, *Righteous Discontent*, 17; "Annual Address of Mrs. S. Willie Layten, President of Women's Convention," cited in ibid., 184.

Chapter Four

1. Berlin, *Slaves without Masters*, 304–5, 288, 296, 302–3; Christopher Phillips, *Freedom's Port*, 117–44.

2. Annals, 1:43; Sherwood, *Oblates' Hundred and One Years*, 81; Rouse, *Study of the Development of Negro Education*, 39; Gillard, *Colored Catholics*, 120–21; Collier-Thomas, "Baltimore Black Community," 79–80; Kauffman, *Tradition and Transformation*, 115–16; Ochs, *Desegregating the Altar*, 24; Posey, "Unwanted Commitment," 288–89; Gillard, "First Negro Parish," 371.

3. Meier and Rudwick, *From Plantation to Ghetto*, 99.

4. Annals, 1:46–47.

5. Ibid., 20, 31, 35, 41, 46, 53, 60, 73.

6. Ibid., 53.

7. Ibid.

8. Ibid., 64, 47.

9. Ibid., 69.

10. All quotes taken from ibid., 72.

11. Ibid., 73.

12. Ibid., 13, 31, 36, 47, 48, 64, 71, 72, 64.

13. Ibid., 64.

14. Ibid., 2.

15. Herbermann, *Sulpicians*, 234; Sherwood, *Oblates' Hundred and One Years*, 15–16; Gillard, *Colored Catholics*, 117; Gregory, "Education of Blacks," 84; McNally, "Minority of a Minority," 263; Spalding, *Premier See*, 108; Kauffman, *Tradition and Transformation*, 114.

16. "A Few Facts," 1.

17. Sherwood, *Oblates' Hundred and One Years*, 14–15, 89.

18. Original Rule.

19. Annals, 1:52, 2, 25, 80.

20. Baptismal Registers of St. Peter's Pro-Cathedral, 1782–1801, 399, 462, 477; 1802–11, 162, 254, 469; 1812–19, 311, 463; 1827–37, 131, AAB microfilm, M1510–11, MdHR; Records of Confraternities: "Rosaire," 3 October 1802; "Auxiliatrice," 5 November 1815, RG 1, Box 17, SAB.

21. Baptismal Registers of St. Peter's Pro-Cathedral, 1782–1801, 399, 462, 477; 1802–11, 162, 254, 469; 1812–19, 311, 463; 1827–37, 131, AAB microfilm, M1510–11, MdHR; *The Baltimore Directory* (John Mullin, 1799): "Arien [*sic*], Gab., baker, S. Calvert st. 52," 4; *The New Baltimore Directory and Annual Register for 1800 and 1801* (Warner and Hanna): "Arieu, Gabriel, baker, 29 Charles st.," 15. Elizabeth Arieu probably brought the old, untitled ledger, which is missing its initial pages, with her when she took up residence in the Oblate convent in 1840. The first section (pp. 3–53), written in French, records the transactions of some unidentified bank or other business from January to June 1791. The second section (pp. 1–60), also written in French, consists of the business journal of Marie Magdeleine Sanite L'Houmeau's bakery from 25 June 1808 to 30 April 1815. The Oblate Sisters' financial accounts from 1 January 1844 to December 1854 form the unpaginated third section, written in English. I infer a familial or otherwise close relationship between Sanite and Arieu for the latter to have the former's business records in her possession.

22. Baptismal Registers of St. Peter's Pro-Cathedral, 1802–11, 87, 257, AAB microfilm, M1510, MdHR.

23. Student Registers.

24. Sherwood, *Oblates' Hundred and One Years*, 33; Student Registers, 5, 4; Original Ledger, 1829–36, 110.

25. Berlin, *Slaves without Masters*, 54–55; Curry, *Free Black*, 250.

26. Curry, *Free Black*, 267–71; Christopher Phillips, *Freedom's Port*, 153–55.

27. Berlin, *Slaves without Masters*, 217–49.

28. "First Foundress," 8.

29. Montpensier to Toussaint, 23 October 1829, typescript copy, AOSP; "Easter Duty Lists"; Records of Confraternities: "Scapulaire," 15 August 1809; "Auxiliatrice," 5 November 1815, RG 1, Box 17, SAB. For Pierre Touissant's life, see Cyprian Davis, *History of Black Catholics*, 91–94. At the present time, the Roman Catholic Church is considering the cause of beatification, the initial step in the process toward canonization or sainthood, for three nineteenth-century African American candidates: Pierre Touissant of New York, Sister Mary Lange, cofounder of the Oblate Sisters of Providence in Baltimore, and Henriette Delille, cofounder of the Sisters of the Holy Family in New Orleans.

30. Montpensier to Toussaint, 21 February 1848, AOSP; Sheehan and Sheehan, *Pierre Toussaint*, 187, 189–91.

31. Original Ledger, 1829–36, 116; April 1855 and December 1861 receipt pages, 1855–61 Ledger; Box 2, Expenses and Cash Received Ledger, 1867–76, September 1872 and July and November 1873 receipts pages, AOSP, for Montpensier contributions. Amelia Warren of New York (1830–31) and Evelina Manuel (1830–33), Elizabeth Andonnes(?) (1832–35), and Aspasia Rissaud (1832–34) of Norfolk, Virginia, as well as students from Maryland and Washington, D.C., enrolled in the Oblate school (Student Registers, 50, 35, 58, 46). No chronicle of Oblate history mentions Fanny Montpensier. Studies of Pierre Toussaint, however, treat Montpensier's relationship with the Oblates in their discussions of her correspondence with Toussaint's wife. See Sheehan and Sheehan, *Pierre Toussaint*, Tarry, *Other Toussaint*, and Norbert, "Pierre Toussaint of New York."

32. Original Ledger, 1829–36, 8, 116, 91, 96; *Seventh Census of the United States* (1850), Maryland, Baltimore City, Ward 6, 200; *Baltimore City Directory* (Matchett, 1831), 328; "Easter Duty Lists," 1818–25.

33. "First Foundress," 4.

34. Misner, *"Highly Respectable and Accomplished Ladies,"* 8, 11, 189, 251; Annals, 1:9, 23, 50, 65.

35. Annals, 1:11, 25 (quote from 15); Student Registers; Original Ledger, 1828–30, 23 June 1828; Sherwood, *Oblates' Hundred and One Years*, 32.

36. Alma, *Thou, Lord, Art My Hope*, 14.

37. "The Triumph of St. John Neumann" sheet, 1977, Mother Louisa Noel Folder, AOSP; James K. Kenneally, *History of American Catholic Women*, 54.

38. Annals, 1:2, 9, 10, 23, 37, 46; "First Foundress," 5.

39. Annals, 1:10, 23–24; "Deluol's Diary," 28 July 1840; Gillard, *Colored Catholics*, 62, *Catholic Church*, 3:14; Ewens, *Role of the Nun*, 56–57.

40. Annals, 1:46, 23, 36.

41. Baptismal Registers of St. Peter's Pro-Cathedral, 1812–19, 230, AAB microfilm, M1511, MdHR; Original Ledger, 23 June 1828; Sherwood, *Oblates' Hundred and One Years*, 32.

42. Quote taken from Annals, 1:60; Student Registers, 22–23; Sherwood, *Oblates' Hundred and One Years*, 85, 222–23. For a discussion of the Gideon manumission irregularities, see Morrow, "Oblate Sisters of Providence," 155 n. 81.

43. Rouse, *Study of the Development of Negro Education*, 42.

44. Stephen West Foreman to Virginia Foreman, 5 November 1834, typescript copy, Box 21, Manumission Documents, no. 7 a-b-c; and James Redpath, "The Colored Nuns," *New York Sun*, 28 September 1884, typescript copy, 5, both in AOSP.

45. Student Registers. Boarder or day status unavailable for three students.

46. Student Registers, 1–3, 6, 12–16, 18, 28, 33, 36, 38, 43, 45, 52, 54, 57; Sherwood, *Oblates' Hundred and One Years*, 33, 30–31; Student Registers, 28, 31, 34, 44, 71.

47. Baumgarten, "Education and Democracy," 175; Brewer, *Nuns and the Education of American Catholic Women*, 47. Tenure data is not available for ten students.

48. Student Registers, 6, 23; *Fifth Census of the United States* (1830), Maryland, Baltimore City, Ward 10, 383; Annals, 1:12 October 1851. Historian Leonard Curry (*Free Black*, 270) has cautioned that census information did not reflect the incidence of free black slaveownership accurately. He has observed that slaves listed in black households may have merely boarded there, allowed by their white owners to make their own living arrangements while they hired out their labor. See Student Registers, 15–16, 26, 24, 34, 31, and Annals, 1:11.

49. Sherwood, *Oblates' Hundred and One Years*, 33; Annals, 1:11. Quote taken from Baptismal Registers of St. Peter's Pro-Cathedral, 1819–27, 394; 1812–19, 290, 478, AAB microfilm, M1511, MdHR.

50. Williamson, *New People*, 24.

51. Franklin and Schweninger, *Runaway Slaves*, 56, 63, 66, 84, 207.

52. *Seventh Census of the United States* (1850) and *Eighth Census of the United States* (1860), Maryland, Baltimore City, Ward 11.

53. Quotes taken from Baptismal Registers of St. Peter's Pro-Cathedral, 1782–1801, 343, 462, AAB microfilm, M1510, MdHR. See also Gould, "Parish Identities," and Hanger, *Bounded Lives*, for further discussion of free black peoples' use of Roman Catholic sacramental records.

54. Goodwin, "Schools and Education," 203; Student Registers, 54–55.

55. Quote taken from Goodwin, "Schools and Education," 204–5; Student Registers, 57; Annals, 1:30, 33, 35, 12, 28.

56. "School for Coloured Girls" advertisement in the *Laity's Directory* (Lucas, 1834), 67, 69–71; Student Registers, 35, 59.

57. Student Registers, 4, 15–16, 7.

58. Ibid., 9; Annals, 1:15, 25.

59. Student Registers, 44–45.

60. "First Foundress," 4.

61. Annals, 1:2–3, 8–9, 16, 32, 43.

62. Original Ledger, 1829–36, 112–13, 118; Antoinette Antoin: "Easter Duty Lists," 1820–31; Eliza Greatfield: "Journal," 17.

63. Annals, 1:43; Eli Arieu: "Easter Duty Lists," 1820, 1825; Mrs. Delatourandai: "Journal," 19, and *Baltimore City Directory* (Matchett, 1829), 190; Hilary LeBarth: "Journal," 19, and Baptismal Registers of St. Peter's Pro-Cathedral, 1827–37, 76, AAB microfilm, M1511, MdHR; Oliver Concklin: *Sixth Census of the United States* (1840), Maryland, vol. 3, City of Baltimore, 316; Jenny [Jane] Russel: *Seventh Census of the United States* (1850), Maryland, City of Baltimore, Ward 6, 356. Anne Clement was Russel's daughter and Concklin's wife (Anne Clement Note 1836/44, "Important Correspondence Folder," Superiors General and Clergy File Cabinet, Drawer 1, AOSP).

64. Quotes taken from Sterling, *We Are Your Sisters*, 114–19.

65. Oates, *Catholic Philanthropic Tradition*, 12, 31.

66. Quotes taken from Annals, 1:52.

67. Ibid.

68. Ibid., 52–53.

69. Sherwood, *Oblates' Hundred and One Years*, 84.

70. Mary Reginald Gerdes, O.S.P., "Providence Moments," 6, unpublished paper, AOSP.

Chapter Five

1. Original Rule.

2. For a thorough discussion of the antebellum church's position on slavery, see Hennesey, *American Catholics*, 143–49; Duncan, "Catholics and the Church"; Miller, "Church in Cultural Captivity" and "Failed Mission"; J. C. Murphy, *Analysis of the Attitudes*, 33–51, 76–79, 136–44; and Cyprian Davis, *History of Black Catholics*, 35–57.

3. Duncan, "Catholics and the Church," 90; Cyprian Davis, *History of Black Catholics*, 43, 38–39; Misner, *"Highly Respectable and Accomplished Ladies,"* 75–88.

4. Cyprian Davis, *History of Black Catholics*, 46–57; Miller, "Church in Cultural Captivity," 15–16, 17; Duncan, "Catholics and the Church," 87–88, 90; Hennesey, *American Catholics*, 146.

5. *Calendar* 1, no. 371; Sophie Barat to Philippine Duchesne, 19 November 1818, cited in Mooney, *Philippine Duchesne*, 130.

6. Philippine Duchesne to Sophie Barat, 28 November 1819, cited in Mooney, *Philippine Duchesne*, 130; 131; Baudier, *Catholic Church in Louisiana*, 397; Cyprian Davis, *History of Black Catholics*, 107.

7. Cyprian Davis, *History of Black Catholics*, 98.

8. Bell, *Revolution, Romanticism*, 128–29; Cyprian Davis, *History of Black Catholics*, 105–6.

9. Mooney, *Philippine Duchesne*, 129.

10. Ibid.

11. Henri Greliche, *Essai sur la vie et les travaux de Monseigneur Flaget* (Paris, 1852), 83–84, cited in Cyprian Davis, *History of Black Catholics*, 283–84 n. 99.

12. Spalding, *Premier See*, 17–19.

13. Annals, 1:4. For a comprehensive treatment of Whitfield's episcopacy, see Panczyk, "James Whitfield," and Spalding, *Premier See*, ch. 5.

14. Spalding, *Premier See*, 109; Misner, *"Highly Respectable and Accomplished Ladies,"* 86; Kauffman, *Tradition and Transformation*, 114–15; Sherwood, *Oblates' Hundred and One Years*, 23–25; Posey, "Unwanted Commitment," 129, 134.

15. Annals, 1:5.

16. Whitfield to Wiseman, 12 June 1829, *Calendar* 7, no. 2315, Baltimore Papers no. 111, MPRF. The *Calendar* cited three entries from James Whitfield. Neither Whitfield to Wiseman, 28 September 1829, nor Whitfield to Propaganda Fide, 27 August 1830, referred to the Oblate Sisters. See [Whitfield], "Statement Concerning the Diocese of Baltimore," 136–37.

17. Currier, *Carmel in America*, 192, 168–69; Shea, *History of the Catholic Church*, 3:106; De Courcy, *Catholic Church*, 141–43.

18. De Courcy, *Catholic Church*, 114–16; Shea, *History of the Catholic Church*, 3:92, 429, 443. Shea followed De Courcy, who dated the Oblate foundation from 1825, not 1829, and credited Archbishop Ambrose Maréchal, not Archbishop James Whitfield, with sanctioning the Oblate formation.

19. [Whitfield], "Statement Concerning the Diocese of Baltimore," 134; "Churches, Pious and Charitable Institutions, Etc. of Baltimore," *Metropolitan* 1 (February 1830): 67.

20. [Whitfield], "Statement Concerning the Diocese of Baltimore," 137.

21. *Fifth Census of the United States* (1830), Maryland, Baltimore City, Ward 10, 365; Gillard, *Catholic Church*, 28.

22. Whitfield to Bishop England, 27 December 1831, cited in Spalding, *Premier See*, 118–19.

23. See Guilday, *History of the Councils*.

24. Quotes taken from Annals, 1:6–7.

25. Guilday, *History of the Councils*, 95–97.

26. Annals, 1:7.

27. Bishop England to P. Cullen, Rome, 23 February 1836, *Calendar* 7, no. 2071, American Papers no. 46, MPRF; Misner, *"Highly Respectable and Accomplished Ladies,"* 49–50.

28. Gould, "Piety, Religious Activism, and Free Women of Color," 6–7, 9.

29. Fichter, "White Church and the Black Sisters," 40.

30. McMaster, "Bishop Barron," 85. For a thorough discussion of Catholic involvement in Liberian colonization in particular and the state of Maryland's efforts at colonization in general, see McMaster, "Bishop Barron," and Campbell, *Maryland in Africa*.

31. Whitfield to Jean-Marie Tessier, 16 January 1832, 23D11b, AAB.

32. Annals, 1:14.

33. "Churches, Pious and Charitable Institutions, Etc. of Baltimore," *Metropolitan* 1 (February 1830): 63–67.

34. Quotes taken from Annals, 1:19–20.

35. Whitfield to Tessier, 2 September 1833, 23D11b, AAB.

36. Annals, 1:32.

37. Spalding, *Premier See*, 127.

38. *Second Census of the United States* (1800), Population Schedules, Maryland, vol. 1, sheet 244.

39. Berlin, *Slaves without Masters*, 183, 182–216. See also Litwack, *North of Slavery*; Meier and Rudwick, *From Plantation to Ghetto*, 90–98, 122–26; and John Hope Franklin and Alfred Moss, *From Slavery to Freedom: A History of Negro Americans*, 6th ed. (New York: Alfred A. Knopf, 1988), 139–42, 154–57.

40. Eccleston to the Clergy and Laity of Baltimore, 23 October 1834, RG 26, Box 10, SAB.

41. "Deluol's Diary," 2 July 1835.

42. Currier, *Carmel in America*, 201–3.

43. Sullivan, *Georgetown Visitation since 1799*, 67; Mannard, "'Maternity of the Spirit,'" 227–28.

44. Annals, 1:46.

45. Spalding, *Premier See*, 120, 123–25, 136.

46. Historian Michael McNally has distinguished racial from ethnic or national parishes, noting that the former lacked black clergy and served less to enhance or preserve ethnicity than to separate blacks from whites ("Peculiar Institution," 74–75).

47. Rouse, *Study of the Development of Negro Education*, 45–46; Gillard, *Catholic Church*, 28.

48. See Raboteau, *Slave Religion*. For a discussion of the exceptional Healy brothers as black priests, see Chapter 11.

49. *Laity's Directory* (1834), 71.

50. Kauffman, *Tradition and Transformation*, 64, 91; Annals, 1:6, 26, 30, 49.

51. Annals, 1:26–27, 30; *Annales de la propagation de la foi*, vol. 7, English translation typescript copy, AOSP.

52. Annals, 1:6, 26, 49.

53. Spalding, *Premier See*, 29; *Cathedral Records*, 26–28, 44, 69, 109; Annals, 1:43, 20, 35, 41, 46, 50, 51. Quote taken from "First Foundress," 11.

54. Goodwin, "Schools and Education," 218.

55. Annals, 1:8.

56. Spalding, *Premier See*, 141, 146; *Cathedral Records*, 60–61; Annals, 1:57.

57. "Dollar-Sterling Mint Parity," *Journal of Economic History* 43, no. 3 (1983): 579–616; Currier, *Carmel in America*, 57, 74–83, 107–8; Misner, "*Highly Respectable and Accomplished Ladies*," 17–18, 257–58.

58. Currier, *Carmel in America*, 184–85.

59. Ibid., 69, 185–87, 225.

60. Spalding, *Premier See*, 66.

61. Sullivan, *Georgetown Visitation since 1799*, 42, 49–51, 72, 98; Misner, "*Highly Respectable and Accomplished Ladies*," 19–20, 145, 260–61.

62. Kauffman, *Tradition and Transformation*, 77; Misner, "*Highly Respectable and Accomplished Ladies*," 28–29; Herbermann, *Sulpicians*, 222–23; Charles L. White, *Life of Mrs. Eliza A. Seton*, 217.

63. [Whitfield], "Statement Concerning the Diocese of Baltimore," 136–37; Misner, "*Highly Respectable and Accomplished Ladies*," 92.

64. Misner, "*Highly Respectable and Accomplished Ladies*," 14, 19, 28, 46, 118–19, 126–27; Gillard, *Catholic Church*, 14–15, and *Colored Catholics*, 63, 88, 99; Ochs, *Desegregating the Altar*, 15.

65. Currier, *Carmel in America*, 184; *Laity's Directory* (1839), 96, (1843), 64, (1847), 80; Sullivan, *Georgetown Visitation since 1799*, 73.

66. Original Ledger, 1829–36, 116, 95; Herbermann, *Sulpicians*, 201; Annals, 1:2–4, 7.

67. Currier, *Carmel in America*, 203–4; Annals, 1:43, 52.

68. Annals, 1:43, 44–45.

69. Ibid., 45.

70. Joubert to Kohlmann, 10 March 1833, *Calendar* 3, no. 742, Congressi: America-Antille, 1820–34, vol. 4, fols. 490r to 493r, MPRF; Annals, 1:35; 56.

71. Annals, 1:28.

72. Ibid., 10.

73. Gillard, *Colored Catholics*, 200.

74. Ewens, *Role of the Nun*, 65, 344 n. 97; Thompson, "Philemon's Dilemma," 5.

75. Correspondence from Sister Mada-anne Gell, V.H.M., archivist of the Sisters of the Visitation, to the author, 14 August 1998.

76. Goodwin, "Schools and Education," 205.

77. Misner, *"Highly Respectable and Accomplished Ladies,"* 191, 203–4; Currier, *Carmel in America*, 82.

78. Specific titles varied among *The United States Catholic Almanac or Laity's Directory, The Catholic Calendar and Laity's Directory; The Metropolitan Catholic Almanac and Laity's Directory;* and *The Catholic Almanac.* See Misner, *"Highly Respectable and Accomplished Ladies,"* 309–10.

79. *Laity's Directory* (1833), 109.

80. Ibid. (Myres, 1834), 124–26; (Lucas, 1834), 69–71.

81. Ibid., 54.

82. Ibid. (1837), 68.

83. Ibid., 97–99.

84. Ibid., 143; quote taken from ibid. (1838), 78.

85. Ibid. (1839), 53.

86. Ibid., 96.

87. Ibid., 94–95, 181.

88. In her informative article "Intelligence, Though Overlooked," Mary Carroll Johansen incorrectly identifies the "School for Girls of Color" notice as an advertisement and its date as 8 January 1829 (456). Internal sections of the 1, 8, 15, and 22 January 1830 issues of the *Genius of Universal Emancipation* incorrectly printed the year 1829. Sister M. Reginald Gerdes, O.S.P., graciously provided a copy of Johansen's article.

89. Annals, 1:18.

90. All quotes taken from ibid., 5.

91. Ibid.

92. Records of the Bureau of the Census, RG 29, National Archives; *Fifth Census of the United States* (1830), Population Schedules, Maryland, vol. 2, sheet 500; *Sixth Census of the United States* (1840), Population Schedules, Maryland, vol. 3, sheet 162; Brackett, *Negro in Maryland*, 32–34; Wright, *Free Negro*, 24–26.

93. All quotes taken from Annals, 1:38.

94. All quotes taken from ibid., 40.

95. Ewens, *Role of the Nun*, 104; Misner, *"Highly Respectable and Accomplished Ladies,"* 262; and author correspondence with John W. Bowen, S.S., Sulpician Archivist Emeritus, 20 October 1996.

96. Chezia Thompson-Cager, "Ntozake Shange's *Sassafras, Cypress, and Indigo*: Resistance and Mythical Women of Power," *National Women's Studies Association Journal* 1, no. 4 (1989): 589–601, cited in Collins, *Black Feminist Thought*, 104.

Chapter Six

1. Original Rule.

2. Fields, *Slavery and Freedom*, 48; Christopher Phillips, *Freedom's Port*, 20–29. Quote taken from Douglass, *My Bondage and My Freedom*, 147–48.

3. Berlin, *Slaves without Masters*, 5, 7; Wright, *Free Negro*, 264.

4. Brackett, *Negro in Maryland*, 235–36, 241; Wright, *Free Negro*, 263–64.

5. Brackett, *Negro in Maryland*, 183.

6. Ibid., 176–83, 187, 198–204, 206–18, 228–29; Wright, *Free Negro*, 122, 123, 124.

7. Spalding, *Premier See*, 113; Brackett, *Negro in Maryland*, 237; Wright, *Free Negro*, 268–70. Quote taken from Christopher Phillips, *Freedom's Port*, 182.

8. Brackett, *Negro in Maryland*, 240.

9. Herbermann, *Sulpicians*, 234–35; Annals, 1:5.

10. Annals, 1:2.

11. Ibid., 5.

12. Ibid., 2–3, 8–9, 16, 32, 4; Misner, *"Highly Respectable and Accomplished Ladies,"* 71, 257–71; Gregory, "Education of Blacks," 90; Herbermann, *Sulpicians*, 226; Wright, *Free Negro*, 200, 215, 218, 237.

13. Sherwood, *Oblates' Hundred and One Years*, 59; Misner, *"Highly Respectable and Accomplished Ladies,"* 47, 229–30; Posey, "Unwanted Commitment," 137–39.

14. Berlin, *Slaves without Masters*, 258–59; Buckler, *History of Epidemic Cholera*, 13–14, 30–32; Gardner, "Free Blacks in Baltimore," 188–97; Christopher Phillips, *Freedom's Port*, 180–82.

15. Buckler, *History of Epidemic Cholera*, 7–9, 27; Curry, *Free Black*, 122, 127.

16. Annals, 1:16.

17. Misner, *"Highly Respectable and Accomplished Ladies,"* 28–29, 227–30; Spalding, *Premier See*, 107; Baltimore City Health Department, "Report of the Commissioner of Health," 31 December 1832, n.p., and "Consulting Physician's Report," 31 December 1832, n.p.

18. Mannard, "1839 Baltimore Nunnery Riot," 194–95.

19. Annals, 1:12.

20. Ibid., 34; Misner, *"Highly Respectable and Accomplished Ladies,"* 6–9.

21. Litwack, *North of Slavery*, 100–102.

22. Quote taken from Mannard, "1839 Baltimore Nunnery Riot," 196–97; Misner, *"Highly Respectable and Accomplished Ladies,"* 47–48; 269; Spalding, *Premier See*, 134.

23. Annals, 1:52–53.

24. Ibid., 52.

25. Litwack, *North of Slavery*, 191.

26. Annals, 1:66.

27. Spalding, *Premier See*, 133; "The Condition of the Colored Population of the City of Baltimore," *Baltimore Literary and Religious Magazine* 4 (April 1838): 170; *Baltimore City Directory* (Matchett, 1833), 46; Annals, 1:52; Student Registers, 33.

28. "The Convent in Aisquith Street—Escape of a Nun—The Doctrine of Celibacy in Popish Priests and Nuns," *Baltimore Literary and Religious Magazine* 6 (January 1840): 2; "Maria Monk," ibid., 2 (September 1836): 359.

29. "Review of the Case of Olevia Neal [*sic*] the Carmelite Nun, Commonly Called Sister Isabella," *Baltimore Literary and Religious Magazine* 5 (October 1839): 436; Annals, 1:60.

30. Spalding, *Premier See*, 57, 113; Hennesey, *American Catholics*, 146.

31. Herbermann, *Sulpicians*, 199–201; Original Ledger.

32. Swisher, *Roger Taney*, 154.

33. Ibid., 94–97.

34. Hennesey, *American Catholics*, 147; Christopher Phillips, *Freedom's Port*, 187–88, 287 n. 37; Swisher, *Roger Taney*, 93, 13.

35. Swisher, *Roger Taney*, 93.

36. Spalding, *Premier See*, 110, 131; Swisher, *Roger Taney*, 471; *Cathedral Records*, 57; Misner, *"Highly Respectable and Accomplished Ladies,"* 17–18, 258; Deluol to Taney, 18 November 1831; Taney to Deluol, 25 November 1831; Deluol to Taney, 12 June 1832; and Chanche to Taney, 16 February 1833, RG 3, Box 16, Letterbook 6, SAB.

37. Gregory, "Education of Blacks," 80.

38. Sherwood, *Oblates' Hundred and One Years*, 5.

39. Spalding, *Premier See*, 109.

40. Annals, 1:2, 3, 10; Student Registers, 5, 55; Original Ledger (1828–30), 11 September 1828, 8 February, 26 April, 5 July, 20 September 1829, 17 January 1830; Original Ledger (1829–36), 116, 97–98, 102, 110; Sherwood, *Oblates' Hundred and One Years*, 15–16, 18–19, 46, 60, 79, 150–51, 161–62, 175, 177; Original Ledger (1829–36), 100, 119.

41. "Easter Duty Lists"; *Cathedral Records*, 51, 53; Sherwood, "America's First Negro Religious Order," *Baltimore Sunday Sun*, 25 August 1929.

42. Herbermann, *Sulpicians*, 234; Sherwood, *Oblates' Hundred and One Years*, 15–16; McNally, "Minority of a Minority," 263; Kauffman, *Tradition and Transformation*, 114; Spalding, *Premier See*, 108; Gregory, "Education of Blacks," 84.

43. Annals, 1:2–3.

44. Ibid., 64.

45. "Beatissime Pater" of Michael Wheeler, 2 October 1831, AOSP; Annals, 1:43; Original Ledger (1829–36), 112; *Cathedral Records*, 76, 73, 109.

46. Annals, 1:1–2; Sherwood, *Oblates' Hundred and One Years*, 9.

47. Spalding, *Premier See*, 132–33.

48. Kennelly, ed., *American Catholic Women*, xiv.

49. McNally, "Peculiar Institution," 74–76; Raboteau, "Black Catholics," 124.

Chapter Seven

1. Sherwood, *Oblates' Hundred and One Years*, 183–84; autobiographical and biographical profiles of Sister M. Theresa Catherine Willigman from Willigman's Superior Files, AOSP. Quotes taken from Annals, 1:74–75, 80.

2. All quotes taken from Annals, 1:86.

3. Posey, "Unwanted Commitment," 218–19, 237–38; Box 21, Manumission Documents, no. 3, AOSP; *Seventh Census of the United States* (1850) and *Eighth Census of the United States* (1860), Population Schedules, Maryland, Baltimore City, Ward 11; Annals, 1:88, 92.

4. Annals, 1:88.

5. Quote taken from Annals, 2: 25 August, 23 October, 21 November 1842. Volume 1 of the Oblate annals ends with the entry dated 15 August 1842. Because of inconsistencies in pagination and disparities between manuscript and typescript copies of volume 2 of the annals, dates entered, rather than page numbers, will identify all references to this work cited in this study. *Laity's Directory* (1842), 72; (1843), 64.

6. Annals, 2: 8 May 1843.

7. Annals, 1:82, 84–85; Annals, 2: 5, 15 March, 5 November 1843.

8. Annals, 1:88–92.

9. Ibid., 42, 91–92.

10. Annals, 1:89. Quote taken from J. B. Fitzpatrick to Sister Stanislaus, 9 June 1841, cited in Currier, *Carmel in America*, 228–29.

11. Annals, 2: 20 April 1843.

12. *Laity's Directory* (1840), 163; (1841), 209; (1842), 188; (1843), 164; (1844), 181.

13. All quotes taken from Annals, 1:91–92.

14. 27 June 1836 Loan Agreements between James Joubert and Oliver Concklin and Jane

Russell (French) and 6 August 1844 Loan Agreements between Louis R. Deluol and Oliver Concklin and Jane Russell (French), Eagle File Box 45, AOSP; Annals, 1:43, 91. "Baptisms and Marriages Registry," by L. R. Deluol, copied by A. J. Elder, under date 19 September 1829, 8–9, SAB, identifies Loiseau as black; Annals, 1:91, notes his donation. Original Ledger, 118. The passive debt total of $1,968.375 cited (Annals, 1:91) does not include the unrepaid loan of $224 that Anne Clement, wife of John Concklin and daughter of Jenny Russel, made to the Oblate Sisters in 1836. Deluol repaid the loan to Clement's mother on 6 August 1844 (Anne Clement Note, Important Correspondence Folder, Drawer 1, Superiors and Clergy File Cabinet, AOSP). Black benefactors thus provided $1,906.05 of the total $2,192.375 Oblate passive debt in 1842. Oblate sources inconsistently identify Jane Russell as Jenny Russel or incorrectly as John Russel. They also misidentify Francis Loiseau as Lorsen.

15. Annals, 2: 20 April 1843.

16. Annals, 1:41, 91; Annals, 2: 6 November 1842 to 2 April 1843.

17. Mother M. Theresa Gerhardinger to Rev. Mathias Siegert, 22 December 1847, in Sister M. Hester Valentine, S.S.N.D., ed., *The North American Foundations, Letters of Mother M. Theresa Gerhardinger, School Sisters of Notre Dame* (Winona, Minn.: St. Mary's College Press, 1977), 67, Letter no. 728, cited in Research of John W. McGrain on the Oblates and Mother Lange, RG 41, Box 3, SAB; Spalding, *Premier See*, 142.

18. Annals, 2: 8 May 1843, Joubert to Mr. John Donelan, cited Jane Somerville.

19. Misner, *"Highly Respectable and Accomplished Ladies,"* 48; Sherwood, *Oblates' Hundred and One Years*, 108; Spalding, *Premier See*, 501 n. 32.

20. Annals, 1:83.

21. Annals, 2: 16 October 1842.

22. Annals, 1:85.

23. Ibid., 57.

24. "Souvenir of Love," 57; "Deluol's Diary," 24 June 1841; Lannon, *Response to Love*, 28; Alma, *Thou, Lord, Art My Hope*, 23.

25. Annals, 1:86.

26. Quote taken from Annals, 1:88, 85–86; "Deluol's Diary," 9 March 1843; Posey, "Unwanted Commitment," 343.

27. Annals, 1:80.

28. Ibid., 82.

29. Ibid., 93.

30. Ibid., 70, 78; Annals, 2: 25 September 1842.

31. Quotes taken from Annals, 1:80.

32. Ibid.

33. Ibid., 93.

34. Annals, 2: 16 May 1843.

35. Annals, 1:87.

36. Ibid., 88.

37. Quotes taken from ibid., 81.

38. Ochs, "Ordeal of the Black Priest," 46, 63–64.

39. Annals, 1:78.

40. Ibid., 81.

41. Annals, 2: 5 September 1842; Ellin M. Kelly, ed., *Numerous Choirs*, 1:279. Quote taken from Annals, 1:86.

42. Annals, 1:96.

43. Annals, 2: 26 July 1843.

44. Annals, 1:74.

45. Ibid., 93.

46. Ibid., 95; "A Circular," 8 June 1842, RG 26, Box 10, SAB.

47. Annals, 2: 11 December 1842, 29 January 1843.

48. Misner, *"Highly Respectable and Accomplished Ladies,"* 277, 204–5; [Daughters of Charity], *1809–1959*, 33, 266.

49. Mother St. John Fournier to the Superior General of the Sisters of St. Joseph, Lyons (1873), cited in Logue, *Sisters of St. Joseph of Philadelphia*, 331–33.

50. Dougherty et al., *Sisters of St. Joseph of Carondelet*, 122–24; Savage, "Congregation of St. Joseph," 63–65; Oliver and Faherty, *Religious Roots*, 4.

51. Annals, 1:76.

52. Annals, 2: 20, 21 May 1843 (quote from 22 May 1843).

53. Annals, 2: 16 May 1843.

54. Cyprian Davis, *History of Black Catholics*, 65.

55. Annals, 1:87; *Calendar* 3:799–800, 809; 4:582, 585–86, 597, 665; "Deluol's Diary," 1 and 8 December 1841. Quote taken from *The Religious Cabinet: A Monthly Periodical* (Baltimore: John Murphy, 1842), "History: Newspapers; Undated, 1829—General" Folder in C/OSP, JFA.

56. Quotes taken from Annals, 1:87.

57. McMaster, "Bishop Barron," 83–85, 87–89, 96–97, 112–25.

58. Annals, 1:57, 66–67, 74, 77, 79, 85, 87, 92–96; Annals, 2: 25 August; 30 October; 20 November; 18 December 1842; 22 January; 2, 26 February; 1, 5, 9, 15, 19 March; 9, 13, 23 April; 25, 28 May; 8, 14 September; 8, 15, 29 October; 1, 5 November 1843.

59. "First Foundress," 11.

60. Annals, 1:95.

61. Anwander to E. J. Sourin, 27 March 1876, Thaddeus Anwander Director File, AOSP. Quote taken from "First Foundress," 11–12.

62. Annals, 2: 15 June 1843.

63. Ibid., 8 September 1843.

64. Ibid., 29 October 1843.

65. Ibid., 7 November 1843.

66. Annals, 1:95; Annals, 2: 14 and 21 July 1843; Spalding, *Premier See*, 137.

67. Annals, 2: 20 August 1843.

68. Ibid., 10 September 1843.

69. Ibid., 12 September 1843; French text of incomplete English translation for 3 September 1843; *Cathedral Records*, 65.

70. Annals, 2: 8 October 1843 (quote); 9 October 1842; Annals, 1:32, 37, 42–43, 45, 51, 59, 71, 79, 86.

71. Annals, 2: 29 October 1843.

72. Ibid., 8 November 1843.

73. "Deluol's Diary," 8 November 1843.

74. Annals, 2: 5 December 1843 (French text).

75. Annals, 2: under date December 1843.

76. "A Few Facts," 6.

Chapter Eight

1. 1844–54 Ledger, 1844–49 entries.

2. Ibid. I calculated the surplus figure by subtracting monthly receipts from monthly expenses during the four-year period.

3. Quote taken from Anwander to E. J. Sourin, 27 March 1876, Thaddeus Anwander Director File, AOSP. See Sherwood, *Oblates' Hundred and One Years*, 109; Lannon, *Response to Love*, 12; and "Where He Leads Me, I Will Follow," 14, pamphlet, n.d., AOSP.

4. 1844–54 Ledger.

5. Ibid., Receipts, November 1844, December 1845, March and November 1847.

6. Ibid., Charleville: August 1844, March 1845, Small: January, February, June, July, October, 1844, January, May, July 1845.

7. Ibid., Smith: April, August, September, October 1844, January 1845, February 1846; Stinecki: June and September 1845, April, June, December 1846.

8. Ibid., Manganos: April, July, December 1845; June and October 1846; September 1847; May and September 1848; "Mary Philomena Magagnos [*sic*], daughter of Joseph Magagnos [*sic*], baptized 26 June 1846 by Peter Chakert," Baptismal Register, 1841–38, Box 8, *Sacramental Registers*, AOSP; *Seventh Census of the United States* (1850), Population Schedules, Maryland, Baltimore City, Ward 11.

9. Berlin, *Slaves without Masters*, 253, 261; Curry, *Free Black*, 58, 78; 1844–54 Ledger, May 1844 Receipts.

10. Annals, 1:32; 1844–54 Ledger, Receipts, Wernerth: February 1844–August 1848; Original Ledger (1829–36), 93, 95.

11. Litwack, *North of Slavery*, 163–67; Douglass quotes cited on 166–67, 165; 1844–54 Ledger, Receipts, Eschbach: February 1844–August 1848; Manuscript 10, Doc. 1–89[1], 1870 Plat A, Baltimore City Archives, Baltimore, Md.; St. John's Parish Records, AAB, M 1525, p. 242, microfilm, MdHR.

12. "Deluol's Diary," 28 December 1843. Following author Grace Sherwood, several sources have conflated the 28 December 1843 and 15 July 1844 constitutional discussions Deluol documented into one event, which they erroneously date December 1844. See Sherwood, *Oblates' Hundred and One Years*, 107; Gillespie, *Mother M. Theresa*, 22–23; Lannon, *Response to Love*, 12; Posey, "Unwanted Commitment," 142, 145–46; and typescript cover sheet by anonymous Oblate source to "Notes."

13. West Chester Notes, 3.

14. Annals, 2: 9 September 1845. See also Gillespie, *Mother M. Theresa*, 22–23; Lannon, *Response to Love*, 12; Cyprian Davis, *History of Black Catholics*, 104; and M. Rosalita Kelly, *No Greater Service*, 43, who cite Duchemin's "Charlottine" proposals.

15. "Deluol's Diary," 15 July 1844.

16. "Notes," II.

17. Ibid., XV.

18. Quote taken from "Notes," XIX; "Notes," XVIII; and Posey, "Unwanted Commitment," 147–48.

19. Spalding, *Premier See*, 147–48; Kauffman, *Tradition and Transformation*, 122; Circular, 24 April 1845, RG 26, Box 10, SAB.

20. "Deluol's Diary," 21 June, 5 July 1844; Kauffman, *Tradition and Transformation*, 115, Annals, 1:68, Posey, "Unwanted Commitment," 183, 212; "Notes," VI.

21. Quotes taken from Deluol to Charles Carroll's granddaughter, n.d., RG 24, Box 9,

SAB; for Deluol's ownership of slaves, see "Article of Agreement," RG 1, Box 7, SAB, cited in Butler, "History of Black Catholics," 8.

22. Daughters of Charity—St. Joseph Provincial House, Emmitsburg, Maryland, Letters III, Deluol to George, 15 and 28 November 1839, cited in Misner, *"Highly Respectable and Accomplished Ladies,"* 78–79.

23. In accepting Sherwood's incorrect date and single occasion of Oblate constitutional debate, Thaddeus Posey and an unidentified twentieth-century Oblate source have predicated their treatment of Oblate constitutional deliberations on the premise of a single constitution co-authored by Duchemin and Deluol. Certain of the Oblate community's rejection of Duchemin's proposals (Annals, 2: 9 September 1845), these two sources have concluded that the Sisters rejected Deluol's rules as well. See Posey, "Unwanted Commitment," 142, 145, and anonymous notation on typescript cover sheet to "Notes."

24. Annals, 1:85.

25. Ibid., 2, 14, 37, 57; Original Rule; "Deluol's Diary," 24 June 1841.

26. "Souvenir of Love," 58–59.

27. "Deluol's Diary," 26 December 1844; Annals, 2: 3 June 1847. Quote taken from "Souvenir of Love," 58–59.

28. Misner, *"Highly Respectable and Accomplished Ladies,"* 101–2. All quotes taken from Ewens, *Role of the Nun,* 34, 107, 118, 206.

29. Annals, 2: under date 1847.

30. Sherwood, *Oblates' Hundred and One Years,* 109–10, 114; Spalding, *Premier See,* 137–38.

31. "Notes of Mother Theresa," cited in Gillespie, *Mother M. Theresa,* 27.

32. Curley, *Venerable John Neumann,* 108–10.

33. Annals, 1:116–17.

34. Quote taken from West Chester Notes, 4; Sherwood, *Oblates' Hundred and One Years,* 98.

35. Quote taken from Alma, *Reverend Louis Florent Gillet,* 136.

36. Peter Czackert, variously spelled Chakert or Tchackert.

37. M. Rosalita Kelly, *No Greater Service,* 45.

38. Ibid., 45–46; Gillespie, *Mother M. Theresa,* 27.

39. Annals, 2: 9 September 1845; under date 1847.

40. "Memories," 3–4. When Thaddeus Anwander assumed the directorship of the Oblate Sisters of Providence in October 1847, there were twelve Sisters in community. Within a month, the death of Sister Catherine Rock reduced the number to eleven. Thus, before the three departures from the community in 1845, the Oblate Sisters numbered fifteen.

41. "Memories," 3.

42. Sister Ann Constance to Mother Louisa Noel, 17 December 1868, AOSP. For full discussions of Duchemin's post-Oblate experiences see Alma, *Thou, Lord, Art My Hope;* Gillespie, *Mother M. Theresa;* M. Rosalita Kelly, *No Greater Service;* and Sisters, *Building Sisterhood.*

43. Annals, 2: 9 September 1845; under date 1847; "Memories," 4.

44. "Deluol's Diary," 13 October, 22 November 1844.

45. Gillespie, *Mother M. Theresa,* 24; see also Shea and Supan, "Apostolate of the Archives," 12, and Code, "Mother Theresa," 318.

46. M. Rosalita Kelly, *No Greater Service,* 91, 764 n. 36.

47. Annals, 2: under date 1847.

48. Patricia Byrne, "Sisters of St. Joseph," 263; Coburn and Smith, *Spirited Lives,* 80–81.

49. Quote taken from Annals, 2: under date 1847; "Deluol's Diary," 26 December 1844; "Memories," 4.

50. Miller, "Slaves and Southern Catholicism," 147; Fichter, "White Church and the Black Sisters," 41.

51. "Memories," 3.

52. Herbermann, *Sulpicians*, 236; Spalding, *Premier See*, 148–49; Sherwood, *Oblates' Hundred and One Years*, 117; Kauffman, *Tradition and Transformation*, 127–29.

53. Eccleston to De Courson, 5 August 1849, RG 29, Box 8, SAB.

54. Kauffman, *Tradition and Transformation*, 116.

55. Annals, 2: 3 September 1843 (French text); *Cathedral Records*, 65. Quotes taken from Annals, 2: under date 1845.

56. Reilly, "Famous Convent," 110.

57. Annals, 2: 9 September 1845.

58. "Deluol's Diary," 5 October 1845.

59. 1844–54 Ledger, Receipts, October 1845, February and September 1846, March, August, and December 1847.

60. Anwander to Sourin, 27 March 1876.

61. "Memories," 4. In 1847, Redemptorist authorities assigned Giles Smulders to Monroe, Michigan (Curley, *Venerable John Neumann*, 126).

62. Annals, 2: 9 September 1845; "Deluol's Diary," 2 and 8 December 1845.

63. Reilly, "Famous Convent," 109–10.

64. Spalding, *Premier See*, 128.

65. Annals, 2: 8 November 1843.

66. Annals, 1:46; 5 December 1843 (French text).

67. Louis Deluol to Francis Lhomme, 1 March 1858, RG 5, Box 11, SAB. Translation from the original French courtesy of Kieran Batts Morrow.

68. "Deluol's Diary," 2 January 1844; Sherwood, *Oblates' Hundred and One Years*, 107; Gillespie, *Mother M. Theresa*, 21–22; "Deluol's Diary," 23 August, 16 November 1844, and 1843–47 passim.

69. Anwander letter fragment, 3 December 1886, Thaddeus Anwander Director File, AOSP.

70. Annals, 2: 12 September, 8, 29 October, 3 December 1843.

71. "Memories," 4; "A Few Facts," 3; "Memories," 3.

72. Annals, 2: 9 September 1845.

73. Ibid., 3 June 1847; "Memories," 3.

74. "First Foundress," 13.

75. Annals, 2: 9 September 1845; "Deluol's Diary," 14 and 15 March 1845; "First Foundress," 11–12.

76. "Deluol's Diary," 19 April 1844.

77. Alma, *Reverend Louis Florent Gillet*, 136.

78. Anwander to Sourin, 27 March 1876.

79. Annals, 1:46, 47.

80. Fields, *Slavery and Freedom*, 63–89. All quotes taken from Brackett, *Negro in Maryland*, 247, 242–44.

81. Brackett, *Negro in Maryland*, 203–4, 244–48.

82. Annals, 1:86; Annals, 2: 5 September 1842. Quote taken from Berlin, *Slaves without Masters*, 231–32.

83. Spalding, *Premier See*, 142–43; *Cathedral Records*, 65; J. A. Frederick, "Old St. Peter's or the Beginning of Catholicity in Baltimore," *Historical Records and Studies* 5, part 2 (1908):

390–91; Brackett, *Negro in Maryland*, 201–2, 205. Quote taken from *Laity's Directory* (1845), 72; (1846), 86. See Cyprian Davis, *History of Black Catholics*, 86–88, for an effective analysis of the Journal of the Society of Coloured People.

84. "Journal," 1–3.

85. Ibid., 11–22.

86. Ibid., 2, 3, 6–7.

87. Records of Confraternities: "Scapulaire," 16 April 1842, RG 1, Box 17, SAB; "Journal," 48–49, 46.

88. "Journal," 44–45.

89. "Constitution and By-Laws of the Cathedral Fund Association," 28 May 1839, RG 26, Box 10, SAB; "Journal," 67, 32, 35, 38, 33, 48.

90. "Subscribers for the Cathedral Fund," appended to "Journal," 4–7; "Journal," 35.

91. "Journal," 61–62.

92. Cyprian Davis, *History of Black Catholics*, 88; *Laity's Directory* (1845), 70; (1857), 73.

93. Gardner, "Free Blacks in Baltimore," 104–9; Christopher Phillips, *Freedom's Port*, 227.

94. "Journal," 65, 66–67.

95. *Laity's Directory* (1834), 69–70.

96. "Deluol's Diary," 7 October 1847.

97. "A Few Facts," 3, 2; "Memories," 3; "First Foundress," 3.

98. Anwander to Sourin, 27 March 1876.

99. Sherwood, *Oblates' Hundred and One Years*, 114–16; Curley, *Venerable John Neumann*, 134.

100. "Deluol's Diary," 7 October 1847; "A Few Facts," 6–7, 3; Reilly, "Famous Convent," 111; Spalding, *Premier See*, 149.

101. Curley, *Venerable John Neumann*, 86, 112, 134; "Deluol's Diary," 7 November 1843; 7 October 1847.

102. Sherwood, *Oblates' Hundred and One Years*, 112–14.

103. Terborg-Penn, "African Feminism," 25.

104. Sherwood, *Oblates' Hundred and One Years*, 118.

Chapter Nine

1. "Notes," VI.

2. Anwander to E. J. Sourin, 27 March 1876, Thaddeus Anwander Director File, AOSP.

3. Annals, 2: 11 October 1847; Anwander to Sourin, 27 March 1876; "A Few Facts," 3, 6–7. Quote taken from Annals, 2: 4 September 1848 (under date 27 July 1848).

4. Oblate Account Books with John Murphy and Co., 1852–59, 1859–61, Box 95, AOSP.

5. Annals, 2: 27 July 1848; 8 October 1848 (under date 3 June 1847).

6. Anwander to Sourin, 27 March 1876.

7. Annals, 2: 14 October 1849.

8. Reilly, "Famous Convent," 111; Sherwood, *Oblates' Hundred and One Years*, 118–19.

9. Anwander to Sourin, 27 March 1876; Annals, 2: 14 October, 25 December 1849.

10. Other Oblate member "children of the house" included Sisters Clotilde (Marie Germaine), admitted in 1836, and Angelica (Angelica Gideon), admitted in 1839.

11. Autobiographical and biographical profiles of Sister M. Theresa Catherine Willigman from Willigman's Superior File, AOSP; Annals, 2: 19 October 1849.

12. Anwander to Sourin, 27 March 1876.

13. Profiles of Sister M. Theresa Catherine Willigman from Willigman's Superior File, AOSP.

14. "Sister Mary James, O.P.," Profile in Willigman's handwriting, Willigman's Superior File, Folder 1, AOSP.

15. Ibid.; Annals, 2: 13 May, 7 June 1850; 8 December 1851; 8 January, 2 February 1853; 2 February 1854.

16. Annals, 1:52; Annals, 2: 10 October 1852; Montpensier to Toussaint(?), 11 October 1852, typescript copy, AOSP.

17. Manumission Documents, no. 1, Box 21, AOSP; *Seventh Census of United States* (1850), Population Schedules, Maryland, Baltimore City, Ward 11.

18. Manumission Documents, no. 5, Box 21, AOSP; Annals, 2: 28 November 1853; 2 February 1854; 2 February 1955.

19. Annals, 2: 29 April 1855; Manumission Documents, no. 4, Box 21, AOSP; 1844–54 Ledger, Receipts, February 1846: "Miss Harper for tuition of Harriet, etc.—$6.75."

20. Annals, 2: 9 March, 15 August 1854; 29 April 1855; 1855–61 Ledger, Receipts, June 1855.

21. Annals, 2: 4 April 1858; 1 May 1859; 9 January, 19 February, 1 June, 9 September 1860.

22. Anwander to Sourin, 27 March 1876.

23. Annals, 2: 30 April 1859; *Laity's Directory* (1857), 72–73.

24. Annals, 1:57, 66–67, 74, 77, 79, 85, 87, 92–104.

25. Annals, 2: 25 December 1849; 13 September [October] 1850; 24 March, 19 August 1849; 7 April, 11 August, 13 September [October] 1850; 12 October, 9 May 1851; 7 May 1852; 2 May 1855.

26. Ibid., 13 September [October] 1850.

27. Ibid., 29 April 1855.

28. "A Few Facts," 4.

29. Annals, 2: 1 January 1856.

30. Ibid., 24 February 1856.

31. "Rule and Constitution," undated manuscript, 42–46, Box 41, AOSP; Annals, 2: 14 March 1856.

32. Annals, 2: 9, 18 March 1857.

33. Anwander letter fragment, 3 December 1886, Thaddeus Anwander Director File, AOSP; Annals, 2: 20 September, 1 October 1857; 5 November 1860.

34. Annals, 2: 9, 11 October 1857; 4 April, 22, 25, 28, 30 May, 17 September 1858.

35. Ibid., 12 October 1851; October 1854; 11 October 1857.

36. Annals, 1:9, 10, 15, 22, 25, 30.

37. Annals, 2: under date 3 September 1856; 27 December 1856; 1 January 1857.

38. Mannard, "'Maternity of the Spirit,'" 251–53; Coburn and Smith, *Spirited Lives*, 149.

39. All quotes from Mother Superior, Sisters of Providence, to Bishop Purcell, 4 December 1857, CACI, II-4-n. I thank Professor M. Christine Anderson for informing me of the existence of this letter.

40. Annals, 2: 12 October 1851; 11 October 1857; 17 September 1858.

41. Anwander to Sourin, 27 March 1876.

42. Sherwood, *Oblates' Hundred and One Years*, 117.

43. 1844–54 Ledger, Expenses and Receipts for September 1847.

44. Annals, 1:91. The correct debt amount, explained in Chapter 7, note 14, was $2,192.375, making the 1847 debt of only $700 even more remarkable.

45. 1844–54 Ledger; 1855–61 Ledger.

46. Kauffman, *Tradition and Transformation*, 129–30; 1844–54 Ledger, 1 February 1850.

47. Louis Deluol to Francis Lhomme, 1 March 1858, RG 5, Box 11, SAB. Translation from the original French courtesy of Kieran Batts Morrow.

48. 1855–61 Ledger; Annals, 2: 30 December 1859.

49. 1855–61 Ledger, January 1857.

50. Ibid., Receipts, January, February 1857, January 1860, March 1857–October 1861.

51. Ibid., Receipts, July 1856, November 1857, May and December 1858; April 1859, January and June 1860, June and October 1861; *Baltimore City Directory* (Matchett, 1831, 60; 1833, 33, 34).

52. *Laity's Directory* (1850), 82.

53. "Colored Schools," *Catholic Mirror*, 26 March 1853, 6.

54. *Laity's Directory* (1854), 72.

55. 1855–61 Ledger, Receipts, September 1856, January, March, August, and December 1858, March and June 1859; Programme for the Distribution of Premiums, St. Frances Schools, 27 July 1859, AOSP.

56. *Laity's Directory* (1834), 70; Original Rule, AOSP.

57. *Catholic Mirror*, 20 August 1853–4 March 1854.

58. *Laity's Directory* (1834), 70; (1836), 168; (1840), 72; "Colored Schools," *Catholic Mirror*, 26 March 1853.

59. Stewart, *Marvels of Charity*, 112.

60. Annals, 2: 27 July 1859; *Laity's Directory* (1859), 272; (1834), 65–71.

61. Annals, 2: 14 December 1866.

62. Ibid., 28 July 1857.

63. Anwander to Sourin, 27 March 1876.

64. *Laity's Directory* (1860), 364; Ripley et al., eds. *Witness for Freedom*, under "Hamilton, Thomas (1823–65), and Robert Hamilton (1819?–),'' 269.

65. *Weekly Anglo-African*, 13 August 1859.

66. Ibid.

67. Programme for the Distribution of Premiums, St. Frances Schools, 27 July 1859, AOSP.

68. Oblate Account Books with John Murphy and Co., 1852–59, 1859–61, Box 95; William Bridges invoice, "Bills and Receipts 1840–1870" Binder, AOSP.

69. Annals, 2: 5 November 1849.

70. Ibid., under date 1 November 1851.

71. Ibid., 3 November 1854.

72. Ibid., 1 November 1855.

73. Ibid., 2 November 1859.

74. 1855–61 Ledger, Expenses, January 1860.

75. Annals, 2: 5 November 1860.

76. Ibid., 4 November 1860.

77. Ibid., 16 January 1861.

Chapter Ten

1. Annals, 2: 4 November 1860.

2. Annals, 1:1, 23, 36, 46; "First Foundress," 5.

3. Annals, 2: 27 August (under date 8 December) 1848.

4. Annals, 2: 30 June 1848 (under date 9 March 1848).

5. Anwander to E. J. Sourin, 27 March 1876, Thaddeus Anwander Director File, AOSP.

6. Annals, 2: 3 June 1847, 30 June 1848 (under 9 March 1848); 24 March 1849.

7. Anwander to Sourin, 27 March 1876; Annals, 2: 24 March 1849.

8. "A Few Facts," 3–4.

9. *Catholic Mirror*, 24 May 1851, 165; Annals, 2: 7 May 1852; *Catholic Mirror*, 19 June 1852, 197; 21 May 1853, 7.

10. *Laity's Directory* (1853), 70.

11. Anwander letter fragment, 3 December 1886, Thaddeus Anwander Director File, AOSP; Annals, 2: 1, 15 February, 9 March 1850.

12. Annals, 2: 12 October 1851; under date 1 November 1851; Anwander to Sourin, 27 March 1876.

13. 1844–54 Ledger, Receipts, May, June, and December 1852; August, September, October 1852; January 1853; 1852–54, passim; 1855–61 Ledger, Receipts, April–June 1857.

14. 3 October 1852 multisignatory note, A. Pompletz Receipts, 10 October 1852–20 May 1853, "Bills and Receipts 1840–1870" Binder, AOSP.

15. 1844–54 Ledger, Receipts, May–December 1852, passim.

16. *Laity's Directory* (1853), 59; (1855), 63; (1857), 62.

17. St. Frances Convent Chapel Baptismal Register, 1853–77, and Confirmation Book for the Oblates of Providence Chapel, St. Frances of Rome, 1849–77, Box 1, AOSP.

18. Anwander to Sourin, 27 March 1876. Sherwood distinguished between this incarnation of the Holy Family Society, approved by Pope Pius IX and entrusted to the Redemptorist order in 1847, and the one established by James Joubert at St. Mary's Lower Chapel in 1827. See Sherwood, *Oblates' Hundred and One Years*, 122–23.

19. "A Few Facts," 3.

20. Annals, 2: 25 December 1855; 9, 15 March 1857; 14, 25 March 1858; under date 2 February, 11 March, 11 October 1859. Archbishop Kenrick established the Forty Hours Devotion in his diocese in 1858 to commemorate the length of time Jesus Christ remained entombed before resurrection. See Shea, *History of the Catholic Church*, 4:378.

21. 1855–61 Ledger.

22. Annals, 2: 7 June 1850; 17 June 1851; 21 June 1854; 14 September 1857; 11 July 1858.

23. 1844–54 Ledger, July 1852; 1855–61 Ledger, Receipts, September 1857; July 1858.

24. Oates, *Catholic Philanthropic Tradition*, 2–3.

25. 1855–61 Ledger.

26. St. Frances Academy Board and Tuition Ledger, 1852–75, 25, Box 7, AOSP; 1855–61 Ledger; Expenses and Cash Received, 1858–64, 2/9/60, 7/4/60, AOSP.

27. Ochs, *Desegregating the Altar*, 456.

28. Christopher Phillips, *Freedom's Port*, 106.

29. Annals, 1:52; Student Registers, 4; Sherwood, *Oblates' Hundred and One Years*, 33; St. Patrick Baptismal Registers, M 1563-1, pp. 275, 312, AAB microfilm, MdHR.

30. St. Frances Confirmation Register, 1849–76, under 1851, AOSP; *Seventh Census of the United States* (1850), Population Schedules, Maryland, Baltimore City, Ward 11, 205, and Ward 2, 177; Annals, 2: 28 July 1854. The custom of bestowing multiple given names at baptism and Confirmation—any one of which could appear alone subsequently on another record—and the distorted spelling characteristic of some census takers frequently obscure family relationships and complicate establishing accurate identities. For example, Emile

Joseph Dubois appeared as "Ameal Dubuys," his wife Adeine as "Amilia," and Philomena as "Phillipa" in *Seventh United States Census*, Maryland, Baltimore City, Ward 2.

31. Sherwood, *Oblates' Hundred and One Years*, 29–30.

32. Anwander to Sourin, 27 March 1876.

33. Dubois note, 16 November 1852, "Bills and Receipts 1840–1870" Binder, AOSP; 1855–61 Ledger, December 1855 expenses; 1855–61 Ledger, May 1855 expenses; Sherwood, *Oblates' Hundred and One Years*, 129; Ruth Hopp note and receipt, "Bills and Receipts 1840–1870" Binder, AOSP.

34. Augustus note, 1844–54 Ledger, on March 1853 Receipt page; *Catholic Mirror*, 6 August 1853, 6.

35. 1844–54 Ledger, Receipts, November 1852 and 1853; December 1854; November 1855; December 1856 and 1857; Mary Jackson receipt, 21 August 1855, "Bills and Receipts" Binder; 1855–61 Ledger, December 1857 receipts and February 1858 expenses.

36. *Catholic Mirror*, 1 June 1850, 171.

37. 1855–61 Ledger, Receipts, April 1855.

38. Annals, 2: 10 January 1859; 1855–61 Ledger, January 1859 expenses: "for masses for R. Green, our benefactor—$5."

39. "A Few Facts," 3; *Laity's Directory* (1853), 58; (1855), 62.

40. "Colored Schools," *Catholic Mirror*, 26 March 1853, 6.

41. Annals, 2: 13 September [October] 1850.

42. Louis Deluol to Francois Lhomme, 4 June 1855, RG 5, Box 11, SAB (translation from the original French in "William A. Williams File," JFA).

43. St. Frances Chapel Sacramental Register, 1849–77, under date 28 May 1852, AOSP.

44. *Calendar* 7, no. 1314, from William Williams in Rome, 27 April 1856.

45. Ibid., 2, no. 686, Francis Patrick Kenrick to PF, 5 August 1853; no. 838, L. A. Rappe to PF, 24 November 1854; no. 877, Thaddeus Anwander to PF, 21 February, 23 July 1855; no. 1364, F. P. Kenrick to PF, 4 October 1858; no. 1402, F. P. Kenrick to PF, 28 November 1858; no. 1595, L. A. Rappe to William Williams, 27 January 1860; Ochs, *Desegregating the Altar*, 29–31.

46. *Calendar* 2, no. 2063, William A. Williams to PF, 2 August 1862.

47. Ochs, *Desegregating the Altar*, 31; Hennesey, *American Catholics*, 144–45. I thank Rev. Peter Hogan, S.S.J., Eva Slezak, Stephen Ochs, and F. P. O'Neill for graciously sharing materials on William Augustine Williams with me.

48. Records of Confraternities: Registre, Confrérie du Rosaire, 6 December 1829, "Harriet Thompson for adoration 15 August," RG 1, Box 17, SAB.

49. Harriet Thompson to Pope Pius IX, 29 October 1853, *Calendar* 2, no. 715, Congressi: America Centrale, vol. 16, fols. 770 rv, 771 rv, 773 rv, 774 rv, 775 r, MPRF.

50. Ibid.

51. Ibid.

52. Ochs, *Desegregating the Altar*, 16–17; Cyprian Davis, *History of Black Catholics*, 60, 97. For a revealing treatment of Irish immigrant attitudes toward African Americans, see Ignatiev, *How the Irish Became White*.

53. Harriet Thompson to Pope Pius IX, 29 October 1853.

54. Ibid.

55. Ibid.

56. Annals, 1:25.

57. Sherwood, *Oblates' Hundred and One Years*, 114; Spalding, *Premier See*, 142; Annals, 2: 7 June 1850.

58. Programme for the Distribution of Premiums, St. Frances Schools, 27 July 1859, AOSP.

59. Anwander to Sourin, 27 March 1876; "A Few Facts," 3.

60. "A Few Facts," 3.

61. "Mrs. Mary A. Jackson for Board and Tuition of God-daughter in acct with the Srs. of Providence, 1852," separate sheet, AOSP.

62. *Catholic Mirror*, 25 December 1858.

63. Misner, *"Highly Respectable and Accomplished Ladies,"* 199–200.

64. *Catholic Mirror*, 26 March 1853, 6.

65. *Laity's Directory* (1853), 69; (1854), 72.

66. Coburn and Smith, *Spirited Lives*, 52, 147; Oates, *Catholic Philanthropic Tradition*, 150–51.

67. 1844–54 Ledger, Receipts, September 1853 and 1854; 1855–61 Ledger, Receipts, July and October 1855; February, July, and September 1856; February, August, and October 1857; July 1858.

68. 1855–61 Ledger, Receipts, September 1857; January, July, and November 1858; April, July, and November 1859; May and July 1860; Programme for the Distribution of Premiums, St. Frances Schools, 27 July 1859, AOSP.

69. 1855–61 Ledger, Receipts, passim, for Mrs. Tompson [*sic*], Mrs. A. Young, or Mrs Warrington on Isa's account; Annals, 2: 9 January, 19 February 1860.

70. Jezierski, *Enterprising Images*, 1, 13–14, 17–22; 1855–61 Ledger, Receipts, October 1855; January and August 1856.

71. Christopher Phillips, *Freedom's Port*, 99; 1844–54 Ledger, Receipts, August 1852; February 1853; September 1854; 1855–61 Ledger, Receipts, July 1855–April 1861; "Journal," 4, 18; St. Frances Confirmation Register, 1849–76, under 1860, AOSP; Programme for the Distribution of Premiums, St. Frances Schools, 27 July 1859, AOSP.

72. *Laity's Directory* (1855), 74–75; (1856), 76–77; (1857) 72–73; (1859), 272; 1855–61 Ledger, Receipts, 1857–59.

73. "Souvenir of Love," 61.

74. Annals, 2: 11 October 1857; "Souvenir of Love," 61; Sherwood, *Oblates' Hundred and One Years*, 128.

75. Annals, 2: 28 May 1858.

76. Ibid.; Revision of 1833, cited in Posey, "Unwanted Commitment," 331.

77. Annals, 2: 4 April; 22, 25 May; 6, 17 September 1858.

78. Annals, 2: 5 August 1859; 1 September 1862; 17 August, 1863.

79. *Laity's Directory* (1861), 57; Annals, 2: 5 August 1859; "St. Benedict's School Prospectus," n.d., AOSP.

80. Spalding, *Premier See*, 142.

81. *Laity's Directory* (1850), 82; "Colored Schools," *Catholic Mirror*, 26 March 1853, 6; Anwander to Sourin, 27 March 1876; Anwander letter fragment, 3 December 1886.

82. Special Historical Papers Binder, AOSP; 1844–54 Ledger, Receipts, October and September 1845; January 1846; 1855–61 Ledger, Receipts, January 1855.

83. Annals, 1:42.

84. Student Registers, 22–23; Annals, 1:60; Sherwood, *Oblates' Hundred and One Years*, 222–23; Expenses and Cash Received, 1867–76, Box 2, AOSP; List of Pupils SFA 1899/Day Book 1880–83, Box 7, AOSP.

85. 1844–54 Ledger, Receipts, December 1852; January, May, December 1853; June, July, August, December 1854; 1855–61 Ledger, Receipts, June, December 1855; June 1856.

86. Oblate Confirmation Register, Box 1, AOSP; Annals, 2: dates cited in text.

87. "Baptisms and Marriages by L. R. Deluol, 1822–49," 24, SAB; "Journal," 19; 1844–54 and 1855–61 Ledgers, Receipts; *Seventh Census of the United States* (1850), Population Schedules, Maryland, City of Annapolis, Anne Arundel Co., 271.

88. 1844–54 Ledger, Receipts, October 1844; *Sixth Census of the United States* (1850), Population Schedules, Maryland, Baltimore City, Ward 11; Annals, 2: 28 July 1854; under date 3 May 1856; 9 January, 19 February 1860.

89. Annals, 2: 25 December 1853.

90. Goodwin, "Schools and Education," 217–18, 211.

91. Ibid., 216.

92. *Boyd's United States City Directories* (Washington, D.C.) for 1867, 283; for 1868, 258; for 1869, 254; for 1870, 154.

93. Goodwin, "Schools and Education," 211.

94. Ibid., 222.

95. Ibid., 211, 222.

96. Berlin, *Slaves without Masters*, 357–59, 377; Brackett, *Negro in Maryland*, 250–52; Fields, *Slavery and Freedom*, 63–89.

97. "Journal," 15; Gardner, "Free Blacks in Baltimore," 331.

98. Berlin, *Slaves without Masters*, 357–59, 377; Fields, *Slavery and Freedom*, 79–80.

99. Goodwin, "Schools and Education," 211.

100. Annals, 2: 29 November 1859.

101. Goodwin, "Schools and Education," 240.

102. Annals, 2: 9 November 1860; 15 May 1861; 15 August 1862; Goodwin, "Schools and Education," 239.

103. Graham, *Baltimore*, 133, 253. The correspondent signed the letter only as Mifflin. Graham identified him as the Reverend John Mifflin Brown.

104. "Some Correspondence," *Weekly Anglo-African*, 13 August 1859.

105. Ibid.

106. Richardson, ed., *Maria W. Stewart*, xiii–xvii, 3–27, 98–100.

Chapter Eleven

1. Annals, 2: 8 May 1852; 30 April 1858.

2. Eccleston to Purcell, 30 March 1850, CACI, II-4-k.

3. For some examples, see Minogue, *Hundred Years of Dominican History*, 63–70; Coburn and Smith, *Spirited Lives*, esp. 46–49, 84, 92–94; and Thompson, "Validation of Sisterhood."

4. Anwander letter fragment, 3 December 1886, Thaddeus Anwander Director File, AOSP; Reilly, "Famous Convent," 112.

5. Mannard, "'Maternity of the Spirit,'" 235. I thank Professor Mannard for bringing this exchange to my attention.

6. Purcell to Eccleston, 3 April 1850, 25Q25, AAB.

7. Sister Mary Louisa Noel to Sister Theresa [Willigman], 28 May 1867, Noel's Superior File, AOSP.

8. Rev. Anthony Deye, "Archbishop John Baptist Purcell of Cincinnati: Pre–Civil War Years" (Ph.D. diss., University of Notre Dame, 1959), 415–16. I thank Professor Christopher Kauffman for this citation.

9. Purcell to Kenrick, 24 November 1857, 31-D-25, AAB.

10. Mother Superior, Sisters of Providence to Bp. Purcell, 4 December 1857, CACI, II-4-n.

11. Annals, 2: 23 September 1858.

12. Spalding, *Premier See*, 154, 163–71, 178.

13. Cyprian Davis, *History of Black Catholics*, 48–50.

14. See Guilday, *History of the Councils of Baltimore*, 168–70, for the former interpretation, and Spalding, *Premier See*, 178, for the latter. See also Marschall, "Francis Patrick Kenrick," 91–92.

15. For detailed discussions of the issue of black Catholic priests in nineteenth-century America, see Foley, *God's Men of Color*; Portier, "John R. Slattery's Vision"; Phelps, "John R. Slattery's Missionary Strategies"; Cyprian Davis, "Black Catholics," 11–12, and *History of Black Catholics*, 145–62; and Ochs, "Ordeal of the Black Priest" and *Desegregating the Altar*.

16. Ochs, *Desegregating the Altar*, 30.

17. Louis R. Deluol to Francis Lhomme, 4 June 1855, RG 5, Box 11, SAB; translation in William A. Williams File, JFA.

18. McMaster, "Bishop Barron," 87–91, 96; Annals, 2: 20, 21, 22 May 1843.

19. Annals, 2: 28 May 1852; 12 May 1853; 9 June 1854; 2 May 1855; 25 June 1858; 11 June 1860.

20. Ibid., 29 July 1853; 28 July 1854; July 1855; under date 3 May 1856; 28 July 1857.

21. Anwander's Subscription Book, January 1853, Box 95, AOSP; 1844–54 Ledger, Receipts, May 1852; 1855–61 Ledger, Receipts, May, November 1855; June, December 1856; August 1857; September 1858.

22. Kenrick to Purcell, 28 November 1857, CACI, II-4-n.

23. Kenrick to Mr. and Mrs. Allen, [13 June] 1860, cited in Zanca, ed., *American Catholics and Slavery*, 238.

24. Ibid.

25. Spalding, *Premier See*, 166, 170.

26. "A New Chapel," *Catholic Mirror*, 26 September 1857.

27. Annals, 2: 25 December 1857; 28 March 1858; 15 May 1859; 24 and 28 February 1860.

28. Spalding, *Premier See*, 135.

29. 1855–61 Ledger, Receipts, October 1857; Spalding, *Premier See*, 136.

30. Annals, 2: 11 October 1857; "Souvenir of Love," 61; Sherwood, *Oblates' Hundred and One Years*, 128.

31. Annals, 2: 4 and 10 November 1860; Sherwood, *Oblates' Hundred and One Years*, 131.

32. Annals, 2: 12 October 1851.

33. Ibid., 10 October 1852; under date 9 September 1853; 9, 11 March, 15 May, 11 October 1859.

34. "Colored Schools," *Catholic Mirror*, 26 March 1853; Anwander Subscription Book, January 1853, Box 95, AOSP; Spalding, *Premier See*, 223, 243; 1844–54 and 1855–61 Ledgers.

35. Spalding, *Premier See*, 168.

36. Ibid., 169.

37. Annals, 2: 28 May 1858.

38. *Catholic Mirror*, 21 July 1855, 4–5.

39. Spalding, *Premier See*, 146–47, 160; *Catholic Mirror*, 26 January 1850, 29.

40. *Catholic Mirror*, 5 July 1851, 213.

41. Ibid., 19 July 1851, 238.

42. Ibid., 13 April 1850, 115; 24 May 1851, 165; 19 June 1852, 197.

43. *Laity's Directory* (1850), 75; (1851), 96; (1852), 67.

44. Ibid., (1853), 59.

45. "Colored Schools," *Catholic Mirror*, 26 March 1853, 6. For an account of black efforts in antebellum Baltimore to secure inclusion in public education, see Christopher Phillips, *Freedom's Port*, 226–27.

46. "Colored Schools," *Catholic Mirror*, 26 March 1853, 6.

47. "St. Francis [*sic*] Female Colored School, Richmond Street," *Catholic Mirror*, 6 August 1853, 6.

48. *Catholic Mirror*, 21 July 1855, 4.

49. *Cathedral Records*, 68.

50. "Churches, Pious and Charitable Institutions, Etc. of Baltimore," *Metropolitan* 1 (February 1830): 67.

51. "Colored Schools," *Catholic Mirror*, 26 March 1853, 6.

52. Ibid.

53. "St. Joseph's," *Catholic Mirror*, 9 July 1853, 6; Manuscript 10, Document 1-89[1], Plat A, 1870, Baltimore City Archives, Baltimore, Md.

54. "St. Francis [*sic*] Female Colored School, Richmond Street," *Catholic Mirror*, 6 August 1853, 6.

55. "First Foundress," 5.

56. *Catholic Mirror*, 21 July 1855, 4–5.

57. Ibid., 5 April 1856, 6.

58. De Courcy, *Catholic Church*, 115.

59. Ibid., footnote.

60. "Judge Taney and his Libelers," *Catholic Mirror*, 25 April 1857, 3; "Roger B. Taney," ibid., 19 September 1857, 2–3.

61. "Roger B. Taney," *Catholic Mirror*, 19 September 1857.

62. *Laity's Directory* (1859), 51, 55–58, 272; (1860), 54, 58–61, 364; (1861), 52, 55–58. The 1858 and 1859 editions of this work did include St. Frances School for Colored Girls and St. Frances Male School in a "Colleges and Academies" addendum concluding each volume, but the 1861 edition omitted the Oblate schools even from this supplement.

63. Ibid., (1861).

64. Brackett, *Negro in Maryland*, 248–49; Fields, *Slavery and Freedom*, 63–89.

65. Brackett, *Negro in Maryland*, 248, 253, 257.

66. Berlin, *Slaves without Masters*, 372–74.

67. Brackett, *Negro in Maryland*, 254.

68. Ibid., 257–58; Fields, *Slavery and Freedom*, 63–89.

69. Brackett, *Negro in Maryland*, 260–62; Fields, *Slavery and Freedom*, 63–89; Wright, *Free Negro*, 315–16.

70. Berlin, *Slaves without Masters*, 375–78; Fields, *Slavery and Freedom*, 63–89.

71. Berlin, *Slaves without Masters*, 349–50; Fields, *Slavery and Freedom*, 63–89; Wright, *Free Negro*, 171–73; Christopher Phillips, "'Negroes and Other Slaves,'" 311–21.

72. Berlin, *Slaves without Masters*, 349–51.

73. Spalding, *Premier See*, 171.

74. Barney, *Passage of the Republic*, 178; Spalding, *Premier See*, 172.

75. Spalding, *Premier See*, 172–73.

76. Ibid., 173–74; Fields, *Slavery and Freedom*, 46–47, 58–60.

77. *Baltimore Republican*, 15 March 1856; John V. McGrain to Sister M. Virginie Fish, O.S.P., 13 May 1993, RG 41, Box 3, SAB.

78. Spalding, *Premier See*, 174; Fields, *Slavery and Freedom*, 47, 58–60; Sherwood, *Oblates' Hundred and One Years*, 128.

79. Sherwood, *Oblates' Hundred and One Years*, 128.

80. Kenrick to Purcell, 28 November 1857, CACI, II-4-n.

81. Manuscript 10, Document 1-89[1], 1870 Plat A, Baltimore City Archives, Baltimore, Md.; 1844–54 Ledger, Receipts, 1844–48; 1855–61 Ledger, Expenses and Receipts, November 1856, and Receipts, June 1857; 1844–54 Ledger, Receipts, March 1853.

82. Manuscript 10, Document 1-89[1], 1870 Plat A, Baltimore City Archives, Baltimore, Md.; Rosensteel Invoices, 31 December 1851; 9 November 1852; 31 December 1856; and 1 January 1858, "Bills and Receipts 1840–1870" Binder, AOSP; 1844–54 Ledger, Receipts, January 1854; 1855–61 Ledger, Receipts, January 1857.

83. 1844–54 Ledger, Receipts, March 1853; John Orhman Invoice, 26 October 1857, and Frederick Bull Invoice, 16 May 1860, "Bills and Receipts 1840–1870" Binder, AOSP.

Conclusion

1. Annals, 1:38–39.

2. *Harper Collins Encyclopedia of Catholicism*, 1995 ed., s.v. "humility."

3. Coburn and Smith, *Spirited Lives*, 81.

4. Ibid., 252 n. 47.

5. Annals, 1:39.

6. Elsa Barkley Brown, "Womanist Consciousness," 278.

7. Collins, *Black Feminist Thought*, 224, 230.

8. Terborg-Penn, "African Feminism," 25.

BIBLIOGRAPHY

Primary Sources

ARCHIVES

Archdiocese of Philadelphia Archives and Historical Collections, Philadelphia, Pa.
Archives of the Archdiocese of Baltimore, Baltimore, Md.
Archives of the Oblate Sisters of Providence, Baltimore, Md.
    Early Student Registers (1828–33), Eagle File Box 44 and Box 95
    Mother Mary Louisa Noel's Superior File
    Mother Theresa Catherine Willigman's Superior File
    "Notes on the Constitutions of the Oblate Sisters of Providence, Established in Balti-
        more, June 1829, by Very Rev. L. R. Deluol, Superior of St. Mary's Seminary," par-
        tially translated from the original French by M. Theresa Catherine Willigman,
        O.S.P., manuscript copy, n.d., Box 52
    Oblate Ledger, 1844–54 (unpaged), Box 51
    Oblate Ledger, 1855–61 (unpaged), marked "Box 10 Ledger #1," Box 1
    "The Original Diary of the Oblate Sisters of Providence," trans., typescript and manu-
        script copies, vols. 1 and 2, Box 47
    Original Oblate Ledger Sheets, 1828–30 (unpaged), 1829–36, Eagle File Box 44
    The Original Rule and Constitutions of the Oblate Sisters of Providence, English
        manuscript copy, Box 41
    Willigman, M. Theresa Catherine, O.S.P. "A Few Facts Relating to the Oblate Sisters
        of Providence of Baltimore, Md.," typescript copy, n.d.
    ————. "First Foundress of the Oblates," typescript copy, n.d.
    ————. "Memories of Sister Theresa Duchemin," typescript copy, n.d.
    ————. "Souvenir of Love and Grateful Remembrance of the Foundress of the
        Oblate Sisters of Providence, Sister Mary, Established in Baltimore, June 5th, 1828,
        Made Their Vows July 2nd, 1829, Celebrated Her Golden Jubilee July 2nd, 1879,
        Died February 3rd, 1882, First Superior of the Oblate Sisters," manuscript copy, n.d.
Baltimore City Archives, Baltimore, Md.
The Catholic University of America Library, Washington, D.C.

The Catholic Mirror (Baltimore, 1850–59), microfilm
The American Catholic Directories, 1817–1879, microfilm
Josephite Archives, Baltimore, Md.
Maryland Hall of Records, State Archives, Annapolis, Md.
   Co-Cathedral—Minor Basilica of the Assumption of the Blessed Virgin Mary (St.
      Peter's Pro-Cathedral) Microfilm Collection
University of Notre Dame Archives, Notre Dame, Ind.
   Archdiocese of Cincinnati Collection
   Congregation of the Propaganda Fide Archives, microfilm
   Diocesan Collections
Redemptorist Provincial Archives, Baltimore Province, Md.
Saint Joseph's University Archives, Philadelphia, Pa.
Sulpician Archives, Baltimore, Md.
   "Excerpts from Louis R. Deluol's Diary Concerning the Oblate Sisters of Providence,"
      compiled by John W. Bowen, S.S.
   "Fr. Tessier's Easter Duty Lists" (1809–33), RG 1, Box 17
   "Journal of the Commencement of the Proceedings of the Society of Coloured Peo-
      ple [Holy Family Society]," 1843–45, Record Group 42, Box 2
   Metropolitan Catholic Calendar and Laity's Directory. Baltimore: James Myres, 1833–37; Field-
      ing Lucas, 1834–57; John Murphy, 1859–61 (specific titles varied among The United
      States Catholic Almanac or Laity's Directory; The Catholic Calendar and Laity's Directory; The
      Metropolitan Catholic Almanac and Laity's Directory; and The Catholic Almanac).
Villa Maria House of Studies, West Chester Motherhouse Archives, Sisters, Servants of
      the Immaculate Heart of Mary, Immaculata, Pa.
   West Chester Notes: "Mother M. Theresa," dictated by Sister Mary James to Sister
      Maria Alma, 22 February 1920, typescript copy

PUBLISHED WORKS

The Baltimore City Directories. Variously compiled by William H. Boyd, Richard J. Matchett,
   and John J. Woods. Baltimore, Md., 1800–1860.
Baltimore Literary and Religious Magazine. Vols. 1–7 (1835–41). Ann Arbor, Mich.: University
   Microfilms, American Periodical Series, 1800–1850.
United States Census Population Schedules, 1830–1880. Washington, D.C.: U.S. Government
   Printing Office.
The Weekly Anglo-African. New York, N.Y.

Selected Secondary Sources

Alma, Maria, C.I.M. The Reverend Louis Florent Gillet: His Life, Letters, and Conferences. Philadel-
   phia: Dolphin Press, 1940.
———. Thou, Lord, Art My Hope! The Life of Mother M. Theresa, a Pioneer of the Sisters, Servants of
   the Immaculate Heart of Mary. Lancaster, Pa.: The Dolphin Press, 1961.
Baltimore City Health Department. The First Thirty-five Annual Reports, 1815–1849. Balti-
   more, 1953.
Baptiste, Mary of Good Counsel, O.S.P. "A Study of the Foundation and Educational
   Objectives of the Congregation of the Oblate Sisters of Providence and of the

Achievements of These Objectives as Seen in Their Schools." M.A. thesis, Villanova University, 1939.

Barney, William L. *The Passage of the Republic: An Interdisciplinary History of Nineteenth-Century America.* Lexington, Mass.: D. C. Heath & Co., 1987.

Baudier, Roger. *The Catholic Church in Louisiana.* New Orleans, La., 1939.

Baumgarten, Nikola. "Education and Democracy in Frontier St. Louis: The Society of the Sacred Heart." *History of Education Quarterly* 34, no. 2 (Summer 1994): 171–92.

Bell, Caryn Cossé. *Revolution, Romanticism, and the Afro-Creole Protest Tradition in Louisiana, 1718–1868.* Baton Rouge: Louisiana State University Press, 1997.

Berlin, Ira. *Slaves without Masters: The Free Negro in the Antebellum South.* New York: Pantheon Books, 1974.

Blassingame, John W. *The Slave Community: Plantation Life in the Antebellum South,* 2d ed., rev. and enl. New York: Oxford University Press, 1979.

Boston, M. Petra, O.S.P. *Blossoms Gathered from the Lower Branches.* St. Louis: Con. P. Curran Printing Co., 1914.

Brackett, Jeffrey R. *The Negro in Maryland: A Study of the Institution of Slavery.* Johns Hopkins University Studies in History and Political Science, edited by Herbert Adams. Extra Vol. 6. Baltimore: Johns Hopkins University, 1889.

—————. *Notes on the Progress of the Colored People of Maryland Since the War.* Vols. 7, 8, 9. Johns Hopkins University Studies in Historical and Political Science, edited by Herbert B. Adams. Baltimore: Johns Hopkins University, 1890.

Brewer, Eileen Mary. *Nuns and the Education of American Catholic Women, 1860–1920.* Chicago: Loyola University Press, 1987.

Brokhage, Joseph D. *Francis Patrick Kenrick's Opinion on Slavery.* The Catholic University of America Studies in Sacred Theology. 2d ser., no. 85. Washington, D.C.: The Catholic University of America Press, 1955.

Brown, Elsa Barkley. "Womanist Consciousness: Maggie Lena Walker and the Independent Order of Saint Luke." Originally published in *Signs* 14 (Spring 1989); reprinted in Ruiz and DuBois, ed. *Unequal Sisters,* 268–83. New York: Routledge, 1994.

Brown, Letitia Woods. *Free Negroes in the District of Columbia, 1790–1846.* New York: Oxford University Press, 1972.

Buckler, Thomas H. *A History of Epidemic Cholera as It Appeared at the Baltimore City and County Alms-house in the Summer of 1849.* Baltimore: J. Lucas, 1851.

Burton, Katherine. *Make the Way Known: The History of the Dominican Congregation of St. Mary of the Springs, 1822 to 1957.* New York: Farrar, Straus, and Cudahy, 1959.

Butler, Loretta M. *History of Black Catholics in the Archdiocese of Washington, D.C., 1634–1898: A Select Bibliography of Works Located in Maryland and Washington, D.C., Archives and Libraries.* Washington, D.C.: Office of Black Catholics of the Archdiocese of Washington, 1984.

Butsch, Joseph, S.S.J. "Negro Catholics in the United States." *Catholic Historical Review* 3 (1917): 33–51.

—————. "The Society of St. Joseph or Josephite Fathers." *The Catholic Church in the United States of America.* Vol. 1. New York: Catholic Editing Company, 1912.

Byrne, John F. "The Redemptorists in America." *American Catholic Historical Society of Philadelphia Records* 41 (1930): 353–84.

Byrne, Patricia, C.S.J. "Sisters of St. Joseph: The Americanization of a French Tradition." *U.S. Catholic Historian* 5, nos. 3 and 4 (Summer/Fall 1986): 241–72.

Cain, James R. *The Influence of the Cloister on the Apostolate of Congregations of Religious Women.* Rome: Lateran University, 1965.

Callan, Louise. *Philippine Duchesne.* Westminster, Md.: Newman Press, 1957.

————. *The Society of the Sacred Heart in North America.* London: Longmans, Green and Co., 1937.

Campbell, Penelope. *Maryland in Africa: The Maryland State Colonization Society, 1837–1857.* Urbana: University of Illinois Press, 1971.

Carbonneau, Robert, C.P. "Society of the Holy Family 1843–45: The Development of Black Spirituality in Baltimore." Unpublished Paper, 1986, Sulpician Archives, Baltimore.

Cathedral Records from the Beginning of Catholicity in Baltimore to the Present Time. Baltimore: The Catholic Mirror Publishing Co., 1906.

The Catholic Church in the United States of America. Undertaken to Celebrate the Golden Jubilee of His Holiness, Pope Pius X. Vols. 1–3. New York: The Catholic Editing Company, 1912–14.

Chatellier, Louis. *The Europe of the Devout: The Catholic Reformation and the Formation of a New Society.* Trans. Jean Birrell. Cambridge: Cambridge University Press, 1989.

Coburn, Carol K., and Martha Smith. *Spirited Lives: How Nuns Shaped Catholic Culture and American Life, 1836–1920.* Chapel Hill: The University of North Carolina Press, 1999.

Code, Joseph B. "A Catholic Colored Educator before the Civil War." *Catholic World* 144 (1938): 437–43.

————. "Mother Theresa Maxis Duchemin." *America* 74 (22 December 1945): 317–19.

————. "Negro Sisterhoods in the United States." *America* 58, no. 14 (January 1938): 318–19.

————. "A Selected Bibliography of the Religious Orders and Congregations of Women Founded within the Present Boundaries of the United States (1727–1850)." *The Catholic Historical Review* 23, no. 3 (October 1937): 331–51; 26, no. 2 (July 1940): 222–45.

Collected Black Women's Narratives. New York: Oxford University Press, The Schomburg Library of Nineteenth-Century Black Women Writers, 1988.

Collier-Thomas, Bettye. "The Baltimore Black Community, 1865–1910." 2 vols. Ph.D. diss., George Washington University, 1974.

————. *Daughters of Thunder: Black Women Preachers and Their Sermons, 1850–1979.* San Francisco: Jossey-Bass Publishers, 1998.

Collins, Patricia Hill. *Black Feminist Thought: Knowledge, Consciousness, and the Politics of Empowerment.* Perspectives on Gender, vol. 2. Boston: Unwin Hyman, Inc., 1990.

Cooper, Anna Julia. *A Voice from the South.* New York: Oxford University Press, The Schomburg Library of Nineteenth-Century Black Women Writers, 1988.

Cosgrove, Joseph J. "Mother Mary Elizabeth Lange, Founder of the Oblate Sisters of Providence." Unpublished paper, 1990, Josephite Archives, Baltimore.

Costin, M. Georgia. *Priceless Spirit: A History of the Sisters of the Holy Cross, 1841–1893.* Notre Dame, Ind.: University of Notre Dame Press, 1994.

Cott, Nancy F. *The Bonds of Womanhood: "Woman's Sphere" in New England, 1780–1835.* New Haven: Yale University Press, 1977.

Curley, Michael J., C.SS.R. *Venerable John Neumann, C.SS.R.: Fourth Bishop of Philadelphia.* Washington, D.C.: The Catholic University of America Press, 1952.

Curran, R. Emmet, S.J. "'Splendid Poverty': Jesuit Slaveholding in Maryland, 1805–1838."

In *Catholics in the Old South: Essays on Church and Culture*, edited by Randall M. Miller and Jon Wakelyn, 124–46. Macon, Ga.: Mercer University Press, 1983.

Currier, Charles Warren. *Carmel in America: A Centennial History of the Discalced Carmelites in the United States*. Baltimore: John Murphy & Co., 1890.

Curry, Leonard P. *The Free Black in Urban America, 1800–1850*. Chicago: University of Chicago Press, 1981.

Dabney, Lillian G. *The History of Schools for Negroes in the District of Columbia, 1807–1947*. Washington, D.C.: The Catholic University of America Press, 1949.

[Daughters of Charity]. *1809–1959*. Emmitsburg, Md.: Saint Joseph's Central House, 1959.

———. *Mother Augustine Decount and Mother Xavier Clark*. Emmitsburg, Md.: Saint Joseph's Central House, 1938.

———. *Mother Etienne Hall*. Emmitsburg, Md.: Saint Joseph's Central House, 1939.

———. *Mother Rose White*. Emmitsburg, Md.: Saint Joseph's Central House, 1936.

Davis, Angela Y. "Reflections on the Black Woman's Role in the Community of Slaves." *Black Scholar* 3 (December 1971): 2–15.

———. *Women, Culture, and Politics*. New York: Random House, 1989.

———. *Women, Race, and Class*. New York: Random House, 1981.

Davis, Cyprian, O.S.B. "Black Catholics in Nineteenth-Century America." *U.S. Catholic Historian* 5, no. 1 (1986): 1–17.

———. "Characteristics of Black Spirituality." *Origins* (4 June 1987): 43–45.

———. "The Future of African-American Catholic Studies." *U.S. Catholic Historian* 12, no. 1 (Winter 1994): 1–9.

———. "God's Image in Black: The Black Community in Slavery and Freedom." In *Perspectives on the American Catholic Church, 1789–1989*, edited by Virginia Geiger and Stephen Vicchio, 105–22. Westminster, Md.: Christian Classics, 1989.

———. *The History of Black Catholics in the United States*. New York: Crossroad, 1990.

———. "The Holy See and American Black Catholics: A Forgotten Chapter in the History of the American Church." *U.S. Catholic Historian* 7, nos. 2 and 3 (1988): 157–81.

Davis, David Brion. *The Problem of Slavery in Western Culture*. Ithaca, N.Y.: Cornell University Press, 1966.

DeCock, Mary, B.V.M. "Turning Points in the Spirituality of an American Congregation: The Sisters of Charity of the Blessed Virgin Mary." *U.S. Catholic Historian* 10, nos. 1 and 2 (1989): 59–70.

De Courcy, Henri. *The Catholic Church in the United States: A Sketch of Its Ecclesiastical History*. Trans. John Gilmary Shea. New York: Edward Dunigan & Bro., 1856.

Dedeaux, M. Liberata, O.S.P. "The Influence of St. Frances Academy on Negro Catholic Education in the Nineteenth-Century." M.A. thesis, Villanova University, 1944.

Dirvin, Joseph I., C.M. *Mrs. Seton: Foundress of the American Sisters of Charity*. New York: Farrar, Straus and Cudahy, 1962.

Dolan, Jay, P. *The American Catholic Experience: A History from the Colonial Times to the Present*. New York: Doubleday, 1985.

Donovan, Mary Ann, S.C. *Sisterhood as Power: The Past and Passion of Ecclesial Women*. New York: Crossroad, 1989.

———. "Spirit and Structure: Historical Factors Affecting the Expression of Charism in an American Religious Congregation." *U.S. Catholic Historian* 10, nos. 1 and 2 (1989): 1–12.

Dorsey, Norbert. "Pierre Toussaint of New York, Slave and Freedman: A Study of Lay Spirituality in Times of Social and Religious Change." S.T.D. diss., Pontifical Gregorian University, Rome, 1986, Josephite Archives, Baltimore.

Dougherty, Dolorita Marie, C.S.J., et al. *Sisters of Saint Joseph of Carondelet*. St. Louis, Mo.: B. Herder Book Co., 1966.

Douglass, Frederick. *My Bondage and My Freedom*. New York: Dover Publications, Inc., 1969.

Dries, Angelyn, O.S.F. "The Americanization of Religious Life: Women Religious, 1872–1922." *U.S. Catholic Historian* 10, nos. 1 and 2 (1989): 13–24.

Du Bois, W. E. B. *Black Reconstruction in America, 1860–1880*. New York: Russell and Russell, 1935. Reprint, New York: Atheneum, 1992.

———. *The Souls of Black Folk*. New York: New American Library, 1969.

Duncan, Richard R. "Catholics and the Church in the Antebellum Upper South." In *Catholics in the Old South: Essays on Church and Culture*, edited by Randall M. Miller and Jon Wakelyn, 77–98. Macon, Ga.: Mercer University Press, 1983.

Ellis, John Tracy. *Documents of American Catholic History*. Vol. 1, 1493–1865. Wilmington, Del.: Michael Glazier, 1987.

———. *A Guide to American Catholic History*. Milwaukee, Wisc.: Bruce, 1959.

———. "A Guide to the Baltimore Cathedral Archives." *The Catholic Historical Review* 32, no. 3 (October 1946): 341–60.

Ellis, John Tracy, and Robert Trisco. *A Guide to American Catholic History*. 2d. ed., rev. and enl. Santa Barbara, Calif.: ABC-Clio, 1982.

Estes-Hicks, Onita. "Henriette Delille: Free Woman of Color, Candidate for Roman Catholic Sainthood, Early Womanist." In *Perspectives on Womanist Theology*. Black Church Scholars Series, Vol. 7, edited by Jacquelyn Grant, 41–54. Atlanta, Ga.: The ITC Press, 1995.

Ewens, Mary, O.P. "The Double Standard of the American Sister." In *An American Church: Essays in the Americanization of the Catholic Church*, edited by David Alvarez, 23–34. Moraga, Calif.: St. Mary's College of California, 1979.

———. "The Leadership of Nuns in Immigrant Catholicism." In *The American Catholic Religious Life: Selected Historical Essays*, edited by Joseph M. White, 14–62. New York: Garland Publishing, 1988.

———. "Political Activity of American Sisters Before 1970." In *Between God and Caesar: Priests, Sisters, and Political Office in the United States*, edited by Madonna Kolbenschlag, 41–59. New York: Paulist Press, 1985.

———. "Removing the Veil: The Liberated American Nun." In *Women of Spirit: Female Leadership in the Jewish and Christian Traditions*, edited by Rosemary R. Ruether and Eleanor McLaughlin, 255–78. New York: Simon and Schuster, 1979.

———. *The Role of the Nun in Nineteenth-Century America*. Salem, N.H.: Ayer Company Publishers, 1984.

———. "Women in the Convent." In *American Catholic Women: A Historical Exploration*, edited by Karen Kennelly, 17–47. New York: Macmillan, 1989.

Faherty, William Barnaby, S.J., and Madeline Barni Oliver. *The Religious Roots of Black Catholics of Saint Louis*. Florissant, Mo.: St. Stanislaus Historic Museum, Inc., 1977.

Fichter, Joseph, H., S.J. "The White Church and the Black Sisters." *U.S. Catholic Historian* 12, no. 1 (Winter 1994): 31–48.

Fields, Barbara J. *Slavery and Freedom on the Middle Ground: Maryland during the Nineteenth Century*. New Haven: Yale University Press, 1985.

————. "Slavery, Race and Ideology in the United States of America." *New Left Review* 181 (May/June 1990): 95–118.

Florian, Mary, O.S.P. "Mother Mary Elizabeth Lange—A Pioneer of the Negro Apostolate in Baltimore." Unpublished paper, n.d., Josephite Archives, Baltimore.

Foley, Albert S., S.J. "Adventures in Black Catholic History: Research and Writing." *U.S. Catholic Historian* 5, no. 1 (1986): 103–18.

————. "Bishop Healy and the Colored Catholic Congress." *Interracial Review* 28 (1954): 79–80.

————. *Bishop Healy, Beloved Outcaste: The Story of a Great Man Whose Life Has Become a Living Legend*. New York: Farrar, Straus, 1954.

————. *Dream of an Outcaste: Patrick F. Healy*. Tuscaloosa, Ala.: Portals Press, 1976.

————. *God's Men of Color: The Colored Catholic Priests of the United States, 1854–1934*. New York: Farrar, Straus, 1955.

Foley, Mary Ann, C.N.D. "Uncloistered Apostolic Life for Women: Marguerite Bourgeoys' Experiment in Ville-Marie." *U.S. Catholic Historian* 10, nos. 1 and 2 (1989): 37–44.

Foner, Eric. *Freedom's Lawmakers: A Directory of Black Officeholders during Reconstruction*. New York: Oxford University Press, 1993.

————. *Reconstruction: America's Unfinished Revolution*. New York: Harper and Row, 1988.

Fox-Genovese, Elizabeth. *Within the Plantation Household: Black and White Women in the Old South*. Chapel Hill: The University of North Carolina Press, 1985.

Frances, Catherine, S.S.J. *The Convent School of French Origin in the United States, 1727–1843*. Philadelphia: Sisters of Saint Joseph, 1936.

Franklin, John Hope. *From Slavery to Freedom: A History of Negro Americans*. 5th ed. New York: Alfred A. Knopf, 1980.

Franklin, John Hope, and Loren Schweninger. *Runaway Slaves: Rebels on the Plantation*. New York: Oxford University Press, 1999.

Friedman, Jean E. *The Enclosed Garden: Women and Community in the Evangelical South, 1830–1900*. Chapel Hill: The University of North Carolina Press, 1985.

Frey, Sylvia R., and Betty Wood. *Come Shouting to Zion: African American Protestantism in the American South and British Caribbean to 1830*. Chapel Hill: The University of North Carolina Press, 1998.

Gardner, Bettye J. "Antebellum Black Education in Baltimore." *Maryland Historical Magazine* 71 (Fall 1976): 360–66.

————. "Free Blacks in Baltimore, 1800–1860." 2 vols. Ph.D. diss., George Washington University, 1974.

Gatewood, Willard B. *Aristocrats of Color: The Black Elite, 1880–1920*. Bloomington: Indiana University Press, 1990.

Geggus, David. "The French Slave Trade: An Overview." Unpublished paper, September 1998.

————. "Racial Equality, Slavery, and Colonial Secession during the Constituent Assembly." *The American Historical Review* 94 (December 1989): 1290–1308.

The Georgia Historical Quarterly 76, no. 2 (Summer 1992). Special Issue: "The Diversity of Southern Gender and Race: Women in Georgia and the South."

Gerdes, M. Reginald, O.S.P. "To Educate and Evangelize: Black Catholic Schools of the Oblate Sisters of Providence (1828–1880)." *U.S. Catholic Historian* 7, nos. 2 and 3 (1988): 183–99.

————. "Service on the Cutting Edge: Unique Experiences of the Foundress of the Oblate Sisters of Providence." Unpublished paper, 1994, AOSP.

Giddings, Paula. *When and Where I Enter: The Impact of Black Women on Race and Sex in America.* New York: William Morrow and Company, 1984.

Gillard, John T., S.S.J. *The Catholic Church and the American Negro.* Baltimore: St. Joseph's Society Press, 1929. Reprint, New York: Johnson Reprint Corp., 1968.

————. *Colored Catholics in the United States.* Baltimore: The Josephite Press, 1941.

————. "First Negro Parish in the United States." *America* 50 (1934): 370–72.

Gillespie, M. Immaculata, C.I.M. *Mother M. Theresa Maxis Duchemin.* Scranton, Pa.: Marywood College, 1945.

Ginzberg, Lori. *Women and the Work of Benevolence: Morality, Politics, and Class in the Nineteenth-Century United States.* New Haven: Yale University Press, 1990.

Glasgow, Betty. "St. Frances Academy Background." Unpublished Paper, n.d., Josephite Archives, Baltimore.

Gomez, Michael A. *Exchanging Our Country Marks: The Transformation of African Identities in the Colonial and Antebellum South.* Chapel Hill: The University of North Carolina Press, 1998.

Goodman, Paul. *Of One Blood: Abolitionism and the Origins of Racial Equality.* Berkley: University of California Press, c. 1998.

Goodwin, Moses B. "Schools and Education of the Colored Population." In *Special Report of the United States Commissioner of Education on the Condition and Improvement of Public Schools in the District of Columbia.* Department of Education. Washington, D.C.: U.S. Government Printing Office, 1871.

Gould, Virginia Meacham. "The Parish Identities of Free Creoles of Color in Pensacola and Mobile, 1698–1860." *U.S. Catholic Historian* 4, no. 3 (Summer 1996): 1–10.

————, ed. *Chained to the Rock of Adversity: To Be Free, Black, and Female in the Old South.* Athens: University of Georgia Press, 1998.

————. "Piety, Religious Activism, and Free Women of Color: The Founding of the Sisters of the Holy Family." Unpublished paper, 1998. Copy in author's possession.

Graham, Leroy. *Baltimore, the Nineteenth-Century Black Capital.* Washington, D.C.: University Press of America, 1982.

Gregory, Clarence K. "The Education of Blacks in Maryland: An Historical Survey." Ed.D. diss., Columbia University Teachers College, 1976.

Guertler, John T., ed. *The Records of Baltimore's Private Organizations: A Guide to Archival Resources.* New York: Garland Publishing, Inc., 1981.

Guilday, Peter. *A History of the Councils of Baltimore, 1791–1884.* New York: Macmillan, 1932.

————, ed. *The National Pastorals of the American Hierarchy, 1792–1919.* Westminster, Md.: Newman Press, 1954.

Gutman, Herbert G. *The Black Family in Slavery and Freedom, 1750–1925.* New York: Vintage Books, 1976.

Guy-Sheftall, Beverly, ed. *Words of Fire: An Anthology of African American Feminist Thought.* New York: The New Press, 1995.

Hadrick, M. Emma, O.S.P. "Contributions of the Oblate Sisters of Providence to Catholic Education in the USA and Cuba, 1829–1922." M.A. thesis, The Catholic University of America, 1964, Josephite Archives, Baltimore.

Halsey, Columba E., O.S.B. "The Life of Samuel Eccleston, Fifth Archbishop of Baltimore." *Records of the American Catholic Historical Society of Philadelphia* 76 (June 1965): 69–156; (September 1965): 131–56.

Hanger, Kimberly S. *Bounded Lives, Bounded Places: Free Black Society in Colonial New Orleans, 1769–1803.* Durham: Duke University Press, 1997.

Hennesey, James, S.J. *American Catholics: A History of the Roman Catholic Community in the United States.* New York: Oxford University Press, 1981.

Herbermann, Charles G. *The Sulpicians in the United States.* New York: The Encyclopedia Press, 1916.

Herskovits, Melville J. *Myth of the Negro Past.* New York: Harper & Brothers, 1941. Reprint, Boston: Beacon Press, 1958.

Higginbotham, Evelyn Brooks. "African-American Women's History and the Metalanguage of Race." *Signs* 17, no. 2 (Winter 1992): 251–74.

————. *Righteous Discontent: The Women's Movement in the Black Baptist Church, 1880–1920.* Cambridge, Mass.: Harvard University Press, 1993.

Hine, Darlene Clark. *HineSight: Black Women and the Re-construction of American History.* New York: Carlson Publishing, 1994.

Hine, Darlene Clark, Elsa Barkley Brown, and Rosalyn Terborg-Penn, eds. *Black Women in America: An Historical Encyclopedia.* 2 vols. New York: Carlson Publishing, 1993.

Hine, Darlene Clark, and David Garry Gaspar, eds. *More Than Chattel: Black Women and Slavery in the Americas.* Bloomington: Indiana University Press, 1996.

Hine, Darlene Clark, William C. Hine, and Stanley Harrold. *The African-American Odyssey.* Combined volume. Upper Saddle River, N.J.: Prentice-Hall, 2000.

Hine, Darlene Clark, Wilma King, and Linda Reed, eds. *"We Specialize in the Wholly Impossible": A Reader in Black Women's History.* New York: Carlson Publishing, 1995.

Hine, Darlene Clark, and Kathleen Thompson. *A Shining Thread of Hope: The History of Black Women in America.* New York: Broadway Books, 1998.

History of Women Religious News and Notes. Vols. 1–14 (1988–2001). Published by the Conference on the History of Women Religious, St. Paul, Minn.

Hogan, Peter E., S.S.J. "Catholic Missionary Efforts for the Negro before the Coming of the Josephites." Unpublished paper, 1947, Josephite Archives, Baltimore.

————. "Toward a Black Catholic Archives." *U.S. Catholic Historian* 5, no. 1 (1986): 91–102.

Hunt, Alfred N. *Haiti's Influence on Antebellum America: Slumbering Volcano in the Caribbean.* Baton Rouge: Louisiana State University Press, 1988.

Ignatiev, Noel. *How the Irish Became White.* New York: Routledge, Chapman, and Hall, 1996.

James, C. L. R. *The Black Jacobins: Toussaint L'Ouverture and the Santo Domingo Revolution.* New York: Vintage Books, 1963.

Jarrell, Lynn, O.S.A. "The Development of Legal Structures for Women Religious between 1500 and 1900: A Study of Selected Institutes of Religious Life for Women." *U.S. Catholic Historian* 10, nos.1 and 2 (1989): 25–35.

Jezierski, John Vincent. *Enterprising Images: The Goodridge Brothers, African American Photographers, 1847–1922.* Detroit: Wayne State University Press, 2000.

Johansen, Mary Carroll. "Intelligence, Though Overlooked: Education for Black Women in the Upper South, 1800–1840." *Maryland Historical Magazine* 93, no. 4 (Winter 1998): 443–65.

Jordan, Winthrop D. *The White Man's Burden: Historical Origins of Racism in America.* London: Oxford University Press, 1974.

Josephite News Letter (November–December 1966; January 1967): 1–10. "Filling in the Background." (The Second Plenary Council of Baltimore, 1866).

The Josephites: A Century of Evangelization in the African-American Community. Commemorative volume. Baltimore: The Josephites, 1993.

Kauffman, Christopher J. *Tradition and Transformation in Catholic Culture: The Priests of Saint Sulpice in the United States from 1791 to the Present*. New York: Macmillan, 1988.

Kelly. Ellin M., ed. *Numerous Choirs: A Chronicle of Elizabeth Bayley Seton and Her Spiritual Daughters*. Vols. 1 and 2. Saint Meinrad, Ind.: Abbey Press, 1981 and 1996.

Kelly, Laurence J. "Negro Missions in Maryland." *Woodstock Letters* 38 (1909): 239–44.

Kelly, M. Rosalita, I.H.M. *No Greater Service: The History of the Congregation of the Sisters, Servants of the Immaculate Heart of Mary, Monroe, Michigan, 1845–1945*. Detroit: Congregation of the Sisters of the Immaculate Heart, 1948.

Kenneally, Finbar, O.F.M., et al., eds. *United States Documents in the Propaganda Fide Archives: A Calendar*. 1st ser., 7 vols. Washington, D.C.: Academy of American Franciscan History, 1966–.

Kenneally, James K. *The History of American Catholic Women*. New York: Crossroad, 1990.

Kennelly, Karen, ed. *American Catholic Women: A Historical Exploration*. New York: Macmillan, 1989.

Kirrane, John. "The Establishment of Negro Parishes and the Coming of the Josephites, 1863–1971." M.A. thesis, Catholic University of America, 1932.

Kolmer, Elizabeth, A.S.C. "Catholic Women Religious and Women's History: A Survey of the Literature." In *The American Catholic Religious Life: Selected Historical Essays*, edited by Joseph M. White, 1–13. New York: Garland Publishing, 1988.

Lancaster, M. Wilhelmina, O.S.P. "Earliest Beginnings of the Oblate Sisters of Providence, 1829–55." Unpublished paper, n.d., AOSP.

———. "Foundress of the Oblate Sisters of Providence." Unpublished paper, n.d., AOSP.

Lannon, Maria M. *Response to Love: The Story of Mary Elizabeth Lange, O.S.P.* Washington, D.C.: Josephite Pastoral Center, 1992.

Law, Robin. "Slave-Raiders and Middlemen, Monopolists and Free Traders: The Supply of Slaves for the Atlantic Trade in Dahomey, c. 1715–1850." *Journal of African History* 30 (1989): 45–68.

Lerner, Gerda, ed. *Black Women in White America: A Documentary History*. New York: Random House, 1972.

Leslie, Shane, ed. *The Letters of Cardinal Vaughan to Lady Herbert of Lea, 1867–1903*. London: Burns, Oates, 1942.

Levine, Laurence. *Black Culture and Black Consciousness: Afro-American Folk Thought from Slavery to Freedom*. Oxford: Oxford University Press, 1977.

Litwack, Leon. *North of Slavery: The Negro in the Free States 1790–1860*. Chicago: The University of Chicago Press, 1961.

Logue, Maria Kostka. *Sisters of St. Joseph of Philadelphia: A Century of Growth and Development, 1847–1947*. Westminster, Md.: The Newman Press, 1950.

Mannard, Joseph G. "The 1839 Baltimore Nunnery Riot: An Episode in Jacksonian Nativism and Social Violence." In *Urban American Catholicism: The Culture and Identity of the American Catholic People*, edited by Timothy Meagher, 192–206. New York: Garland Publishing, 1988.

———. "Maternity . . . of the Spirit: Nuns and Domesticity in Antebellum America." *U.S. Catholic Historian* 5, nos. 3 and 4 (Summer/Fall 1986): 305–24.

———. "'Maternity of the Spirit': Women Religious in the Archdiocese of Baltimore, 1790–1860." Ph.D. diss., University of Maryland, College Park, 1989.

Marschall, John Peter, C.S.V. "Francis Patrick Kenrick, 1851–1863: The Baltimore Years." Ph.D. diss., The Catholic University of America, 1965.

McFeely, William S. *Frederick Douglass*. New York: Simon and Schuster, 1991.

McMaster, Richard K. "Bishop Barron and the West African Missions." *Historical Records and Studies* 50 (1964): 83–129.

McNally, Michael J. "A Minority of a Minority: The Witness of Black Women Religious in the Antebellum South." *Review for Religious* 40 (1981): 260–69.

———. "A Peculiar Institution: Catholic Parish Life and the Pastoral Mission to the Blacks in the Southeast, 1850–1980." *U.S. Catholic Historian* 5, no. 1 (1986): 67–80.

McNamara, Jo Ann Kay. *Sisters in Arms: Catholic Nuns through Two Millenia*. Cambridge: Harvard University Press, 1996.

Meehan, Thomas F. "Mission Work among Colored Catholics." *United States Catholic Historical Society Records and Studies* 8 (1915): 116–28.

Meier, August, and Elliot Rudwick. *From Plantation to Ghetto*. 3d ed. New York: Hill and Wang, 1976.

Melville, Annabelle McConnell. *Elizabeth Bayley Seton, 1774–1821*. New York: Charles Scribner's Sons, 1951.

Miller, Randall M. "Black Catholics in the Slave South: Some Needs and Opportunities for Study." *Records of the American Catholic Historical Society of Philadelphia* 86 (March 1975– December 1975): 93–106.

———. "A Church in Cultural Captivity: Some Speculations on Catholic Identity in the Old South." In *Catholics in the Old South: Essays on Church and Culture*, edited by Randall M. Miller and Jon Wakelyn, 11–52. Macon, Ga.: Mercer University Press, 1983.

———. "The Failed Mission: The Catholic Church and Black Catholics in the Old South." In *Catholics in the Old South: Essays on Church and Culture*, edited by Randall M. Miller and Jon Wakelyn, 149–70. Macon, Ga.: Mercer University Press, 1983.

———. "Slaves and Southern Catholicism." In *Masters and Slaves in the House of the Lord: Race and Religion in the American South, 1740–1870*, edited by John B. Boles, 127–52. Lexington: University of Kentucky Press, 1988.

Minogue, Anna C. *Pages from a Hundred Years of Dominican History: The Story of the Congregation of Saint Catharine of Sienna*. New York: Frederick Pustet & Co., 1921.

Misch, Edward. "The American Bishops and the Negro from the Civil War to the Third Plenary Council of Baltimore, 1865–1884." Ph.D. diss., Pontifical Gregorian University, Rome, 1968, Josephite Archives, Baltimore.

Misner, Barbara, S.C.S.C. *"Highly Respectable and Accomplished Ladies": Catholic Women Religious in America, 1790–1850*. New York: Garland Publishing, 1988.

Mooney, Catherine M., R.S.C.J. *Philippine Duchesne: A Woman with the Poor*. New York: Paulist Press, 1990.

Morrow, Diane Batts. "Francophone Residents of Antebellum Baltimore and the Origins of the Oblate Sisters of Providence." In *Slavery in the Caribbean Francophone World: Distant Voices, Forgotten Acts, Forged Identities*, edited by Doris Kadish, 122–39. Athens: University of Georgia Press, 2000.

———. "The Oblate Sisters of Providence: Issues of Black and Female Agency in Their Antebellum Experience, 1828–1860." Ph.D. diss., University of Georgia, 1996.

———. "'Our Convent': The Oblate Sisters of Providence and the Antebellum Black Community." In *Dealing with the Powers That Be: Negotiating the Boundaries of Southern Womanhood*, edited by Janet Coryell et al., 27–47. Columbia: University of Missouri Press, 2000.

———. "Outsiders Within: The Oblate Sisters of Providence in 1830s Church and Society." *U.S. Catholic Historian* 15, no. 2 (Spring 1997): 35–54.

Morton, Patricia. *Disfigured Images: The Historical Assault on Afro-American Women.* New York: Praeger, 1991.

———, ed. *Discovering the Women in Slavery: Emancipating Perspectives on the American Past.* Athens: The University of Georgia Press, 1996.

Murphy, J. C. *An Analysis of the Attitudes of American Catholics toward the Immigrant and the Negro, 1825–1925.* Washington, D.C.: Catholic University Press of America, 1940.

Murphy, Miriam T. "Catholic Missionary Work among the Colored People of the United States, 1766–1866." *American Catholic Historical Society of Philadelphia Records* 35 (1924): 101–36.

Oates, Mary J. *The Catholic Philanthropic Tradition in America.* Bloomington: Indiana University Press, 1995.

Ochs, Stephen J. *A Black Patriot and a White Priest: André Cailloux and Claude Paschal Maistre in Civil War New Orleans.* Baton Rouge: Louisiana State University Press, 2000.

———. *Desegregating the Altar: The Josephites and the Struggle for Black Priests, 1871–1960.* Baton Rouge: Louisiana State University Press, 1990.

———. "The Ordeal of the Black Priest." *U.S. Catholic Historian* 5, no. 1 (1986): 45–66.

Oliver, Madeline, and William Faherty. *The Religious Roots of Black Catholics of Saint Louis.* Florissant, Mo.: St. Stanislaus Historic Museum, Inc., 1977.

Palmer, Colin A. *Passageways: An Interpretive History of Black America.* Vol. 1, 1619–1865. New York: Harcourt Brace College Publishers, 1998.

Panczyk, Matthew Leo. "James Whitfield, Fourth Archbishop of Baltimore." *Records of the American Catholic Historical Society of Philadelphia* 75 (December 1964): 222–51; 76 (March 1965): 21–53.

Paul, William George. "The Shadow of Equality: The Negro in Baltimore, 1864–1911." Ph.D. diss., University of Wisconsin, 1972.

Pease, William H., and Jane Pease. "The Negro Convention Movement." In *Key Issues in the Afro-American Experience.* Vol 1, edited by Nathan I. Huggins, Martin Kilson, and Daniel M. Fox, 191–205. New York: Harcourt, Brace, Jovanovich, Inc., 1971.

Perry, Ashley J., S.S.J. "Oblate Sisters of Providence: First Fifty Years." M.S. thesis, 1977, Josephite Archives, Baltimore.

Phelps, Jamie T., O.P. "John R. Slattery's Mission Strategies." *U.S. Catholic Historian* 7, nos. 2 and 3 (1988): 201–14.

Phillips, Christopher. *Freedom's Port: The African American Community of Baltimore, 1790–1860.* Urbana: University of Illinois Press, 1997.

———. "'Negroes and Other Slaves': The African-American Community of Baltimore, 1790–1860." Ph.D. diss., University of Georgia, 1992.

Phillips, Glenn O. "Maryland and the Caribbean, 1634–1984: Some Highlights." *Maryland Historical Magazine* 83, no. 3 (Fall 1988): 199–214.

Poole, Strafford, C.M., and Douglas J. Slawson, C.M. *Church and Slave in Perry County, Missouri, 1818–1865.* Lewiston, N.Y.: The Edwin Mellen Press, 1986.

Porter, Dorothy B. "The Organized Educational Activities of Negro Literary Societies, 1828–1846." *Journal of Negro Education* 5, no. 4 (October 1936): 555–76.

Portier, William. "John R. Slattery's Vision for the Evangelization of American Blacks." *U.S. Catholic Historian* 5, no. 1 (1986): 19–44.

Posey, Thaddeus John, O.F.M., Cap. "Praying in the Shadows: The Oblate Sisters of Providence, a Look at Nineteenth-Century Black Spirituality." *U.S. Catholic Historian* 12, no. 1 (Winter 1994): 11–30. Reprinted in *This Far by Faith: Readings in African American*

Women's Religious Biography, edited by Judith Weisenfeld and Richard Newman, 73–93. New York: Routledge, 1996.

———. "An Unwanted Commitment: The Spirituality of the Early Oblate Sisters of Providence, 1829–1890." Ph.D. diss., St. Louis University, 1993.

Raboteau, Albert J. "Black Catholics and Afro-American Religious History: Autobiographical Reflections." *U.S. Catholic Historian* 5, no. 1 (1986): 119–27.

———. *A Fire in the Bones: Reflections on African American Religious History*. Boston: Beacon Press, 1995.

———. *Slave Religion: The Invisible Institution in the Antebellum South*. New York: Oxford University Press, 1978.

Rapley, Elizabeth. *The Dévotes: Women and Church in Seventeenth-Century France*. Montreal: McGill-Queen's University Press, 1990.

Rawick, George P., ed. *The American Slave: A Composite Autobiography*. Vol. 14, Maryland Narratives. Westport: Greenwood Publishing Co., 1972.

Reilly, L. W. "A Famous Convent of Colored Sisters." *Annales Congregationis SS. Redemptoris*, 105–16. Provinciae Americanae, Supplementum, Pars II, 1903.

Reuther, Rosemary R., and Rosemary S. Keller, eds. *Women and Religion in America*. Vol. 1. New York: Harper and Row, 1981.

Richardson, Marilyn, ed. *Maria W. Stewart, America's First Black Woman Political Writer: Essays and Speeches*. Bloomington: The University of Indiana Press, 1987.

Riggs, Marcia Y., ed. *Can I Get A Witness? Prophetic Religious Voices of African American Women, an Anthology*. Maryknoll, N.Y.: Orbis Books, 1997.

Ripley, C. Peter, et al., eds. *Witness for Freedom: African American Voices on Race, Slavery, and Emancipation*. Chapel Hill: The University of North Carolina Press, 1993.

Rouse, Michael F. (Brother Bede, C.F.X.). *A Study of the Development of Negro Education under Catholic Auspices in Maryland and Washington, D.C.* Baltimore: Johns Hopkins University Press, 1935.

Ruiz, Vicki L., and Ellen Carol DuBois. *Unequal Sisters: A Multicultural Reader in U.S. Women's History*. New York: Routledge, 1994.

Ryan, John A. *Chronicle and Sketch of the Church of St. Ignatius of Loyola, Baltimore, 1856–1906*. Baltimore: Press of A. Hoen & Co., 1907.

Sagers, Yvonne. "A History of the Oblate Sisters of Providence, Black Catholic Educators." M.A. thesis, 1973, Josephite Archives, Baltimore.

Savage, Mary Lucida. "The Congregation of Saint Joseph of Carondelet: A Brief Account of Its Origin and Its Work in the United States (1650–1922)." Ph.D. diss., Catholic Sisters College of the Catholic University of America, 1923.

Scharf, Thomas J. *History of Baltimore City and Baltimore County*. Baltimore, 1881. Reprint, Baltimore: Baltimore Regional Publishing Co., 1971.

Schmandt, Raymond H. "An Overview of Institutional Establishments in the Antebellum Southern Church." In *Catholics in the Old South: Essays on Church and Culture*, edited by Randall M. Miller and Jon Wakelyn, 53–76. Macon, Ga.: Mercer University Press, 1983.

Sharps, Ronald L. "Black Catholics in the United States: A Historical Chronology." *U.S. Catholic Historian* 12 (Winter 1994): 119–41.

Shea, John Gilmary. *A History of the Catholic Church within the Limits of the United States, from the First Attempted Colonization to the Present Time*. 4 vols. New York: J. G. Shea, 1886–92.

Shea, Diane Edward, I.H.M., and Marita Constance Supan, I.H.M. "Apostolate of the Archives—God's Mystery through History." *Josephite Harvest* 85 (1983): 10–13.

Sheehan, Arthur, and Elizabeth Sheehan. *Pierre Toussaint: A Citizen of Old New York*. New York: P. J. Kenedy, 1955.

Sherwood, Grace. *The Oblates' Hundred and One Years*. New York: Macmillan, 1931.

———. "The Oblate Sisters of Providence." *America* 42, no. 8 (30 November 1929): 179–80.

Simmons, William J., D.D. *Men of Mark: Eminent, Progressive and Rising*. Cleveland: George M. Rewell & Co., 1889. Reprint, New York: Arno Press, 1968.

Sisters, Servants of the Immaculate of Mary. *Building Sisterhood: A Feminist History of the Sisters, Servants of the Immaculate Heart of Mary, Monroe, Michigan*. Syracuse, N.Y.: Syracuse University Press, 1997.

Six Women's Slave Narratives. New York: Oxford University Press, The Schomburg Library of Nineteenth-Century Black Women Writers, 1988.

Skerrett, J. Taylor. "'Is There Anything Wrong with Being A Nigger?' Racial Identity and Three Nineteenth-Century Priests." *Freeing the Spirit* 5 (1977): 27–37.

Snead-Cox, J. G. *The Life of Cardinal Vaughan*. 2 vols. London: Herbert and Daniel, 1910.

Spalding, Thomas. "The Negro Catholic Congresses, 1889–1894." *Catholic Historical Review* 55 (1969): 337–57.

———. *The Premier See: A History of the Archdiocese of Baltimore, 1789–1989*. Baltimore: The Johns Hopkins University Press, 1989.

Spiritual Narratives. New York: Oxford University Press, The Schomburg Library of Nineteenth-Century Black Women Writers, 1988.

Steins, Richard H. "The Mission of the Josephites to the Negro in America, 1871–1893." M.A. thesis, Columbia University, 1966, Josephite Archives, Baltimore.

Sterling, Dorothy. *We Are Your Sisters: Black Women in the Nineteenth Century*. New York: W. W. Norton & Company, 1984.

Stewart, George C., Jr. *Marvels of Charity: History of American Sisters and Nuns*. Huntington, Ind.: Our Sunday Visitor Publishing Division, Our Sunday Visitor, Inc., 1994.

Stopak, Aaron. "The Maryland Colonization Society: Independent State Action in the Colonization Movement." *Maryland Historical Magazine* 63 (Fall 1968): 275–98.

Stratton, Robin, O.C.D. *The Carmelite Sisters of Baltimore and the Education of Young Ladies, 1831–1851*. Baltimore: Carmelite Monastery, 1990.

Sullivan, Eleanore C. *Georgetown Visitation since 1799*. Privately printed, 1975.

Swisher, Carl Brent. *Roger Brooke Taney*. New York: Macmillan, 1936.

Tarry, Ellen. *The Other Toussaint: A Post-Revolutionary Black*. Boston: St. Paul Editions, 1981.

Terborg-Penn, Rosalyn. "African Feminism: A Theoretical Approach to the History of Women in the African Diaspora." In *Women in Africa and the African Diaspora: A Reader*. 2d ed., edited by Rosalyn Terborg-Penn and Andrea Benton Rushing, 23–41. Washington. D.C.: Howard University Press, 1996.

Thomas, Evangeline, C.S.J. *Women Religious History Sources: A Guide to Repositories in the United States*. New York: R. R. Bowker Co., 1983.

Thompson, Margaret Susan. "Discovering Foremothers: Sisters, Society, and the American Catholic Experience." In *The American Catholic Religious Life: Selected Historical Essays*, edited by Joseph M. White, 63–80. New York: Garland Publishing, 1988.

———. "Philemon's Dilemma: Nuns and the Black Community in Nineteenth-Century America: Some Findings." In *American Catholic Religious Life: Selected Historical Essays*, edited by Joseph M. White, 81–96. New York: Garland Publishing, 1988.

———. "Sisterhood and Power: Class, Culture, and Ethnicity in the American Convent." *Colby Library Quarterly* 25, no. 3 (September 1989): 149–75.

———. "The Validation of Sisterhood: Canonical Status and Liberation in the History of American Nuns." In *A Leaf from the Great Tree of God: Essays in Honour of Ritamary Bradley, S.F.C.C.*, edited by Margot H. King, 38–78. Toronto, Ontario: Peregrina Publishing Co., 1994.

———. "Women and American Catholicism, 1789–1989." In *Perspectives on the American Catholic Church, 1789–1989*, edited by Virginia Geiger and Stephen Vicchio, 123–42. Westminster, Md.: Christian Classics, 1989.

———. "Women, Feminism, and the New Religious History: Catholic Sisters as a Case Study." In *Belief and Behavior: Essays in the New Religious History*, edited by Philip R. Vandermeer and Robert P. Swierenga, 136–63. New Brunswick: Rutgers University Press, 1991.

Three Catholic Afro-American Congresses. Cincinnati: American Catholic Tribune, 1893. Reprint, New York: Arno Press, 1978.

Tourscher, F. E., ed. and trans., *Diary and Visitation Record of the Rt. Rev. Francis Patrick Kenrick, Administrator and Bishop of Philadelphia, 1830–1851*. Lancaster, Pa.: Wickersham Printing Co., 1916.

"Two Nuns and 120 Years of Cloistered Service." *America* 56, no. 18 (6 February 1937): 411.

U.S. Department of Commerce, Bureau of Census. *200 Years of U.S. Census Taking: Population and Housing Questions, 1790–1990*. Washington, D.C.: U.S. Government Printing Office, 1989.

Varle, Charles. *View of Baltimore*. Baltimore: S. Young, 1833.

Vollmar, Edward R., S.J. *The Catholic Church in America: An Historical Bibliography*. New Brunswick: The Scarecrow Press, 1956.

———. *The Catholic Church in America: An Historical Bibliography*. 2d ed. New Brunswick: The Scarecrow Press, 1963.

Wakelyn, Jon L. "Catholic Elites in the Slaveholding South." In *Catholics in the Old South: Essays on Church and Culture*, edited by Randall M. Miller and Jon Wakelyn, 211–39. Macon, Ga.: Mercer University Press, 1983.

Washington, Booker T. *Up from Slavery*. New York: Airmont Publishing Co., 1967.

Weisenfeld, Judith, and Richard Newman, eds. *This Far by Faith: Readings in African American Women's Religious Biography*. New York: Routledge, 1996.

White, Charles L., D.D. *Life of Mrs. Eliza A. Seton, Foundress and First Superior of the Sisters or Daughters of Charity in the United States of America*. 3d ed. Baltimore: Kelly, Piet & Co., 1879.

White, Deborah Gray. *Ar'n't I a Woman? Female Slaves in the Antebellum South*. New York: W. W. Norton & Co., 1985.

[Whitfield, James]. "A Statement Concerning the Diocese of Baltimore Prepared and Forwarded to the Editor of the Annals of the Propagation of the Faith by Archbishop Whitfield (June 27, 1829)." *Historical Records and Studies* 2 (1900): 131–38.

Williamson, Joel. *New People: Miscegenation and Mulattoes in the United States*. New York: New York University Press, 1980.

Woods, Frances Jerome, C.D.P. "Congregations of Religious Women in the Old South." In *Catholics in the Old South: Essays on Church and Culture*, edited by Randall M. Miller and Jon Wakelyn, 99–123. Macon, Ga.: Mercer University Press, 1983.

Woodson, Carter G. *The Education of the Negro prior to 1861*. New York: G. P. Putnam's Sons, 1915.

Wright, James M. *The Free Negro in Maryland, 1634–1860*. Studies in History, Economics and Public Law, no. 222. New York: Columbia University, 1921.

Zanca, Kenneth J., ed. *American Catholics and Slavery, 1789–1866: An Anthology of Primary Documents*. Lanham, Md.: University Press of America, 1994.

Boarders, nonpupil, 74–75, 181, 215

Boegue, Rosine (Sister Mary Rose), 11, 16, 17, 22–23, 25, 29–30, 184

Book purchases, 222–23

Boston, Sister Mary Petra: *Blossoms Gathered from the Lower Branches*, 10

Bourgoin, Cecile (Sister Mary Bridget), 61, 92–93

Bourgoin, Claire (Sister Scholastica), 61, 72, 185, 217

Bourgoin, Clara (Sister Elizabeth), 61, 212

Bourgoin, Helen, 75

Boyd, Agnes (Sister Mary Martha), 212

Boyer, Jean Pierre, 173

Breckinridge, Robert J., 152–53

Brown, Elizabeth, 244

Brown, Elsa Barkley, 274

Brown, Rev. John Mifflin, 220, 221, 245, 246, 309 (n. 103)

Bruté, Rev. Simon, 130

Butler, Cassandra (Sister Mary Stanislaus), 61, 77, 82, 131–32

Byrne, Patricia, 191

Capot, Jeanne, 65–66

Carmelite Nuns, 44, 48, 79, 128, 132–33, 134, 150–51, 166

Carroll, Charles, 153–54, 157, 182

Carroll, John (archbishop of Baltimore), 3, 6, 116, 118

Catechetical classes. *See* Instruction, religious

Cathedral Fund Association, 200

Catholic Church, 3, 5; and accommodation to racism, 116, 117–18, 138; and colonization, 124, 173–74; and racial inclusion, 117–18, 254; and racial segregation, 20–21, 95, 113–14, 151, 200–201, 233–35; and slavery, 8, 40, 69–70, 79, 116–17, 184, 250–51, 256–57; southern origins of, 8

Catholic Mirror, 132, 232, 237; inclusion of black Catholics, 254–55, 257–62; Oblate advertisement in, 218; on slavery, 256–57

Chanche, Rev. John Joseph, 42, 43, 44, 88

Chapel, Oblate (St. Frances): financing of, 111–12; French liturgies in, 77–78, 166–67; parish life of, 229–32, 236, 245; public use of, 94–95, 98–100, 129, 208, 226

Charism, 13, 15; of Balas, 14, 15–16, 19–20, 21, 22–23; of Duchemin, 22–23, 168–69, 187, 188; of Lange, 13–14, 15–16, 19–20, 21, 22–23, 28; Oblate, 11, 14, 28, 35, 65, 67–69, 70–72, 78, 93

Chatard, Luke Tiernan, 256–57

Chatard, Madame, 100–101

Chatard, Peter, 147, 156

Cholera, 71–72, 147–49

Clark, Emily, 45

Clarke, Rev. William, 239, 253–54, 256

Claver chapel, 253, 254

Clerical recognition: of the Oblates, 130–32, 172–74, 193–94, 197, 247–48, 250

Clerical requests: for Oblate missions, 72, 215, 248–50

Clerical support: of white sisterhoods, 132–33

Coburn, Carol K., 270, 277 (n. 2)

Collins, Patricia Hill, 2

Colonization, 144, 145, 263; black responses to, 146, 174, 243–44

Coloured Female Roman Catholic Beneficial Society, 22

Communal identity, 11, 14, 28, 65–67, 95–96

Confraternities, religious, 18–20, 31

Constitutional issues, Oblate, 182–85, 300 (n. 12), 301 (n. 23)

Cook, Henrietta, 152

Cooper, Anna Julia, 36

Costin, William, 109

Cross, Rev. Andrew B., 152–53, 265

Cuba, 17, 26, 279 (n. 16)

Currier, Charles Warren, 120, 121, 128

Curry, Leonard, 291 (n. 48)

Czackert, Rev. Peter, 188, 193, 194, 197

Czvitkovicz, Rev. Alexander, 202, 203–4

Dahomey: women in, 33–34, 35

Damphoux, Rev. Jean-Baptiste Edward, 42, 43, 67, 174

Davis, Rev. Cyprian, 11, 68–69

Debt reduction, 216, 304 (n. 44)

De Courcy, Henri, 121, 261

Delille, Henriette, 118

Deluol, Rev. Louis Regis, 42, 43, 67; attitude toward black people, 184, 251; diary entries on Oblates, 44, 51, 128, 176, 182, 183, 184, 190, 193, 202; and Oblate Rule revisions, 183–84; and Oblates at St. Mary's, 27, 28, 140–41; relationship with the Oblates, 176–77, 180, 190–91, 191–92, 194–95, 202, 217

Deposits: at St. Mary's Seminary, 179–80, 216–17

Deshais, Hospiliene, 61

Diocesan approval of the Oblates, 51–52, 54, 56

Diocesan neglect of the Oblates, 175–77, 186–87, 192–96

Diocesan reconciliation to the Oblates, 203, 204, 207, 208

Diocesan sisterhoods: and the Oblates, 135–36, 248–49

Diocesan status of the Oblates, 121, 133–35, 255–56, 257–62, 267

Dominican Sisters of St. Catharine, Kentucky, 49

Donaldson, Charlotte (Sister Mary Agnes), 212

Douglass, Frederick, 144, 182

Dowries, 50–51, 63, 72–73, 104, 165

Dred Scott v. Sanford, 155, 262, 263

Dubois, Emile Joseph, 230, 231

Dubois, Philomena, 230, 306 (n. 30)

Du Bois, W. E. B., 36–37; *Souls of Black Folk, The*, 37

DuBourg, Louis (bishop of Louisiana), 116, 118

Ducatel, Edward, 156

Ducatel, Madame, 100–101, 103

Duchemin, Betsy (Sister Mary Anthony), 30–31, 61, 72, 73, 92, 125–26

Duchemin, Marie Therese Almaide (Sister Marie Therese), 11, 16–17, 60, 92, 185; baptismal records of, 31; concern about religious status, 185–86, 188, 189, 190; early life of, 30, 31–33; and French cultural identity, 32, 77–78, 166–67, 187,

191; as Oblate annalist, 80–82, 99, 166–69, 187; as Oblate superior, 167–69, 182–83; Willigman's accounts of, 32, 188–89

DuMoulin, Elizabeth, 75

Easter Duty Lists, 20, 31

Eccleston, Samuel (archbishop of Baltimore), 42, 43, 98, 127, 164, 173; on black evangelization, 129, 227; behavior toward the Oblates, 127–28, 131, 171, 194, 202, 203, 204, 248–49; mental health of, 183–84; and Visitation Sisters, 128

Education, 17, 48, 49; in Baltimore, 45–46, 97, 257–58; black initiatives in, 14–15, 32, 45, 97, 201; in Charleston, 123, 171; in Cincinnati, 249–50; in New Orleans, 45, 171; in New York, 233–35; in Saint Domingue, 17–18, 32; in St. Louis, 172; in Washington, D.C., 45, 136; in Wilmington, 64. *See also* Academies; Instruction, religious; Schools, parochial; Teaching ministry 1844-54 Ledger, 179-82, 216

Elections, 25, 167, 185, 208, 214

Employment: at St. Mary's Seminary, 27–28, 139, 140–41, 180

England, John (bishop of Charleston), 51, 116, 123, 284 (n. 49)

Eschbach, John and Margaret, 181–82

Ethnicity, 9, 77–78, 105–6, 129, 155–58, 166–67, 189–90, 219–20, 234–35

Exercise, 83

Fair, 112–14, 151

Female associations, voluntary, 21, 96, 112, 273

Fenwick, Benedict J. (bishop of Boston), 131

Finances, 64, 72–76, 100–101, 111–12, 163–66, 179–82, 216–18, 227–30, 231

Finnall, William, 107

First Provisional Council, 122–23

Flaget, Benoit Joseph (bishop of Kentucky), 61, 116, 118, 123

Forman, Stephen West, 107

Fortière, Sister Marthe, 45, 117–18

Frances of Rome, Saint, 16, 50, 53
Free School for Girls, 200–201
French Black Codes, 26
French cultural identity: and the Oblates, 33, 77–78, 166–67
French Revolution, 3
Frey, Sylvia, 34

Gallicanism, 58
Gaudin, Juliette, 118
Gender, 2–3, 16, 21, 35–36, 71, 90, 140–41, 251; restricted roles for women, 24–25. *See also* White attitudes: toward black women
Generational issues, 79, 80–82, 167–68
Genius of Universal Emancipation (abolitionist weekly), 138–39, 295 (n. 88)
Gerhardinger, Mother M. Theresa, 166
German immigrants, 78, 181–82
Gideon, Almira (Almaide), 107, 241
Gideon, Angelica (Sister Mary Angelica), 62, 69, 107, 212, 217
Gillet, Rev. Louis, 175, 187–88, 197
Gomez, Michael, 34
Goodridge, William C., 238
Goodwin, Moses, 243
Graham, Leroy, 309 (n. 103)
Gregory XVI, 53, 55

Habit: Oblate, 60, 153
Haiti, 3, 40, 56, 173
Harker, Ann (Sister Anna Theresa), 211
Harper, Emily, 211, 255
Health issues, 79, 82–83
Herbermann, Charles, 146
Hickey, Rev. John, 174, 175, 193; and Society of Coloured People, 198, 199, 200–201
Higginbotham, Evelyn Brooks, 96
Holy Family Society, 57–58
Howard, Arthur, 31–32, 33
Hughes, John (archbishop of New York), 116, 234, 235
Humility, 29, 67–68, 260, 269–70

Immigrant priests, 186
Immigration: in Baltimore, 3–4, 6, 11, 78, 129, 181–82, 186, 198

Incorporation, 147
Infirmarian, 83
Institute, pontifical, 55
Instruction, religious, 4, 44–45, 77, 96, 106, 138, 226–27
Integration, residential: in Baltimore, 181
Interaction, lay/religious, 90–95, 169

Jakes, Henry, 239
James, Mary Louise (Sister Mary Aloysius), 61, 62, 82–83
Jesuits, the, 253, 254
Johansen, Mary Carroll, 295 (n. 88)
Johnson, Ann, 163, 177
Johnson, Maria (Sister Frances Catherine), 211
Jones, Arabella, 242–44
Josephine Amanda (Sister Mary Stanislaus), 62, 75, 188–89, 191–92
Joubert de la Muraille, Rev. James Hector Nicholas, 42, 43, 46, 62, 173, 269; attitudes toward black people, 57–58, 113; and black female education, 46, 57, 85; early life of, 39–40; and Gallicanism, 58; health of, 82, 170, 174–75; as Oblate annalist, 14, 82; Oblate cofounder, 1–2, 11, 14, 15–16, 30; and Oblate Rule and Constitutions, 49–50, 51; as Oblate spiritual director, 23–24, 40–42, 67, 71, 139–40, 168, 186; relationship with Oblate Sisters, 40–42, 58; seeks church approval of Oblates, 51–52, 55–56; and slavery, 57; Willigman's accounts of, 131, 174, 260

Kauffman, Christopher J., 277 (n. 4)
Kelly, Rev. John, 173–74
Kenrick, Francis Patrick (archbishop of Baltimore), 5, 131, 232–33; attitude toward black people, 251, 252; and the Oblates, 172, 252–53, 265; on slavery, 116, 250–51
Kenrick, Peter Richard (archbishop of St. Louis), 172, 247
Kinship policies, 91–94, 215
Kohlmann, Rev. Anthony, 53, 56
Kraus, Rev. Dominic, 214

Labor, free black, 7, 143–44, 198, 230, 263, 264
Lafont, Rev. Annet, 234–35
Lake, Mary, 220, 242
Lange, Nannette, 75
Lange, Elizabeth Clarisse (Sister Mary Elizabeth), 61, 72, 74, 75, 174, 184, 215–16, 269; and Duchemin, 32, 33; early life of, 11, 15–16, 17, 18–20, 21, 22–23, 279 (n. 16); as free woman of color, 18, 26, 27, 36; and French cultural identity, 26–27, 36; letter to Deluol of, 27–28; Oblate cofounder, 1–2, 15–16; as Oblate superior, 27–28, 68, 87, 93–94, 139, 161; offices held, 28; personal charism of, 13–14, 15–16, 19–20, 21, 22–23, 25, 28; religious vocation of, 4, 15; and slavery, 18; Willigman's accounts of, 23, 25, 26, 30
Lay organizations, 121, 125, 126
LeBarth, Eugenie (Sister Mary Benedict of San Philadelpho), 61, 93, 212
LeBarth, Hilary, 93
Lefevre, Peter Paul (bishop of Detroit), 172
Legal restrictions: on free black people, 127, 140, 144–46, 197–98, 201, 263–64
Lenten fasting, 83–84
Lhomme, Rev. Francis, 216–17
Liberian Mission, 124, 173–74
Loras, Rev. Mathias, 72, 172
Lorde, Audre, 269
Loughlin, Rev. John, 234

Manganos, Charlotte, 181
Mannard, Joseph, 70, 151
Maréchal, Ambrose (archbishop of Baltimore), 4, 157
Marie Germaine (Sister Mary Clotilde), 62, 66, 69, 107, 212
Maryland, 5–6, 7, 46, 140, 144–46, 197–98, 263–64
Maternal feminism, 270
Maturation: of the Oblate community, 223–24
Maxis, Anne Marie. See Duchemin, Betsy
Maxis, Sister Mary Theresa. See Duchemin, Marie Therese Almaide

McColgan, Rev. Edward, 201, 233, 234
McElroy, Rev. John, 131–32
McKanna, Patrick, 266
McNally, Michael, 294 (n. 46)
Membership, criteria of Oblate, 63–67
Messonier, Frances (Sister Mary Alphonsa), 209, 210
Messonier, Henriette (Sister Theresa Victoria), 209, 210, 220, 228
Metropolitan (Catholic monthly), 21, 125, 139
Misner, Barbara, 73, 136, 150–51, 284 (n. 49)
Montpensier, Fanny, 104–6, 211
Mortification, 83–84
Mulattoes, 4, 20, 26, 30, 73, 109, 191, 277 (n. 9)

National Catholic directories: inclusion of black Catholics, 136–38, 198, 237, 257, 262
National parishes, 129, 294 (n. 46)
Nativism, 9, 149–51, 152–53, 190, 239, 253–54, 264–65
Neale, Leonard (archbishop of Baltimore), 133
Neale, Rev. Charles, 132
Needlework. See Sewing
Nerinckx, Rev. Charles, 49, 117
Neumann, Rev. John, 203, 247
Noel, Andrew, 63
Noel, Angela (Sister Mary Seraphina), 112, 195, 210–11, 232, 239–40
Noel, Jane Laurette (Sister Mary James), 64, 65, 83, 93–94
Noel, John, 107, 198–99, 231, 255
Noel, Laurette Jane (Sister Mary Chantal), 63, 64–66, 69, 93–94, 167
Noel, Marie Louise (Sister Marie Louise), 64, 65, 93–94, 185, 195, 249
Novice mistress, 70–71

Oates, Mary, 112, 229
Oblate, defined, 16
Oblate Sisters of Providence: and African cultural traditions, 9, 33–35; Caribbean origins of, 33; communal growth of, 60–63, 81, 161–63, 209–12; and historical record, 10, 11–12; as indigenous sister-

46, 96, 169–70, 208, 218–23; curriculum, 77, 88–89, 90, 180–81, 218–19; prospectus (1834), 54, 75, 84–85
School Sisters of Notre Dame, 79, 166
Schools, parochial, 86, 87, 200–201, 236, 237
Schools, public: and black people, 201, 234, 258
Seguin, Peter, 109
Seton, Mother Elizabeth, 48, 133, 135
Sewing, 75–76, 163–64, 180, 216, 217, 220–21
Shea, John Gilmary: *History of the Catholic Church*, 121
Sherwood, Grace, 28, 33, 101, 102–3, 113, 187, 205, 216, 230, 300 (n. 12); *Oblates' Hundred and One Years, The*, 12
Sister Clara, 212
Sister Mary James, I. H. M., 31–32
Sisters of Charity, 48–49, 51, 71, 74, 89–90, 148, 149, 171, 184, 256
Sisters of Loretto, Kentucky, 49, 117
Sisters of Mercy, 79, 172, 255
Sisters of Mount Carmel, 45, 171
Sisters of Notre Dame du Cap-Français, 17–18
Sisters of St. Joseph, 171–72
Sisters of the Holy Cross, 79, 236–37
Sisters of the Holy Family, 117, 118, 124, 192
Sisters, Servants of the Immaculate Heart of Mary (I. H. M.), 30, 31, 32–33, 187–88, 191
Skin color: references to, 20, 30, 109, 162, 188–89, 192
Slavery, 106–7, 127, 144, 184; and the Catholic Church, 79, 116–17, 250–51, 256–57; and the Oblates, 69–70, 211–12
Smith, Julia, 244
Smith, Martha, 270, 277 (n. 2)
Smulders, Rev. Giles, 193, 194, 196
Social status, black, 14–15, 20, 26, 73–74
Society for the Propagation of the Faith, 119–20, 130
Society of Coloured People (Holy Family Society), 198–202
Solomon, 81, 151–52

Spalding, Thomas, 129
Spirituality, 2, 68–69, 141, 208. *See also* Charism
Stewart, Maria, 246
Stirling, Archibald, 72, 147
Sulpicians, the (Society of St. Sulpice), 3, 46; "Americanist" faction of, 42; "revolution" of 1829, 42–43; traditionalist faction of, 42; withdrawal from the Oblates, 192–93, 194

Taney, Roger B., 154–55, 262
Teaching ministry, 3, 17, 35–36, 72, 84–90, 215, 220–23, 236–37, 239–40, 245–46
Terborg-Penn, Rosalyn, 3
Tessier, Rev. Jean-Marie, 4, 20, 30, 42, 43, 49
Thomas, Sister Dominica, 212
Thomas, Marie Helen (Sister Mary Gertrude), 61–62; letters to Purcell, 215, 249; as Oblate superior, 214–15, 239
Thompson, Harriet, 233–35
Thompson, Jane, 199
Timon, John (bishop of Buffalo), 250
Tobias Society, the, 21, 121, 125, 126, 259
Tritt, Mary, 66, 75
Trustees of the Bureau of the Poor, the, 71, 72
Tuition, 74, 103, 110–11, 216, 217, 237, 240

Uncles, Lorenzo, 230
Uncles, Rev. Charles Randolph, 230
United States Catholic Miscellany (newspaper), 51, 139
Ursuline Nuns, 44–45, 48

Van Emstede, Rev. Nicholas, 214
Visitation Sisters of Georgetown, 48, 54, 79, 87–88, 128, 133, 136, 248–49
Vogien, Rev. John B., 214
Vows, religious, 50, 51, 52, 53, 55, 56

Walker, Maggie Lena, 274
Waters, Margaret (Sister Mary Agatha), 212
Weekly Anglo-African, The (newspaper), 220, 245, 246

Wernerth, Rosine, 181

Wernerth, Rutherton, 181

West, Marie (Sister Helen Joseph), 62, 69, 217

West African societies: women in, 33–35

Wheeler, Rev. Michael, 42, 43, 88; and papal endorsement of Oblate Sisters, 52, 53, 54, 55

Whelan, Richard Vincent (bishop of Wheeling), 248

Whipper, Adalina, 152

Whipper, Sarah Helena, 152

White, Rev. Charles, 132

White patronage: of the Oblates, 76, 100–101, 132, 134, 147, 153, 156, 254–56

White attitudes: toward black people, 7, 26, 118, 127, 144, 145–46, 154, 155, 211, 263–64; toward black women, 1, 9, 35, 66–67; toward the Oblates, 11, 100–101, 112, 146–47, 153–55, 181–82, 189, 254, 266–67

Whitfield, James (archbishop of Balti-more), 4, 6, 86, 132–33; bequest to Oblates, 124–25, 126; and cholera, 125–26; and commitment to Oblates, 119–20, 121, 122, 123, 125, 126–27; and establishment of Oblate Sisters, 50–51, 52, 54, 56; and historical record, 120–21; racial attitudes of, 121–22

Williams, William Augustine, 232–33

Williamson, Rev. Adolphus, 80, 131, 134

Williamson, Charles, 112, 157

Willigman, Sarah (Sister Mary Theresa Catherine), 185, 213, 217; early life of, 161, 209–10; as Oblate historian, 14–15, 76, 79, 101, 114, 177, 236; portrayal of Deluol, 202–3

Wilson, Rev. Thomas, 49

Wissel, Rev. Joseph, 55

Women religious, 1, 8–9, 47–49, 60, 68, 70, 78–79, 186, 273, 277 (n. 2). *See also individual orders*

Women of virtue, 1, 35–36, 270

Wood, Betty, 34